Trees of the
Central Hardwood Forests
of North America

Trees of the Central Hardwood Forests of North America

AN IDENTIFICATION AND CULTIVATION GUIDE

Donald J. Leopold

COLLEGE OF ENVIRONMENTAL SCIENCE AND FORESTRY,
STATE UNIVERSITY OF NEW YORK, SYRACUSE

William C. McComb

DEPARTMENT OF FORESTRY AND WILDLIFE MANAGEMENT,
UNIVERSITY OF MASSACHUSETTS, AMHERST

Robert N. Muller

DEPARTMENT OF FORESTRY,
UNIVERSITY OF KENTUCKY, LEXINGTON

Timber Press
Portland, Oregon

To
Kay and Mark
Kevin and Michael
Jon and Neil

ISBN 0-88192-406-7

Printed in Hong Kong

Timber Press, Inc.
The Haseltine Building
133 S.W. Second Avenue, Suite 450
Portland, Oregon 97204, U.S.A.

Library of Congress Cataloging-in-Publication Data

Leopold, Donald Joseph. 1956–
Trees of the central hardwood forests of North America : an identification and
cultivation guide / Donald J. Leopold, William C. McComb, Robert N. Muller.
        p.   cm.
Includes bibliographical references (p.   ) and index.
        ISBN 0-88192-406-7
1. Trees—East (U.S.)—Identification. 2. Trees—Canada, Eastern—Identification.
    3. Hardwoods—East (U.S.) 4. Hardwoods—Canada, Eastern.
    5. Forest ecology—East (U.S.) 6. Forest ecology—Canada, Eastern.
    7. Landscape plants—East (U.S.) 8. Landscape plants—Canada, Eastern.
    I. McComb, William C. II. Muller, Robert N. (Robert Neil), 1946–
                III. Title.
            QK115.L43   1998
        582.16′097—dc21   97-6200
                CIP

Contents

Color plates follow page 272

Preface

"To keep every cog and wheel is the first precaution of intelligent tinkering" (Leopold 1966, p. 190). We have "tinkered" with forested ecosystems throughout the eastern United States. We have cut them, burned them, cleared them, and then allowed some to regrow. Some of the "tinkering" was less direct, yet it profoundly influenced the character of these forests. Introduction of *Cryphonectria parasitica*, the causal agent of the chestnut blight, greatly influenced the species composition of these forests. The result of these disturbances is that we now have few forest stands remaining in the eastern United States that appear as they might have appeared before the arrival of Europeans on the continent. Those that have been placed in reserve as exemplary "pieces" have been influenced by insidious human effects such as the chestnut blight, Dutch elm disease, grazing, and incendiary fire. Consequently, we have little basis for stating that these forests are more diverse or less diverse than they might have been without these disturbances.

Certainly we can say that the richness or number of species within the eastern forests has changed. Some species have dropped out of many stands (e.g., American chestnut, *Castanea dentata*) while others have been added (e.g., kudzu-vine, *Pueraria lobata*; Japanese honeysuckle, *Lonicera japonica*; and tree-of-heaven, *Ailanthus altissima*). Invariably, the added species are exotics that aggressively inhabit areas following disturbance. In this manual, we hope to raise the reader's awareness of native and exotic species in the Central Hardwood Forests of North America as well as promote the use of native species in the landscape. Development of the awareness of native plant species, where they grow, and what their uses are should bring about an appreciation for the richness of species in native Central Hardwood Forest communities.

Not only are these forest communities of interest in themselves, but they also provide the food, cover, and space for a variety of animal species. The mixed mesophytic forest contains one of the richest assemblages of plant species and very complex insect, bird, and amphibian communities. We have attempted to provide examples of the values of trees not only to humans, but also to other animals that inhabit the region. It is important to recognize that many animals require forest stands of sufficient size to support viable populations in the Central Hardwood Forests. The natural complexity of plant and animal communities declines as the forest becomes fragmented into smaller and smaller pieces. Thus, it is not only important that we save the pieces of our ecological machine as we tinker with it, we must also save pieces of sufficient size that we do not lose any more of the cogs and gears that keep it rolling along a natural trajectory. The use of native trees in the landscape, in stands, and in forests would be one step toward maintaining complexity in the structure and function of Central Hardwood Forests.

Donald J. Leopold
William C. McComb
Robert N. Muller

Acknowledgments

Although all the authors of articles and books listed in the bibliography have facilitated the development and completion of this book, two authors and their books deserve special mention: Charles Sargent, *Manual of the Trees of North America*, and Michael Dirr, *Manual of Woody Landscape Plants*. A true admirer and lifelong learner of woody plants could hardly do without either. Sargent's manual, although often difficult to read because of the changes in plant nomenclature since 1922 and seemingly endless technical terms, is incomparable in amount of botanical detail for the trees native to North America. Dirr's book, unsurpassed for botanical and horticultural detail (and wit) on woody plants, has inspired me and apparently uncounted individuals since the first edition was published in 1975. I do not think that our book would have ever happened if not for these truly outstanding plantsmen.

Inda Kidd typed the first drafts of this manuscript. Sandra Polimino worked on numerous later drafts and, with Gwynne May, converted the manuscript into forms that I could use; she also provided much logistical support throughout the last ten years of this project. I thank David Apsley, Larry Doyle, Clarence Hubbuch, Mark A. Leopold, George Parker, and Mary Witt for reviewing earlier drafts of this manuscript.

Amy Edwards prepared all the line drawings. Greg McGee produced all the range maps, based on species distribution maps from Volumes 1 and 4 of the *Atlas of United States Trees* (Little 1971, 1977).

Doug Pearsall assisted in taking some of the black-and-white close-up photographs, otherwise I am responsible for all the color and black-and-white photography. I thank Mark A. Leopold for accompanying me on trips to take photographs. My family—Nancy, Kay, and Mark F.—willingly has accepted many detours to final destinations so that I could photograph particular specimens. I appreciate the support for photographs provided by The New York State/United University Professions Professional Development and Quality of Worklife Committee, and the State University of New York College of Environmental Science and

Forestry (SUNY-CESF). Industrial Color Labs, Syracuse, New York, was very helpful in printing the black-and-white photographs. The SUNY-CESF Instructional Services Department, particularly Stella Kroft, Tom Reagan, and George Snyder, have been very helpful with the production of the photographs.

SUNY-CESF and the Faculty of Environmental and Forest Biology have been supportive of this project throughout, principally by allowing me a sabbatical to focus on this manuscript. I especially thank my colleagues Dudley Raynal and Robert Burgess for their support and encouragement.

Donald J. Leopold

Introduction

Trees may have different values to different people. To recreationists trees are a source of the natural beauty and aesthetic quality which are important in our everyday life. To wildlife biologists trees are the sources of food and cover required by many animals that occur in forested ecosystems. To ecologists trees are the basis for storage of 90% of the biosphere's fixed energy and are the dominant species of complex ecosystems. To foresters trees supply food, fiber, and energy necessary to support the world's growing population.

What is a tree? A clear definition may be elusive because species and even individuals within a species gradually change from low-lying shrubs into full-statured trees. The extreme conditions are, or course, obvious. It is in the middle, where a line must be drawn, that the difficulty arises. One definition is that a tree is a "woody plant having one erect perennial stem or trunk at least 3 in. (8 cm) in diameter at breast height (4.5 ft or 1.4 m), and a height of at least 13 ft (4 m)" (Little 1979). Using this definition, Little has described 679 species of trees as native to the continental United States. An additional 69 species are described as being naturalized, that is, having been introduced either by accident or design and are now maintaining established populations capable of successful reproduction.

The Central Hardwood Forests of North America (see map) have more than 200 species of native trees. These are not evenly distributed throughout the region. Some are found in more northerly locations, others in the south. Still others may be endemic, or restricted to only very localized sites. These broad distributional patterns reflect the geographic ranges of the species in the Central Hardwood Forests. Within more local areas, however, important patterns of species distribution are still apparent. These patterns may be associated with environmental conditions such as moisture status or nutrient availability of a site, or they may be associated with historical factors influencing a site such as past disturbance.

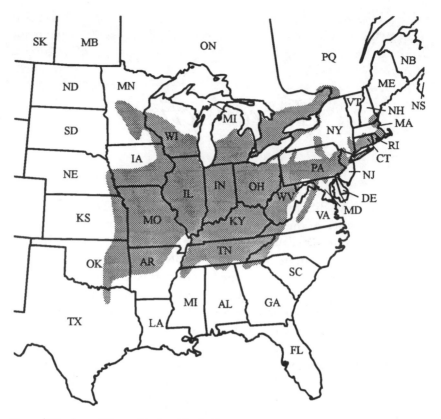

Central Hardwood Forest Region (shaded).

All plants are constrained by environmental and disturbance factors. Some exhibit similar responses to these constraints and are frequently observed in association with one another on particular sites. These associations are so repetitive that "communities" of organisms are recognized. Thus, within any phytogeographic region of the Central Hardwood Forests, trees, shrubs, and herbs are assembled into identifiable groups. It is important to recognize that this sorting is a growth response to changing environmental conditions. Where important environmental factors such as moisture and fertility change gradually, species composition may be expected to change gradually as well. Thus, forest communities are actually gradients of species responding to gradients of environmental change. A brief discussion of the vegetation in the Central Hardwood Forests and important species associations follows in the next section.

The ability to identify trees is important to several interests. Certainly, there are numerous practical applications of the knowledge that relate to the management of our natural renewable resources. Land managers, be they foresters, wildlife biologists, farmers, or horticulturists, utilize the knowledge in varying intensities as part of their professional activities. Scientists seeking to understand the complexities and important inter-relationships of the biosphere require a working knowledge of the species with which they are dealing. Not least, we all express a native curiosity about the environment in which we live. It is hoped that the Keys and Species Descriptions of this manual will contribute to the working needs of land managers and scientists, and will stimulate and satisfy some of the environmental curiosity that lies in us all.

Trees have an aesthetic character that adds to the quality of life in our daily existence. As a result, they are frequently used along with shrubs and herbs in planting in areas where we live and work. To fully appreciate the flowers, fruits, and foliage of native trees planted in the landscape, the environmental requirements and growth characteristics of each species must be fully considered before planting and propagation. The Species Descriptions, including the category of Landscape Value, provide information that should be considered in choosing species for ornamental use.

THE CENTRAL HARDWOOD FOREST REGION

The Central Hardwood Forests are a broad band of forests in eastern North America that are distinguished by dominance of broad-leaved, deciduous species. Evergreen forests exist to the north and south. The needle-leaved, coniferous forests of the Canadian Shield reflect adaptations to shortened growing seasons and extreme winter temperatures. In contrast, the more tropical evergreen, broad-leaved forests of southern Florida and Central America exhibit adaptations to continual growing seasons without the danger of damage by frost.

On both the northern and southern boundaries of the Central Hardwood Forests, transitions to these predominantly evergreen forests exist. The mixed deciduous-evergreen forests of the Hemlock–White Pine–Northern Hardwoods region, extending from northern Wisconsin to Maine, represent the transition from the predominantly broad-leaved, deciduous Central Hardwood Forests to the predominantly evergreen, needle-leaved forests of the Boreal Forest. To the south, the mixed forests of the Oak-Pine and Southeastern Evergreen Forest regions are transitional to the predominantly evergreen, broad-leaved forests of the tropics. For the purposes of this book the Central Hardwood Forests include only those portions of eastern North America that are dominated by deciduous species.

Climate

The climate of the Central Hardwood Forests is classified as humid, mid-continental with no strong seasonal variation in precipitation. The boundaries of the region and the shift to vegetation of different physiognomic character are, in part, delineated by important shifts in climatic pattern, which are associated with the yearly cycle of atmospheric movement across the continent. The northern boundary and transition to boreal forest are related to the arctic airstream as it crosses the Canadian land mass from west to east. Areas which are influenced by arctic air masses for 3½ months or more (principally during the winter) are covered by boreal forest. More southerly regions contain deciduous forest. The transition to grasslands in the west is associated with the winter rainshadow on the lee side of the Rocky Mountain Cordillera and resultant decreased precipitation in the prairie lands of the Great Plains. This rainshadow is provided by the strong influence of Pacific air masses moving across the mid-continental region in winter. In summer, the Pacific air masses are replaced by movement of moisture-laden atmosphere derived from the Gulf of Mexico, which produces the frontal precipitation characteristic of both the Great Plains grasslands and the Central Hardwood Forests. The southern transition of the Central Hardwood Forests to a mixed forest with a greater importance of evergreen species, especially laurels and conifers, is associated with the continuous influence of warm, moist, tropical air masses from the Gulf of Mexico. Major climatic shifts to the east are the result of maritime influences of the Atlantic Ocean. These changes are not significant enough alone, however, to change the physiognomy of the resulting forest vegetation; species composition is the product of both geologic and climatic influences.

Within the Central Hardwood Forests the principal climatic variations are associated with north-south gradients of precipitation and temperature. Mean annual precipitation is more than 47 in. (120 cm) per year in Tennessee, but less than 32 in. (80 cm) per year in central Wisconsin and the lower peninsula of Michigan. Similarly, temperature declines with increasing latitude. Mean January and July temperatures are 40 and 78°F (4.4 and 25.7°C), respectively, in Nashville, Tennessee, and 24 and 70°F (-4.3 and 22.1°C) in Lansing, Michigan. Higher temperatures in the southern portion of the region where precipitation is greatest, of course, imply greater evaporative demand. Average annual pan evaporation is about 40 in. (100 cm) per year in Tennessee and declines to about 28 in. (70 cm) per year in central Wisconsin. Thus, higher evaporation compensates in part for increased precipitation in the South, and gradients in available moisture for vegetation within the Central Hardwood Forests are reasonably shallow. Dates of first and last frost, of course, are closely aligned with average temperatures. As a result, length of the growing season is considerably longer in the southern portion of the region (more than 200 days in Tennessee) than in the northern (140 days in central Wisconsin).

PHYSIOGRAPHY AND GEOLOGY

The Central Hardwood Forests include five major physiographic provinces that are closely tied to the geologic and glacial history of the region. These include the Appalachian Plateaus of eastern Tennessee and Kentucky, southeastern Ohio, Pennsylvania, and New York; the Central Lowlands Province of Ohio, Indiana, Illinois, Wisconsin, and Michigan; the Interior Low Plateau Province of central Tennessee and Kentucky; and the Ouachita Province and Ozark Plateaus of Arkansas and southern Missouri. The geologic substrates represented in these physiographic provinces are all of marine sedimentary origin and are extremely variable in age and composition. Deposition of these sediments occurred during various periods of the Paleozoic Era, some 225–600 million years ago. At that time the central United States was submerged under a vast inland sea that accumulated materials eroded from surrounding upland regions. The present-day Appalachian Mountains and associated plateaus are comprised of deep sediments deposited in an oceanic trough (geosyncline), and the balance of the central United States consists of deposits made in shallower seas. Subsequent uplift brought these consolidated sediments to the surface where they were eroded and modified by further mountain-building processes and more recently by glacial action.

The physiography of the Appalachian Plateaus and Central Lowlands Provinces has been modified by four glacial advances during the Pleistocene. The major effect of these glacial epochs was through sculpting of the landscape during and following each advance. As subsequent glacial advances developed, the influences of earlier advances were obliterated and new landforms were established. The oldest advance, the Nebraskan, occurred one million years ago and is evident only in a narrow band along the southwestern margin of the glaciated region in Missouri, Kansas, and Nebraska. Drift from the Kansan advance (750,000 years ago) occurs in a slightly larger area in Missouri, Kansas, Nebraska, Iowa, Minnesota, and South Dakota. The Illinoian drift (350,000 years ago) occurs in a band along the southern border of the glaciated region in Illinois, Indiana, Ohio, and parts of Pennsylvania and New York. More recently, the Wisconsin advance (25,000 years ago) reached its southern limit in South Dakota and the central parts of Iowa, Illinois, Indiana, and Ohio. Most of New York is covered by glacial till from the Wisconsin ice sheet. It is interesting that a large area of southwestern Wisconsin was never covered by glacial ice. The driftless area covers some 10,000 mi^2 (25,900 km^2) and was protected from the continental ice sheets by the Superior Highlands in northern Wisconsin.

An additional important feature of the glacial retreat was the development of large deposits of wind-blown silt (loess). Following each glacial retreat, alluvial deposits in the floodplains of major drainage systems provided a source of fine-grained material exposed to movement by wind. This air-borne material was subsequently deposited in grasslands, which provided a matrix for trapping the material. The most significant loess movement occurred during the interglacial periods following the Illinoian and Wisconsin glaciations. Large deposits of loess can be found throughout the Central Hardwood Forests, principally near the Mississippi and Missouri Rivers.

The Appalachian Plateaus

The Appalachian Plateaus were formed as part of the massive uplift of marine sediments that was responsible for the formation of the upland regions encompassing all the United States east of the Central Lowlands. In the Appalachian Plateaus this uplift occurred with relatively little of the folding characteristic of the Ridge and Valley and other provinces to the east. As a result, most of the exposed sediments are horizontally bedded. The Appalachian Plateaus are bounded on the east by the Appalachian Front, a southeast-facing escarpment facing the Ridge and Valley Province. On the west, the boundary is frequently less obvious and consists of an escarpment of Mississippian and Pennsylvanian materials that extends from Ohio south to Alabama and forms scattered promontories known as "knobs." In central and northern Ohio the escarpment is apparent principally in the topographic contrast between the low relief of the glacial till plains in the west and the more eroded contours of the plateau on the east.

Throughout the Plateaus, local physiography is a product of geologic substrate and erosional and glacial history. In the north the Catskill Mountains exhibit greater relief than any other part of the province because of the erosion-resistant nature of the exposed rock. Maximum elevations reach 4000 ft. (1219 m) and, locally, mountain tops may be as much as 2000 ft. (607 m) above valley bottoms.

The remainder of the northern portion of the Appalachian Plateaus, known as the Allegheny Plateau, consists principally of shales and sandstones. Frequently, where beds of limestone did occur at the surface, the softer nature of this rock led to its solution and erosion, leaving the harder sandstone material behind. Glacial scouring of the northern Allegheny Plateau in New York and northern Pennsylvania has modified many of its features. Altitudes throughout range from 1000 to 2000 ft. (305 to 607 m), and relief is rarely greater than 400 ft. (122 m). The surface of the Allegheny Plateau is gently undulating with steepest slopes occurring close to the valley bottoms.

South of the Allegheny Plateau lies the Cumberland Plateau, a more dissected, rougher landscape. The northern boundary of the Cumberland Plateau is generally considered to be the topographic divide between the Kentucky River drainage and the upper Ohio River watershed. On the west it is bordered by the Pottsville escarpment overlooking the Interior Low Plateaus and on the east by the Cumberland Mountains, an extension of the Allegheny Front. Geologic exposures consist throughout of Pennsylvanian materials, principally interbedded layers of sandstone, siltstone, and shale with interspersed beds of coal. However, outcrops of limestone may occur. The notable feature of the Cumberland Plateau is the degree of dissection of the landscape. Erosional networks are dendritic and consist of long, steep slopes with narrow ridge tops and narrow valley bottoms. The maturity of dissection increases to the east and reaches its peak adjacent to the Cumberland Mountains. This dissection provides an array of site conditions and optimum growing conditions for many tree species.

The Central Lowlands

The Central Lowlands are one of the most extensive physiographic provinces of the contiguous United States, covering approximately 650,000 mi^2 (1,683,500 km^2). The surface of the province slopes inwardly from elevations of about 1000 ft. (305 m) at its eastern margin adjacent to the Appalachian Plateaus to 500 ft. (152 m) along the Mississippi River and then rises again to about 2000 ft. (610 m) at the 100th meridian, the approximate western margin of the province. There are no outstanding physiographic features, and relief throughout the province is extremely gentle. The characteristic attributes of the province are its great extent, low elevation and relief, continental climate, great lakes and rivers, and its overlying mantle of glacial deposits that provide a uniform ground surface and mask much of the underlying geologic features.

Most of the Central Lowlands was glaciated during the various ice advances of the Pleistocene, and the landscape as seen today reflects the glacial histories of the region. The Great Lakes Section of this province lies at the northern margin of the Central Hardwoods Forests and consists of a plain of late Wisconsin glacial till with interspersed morainal ridges occurring in concentric rings around the bases of the Great Lakes. Between the morainal ridges the terrain is varied, consisting of knobs and water-filled kettle holes.

The Till Plain Section occurring to the south consists mostly of till from the Illinoian and, to the west, Kansan ice advances. Because of its older age and longer erosional history, there are few lakes and ponds. The drainage networks are well integrated, and the landscape consists of broad uplands between steep-sided valleys with broad floodplains. That portion of the Till Plain Section adjacent to the Mississippi River is covered by a blanket of loess (wind-blown silt), which is commonly more than 30 ft. (9.1 m) thick. The thickness of the deposit lessens at greater distances from the river, which was the original source of material. Because of the predominance of small-sized particles in the soil and the lack of internal structure, the loess deposits are subject to severe erosion, which has been intensified by misuse of the resource.

The driftless area of southwestern Wisconsin was not glaciated because it lay between two major channels of ice flow, the valleys of Lake Superior and Lake Michigan, and because it was protected by the prominence of the Superior Upland to the north. Glacial deposits are lacking throughout the area, and the presence of fine physiographic details (e.g., natural bridges, rock towers) point to the lack of glacial scouring.

Other sections of the Central Lowland Province (i.e., the Small Lakes Section and the Manitoba Plain to the northwest, and the Osage Plain to the southwest) lie outside the Central Hardwood Forests and are not considered here.

The Interior Low Plateau

The Interior Low Plateau Province lies south of the glaciated region of the Central Lowlands. The striking geologic feature of the province is the presence of a broad anticline, the Cincinnati Arch, which runs along a north-south axis from northwestern Alabama to northwestern Ohio. In the north, glacial outwash dictates the character of the landscape, which is generally considered to be part of the Central Lowlands Till Plains.

The unglaciated region of the Arch south of the Ohio River constitutes the Interior Low Plateaus.

The Lexington Plain and the Nashville Basin are on geologic domes of Ordovician limestone exposed by the Cincinnati Arch. These limestone regions contain some karst topography with its sinkholes and subterranean drainage systems.

The bulk of the remainder of the Interior Low Plateaus is included in the Highland Rim Section, which surrounds the Nashville Basin and lies on three sides of the Lexington Plain. The Highland Rim is a cuesta with escarpments facing inward towards the two geologic domes. Surrounding the Lexington Plain the escarpment of Silurian and Devonian materials has been eroded to form the distinctive Knobs Region, an area of conical prominences whose form is attributable to the presence of the highly erosive, oil-bearing Ohio Shale. The escarpment surrounding the Nashville Basin is one of limestone, incised by drainage systems, with elevations ranging from 500 to 1000 ft. (152 to 305 m). The bulk of the Highland Rim is of Mississippian origin and contains large areas of limestone; however, only about one-half of the section contains karst topography.

Separated from the Highland Rim by a prominent escarpment to the northwest lies the Shawnee Hills Section in western Kentucky. This section contains the same coal-bearing strata of Pennsylvanian-aged sandstone and shale which occur in the Appalachian Plateaus. The similarity in geologic exposures in the Shawnee Hills and the Appalachian Plateaus is echoed by many similarities in composition of the vegetation.

The Ouachita Province and Ozark Plateaus

The Ouachita Province and Ozark Plateaus are two adjacent upland areas in the southwestern corner of the Central Hardwood Forests, lying west of the Mississippi River and south of the Missouri. The southerly Ouachita Mountains are formed from thick sandstone sediments deposited throughout the Paleozoic. Subsequent uplift involving multiple thrusts and folds of the deposits have formed the present-day mountains, which lie in a more or less linear arrangement of ridges and valleys with maximum elevations of about 2600 ft. (793 m). The Arkansas River Valley north of the Ouachita Mountains separates them from the Ozark Plateaus. The geologic exposures of the Arkansas River Valley contain Pennsylvanian sandstones and shales with interbedded coal deposits similar to the Appalachian Plateaus and the Shawnee Section of the Interior Low Plateaus.

The Ozark Plateaus are a broad upwarped plain with maximum

elevations ranging between 1700 and 2000 ft. (518 and 610 m). The geologic structure of the plateau is similar to the domes created by the Cincinnati Arch in the Interior Low Plateaus. The exposed strata are predominantly limestone materials derived from Cambrian and Ordovician deposits in the center of the dome and from surrounding Mississippian deposits. Pennsylvanian sandstones and shales occur in northern and southern parts of the province. Their greatest importance occurs at the southern margin where greater elevations and subsequent erosion have produced the Boston Mountains, an area of increased relief and steep slopes. Besides the Boston Mountains the bulk of the Ozark Plateaus exhibits only shallow relief, and most of the topography is the product of solution processes acting on the calcareous substrate.

The Ridge and Valley and the Blue Ridge

Both the Ridge and Valley and the Blue Ridge Provinces are narrow, longitudinally oriented physiographic units that encompass the Appalachian Crest and constitute the divide between the Atlantic coastal watersheds and those draining to the Mississippi Basin. The Ridge and Valley Province extends from central Alabama through Vermont and is limited by the Coastal Plain to the south and the St. Lawrence Lowland to the north.

As its name implies, this is a region of parallel ridges and valleys produced from marine deposits occurring through much of the Paleozoic. Continental movement at the end of the Paleozoic pushed the Blue Ridge and Piedmont Provinces against the eastern side of the oceanic trough in which these deposits had occurred. Compression of the sediments caused folding, resulting in the linear ridges and valleys observed today. Because of the long history of deposition (from the Cambrian through the Pennsylvanian) the Ridge and Valley Province includes much sandstone and shale along the eastern margin, and shale and limestone on the west. During the Pennsylvanian, organic materials originating from coastal swamps contributed to deposits, which now make up the desirable anthracite coal beds of the province.

The Blue Ridge Province is similar to the Ridge and Valley Province in geographic boundaries. It extends from northern Georgia to central Pennsylvania in a narrow band, never more than 50 mi (80 km) wide. It includes the central and southern portions of the Appalachian Crest overlooking the Piedmont Province to the east. As such it contains the highest peaks of the Appalachian Highlands, which reach a maximum elevation of 6684 ft. (2037 m) on Mt. Mitchell in North Carolina. The high elevations contained in the province provide cooler climates in the south, which support more northern vegetation types. Exposed geologic substrates include granite and gneiss of Precambrian origin, which are believed to have formed the original oceanic trough in which sediments of today's Appalachian Highlands were deposited. In the southern Blue Ridge some of the early sediments from Precambrian origin are exposed as siltstones, sandstones, and conglomerates.

FOREST VEGETATION

The vegetation of the Central Hardwood Forests has an ecological history of about 18,000 years, the time that has elapsed since the last full glacial maximum. The evolutionary history of the flora is much older and traces much of its origin to the Arcto-Tertiary Geoflora, which covered much of the northern half of the United States and all Canada during the Tertiary, some 65 million years ago. Prominent genera of that period included the hickories, elms, maples, and ashes that are found in the eastern United States today.

During the last full glacial period, species were not only exterminated from regions north of the glacial boundary, but to the south, species were redistributed in accord with the altered regional climatic regimes. Thus, immediately adjacent to the glacial boundary a narrow band of tundra existed. South of this, a broad distribution of spruce-dominated forest existed with eastern larch (*Larix laricina*) as an associate to the west of the Mississippi River and jack pine (*Pinus banksiana*) to the east. The southern region in what is now the Gulf Coastal Plain was covered by an oak–hickory–southern pine forest. However, along the bluffs of the major rivers, which were created from loess deposits of an earlier glacial age, lay habitats covered with a mixed mesophytic forest whose composition included a mixture of deciduous taxa (*Acer saccharum, Alnus, Betula, Carpinus caroliniana, Carya, Fagus grandifolia, Fraxinus, Juglans nigra, Liriodendron tulipifera, Magnolia acuminata, Quercus,* and *Ulmus*). The richness and composition of these late-glacial species assemblages have been taken as evidence that the blufflands of the lower Mississippi River served as a refuge for cool-temperate taxa during the last full-glacial maximum. The diverse array of cool-temperate species contained in these habitats provided the genetic pool from which the species of today's Central Hardwood Forests were drawn.

The vegetation of the Central Hardwood Forests has been classified variously over the last 100 years. However, the general outlines of each classification remain approximately the same. Three broad regions may be considered within the Central Hardwood Forests: northern forests in which sugar maple (*Acer saccharum*) is an important dominant; southern forests in which a variety of oaks (*Quercus* spp.) are dominant; and central forests of the Appalachian Highlands, which are characterized by a high diversity of species and dominance by none. Each of these regions may be further divided into associations or vegetational complexes that form descriptive units upon which the following discussion is based. While forests to the north and south may contain large components of broad-leaved deciduous species, they also contain a significant evergreen component. The Central Hardwood Forests are distinguished by the dominance of broad-leaved deciduous species. The mixed deciduous-evergreen forests to the north and south are not considered here.

Mixed Mesophytic Forests

The Mixed Mesophytic Forest Region encompasses much of the Appalachian Highlands, including the Cumberland Mountains and Cumberland Plateau to the south, and the Allegheny Mountains and the unglaciated portion of the Allegheny Plateau to the north. Perhaps the finest examples of mixed mesophytic forest occur in the Cumberland Mountains, which combine the environmental features of optimal climate, high diversity of site conditions due to physiographic development, and fully developed soils. In the more northerly Allegheny Mountains the influence of cooler climates is reflected in the occurrence of northern species. On the Cumberland and Allegheny Plateaus moisture availability and diversity of sites circumscribe the occurrence of mixed mesophytic forest.

Mixed mesophytic forests are characterized by (1) a rich diversity of plants, which spans all strata of the forest and in which no individual species exerts clear dominance; (2) the presence of the indicator species white basswood (*Tilia heterophylla*) and yellow buckeye (*Aesculus octandra*); and (3) the occurrence of rich, dark soil horizons developed from rapid decomposition of forest litter and incorporation of organic matter into the mineral soil. In today's forests the most abundant species are sugar maple, white basswood, yellow-poplar (*Liriodendron tulipifera*), American beech (*Fagus grandifolia*), yellow buckeye, northern red oak (*Quercus rubra*), and white oak (*Q. alba*). These seven species may share 70–95% of the importance or dominance (i.e., relative density or basal area) within a forest stand. However, a complete list of trees would include more than 30 species. Among the important understory arborescent species are American hornbeam (*Carpinus caroliniana*), flowering dogwood (*Cornus florida*), eastern redbud (*Cercis canadensis*), and, on drier sites, sourwood (*Oxydendrum arboreum*) and downy serviceberry (*Amelanchier arborea*).

Within mixed mesophytic forests an underlying pattern of species distribution exists which is most easily described as a gradient related to slope position and aspect. This is most evident in the Cumberland Mountains, which have the greatest physiographic diversity and most equable climates. In protected coves on north- and east-facing slopes, sugar maple, white basswood, and yellow buckeye are the principal species with secondary dominants consisting of the species previously mentioned. The herbaceous layer consists of a diverse array of species that are typically restricted to moist, fertile sites. Important among these are several species in the lily family, including trilliums (*Trillium erectum* and *T. grandiflorum*), bellwort (*Uvularia perfoliata*), and spotted mandarin (*Disporum maculatum*).

On lower slopes and ravines, American beech becomes increasingly important and, in extreme situations, may account for 80% of the overstory composition. Although American beech and sugar maple form extensive forests in regions to the northwest, these species are infrequently in close association as dominant species in mixed mesophytic forests. Secondary species associated with American beech in lower slope stands include yellow-poplar, sugar maple, cucumbertree (*Magnolia acuminata*), white basswood, and yellow buckeye. In very protected ravines, American beech may be replaced by pockets of eastern hemlock (*Tsuga canadensis*). Significant changes related to soil character are easily noted on these beech-dominated lower slopes, where increased accumulation of undecomposed leaves on the forest floor is accompanied by shifts in herbaceous composition away from dominance by lilies. Important herbaceous species here are Christmas fern (*Polystichum acrostichoides*), beggar's ticks (*Desmodium nudiflorum*), Virginia creeper (*Parthenocissus quinquefolia*), false goat's-beard (*Astilbe biternata*), and heart-leaved aster (*Aster divericatus*). On more exposed lower slopes the dominance by American beech is reduced and other species, especially white oak, may become important.

The role of eastern hemlock is variable. It may form pure stands, which frequently are the result of prior disturbance. However, it also is an associate of mixed deciduous species. This forest is similar in many respects to the all-deciduous mixed mesophytic forest previously described. In particular, species composition is varied with none being dominant. However, sugar maple, white basswood, and yellow buckeye are poorly represented when eastern hemlock is present. At densities below 30% of stand composition eastern hemlock seems to have little influence on herbaceous composition. However, at greater densities the combination of reduced light and altered soil character (hemlock litter is acidic) serve to modify understory composition. As in beech-dominated sites, lilies are poorly represented and ericaceous species (i.e., members of the Ericaceae or heath family) are more abundant. Rosebay rhododendron (*Rhododendron maximum*) is a common associate of dense hemlock stands along with partridge berry (*Mitchella repens*), round leaf yellow violet (*Viola rotundifolia*), and in some cases mountain-laurel (*Kalmia latifolia*), sweet pepperbush (*Clethra acuminata*), and mountain-camellia (*Stewartia ovata*).

On more exposed upper slopes and ridges of the Cumberland Mountains the mixed mesophytic character gives way to an oak forest strongly dominated by oaks in the overstory and the ericaceous species in the understory. Five species of oak regularly occur in the region, and these tend to be segregated by moisture requirements. Northern red oak is generally restricted to mesic conditions, where it is a typical associate of American beech, sugar maple, yellow-poplar, and other mesophytic species. White oak is also an important component of mesophytic associations; however, typically it is restricted to drier conditions. Although black oak (*Quercus velutina*) is rarely a dominant species, it occurs frequently on drier slopes and ridges in association with white oak, chestnut oak (*Q. prinus*), and scarlet oak (*Q. coccinea*). The latter two are the principal species of dry upper slopes and ridges. Chestnut oak occurs on slightly less exposed north-facing slopes and ridge tops, and scarlet oak occurs on drier south- and west-facing upper slopes. Secondary species of these oak forests include red maple and downy serviceberry. The understory is dominated by ericaceous shrubs and herbs, including mountain-laurel, flame azalea (*Rhododendron calendulaceum*), trailing arbutus (*Epigaea repens*), wintergreen (*Gaultheria procumbens*), lowbush blueberry (*Vaccinium vacillans*), and farkleberry (*V. arboreum*). The open herbaceous layer frequently includes pink lady's-slipper (*Cypripedium acaule*), alum-root (*Heuchera longiflora*), whorled loosestrife (*Lysimachia quadrifolia*), smooth false foxglove (*Aureolaria laevigata*), large coreopsis (*Coreopsis major*), and hawkweed (*Hieracium venosum*).

On extremely dry ridges a pine or pine-oak forest may prevail. Pitch pine (*Pinus rigida*) and shortleaf pine (*P. echinata*) are prominent on extremely dry sites with shallow, sandy soil. Scarlet oak is a frequent associate along with chestnut oak, black oak, blackgum (*Nyssa sylvatica*), and sourwood. The understory is frequently dominated by lowbush blueberry and farkleberry.

Riparian forests are not a prominent feature of the more mountainous portions of the Mixed Mesophytic Forest Region; however, the forested floodplains of continuously flowing streams contain river birch (*Betula nigra*), American sycamore (*Platanus occidentalis*), American hornbeam, and umbrella magnolia (*Magnolia tripetala*). Overgrown agricultural fields of wet floodplains may also contain thickets of smooth alder (*Alnus serrulata*). In less deeply dissected portions of the Cumberland and Allegheny Plateaus broad valleys support a variety of swamp species including pin oak (*Quercus palustris*), swamp white oak (*Q. bicolor*), swamp chestnut oak (*Q. michauxii*), sweetgum (*Liquidambar styraciflua*), and red maple (*Acer rubrum*). Many of these swamp forests contain disjunct species from the Coastal Plain.

Mixed mesophytic forests have been described as a center of distribution for species of the eastern deciduous forest. Certainly the mixed mesophytic forest contains the forest communities with the greatest diversity of species, and many of the dominants and subdominants from other regions of the deciduous forest region are found as dominants of the mixed mesophytic forest. To the north, glacial soils and cooler temperatures restrict the distribution of species with southerly affinities. To the west, more mesophytic species are limited by the increasing aridity of the forest environment.

Oak-Hickory Forests

The westernmost boundary of the eastern deciduous forest is reached at approximately the 98th meridian. Along its extent from the boreal forest region to the Gulf of Mexico the expansive oak-hickory forest prevails. Much of this is included within the Central Hardwood Forests. As its name implies oak-hickory forest is characterized by dominance of oak and hickory (*Carya*) species. However, substantial variation in composition does occur and relates both to regional variation in glacial history as well as localized variation in site quality.

White oak, northern red oak, black oak, bitternut hickory (*Carya cordiformis*), and pignut hickory (*C. glabra*) are broadly spread and contribute significantly to composition of oak-hickory forests. Migrational histories of species originating in the Ozark Upland, first onto the Kansan till and then onto the younger Wisconsin drift, have segregated species composition. For instance, gum bumelia (*Bumelia lanuginosa*) and Shumard oak (*Quercus shumardii*) occur only rarely north of the glacial boundary. Other oaks, such as post oak (*Q. stellata*) and blackjack oak (*Q. marilandica*), extend some distance onto the Kansan drift, but are not found around the younger Wisconsin drift. Bur oak (*Q. macrocarpa*) occurs throughout the glaciated and unglaciated regions of the oak-hickory forest. Finally, northern pin oak (*Q. ellipsoidalis*) and swamp white oak are generally restricted to regions north of the glacial margin. These segregations strongly influence forest composition of the glaciated and unglaciated portions of the oak-hickory forests.

The strongest site-related gradients in species composition are found in the southern portion of the oak-hickory forests where decreased moisture and increased topographic relief provide variety of site conditions. On more exposed ridges and slopes, drier conditions favor almost pure stands of post oak and blackjack oak. Secondary species may include shortleaf pine, black oak, Shumard oak, black hickory (*Carya texana*), winged elm (*Ulmus alata*), flowering dogwood, and common persimmon (*Diospyros virginiana*). On less extremely xeric sites black oak may become an important associate of post oak and blackjack oak. White oak may be an associate of post oak and black oak on exposed ridges and upper slopes, but is most abundant on less xeric, north-facing slopes where it may be clearly the dominant species. Throughout all these oak forests the understory may include flowering dogwood, New Jersey tea (*Ceanothus americanus*), and fragrant sumac (*Rhus aromatica*). In the more mesophytic white oak forests, associated species include eastern redbud, eastern hophornbeam (*Ostrya virginiana*), American hornbeam, red mulberry (*Morus rubra*), serviceberry, pawpaw (*Asimina triloba*), and gum bumelia. The occurrence of truly mesophytic forests is restricted to the most protected sites found in ravines and north-facing lower slopes. On these sites, white oak may remain as a dominant species of the overstory. However, it shares dominance with several more mesophytic species including northern red oak, sugar maple, black walnut (*Juglans nigra*), white ash (*Fraxinus americana*), and bitternut hickory. The shrub layer of these mesophytic forests contains species frequently found in more mesophytic forests to the east. These include wild hydrangea (*Hydrangea arborescens*), Virginia creeper, and spicebush (*Lindera benzoin*). Finally, in the moister bottoms water oak (*Quercus nigra*), overcup oak (*Q. lyrata*), pecan (*C. illinoensis*), nutmeg hickory (*C. myristiciformis*), and water hickory (*C. aquatica*) are important, as are the successional associates silver maple (*Acer saccharinum*), American sycamore, black willow (*Salix nigra*), river birch, and green ash (*Fraxinus pennsylvanica*).

Because of its prolific reproductive capacity sugar maple is frequently found in the understories of the less xeric oak and hickory-dominated sites. This has led to recent speculation that the oak-hickory forest is fundamentally a successional forest that will eventually be replaced by sugar maple-dominated stands. However, successful establishment of sugar maple forests is dependent upon several factors, of which seedling establishment is only one. Mortality of sugar maple saplings during recent droughts suggests that infrequent events such as these may be far more important determinants of final species composition than simply seedling establishment.

Within the unglaciated region of the oak-hickory forest the Boston Mountains are of considerable interest for their geologic and vegetational similarities to the Shawnee Hills of the Interior Low Plateau Province and the Appalachian Plateaus. The surficial geology of all these regions is dominated by sediments of Pennsylvanian age, and in spite of increasing aridity in the more western areas, they all contain very similar vegetation. American beech may dominate the mesic sites of deep ravines, but may extend up the talus slopes above those ravines as well. Associated species may include northern red oak, white oak, chinkapin oak (*Quercus muehlenbergii*), blackgum, American elm (*Ulmus americana*), and Carolina basswood (*Tilia caroliniana*). The understory includes eastern redbud and flowering dogwood. Notable along with the high diversity of mesophytic species is the occurrence of cucumbertree and umbrella magnolia. Magnolias, which are commonly found in the mixed mesophytic forest region, are restricted from forests to the west of the Appalachian Plateaus except where Pennsylvanian substrates occur.

Within the glaciated region of oak-hickory forests, moisture availability is an important determinant of species distribution. In the moister regions to the east the mesophytic forests are dominated by sugar maple and American basswood (*Tilia americana*). However, as sugar maple reaches its physiological moisture limits in the more westerly areas, it is replaced by northern red oak, and northern red oak–basswood communities dominate the more mesic sites. On more xeric sites of the glaciated region several varieties of oak-hickory dominated vegetation occur. White oak, an ever important species of the deciduous forest, may be a dominant on the most xeric sites. Associates may include a variety of oaks and hickories, as well as more mesophytic species such as sugar maple and white ash. On moister upland sites white oak may share dominance with red oak and black oak. Bur oak, pignut hickory, and bitternut hickory are among the species that extend furthest west into the dry prairie regions of the plains.

Western Mesophytic Forests

The vegetation of the Interior Low Plateau Province has been described as a zone of transition between the mixed mesophytic forest to the east and the oak-hickory forest to the west. Thus, it is a region in which mesophytic communities prevail on protected sites and oak-hickory communities occur on exposed ridges and slopes. The overlying influence of declining moisture is responsible for a progressive reduction in the mesophytic character of the eastern forests. Along with this, the substantially different geologic character of the Interior Low Plateaus is responsible for additional differentiation of vegetation. This zone of transition has been termed the Western Mesophytic Forest Region.

Much of the geologic influence on vegetation composition relates to the general absence of sandstones and siltstones of Pennsylvanian origin and the presence of limestones of Ordovician or Mississippian age. Typical indicator species of mixed mesophytic forest do not occur on the older limestones. For instance, yellow buckeye and white basswood are replaced by Ohio buckeye (*Aesculus glabra*) and American basswood, and chestnut oak is replaced by chinkapin oak on the extensive limestones of the Interior Low Plateaus. Ericaceous species, especially rosebay rhododendron and lowbush blueberry, are not found west of the Appalachian Plateaus. Finally, *Magnolia* spp. are severely restricted in these limestone regions. Where Pennsylvanian material does outcrop, such as in the Shawnee Hills Section, many of these Appalachian species reappear. Characteristic species of the limestones of the Interior Low Plateaus, which are not found in the mixed mesophytic forest, include blue ash (*Fraxinus quadrangulata*), yellowwood (*Cladrastis kentukea*), eastern burningbush (*Euonymus atropurpureus*), shingle oak (*Quercus imbricaria*), Carolina buckthorn (*Rhamnus caroliniana*), and fragrant sumac.

A strong gradient of declining moisture availability from east to west overlies these influences of geologic substrate on species composition. Mixed mesophytic communities clearly occur within the Western Mesophytic Forest Region. However, they are characterized by increasing restriction to highly protected sites such as ravines and sheltered north-facing slopes or coves. Diversity within these mesophytic communities declines along the east-west gradient of declining moisture availability. Along the eastern margin of this region, especially on the shales and sandstones of the Knobs, the original mesophytic communities may be indistinguishable from those of the Appalachian Plateaus. Important canopy species include American beech, sugar maple, white ash, yellow-poplar, white oak, northern red oak, black walnut, shagbark hickory (*Carya ovata*), mockernut hickory (*C. tomentosa*), and American elm. In isolated locations the Appalachian indicator species white basswood and yellow buckeye may be present rather than their more dominant western counterparts, American basswood and Ohio buckeye. The influence of declining moisture on mesophytic communities of the West is evident in reduced diversity of species in mesophytic communities, increased dominance by one species (frequently American beech), and loss of some of the more mesophytic species such as buckeye and ash.

On more xeric sites throughout the region, oaks and hickories prevail. On limestone, white oak, black oak, southern red oak (*Quercus falcata*), and chinkapin oak predominate. On sandstones and shales of the Shawnee Hills and the Knobs scarlet oak is also prominent and chinkapin oak is replaced by chestnut oak. Among the hickories, shellbark (*Carya laciniosa*) replaces shagbark on the limestones of the Mississippian Plateaus while pignut, mockernut, and bitternut are found throughout. Associated species of these oak-hickory forests include eastern redbud, persimmon, flowering dogwood, fragrant sumac, dwarf hackberry (*Celtis tenuifolia*), and Carolina buckthorn.

Several edaphic variations exist within western mesophytic forests. Most prominent among these is in the Blue Grass Region, which is distinctive because of the occurrence of Ordovician-aged limestone, much of which contains high levels of phosphorus. The vegetation of this region has been heavily disturbed by humans, and in the Inner Blue Grass the remnants consist of widely spaced dominant trees of bur oak, chinkapin oak, and blue ash. Chestnut oak, yellow buckeye, and pines are missing, and species such as shagbark hickory, red maple, American beech, and yellow-poplar occur only along the cliffs of the Kentucky River. Especially fertile sites contain black walnut, Kentucky coffee-tree (*Gymnocladus dioicus*), pawpaw, spicebush, hawthorns (*Crataegus* spp.), American hornbeam, and eastern redbud, while poorer sites are dominated by white oak, Shumard oak, chinkapin oak, and flowering dogwood. In the shaly portions of the Blue Grass, eastern redcedar (*Juniperus virginiana*) is a frequent successional species on disturbed sites; however, it is restricted from the limestone of the Inner Blue Grass. The Nashville Basin of central Tennessee has similar vegetation. On deeper soils on top of the Ordovician limestone, forests with dominants of white oak and yellow-poplar occur. Sugar maple is more frequent on slopes. Secondary species include several limestone species such as sugarberry (*Celtis laevigata*), chinkapin oak, and bur oak. American elm, winged elm, black walnut, northern red oak, shagbark hickory, blackgum, black cherry, and sweetgum are also significant. On more shallow soils of the Nashville Basin, glades dominated by eastern redcedar may occur. Scattered throughout these glades may be individuals of post oak, chinkapin oak, shagbark hickory, eastern redbud, gum bumelia, fragrant sumac, and Carolina buckthorn. A distinctive assemblage of herbaceous species occurs in these glades, which does not occur in the gladelike communities developing on shallow soils following cutting. This suggests that the true cedar glades are a naturally occurring and stable community.

Surrounding the Blue Grass and extending north into south-central Indiana and eastern Ohio lies the Knobs, a region of distinct geologic character. Outcrops of relatively infertile shales and sandstones of Devonian and Silurian age provide an edaphic basis for westward extension of the Appalachian flora. Mixed mesophytic forest communities may occur on protected north- and northeast-facing slopes. Many of these sites, however, show the influence of the westward transition to oak-hickory forest through reduced overall species diversity, and replacement of some of the Appalachian species by their western counterparts. Upper slopes are strongly dominated by white or chestnut oak. Secondary species include red oak, black oak, mockernut hickory, pignut hickory, and shagbark hickory. Notably distinct in this vegetation is the presence of ericaceous species, which are restricted from the limestone region of the Interior Low Plateaus. The Knobs vegetation extends briefly into the unglaciated portion of southeastern Ohio along the escarpment of the Cumberland Plateau and covers a significant region of unglaciated south-central Indiana. In Indiana, this area has been referred to as the Chestnut Oak Upland because of the strong dominance of that species on the upper slopes and ridges.

The limestone soils of the broad Highland Rim contain most typical western mesophytic forests. Protected slopes harbor mesophytic species dominated frequently by American beech, while upper slopes and ridges contain oak, oak-hickory, and, formerly, oak-chestnut forests. The xerophytic oaks include white oak, chinkapin oak, black oak, southern red oak, and, on the poorest sites, post oak and blackjack oak. Associates may include redbud, persimmon, flowering dogwood, and shrubs such as fragrant sumac and Carolina buckthorn.

The Mississippi Embayment encompasses that region along the Mississippi River in Kentucky and Tennessee that was submerged as part of the coastal plain during the Tertiary (70 million years ago). Immediately adjacent to the Mississippi River the vegetation has been classified as Southern Mixed Evergreen Forest. However, the uplands of this region covered with soils of loess origin are clearly a part of the western mesophytic forests. The vegetation of the region is dominated by oaks and hickories, and distinctions among forest types occur principally as a function of geologic substrate as well as localized topographic influences. The rolling uplands with gravelly substrates from the period of embayment contain several oak species, including post oak, black oak, blackjack oak, white oak, northern red oak, and southern red oak. Important hickories are pignut, bitternut, and shagbark. Mesophytic forests occur where loess soils are important and are often dominated by American beech, but may contain sugar maple, American basswood, yellow-poplar, white oak, shagbark hickory, and black walnut. The presence of pawpaw in the understory reflects the mesophytic nature of these forests. The wet to mesic bottoms may contain a variety of swamp forests whose specific character depends upon the degree of flooding.

Throughout the region poorly drained flats and floodplains of slowly flowing streams and rivers provide environments conducive to growth of swamp forests. Species composition, of course, is determined by degree of tolerance for flooded conditions. In the extreme condition of continuous flooding, baldcypress (*Taxodium distichum*) may be almost exclusively dominant, or may occur with water tupelo (*Nyssa aquatica*). These southern species are found along the Mississippi and lower Ohio Rivers, as well as the Wabash River floodplain in Indiana and the Green River of Kentucky. Freely flowing streams may be bordered by eastern cottonwood (*Populus deltoides*), swamp cottonwood (*P. heterophylla*), sycamore, black willow, and silver maple. Less extensively flooded areas contain a diverse mixture of the above species and hydrophytic oaks, such as willow oak (*Quercus phellos*), swamp chestnut oak, pin oak, overcup oak, and water oak, as well as American elm, winged elm, pecan, sweetgum, and boxelder (*Acer negundo*). The variety of southern species contained in these swamp forests reflects the importance of riparian forest zones as migrational corridors for biotic species. Many of these species have their centers of distribution in the Coastal Plain and reach into the Central Hardwood Forests only by the circuitous migrational routes provided by the Mississippi River drainage basin.

Appalachian Oak Forests

Central Hardwood Forests of the Appalachian Crest and much of the eastern slope are all classified as Appalachian oak forests. Previously, these were referred to as oak-chestnut forests because of the abundance of American chestnut which has been subsequently removed, as a canopy dominant, by the chestnut blight. The region today contains a variety of forest types; however, the abundance of oaks is predominant throughout and is especially notable in the Ridge and Valley Province.

Important species of mixed oak forests include northern red oak, chestnut oak, white oak, and scarlet oak. Associates include red maple in the overstory, and sourwood, flowering dogwood, black cherry (*Prunus serotina*), sassafras (*Sassafras albidum*), hawthorns, and serviceberry. Besides the dominance of oaks in the overstory a distinctive feature of Appalachian oak forests is the presence of a well-developed understory of ericaceous shrubs. Flame azalea, in particular, is abundant throughout the region. Other ericaceous species include mountain-laurel, various blueberry species, hobble-bush (*Leucothoe* spp.), and minnie-bush (*Menziesia pilosa*). As in other regions the actual composition of the mixed oak forest reflects a gradient of moisture availability. White oak may be dominant on lower, somewhat more mesic, slopes. Under these conditions the ericaceous layer may or may not occur. Associates may include mockernut hickory, shagbark hickory, pignut hickory, witch-hazel (*Hamamelis virginiana*), maple-leaf viburnum (*Viburnum acerifolium*), and beaked hazel (*Corylus cornuta*). On more extreme, drier slopes and ridges chestnut oak or scarlet oak may prevail and frequently grade into an oak-pine forest with pitch pine, Table Mountain pine (*Pinus pungens*), short-leaf pine, and Virginia pine (*P. virginiana*).

On more protected, northerly slopes and coves a mesophytic community may exist, which is frequently marked by the presence of sugar maple. Associates may include American beech, yellow buckeye, white basswood, eastern hemlock, cucumbertree, white ash, yellow-poplar, sweet birch (*Betula lenta*), yellow birch (*B. alleghaniensis*), and black walnut. In the southern Appalachians, especially near the Great Smoky Mountains, silverbell (*Halesia monticola*) is a frequent associate of the indicator species of mixed mesophytic forest, yellow buckeye and white basswood.

The broad geographic and latitudinal extent of Appalachian oak forest necessarily includes significant climatic variation. At higher elevations along the Appalachian Crest a northern hardwood forest dominated by sugar maple, yellow birch, American beech, and yellow buckeye occurs. Associates include white ash, black cherry, silverbell, and cucumbertree. In the understory, hobblebush (*Viburnum alnifolium*), striped maple (*Acer pensylvanicum*), and mountain maple (*A. spicatum*) are frequently present. These distinctly northern species along with northern herbaceous species reflect this transition to cooler, more boreal climates at higher elevations. At extreme elevations along the Appalachian Crest, a true boreal forest may occur in which the dominant species are Fraser fir (*Abies fraseri*) and red spruce (*Picea rubens*).

Besides the cutting that has occurred in all deciduous forests, the Appalachian oak forest was significantly influenced by the loss of chestnut in the 1930s and 1940s. American chestnut was a dominant species of this region, and its loss initiated a period of ecological resorting of the remaining species. The future of these forests has been subject to debate. Some investigators have argued that future forests will remain a complex of the important oak species left behind following the blight. Others have suggested that expansion by hickories will occur, creating an oak-hickory forest type. Recent studies in Virginia have shown a significant increase in pignut hickory in a chestnut oak–northern red oak–white oak forest. However, much of the region remains a mixed oak forest with principle dominance by chestnut oak. The presence of oak-hickory forest frequently occurs with white oak as the dominant oak, suggesting that white oak dominance may open the way for hickory invasion.

Beech-Maple Forests

The beech-maple association is one of two associations characterized by considerable importance of sugar maple. Throughout beech-maple forests, dominance of forest stands is generally by the two species, sugar maple and American beech. The southern boundary of the beech-maple forests coincides closely with the Wisconsin glacial advance, which reached its maximum extent 21,000 years ago. The soils of the glaciated region are youthful compared to those occurring south of the glacial limit. The more diverse mixed mesophytic and western mesophytic forests are associated with fully developed soils, rich in nutrients and organic matter.

Thus, at the southern boundary of the beech-maple forests, strongly different forest types may be observed within a few miles of each other and are distinguished solely by the different substrates upon which they occur, not by any significant climatic change. An additional factor that limits the diversity of species in beech-maple forests is the time that has been available for migration since the last glacial retreat. Although the Wisconsin glaciation reached its maximum extent 21,000 years ago, the northern parts of the region were still glaciated as recently as 12,000 years ago. Further, the slow climatic change following the glacial retreat meant that invasion of the glaciated region by deciduous forest species was retarded another three to four thousand years.

Revegetation of this region was determined by three factors. The first potential migrants into the region were characterized by tolerance of the cooler climates associated with the more northerly region. Among these were sugar maple, American beech, eastern hemlock, and yellow birch. Second, the same species are also tolerant of the less fertile soils north of the glacial limit. Finally, the successful migrants were species with reproductive characteristics that allowed successful colonization on the glaciated sites. Sugar maple is well known for its prolific production of wind-dispersed seeds, which can establish on a variety of sites. American beech also produces large quantities of seed that are animal dispersed. It has the additional feature of successfully reproducing by means of root sprouts. While both eastern hemlock and yellow birch produce large numbers of seeds, they contain little stored food and are incapable of germinating through thick forest litter.

While beech-maple forests overall exhibit strong dominance by sugar maple and American beech, local variation in composition occurs that is principally related to edaphic conditions. Sugar maple is more frequently associated with better drained, more aerated soils of loam or silt-loam texture where reproduction is more effective. American beech, on the other hand, exhibits greater tolerance of poorly drained soils, and its seedlings are less tolerant of moisture stress than is sugar maple reproduction. Thus, on more poorly drained sites American beech may prevail, while on better drained upland sites sugar maple may be the dominant species. Associated species in the southern part of the region include yellow-poplar, white ash, blackgum, northern red oak, and white oak. Hackberry (*Celtis occidentalis*), black cherry, and eastern hophornbeam are occasional associates. In the northern part of the region American basswood, American elm, white ash, yellow birch, eastern hophornbeam, northern red oak, and bitternut hickory are more common associates. Because of the dense shade cast by both sugar maple and American beech, the understory layer may be poorly developed. Understory shrubs may include pawpaw, spicebush, red-berried elder (*Sambucus racemosa*), leatherwood (*Dirca palustris*), and maple-leaf viburnum. In the herbaceous layer, spring-flowering, ephemeral species are most common. These species are successful because of their habit of above-ground growth in the spring when light intensity at the forest floor is high. These include spring beauty (*Claytonia virginica*), cutleaf toothwort (*Dentaria laciniata*), bloodroot (*Sanguinaria canadensis*), sweet cicely (*Osmorhiza claytonii*), squirrel corn (*Dicentra canadensis*), Dutchman's breeches (*Dicentra cucullaria*), and troutlily (*Erythronium americanum*).

Physiographic dissection of the region is poorly developed; however, some differentiation does exist. In particular, wetlands of some considerable extent exist, which were derived from glacial modifications of the landscape. In northwestern Ohio the Great Black Swamp is a remnant glacial lake. Poorly drained conditions restrict the beech-maple forest to uplands where topographic dissection has produced adequately drained soils. In the wetter lowlands, an elm-ash-maple forest occurs, which may be characterized by red maple, silver maple, green ash, black ash (*Fraxinus nigra*), sweetgum, blackgum, American sycamore, pin oak, swamp white oak, and American elm.

On especially well-drained sites and along the western margin of beech-maple forests a transition to oak-hickory forest occurs. American beech, being the least tolerant of low-moisture availability, declines in importance. Sugar maple may occur in varying importance in association with the oak and hickory dominants. On these more xeric sites, white oak, black oak, chestnut oak, shagbark hickory, and pignut hickory are the most frequent dominants.

Throughout beech-maple forests, species of more northern affinity may be found locally. Arborvitae, or northern white-cedar (*Thuja occidentalis*), and Canada yew (*Taxus canadensis*) are found in Cedar Swamp of central Ohio. In the upland forests, several species of the herbaceous layer have predominantly more northern distributions. These include false lily-of-the-valley (*Maianthemum canadense*), wild sarsaparilla (*Aralia nudicaulis*), the spinulose shield fern (*Dryopteris spinulosa*), and the shrubs red-berried elder, bush-honeysuckle (*Diervilla lonicera*), and fly-honeysuckle (*Lonicera canadensis*). However, most species of beech-maple forests have more southern distributions as well. Thus, the beech-maple forest is characterized not so much by its differential species composition as it is by the importance with which these species occur. Sugar maple and beech may account for as much as 80% of the forest canopy in the beech-maple region, but only 50–60% of the canopy in the western mesophytic forests. In mixed mesophytic forests, these two species make up on average 35% of the forest canopy. The predominance of sugar maple and beech in this region relates primarily to edaphic conditions, which provide the moderately to poorly drained soils upon which these species thrive.

Maple-Basswood Forests

The distinction between maple-basswood forests and beech-maple forests relies principally on the presence or absence of American beech. From the center of the beech-maple forests westward, American beech becomes progressively less important as available moisture becomes more limiting. With this decline, associated species become more important. American basswood is especially significant in this regard. Throughout the beech-maple forests it is an important subdominant and increases in importance from east to west. In areas where beech is eliminated, American basswood replaces it. However, the common occurrence of several associated subdominant canopy species, understory shrubs, and herbaceous species between beech-maple and maple-basswood forests suggests that the differences between the two regions are gradational, relating principally to moisture availability. The principal effect of this moisture gradient lies in the presence or absence of American beech.

Maple-basswood forests include both the unglaciated driftless area of southwestern Wisconsin as well as the glaciated area to the northwest. The historical differences associated with glaciation have had significant effects upon the history of these two areas. However, today they are similar in forest composition. The two dominant species are sugar maple and American basswood. Frequent associates include northern red oak, American elm, slippery elm (*Ulmus rubra*), and bitternut hickory. The understory is frequently poorly developed, but most often includes eastern hophornbeam. In the herbaceous layer, spring ephemeral species are characteristic. Early in the season, these include sharp-lobed hepatica (*Hepatica acutiloba*), false rue anemone (*Isopyrum biternatum*), spring beauty, bloodroot, Dutchman's breeches, squirrel corn, cutleaf toothwort, and trout lily. Later, sweet cicely, fragile fern (*Cystopteris fragilis*) and maidenhair fern (*Adiantum pedatum*) are common. The composition of the herbaceous layer reflects as much about the character of the canopy dominants as it does about geographic location of the region and soil condition. As in beech-maple forests, sugar maple and American basswood cast dense summer shade that limits the growth of summer-green herbaceous species. The rich litter produced by these two canopy dominants creates nutrient-rich surface soils favorable to the growth of these nutrient-demanding herbs.

Throughout maple-basswood forests the same declining moisture availability that was responsible for the decline of beech continues to modify the composition of the forest. On the western margin of the region sugar maple reaches its physiological limits and a significantly drier forest appears, which is transitional to oak-hickory forests. As sugar maple declines, a basswood–northern red oak forest becomes more important. Additional oaks and hickories include bur oak, white oak, and shagbark hickory. In areas subject to frequent fire or on sites with especially poor moisture conditions, a modified prairie may have developed. However, today agriculture and fire control have led to the elimination of these sites.

How to Use this Guide

Two names accompany each tree species; a scientific name, which should be written either in italics or underlined, and a common name. Scientific names consist of two words, one for the genus and one for the specific epithet of each plant. Throughout the world each plant has only one accepted scientific name so that it cannot be confused with any other plant. Each tree often has more than one common name, and we have presented the one that the U.S. Forest Service (Little 1979) considers proper, along with a few other commonly used names.

TREE IDENTIFICATION

Before attempting to identify a tree using the included keys, it is essential to become familiar with the gross features of a tree.

Trees may be separated into two groups based upon their growth form. Excurrent trees have a strong central leader and pyramidal shape composed of branches which point down at the bottom of the tree and are horizontal in the middle and upright at the top of the tree. With age, the tree usually loses the tendency towards excurrent growth and it becomes more open and rounded. Deliquescent trees usually have branches that initially ascend. The shape of the crown (branches and leaves) and the length of the bole (trunk) often are of aid in identification. The form of each tree varies much with the tree's growing space (i.e., whether the tree is in a forest or open area).

Bark characteristics such as color, texture, and thickness are very useful in tree identification, so much in fact that trained foresters usually rely exclusively on this outer protective covering of the tree for identification. Bark may appear tight or loose, furrowed, blocky, scaly, shaggy, ridged, or smooth. Bark characteristics usually change with the age of the tree, so photographs are included with the descriptions showing the transition from sapling to mature trees. Once one is familiar with bark characteristics and changes that occur due to growth and the location or site, most trees can be identified, in summer or winter, on this basis alone.

Twigs and buds are particularly important for identifying trees in the fall and winter (Figure 1). Besides twig color, taste, and odor, characteristics of the buds, pith, leaf scars, and stipule scars are helpful identification aids. Because leaf shape and bark vary greatly within a given tree species, twig and bud characteristics are often the most reliable features by which to identify a tree. Twigs may also exhibit hairiness (pubescence), corky projections, and thorns or spines.

Stipule scars on the twig are common to some tree genera and are caused by stipules (modified leaves) attached to the twig on both sides of the leaf scar. These structures are lost with the leaves, resulting in paired stipule scars near the leaf scar. Some stipule scars even encircle the twig.

Leaf scars on the twig either encircle the bud, or more commonly are located just below the bud. Within this scar will be found one or more minute dots or bundle scars that indicate where the conducting tissue of the leaf was once connected to the stem. The number of bundle scars and their arrangement are very important in keying trees in leafless condition.

The central portion of a twig, the pith, is distinctively formed depending on the genus or species. Pith may be absent, resulting in a hollow twig, or if present it may be continuous or chambered. Diaphragmed pith is continuous and is composed of elongated disks that appear to be separated by bars.

The presence of thorns and spines may readily give away the identity of some species. Thorns are modified twigs and may be single or branched. Spines are modified stipules, bud scales, or leaf parts, and are never branched.

Buds may be of two types, terminal or lateral. Terminal buds are borne at the end of the twig after each year's growth, and they are usually larger than the laterals. Lateral buds are either borne in the axils of the leaves or are enclosed by the leaf petiole. Lateral buds, like leaves, can be arranged on a twig in these ways: alternate, opposite, or whorled. Some species have false terminal buds (pseudo-terminal) or end buds that are the last lateral buds formed at the end of the growing season. These false terminal buds resemble the remaining lateral buds and are characteristic of certain genera. Collateral buds are small buds found on either side of lateral buds on a few species. Buds may be either naked or covered with one or more scales. These scales overlap in many genera and are referred to as imbricate; or they may meet and not overlap, termed valvate.

Leaves consist of a blade, or photosynthetic portion, and the petiole,

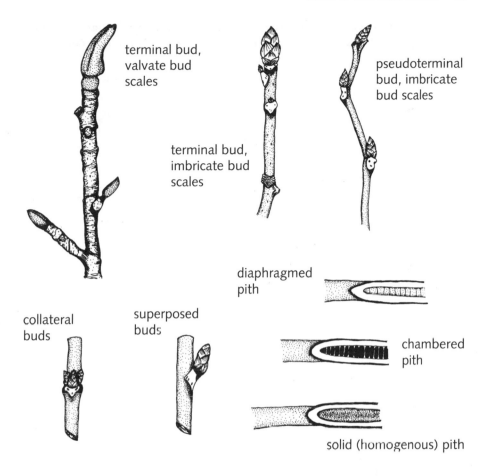

terminal bud,
valvate bud
scales

terminal bud,
imbricate bud
scales

pseudoterminal
bud, imbricate
bud scales

diaphragmed
pith

collateral
buds

superposed
buds

chambered
pith

solid (homogenous) pith

Figure 1. Twig and bud characteristics

or stalk, which attaches the leaf to the twig. Leaf characteristics, particularly shapes, are most frequently used to identify trees, but leaf shapes even on a single tree can be confusingly variable depending upon the species and where the leaf is located in the crown. Leaf shape (i.e., the shape of the blade) can include the following: scale, linear, oblong, lanceolate, oblanceolate, ovate, obovate, elliptical, oval, and deltate (Figure 2). Many leaf shapes are intermediate between these more general shapes. Leaf margins vary considerably among species, but in general are either entire or toothed. An entire margin may be revolute (slightly rolled) or undulate (wavy). Leaves with teeth often have serrate margins and may be singly serrate or doubly serrate (teeth with smaller teeth), or crenate (rounded) or dentate (sharp-pointed, outward) (Figure 3). The top of the blade, or apex, can be acuminate (sharp pointed with long tip), acute (sharp pointed), obtuse (blunt), rounded, or emarginate (notched) (Figure 4). The base of the leaf blade can be acute, cordate (heart-shaped), oblique (asymmetrical), obtuse, rounded, truncate (squared-off), or auriculate (earlobelike) (Figure 5). Leaf venation may be pinnate, with one main vein branching into secondary veins which lead to the leaf margin, or palmate, with all veins originating at the base of the leaf blade (Figure 6). Other types of leaf margins, leaf venation, and so forth are also possible.

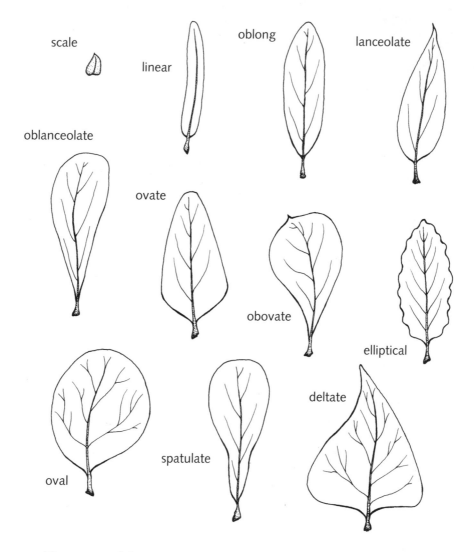

Figure 2. Leaf shapes

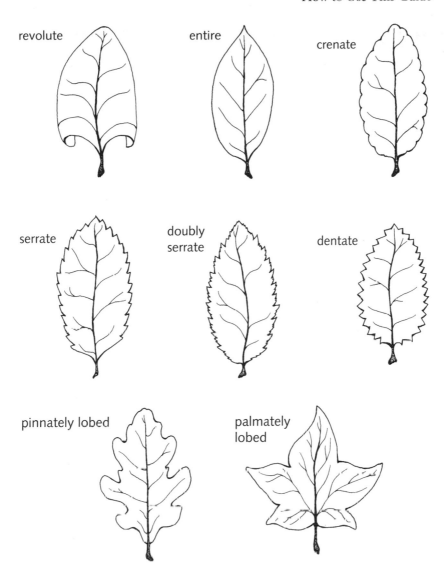

revolute

entire

crenate

serrate

doubly serrate

dentate

pinnately lobed

palmately lobed

Figure 3. Leaf margins and lobing

Leaves and buds have a definite arrangement along the twig (Figure 7). They may be borne opposite to one another or they may be alternate; occasionally leaves are arranged in a whorled fashion. Leaves may be simple (one blade per petiole) or compound (two or more blades or leaflets per petiole, attached to a rachis). Compound leaves may be pinnate (arranged laterally along the rachis), bipinnate (twice pinnate), or palmate (leaflets radiating out from the end of the rachis).

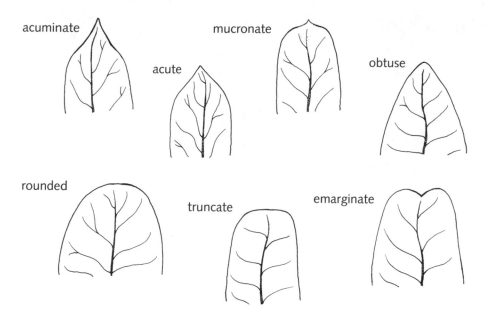

Figure 4. Leaf apices

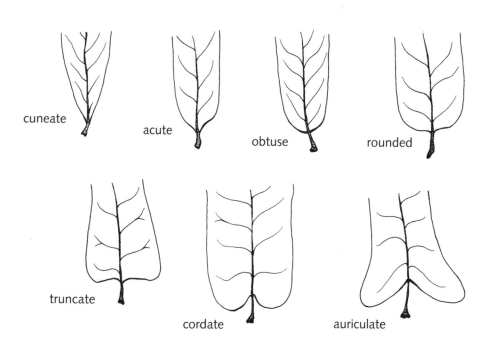

Figure 5. Leaf bases

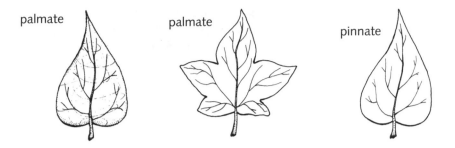

Figure 6. Leaf venation

Autumn coloration is noted for species that have a noteworthy display. Brilliant leaf color in the fall is promoted by cool, clear nights and warm, sunny days. Some species exhibit much variation in color from individual to individual and from year to year; others are more consistent. Soil and climate influence what specific pigments in a leaf will be allowed to show.

All woody species in this guide belong to either one of two groups of plants: angiosperms, or plants whose seeds are borne within a matured

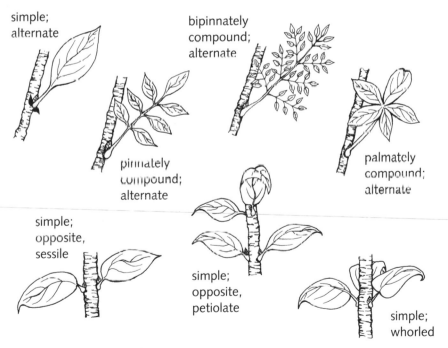

Figure 7. Leaf types and arrangement

ovary, and, gymnosperms, or plants that lack a protecting case, like the ovary wall, around the seeds. Angiosperms are the true flowering plants and many have very showy flowers, a characteristic that generally facilitates pollination by animals. Gymnosperms lack flowers, but have staminate (male) and ovulate (female) cones; the latter, upon fertilization and maturation, are the familiar cones of pines, spruces, firs, and so forth.

This field guide places little emphasis on identifying trees according to flower structure since flowers are generally located at heights which make them inconspicuous and because these structures are relatively short-lived. It should be mentioned, however, that the natural classification system of plants is indeed based on floral characteristics, therefore flowers should not be ignored and we have included information on the flowers of each species. We have indicated which species have a high landscape value because of showy flowers.

Some angiosperms bear flowers that have both stamens (male) and pistils (female). These flowers are said to be perfect. If perfect flowers have petals and sepals, then they are also complete. Flowers that lack either stamens or pistils are imperfect, or unisexual. An imperfect flower bearing stamens is known as a staminate flower, while one bearing pistils is a pistillate flower. A species that bears both staminate and pistillate flowers on the same tree is monoecious (Greek for "one house"), while a species bearing staminate and pistillate flowers on separate trees is dioecious (Greek for "two houses"). Flowers may also be terminal (borne at the end of a branch) or axillary (borne in the leaf axis). Several flowers can be arranged within a branched system called an inflorescence. Types of inflorescences are catkin, raceme, panicle, cyme, and umbel (Figure 8).

The actual period of flowering given for each species will vary because of a species' exposure to the sun, the air and soil temperature, and available moisture. Therefore, one can expect some deviation on a year-to-year basis. Trees in the northern portion of the Central Hardwood Forests may flower two to four weeks later than those in southwestern portion of this region. A particular species planted in the city will often begin flowering a few days to one week before the same species flowers in a nearby forest.

Fruits of trees are another good aid in identification since they are usually conspicuous and often persist for many months. Fruit is not only useful to wildlife, but some fruits provide refreshing color in the often drab fall and winter landscape. Such decorative species are indicated in this guide.

The fruit of a conifer is called a cone, which is often present during most or all the year. A series of cone scales attached spirally to a central axis is the typical composition of cones. The size, shape, and color of a cone,

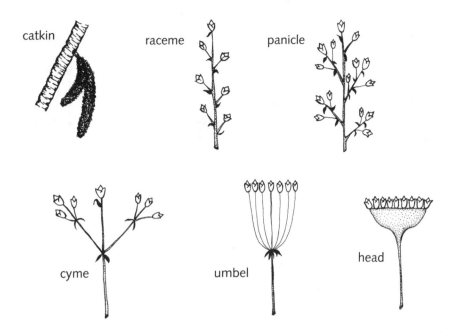

catkin   raceme   panicle

cyme   umbel   head

Figure 8. Inflorescence types

and the presence or absence of a prickle at the end of each cone scale are all characteristics used to separate many coniferous species. Other conifers, such as eastern redcedar, produce a fleshy, one-seeded fruit.

Fruits of angiosperms (broadleaved trees) are of many types (Figure 9). Dry, one-seeded fruits are of three forms: achenes (small, unwinged), samaras (small, winged), and nuts (large, enclosed in a husk). Multi-seeded fruits may be either dry or fleshy. Dry multiseeded fruits include legumes (podlike, splitting open along two lines), follicles (podlike, splitting open along one line), and capsules (splitting open along two or more lines). Fleshy fruits include pomes (seeds enclosed in a papery wall, surrounded by an outer fleshy wall), drupes (a single seed surrounded by a fleshy pulp), and berries (seeds embedded in a fleshy wall). These fruit types occasionally occur as aggregates of one particular type and may resemble a cone.

Characteristics of wood are mentioned because we have often had to identify trees based on cut stumps, standing or down dead boles, and pieces of firewood. Excellent guides to wood identification are available (e.g., Core et al. 1976). We have also included some traditional uses for the wood of most species. Some of the smaller tree species may have no or only local value for wood products.

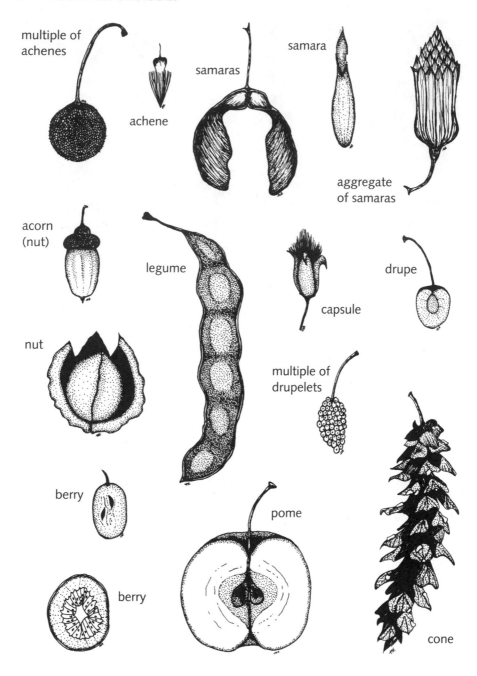

multiple of achenes

achene

samaras

samara

aggregate of samaras

acorn (nut)

legume

capsule

drupe

nut

multiple of drupelets

berry

pome

berry

cone

Figure 9. Fruit types

HABITAT AND RANGE

Accompanying each species description is a map of the Central Hardwood Forests, with shading to indicate the approximate natural and/or naturalized distribution of a species. Ranges are primarily based on maps by Little (1971, 1977). Although these maps may give the impression that a species is locally abundant, this is often not so. A particular habitat for a species may or may not be widespread at any given location, and this greatly influences a plant's distribution.

The habitat for each species is that set of conditions, especially soil characteristics and microclimate (due to local effects of area in which a tree occurs) under which that species is naturally found. Habitat information should suggest the type of conditions a species should at least tolerate when planted. For example, the habitat for flowering dogwood (*Cornus florida*) is described here as "rich, well-drained soils in the understory," suggesting correctly that poorly drained soils in full sun might be a problem for this species. On the other hand, many species are found naturally under less than ideal conditions, but will grow well or better under average soil conditions in the landscape. For example, baldcypress (*Taxodium distichum*) occurs naturally in permanently and deeply flooded conditions, but has been widely planted successfully throughout the eastern United States as an ornamental on well-drained soils. In general, species that naturally occur under ideal growing conditions (i.e., rich, moist, but well-drained soils) should have similarly good conditions if planted in the landscape. Species that occur on extreme sites (e.g., excessively drained or saturated soils) generally thrive under less extreme situations, but can better tolerate extremes that might be encountered in urban plantings.

PROPAGATION

Although some native trees of the Central Hardwood Forests have been planted extensively across the eastern United States, many are rarely considered for planting, although these species may be highly prized for planting elsewhere (e.g., throughout Europe). It is relatively simple to grow most of our native species from seed, and generally a much wiser and successful alternative to gathering seedlings and saplings from a woodlot or forest.

The key to propagating any of the following species is to imitate what naturally stimulates a seed to germinate in the forest. Plants have evolved different seed germination requirements, which allow them to survive extremes in the environment, including predation by herbivores, competition from other germinating seeds, and attack by insects or disease.

Some species such as white oak (*Quercus alba*) germinate immediately after they mature. Seeds of these species require no special treatment as long as fresh, mature, sound seed is planted soon after collecting.

Seeds of many species such as northern red oak (*Quercus rubra*) require a period of moist and cold conditions to overcome the inhibition against germination (known as dormancy). These seeds should be thoroughly mixed with moist (not sopping) peat moss, stored in a tied plastic bag, and placed in a refrigerator for a specific number of days depending on the temperature. This technique is referred to as cold stratification and is an effective means to overcome dormancy in most seeds. Fewer species require a warm stratification period in moist peat moss, followed by a cold stratification period. Room temperature is generally sufficient in these cases, especially if the temperature fluctuates from day to night (generally 86/68°F or 30/20°C day/night).

The seedcoat of some species such as Kentucky coffeetree (*Gymnocladus dioicus*) is so hard that little oxygen and water can reach the embryo within the seed and so germination is prevented. This seedcoat must be broken down either by mechanical or chemical (acid) scarification to allow entry of water and air (oxygen). Mechanical scarification involves creating an opening into the seed by means of a file or sandpaper. This is rather tedious for large amounts of seed, but nevertheless is successful if the embryo is not severely damaged. Acid scarification is more hazardous to the inexperienced and ill-equipped person, but is more passive and efficient, particularly for large quantities of seed. In this technique, seeds are placed in a heat resistant, glass container, then sulfuric acid (H_2SO_4-95% pure) is slowly poured over the entire batch so that the seeds are completely covered. After a certain period of time (usually an hour) the seeds are thoroughly rinsed in cold water to remove all acid residue. Of course extreme caution must be used while using sulfuric acid as it will be equally effective in indiscriminately dissolving skin tissue, clothing, and other desirable items. A safer method, which sometimes substitutes for scarification, is to soak seeds in hot water. Seeds are completely covered with boiling water and are left to soak for 12 to 24 hours as the water cools to room temperature.

The methods outlined above are suitable for nearly all the native species in this guide (at least non-commercially). Some species such as junipers are commercially propagated by taking young stem cuttings, treating them with a rooting compound, and waiting for the cuttings to

root in a greenhouse or mist bed. Propagation by cuttings (asexual propagation) is sometimes an art in itself. Those readers interested in a more
detailed account of seed propagation (sexual) should consult Young and
Young (1986, 1992). Propagation by seed, cuttings, grafting, and so
forth is thoroughly discussed by Hartmann and Kester (1990).

WILDLIFE VALUE

Trees provide much food and cover to many wildlife species in this region.
In general, one should expect a greater value to wildlife species, where
more and larger individuals of a species are in the landscape. To attract a
greater diversity of wildlife species, plant a diversity of native trees, choosing tree species that flower and fruit at different times, offer various types
of fruit (e.g., nuts vs. berries), have an evergreen versus deciduous canopy,
and can occupy an understory or comprise the overstory.

LANDSCAPE VALUE

The failure of many trees in the landscape is usually due to planting them
in the wrong location, which predisposes them to biotic (e.g., insects,
disease) and abiotic (e.g., freezing, drought) factors. Most of the tree species listed in this guide would grow well in the home or urban landscape
if planted in a rich, moist, well-drained soil; sheltered from drying winds
and injurious pathogens; and protected from urban lighting, pollutants,
soil compaction, and salt spray. Such ideal growing conditions, however, are not common. We have tried to include information about species tolerance and susceptibility to a variety of conditions common in a
landscape. Since an objective of this tree guide is to encourage the planting of native trees, we wish to ensure that trees are planted on suitable
sites.

Many of these tree species have great potential for reclaiming badly
degraded land and ultimately restoring damaged ecosystems. Thus we
have indicated which species deserve attention for land reclamation and
wetland restoration, and which species should tolerate urban conditions.

Before selecting a tree for the landscape, carefully consider the proposed planting site and the desired type of tree. Regarding the site, the
kind of soil (e.g., sand, clay, loam) is important in that it determines the
potential moisture and oxygen supply to the plant. The exposure (north,

south, east, west) will influence the success of some species since some (e.g., eastern hemlock, *Tsuga canadensis*) naturally occur protected from harsh, desiccating, southwest winds. If the specimen is to be located near pavement, brick, or concrete, will it be able to withstand the heat resulting from these conditions? Will the proposed site physically limit the species height (utility lines) or width (too close to building or sidewalks)? Most trees that are short when planted become tall (much to some people's surprise), and when placed under utility lines they are later topped out of necessity. Topping is not only deleterious to a tree, but is avoidable and particularly ugly.

Also, what purpose will the selected tree serve on the site? Will it be used as a screen, a single specimen, in groups, as an accent, a large shade tree, or in naturalizing? Surprisingly, most trees conform to specific roles in the landscape, since they exist in unique niches in the forest.

Questions regarding the individual tree (species) might be as follows: Is it able to survive extremes in the climate (nearly all native plants will)? Are insects and disease such a problem to it that a regular spray program will be needed? What are the ornamental attributes of the species (e.g., form, bark, flowers, fruit, fall color)? Is it useful as a source of wildlife food and cover? Is it evergreen or deciduous? What size could this tree reach with or without maintenance? Most of these questions are answered in this field guide. Some questions can be answered by simply observing these species year round in their native habitat.

In the forest, trees are limited to specific soil types, aspects, slopes, stages of succession, and so forth due to their competitive ability under a particular set of conditions. But, although a species may naturally occur only in a very specific area, it often will grow well in a variety of habitats if competing species are removed. As mentioned earlier, there are numerous tree species that are found naturally on the driest or wettest sites, but grow well (usually better) on moist, but well-drained soils.

BEST RECOGNIZABLE FEATURES

The characteristics of trees mentioned thus far represent only a small sample of the ones described in many tree identification guides, but a knowledge of these basic characteristics should allow one to identify any tree common to Central Hardwood Forests by using the enclosed keys, photographs, and written descriptions. To summarize what we feel are often the most obvious or useful characteristics of each species, we have included a brief recapitulation for easy reference, called Best Recognizable Features. In teaching dendrology at various institutions, we have followed the philosophy that one does not need to know every bit of detail on each species to identify it. You may find other characteristics of each species that are most useful to you in keeping the various species distinct in your mind.

Keys

The keys that follow are dichotomous keys, that is, there are always two choices or leads presented to you at each step or couplet. If the tree you are keying has leaves or needles, then proceed through the summer key. If leaves are not available, use the winter key. Read the leads in the first couplet and select the lead that best describes the specimen you are keying. The number following the selected lead directs you to the next couplet. Read both leads of this couplet and again select the one that best describes the plant. Proceed in this manner until you arrive at an answer, then check that answer by referring to the designated page for that species. If you have the wrong answer, repeat the keying process again, checking each characteristic more carefully. Remember, these keys only work for trees, not shrubs or vines, so be careful when keying what may appear to be a seedling or sapling—it may be a shrub. Also, keep in mind that no two features on a tree appear exactly alike, so look at several leaves, twigs, buds, and so forth, before making your selection.

SUMMER KEY TO GENERA

Key to Subgroups

1.	Leaves needlelike, scalelike, or awl-like	Group A
1.	Leaves broad	2
2(1).	Leaves alternate	3
2.	Leaves opposite or whorled	Group B
3(2).	Leaves simple	Group C
3.	Leaves compound	Group D

Key to Group A (Conifers)

1.	Leaves needlelike	2
1.	Leaves scalelike or awl-like	7

2(1). Needles borne separately 3
2. Needles in clusters .... *Pinus*
3(2). Needles with 2 white lines on undersurface 4
3. Needles lacking 2 white lines on undersurface 5
4(3). Needles ≥ ½ in. (≥ 13 mm) long; cones held upright; stems with large, round leaf scars where needles fall ....*Abies*
4. Needles < ½ in. (< 13 mm) long; cones pendent; stems lacking round leaf scars where needles fall .... *Tsuga*
5(3). Peglike projections distinct on stems where needles absent; ever-green..*Picea*
5. Peglike projections absent; deciduous 6
6(5). Needles 2-ranked; cones globose, about 1 in. (2.5 cm) diameter, and fall apart at maturity ....*Taxodium*
6. Needles arranged in spiral fashion along twig or whorled on spur shoots; cones elliptical, about ½ in. (13 mm) diameter, and persist on tree ....*Larix*
7(1). Leaves scalelike only and borne in flat sprays; cone woody ....*Thuja*
7. Leaves scalelike and/or awl-like and whorled; cone berrylike ....*Juniperus*

Key to Group B (Leaves opposite or whorled)

1. Leaves compound 2
1. Leaves simple 6
2(1). Leaves pinnately compound or trifoliate 3
2. Leaves palmately compound ....*Aesculus*
3(2). Leaves pinnately compound; terminal bud present 4
3. Leaves trifoliate; terminal bud absent ....*Staphylea*
4(3). Pith large, spongy; twig with raised lenticels ......*Sambucus*
4. Pith small, not spongy; twig lacking lenticels 5
5(4). Twig with thick glaucous bloom; bud covered with white pubescence ....*Acer negundo*
5. Twig lacking thick glaucous bloom; bud lacking white pubes-cence ....*Fraxinus*
6(1). Leaves lobed 7
6. Leaves unlobed 8

7(6).	Broken stems and leaves exude milky sap	*Broussonetia*
7.	Broken stems and leaves lacking milky sap	*Acer*
8(6).	Leaves opposite	9
8.	Leaves whorled	18
9(8).	Broken stems and leaves exude milky sap	*Broussonetia*
9.	Broken stems and leaves lacking milky sap	10
10(9).	Leaves 6–12 in. (15–31 cm) long; pith large diameter	11
10.	Leaves ≤ 6 in. (15 cm) long; pith relatively small diameter .	12
11(10).	Pith hollow or chambered; fruit an ovoid capsule to 1½ in. (4 cm) long	*Paulownia*
11.	Pith solid; fruit a slender capsule to 18 in. (46 cm) long	*Catalpa*
12(10).	Leaves thick, glossy, evergreen; fruit a persistent 5-celled capsule	*Kalmia*
12.	Leaves not evergreen; not as thick or glossy; fruit not a capsule	13
13(12).	Leaf margin entire	14
13.	Leaf margin toothed	16
14(13).	Leaves often in whorls of 3–4; fruit a globose head of achenes	*Cephalanthus*
14.	Leaves only opposite; fruit a red, white, or blue drupe	15
15(14).	Leaves 4–6 in. (10–15 cm) long; bark with lenticels	*Chionanthus*
15.	Leaves generally to 4 in. (10 cm), rarely 5 in. (13 cm) long; bark lacking lenticels	*Cornus*
16(13).	Leaf margin toothed only above middle of leaf	*Forestiera*
16.	Leaf margin toothed completely	17
17(16).	Stems green; fruit a deeply 4-lobed capsule	*Euonymus*
17.	Stems not green; fruit a drupe	*Viburnum*
18(8).	Leaves 6–12 in. (15–31 cm) long; pith large diameter	19
18.	Leaves ≤ 6 in. (15 cm) long; pith relatively small diameter .	20
19(18).	Pith hollow or chambered; fruit an ovoid capsule to 1½ in. (4 cm) long	*Paulownia*
19.	Pith solid; fruit a slender capsule to 18 in. (46 cm) long	*Catalpa*
20(18).	Leaves thick, glossy, evergreen; fruit a persistent 5-celled capsule	*Kalmia*
20.	Leaves not evergreen; fruit a globose head of achenes	*Cephalanthus*

Key to Group C (Alternate, simple leaves)

1. Leaves lobed 2
1. Leaves unlobed 11
2(1). Buds clustered at end of twig; pith stellate in cross section; fruit an acorn . . . . *Quercus*
2. Buds not clustered at end of twig; pith not stellate in cross section; fruit not an acorn 3
3(2). Leaf margin entire 4
3. Leaf margin toothed 6
4(3). Leaves tulip-shaped; buds valvate; stems with stipule scars that encircle twig . . . . *Liriodendron*
4. Leaves not tulip-shaped; buds with imbricate scales or naked; stipule scars absent or inconspicuous 5
5(4). Bud scales imbricate; stems green and very aromatic when crushed; flowers in early spring; fruit a blue drupe . . . *Sassafras*
5. Buds naked; stems brown and not aromatic; flowers in autumn; fruit a brown, woody capsule . . . . *Hamamelis*
6(3). Petiole exudes milky sap when broken 7
6. Petiole lacking milky sap when broken 8
7(6). Leaves often opposite; pith interrupted at node by very thin green diaphragm . . . . *Broussonetia*
7. Leaves never opposite; pith continuous . . . . *Morus*
8(6). Stems typically with sharp thorns or spine-tipped spur shoots; fruit a pome; tree small at maturity 9
8. Stems lacking thorns or spine-tipped spur shoots; fruit not a pome; tree large at maturity 10
9(8). Stems have sharp thorns and bud at base of thorn; stems typically glabrous . . . . *Crataegus*
9. Stems have spine-tipped spur shoots and bud is often located along spur shoot; stems often covered by whitish pubescence . . . . *Malus*
10(8). Leaves to 6 in. (15 cm) diameter, margin finely serrate; base of petiole does not enclose bud; fruit a multiple of capsules . . . . *Liquidambar*
10. Leaves to 8 in. (20 cm) diameter, margin very coarsely toothed; base of petiole encloses bud; fruit a multiple of achenes . . . . *Platanus*
11(1). Apex of leaves bristle tipped . . . . *Quercus*
11. Apex of leaves not bristle tipped 12
12(11). Leaf margin entire 13
12. Leaf margin toothed 27

13.   Leaves evergreen, or tardily deciduous; habit shrubby 14
13.   Leaves not evergreen; habit of individuals arborescent 16
14.   Fruit a persistent 5-celled capsule 15
14.   Fruit a 10-seeded berry .... *Vaccinium*
15(14). Leaves < 4 in. (10 cm) long; flower buds inconspicuous .....
          .... *Kalmia*
15.   Leaves ≥ 4 in. (10 cm) long; flower buds very large ....
          .... *Rhododendron*
16(13). Stems armed; broken twigs and petioles exude sap 17
16.   Stems unarmed; broken twigs and petioles lacking sap 18
17(16). Leaves ovate; broken petiole exudes milky sap; fruit a very large
          aggregate of drupes to 5 in. (13 cm) diameter ...... *Maclura*
17.   Leaves more or less elliptical; broken petiole exudes gummy sap;
          fruit a drupelike berry to ½ in. (13 mm) long .... *Bumelia*
18(16). Pith diaphragmed or chambered 19
18.   Pith continuous 21
19(18). Leaves ≥ 10 in. (25 cm), very aromatic when crushed; terminal
          bud naked; fruit a berry to 5 in. (13 cm) long .... *Asimina*
19.   Leaves ≤ 7 in. (18 cm), lacking strong odor when crushed; ter-
          minal bud with scales; fruit a drupe ≤ 1 in. (2.5 cm) long .. 20
20(19). Pith diaphragmed .... *Nyssa*
20.   Pith chambered .... *Symplocos*
21(18). Leaves ≥ 6 in. (15 cm) long; stipule scars encircle twig ....
          .... *Magnolia*
21.   Leaves < 6 in. (15 cm) long; stipule scars absent, inconspicu-
          ous, or do not encircle twig 22
22(21). Leaves distinctly heart shaped; fruit a legume .... *Cercis*
22.   Leaves not heart shaped; fruit not a legume 23
23(22). Pith golden-brown in cross section .... *Cotinus*
23.   Pith white in cross section 24
24(23). Buds naked .... *Styrax*
24.   Buds with 1 or more scales 25
25(24). Bud scale single and caplike .... *Salix*
25.   Bud scales 2 or more 26
26(25). Bud scales 2; stems brown, not aromatic when crushed; fruit a
          large orange berry .... *Diospyros*
26.   Bud scales more than 2; stems green, aromatic when crushed;
          fruit a small blue drupe .... *Sassafras*
27(12). Buds naked 28
27.   Buds with 1 or more scales 29
28(27). Leaves oblong; leaf scar with 3 distinct bundle scars . *Rhamnus*
28.   Leaves broader; leaf scar with 1 central bundle scar .... *Styrax*

29(27). Bud scale single and caplike .... *Salix*
29.   Bud scales 2 or more 30
30(29). Pith interrupted at node by green diaphragm ... *Broussonetia*
30.   Pith not interrupted at node by green diaphragm 31
31(30). Pith diaphragmed throughout or chambered 32
31.   Pith solid 35
32(31). Pith diaphragmed .... *Nyssa*
32.   Pith chambered 33
33(32). Twigs ridged with scattered hairs .... *Symplocos*
33.   Twigs lacking hairs 34
34(33). Leaves asymmetrical at base, margin coarsely serrate; fruit a round drupe; bark irregular, warty .... *Celtis*
34.   Leaves even at base, margin finely serrate; fruit a 4-winged, nut-like drupe; bark ridged and furrowed, somewhat blocky .... *Halesia*
35(31). Broken petiole exudes milky sap; fruit a multiple of small drupes (berrylike) .... *Morus*
35.   Broken petiole lacking sap; fruit not a multiple of small drupes 36
36(35). Stems with thorns or spine-tipped spur shoots 37
36.   Stems not armed 40
37(36). Stems with prominent thorns and bud at base of each thorn .. .. *Crataegus*
37.   Stems with spine-tipped shoots 38
38(37). Petioles glandular .... *Prunus*
38.   Petioles lacking glands 39
39(38). Stems often covered with white pubescence; fruit an apple ... . *Malus*
39.   Stems glabrous; fruit a pear .... *Pyrus*
40(36). Pith round 43
40.   Pith triangular or stellate 41
41(40). Pith triangular; buds stalked and valvate .... *Alnus*
41.   Pith stellate; buds not stalked nor valvate 42
42(41). Leaves elongate; leaf scar half round; fruit a nut; habit typically small .... *Castanea*
42.   Leaves broad; leaf scar triangular to crescent shaped; habit typically large trees .... *Populus*
43(40). Petiole with glands .... *Prunus*
43.   Petiole lacking glands 44
44(43). Leaves with pinnate venation 45
44.   Leaves lacking pinnate venation 49

45(44).   Leaf margin doubly serrate 46
45.   Leaf margin with single very large teeth . . . . *Fagus*
46(45).   Buds of similar size; bark not fluted 47
46.   Buds of 2 sizes; bark fluted . . . . *Carpinus*
47(46).   Staminate catkins present 48
47.   Staminate catkins absent; fruit a samara . . . . *Ulmus*
48(47).   Spur shoots on older stems; bud scales not striated; bark
           smooth, exfoliating in large strips, or with large ridges . *Betula*
48.   Spur shoots absent; bud scales striated; bark broken into very
           small ridges . . . . *Ostrya*
49(44).   Leaves evergreen, margin tipped with sharp prickles *Ilex opaca*
49.   Leaves not evergreen, margin lacking sharp prickles 50
50(49).   Lateral buds recurved; fruit a pome, maturing in early summer;
           bark smooth slate gray, often with thin black vertical lines . . .
           . . . . *Amelanchier*
50.   Lateral buds not recurved; fruit not a pome; bark not smooth
           slate gray 51
51(50).   Leaves broad and typically ≥ 6 in. (15 cm) long, base very asym-
           metrical, margin very coarsely serrate; often a very large tree . .
           . . . . *Tilia*
51.   Leaves less broad and typically < 6 in. (15 cm) long, base sym-
           metrical, margin less coarse; bole generally < 12 in. (31 cm)
           diameter at maturity 52
52(51).   Leaves 2-ranked, typically ≤ 2½ in. (6 cm) long; bark gray or
           brown and very shaggy . . . . *Planera*
52.   Leaves not 2-ranked, generally > 3 in. (8 cm) long; bark not
           dark and shaggy 53
53(52).   Leaves minutely or obscurely toothed 54
53.   Leaves with more conspicuous teeth 55
54(53).   Leaves to 7 in. (18 cm) long, sour tasting; individual flowers
           small but in long clusters; fruit a small capsule in long clusters;
           bark with thick ridges and deep furrows . . . . *Oxydendrum*
54.   Leaves to 5 in. (13 cm) long, not sour tasting; individual flow-
           ers large, ≥ 2½ in. (6 cm) long and not in long clusters; fruit a
           larger capsule; bark lacking deep furrows . . . . *Stewartia*
55(53).   Leaves to 6 in. (15 cm) long, margin serrate; fruit a capsule;
           bark exfoliating into red and brown strips . . . . *Clethra*
55.   Leaves ≤ 4 in. (10 cm) long, margin serrate or crenate; fruit a red
           drupe; bark gray, non-exfoliating . . . . *Ilex*

Key to Group D (Alternate, compound leaves)

1.	Leaves trifoliate . . . . *Ptelea*
1.	Leaves pinnately or bipinnately compound 2
2(1).	Leaves pinnately compound 7
2.	Leaves bipinnately compound 3
3(2).	Rachis with prickles; habit short, often shrubby . . . . . . *Aralia*
3.	Rachis lacking prickles; habit relatively large tree at maturity . 4
4(3).	Leaflets generally < 1 in. (2.5 cm) long 5
4.	Leaflets generally ≥ 1 in. (2.5 cm) long 6
5(4).	Flowers pink, very showy and pincushion-like; bark light colored; thorns absent; tree typically branches into many main stems near ground . . . . *Albizia*
5.	Flowers yellow-green, not showy; bark dark colored; branched thorns typically present on wild specimens; tree has single stem . . . . *Gleditsia*
6(4).	Leaflets dull bluish green; leaves to 36 in. (91 cm) long; fruit a legume . . . . *Gymnocladus*
6.	Leaflets shiny dark green; leaves ≤ 18 in. (46 cm) long; fruit a yellow berry . . . . *Melia*
7(2).	Leaflets gland tipped at base; fruit a twisted samara . *Ailanthus*
7.	Leaflets lacking glands; fruit not a samara 8
8(7).	Cut stems exude milky sap . . . . *Rhus*
8.	Cut stems lacking milky sap 9
9(8).	Pith chambered . . . . *Juglans*
9.	Pith solid 10
10(9).	Spines or thorns along stem 11
10.	Stems unarmed 13
11(10).	Spines in pairs 12
11.	Thorns branched, not in pairs . . . . *Gleditsia*
12(11).	Spine on either side of minute, glabrous bud; leaflet bristle tipped; rachis lacking prickle; fruit a legume . . . . *Robinia*
12.	Spine on either side of rusty red, tomentose bud; leaflet lacking bristle; rachis with 1–2 prickles; fruit a capsule . . *Zanthoxylum*
13(10).	Leaflets < 1 in. (2.5 cm) long; leaves often bipinnately compound . . . . *Gleditsia*
13.	Leaflets > 1 in. (2.5 cm) long; leaves only pinnately compound 14
14(13).	Leaves even pinnately compound; bud not densely hairy; fruit not a legume 15
14.	Leaves odd pinnately compound; bud densely hairy; fruit a legume . . . . *Cladrastis*

15(14). Buds resinous; fruit a small, red pome .... *Sorbus*
15.   Buds lacking resin; fruit yellow and berrylike or a dehiscent nut
        16
16(15). Pith white; fruit berrylike .... *Sapindus*
16.   Pith pale to brown; fruit a dehiscent nut .... *Carya*

WINTER KEY TO DECIDUOUS GENERA

1.   Leaf scars opposite or whorled 2
1.   Leaf scars alternate 17
2(1).   Bundle scars 4 or more 3
2.   Bundle scars 1–3 9
3(2).   Terminal buds paired 4
3.   Terminal buds 1 or 3 7
4(3).   Habit shrublike; fruit a small drupe or 3-lobed capsule 5
4.   Habit arborescent; fruit a follicle or unlobed capsule 6
5(4).   Stems smooth, maroon and developing narrow white vertical
        stripes; fruit a 3-lobed capsule in open cluster ..... *Staphylea*
5.   Stems with numerous, warty lenticels and always lacking white
        vertical stripes; fruit remnant a small drupe on flat or pyramidal
        cluster .... *Sambucus*
6(4).   Pith hollow or chambered; fruit an ovoid capsule; bark gray and
        not furrowed .... *Paulownia*
6.   Pith solid; fruit a long, slender capsule; bark brown and ridged
        and furrowed .... *Catalpa*
7(3).   Pith green, diaphragmed at nodes .... *Broussonetia*
7.   Pith continuous 8
8(7).   Buds with 2–3 pairs of not keeled scales; fruit a samara ......
        .... *Fraxinus*
8.   Buds with 4 or more pairs of keeled scales; fruit a large capsule
        .... *Aesculus*
9(2).   Terminal bud absent .... *Cephalanthus*
9.   Terminal bud present 10
10(9). Bundle scar 1 11
10.   Bundle scars 2–3 13
11(10). Leaf scars white; twigs bright green .... *Euonymus*
11.   Leaf scars not white; twigs not green 12
12(11). Twigs slightly 4-angled .... *Chionanthus*
12.   Twigs round .... *Forestiera*

13(10). Bud scales 2 14
13.   Bud scales 3 .... *Acer*
14(13). Buds stalked .... *Acer*
14.   Buds sessile 15
15(14). Bud scales imbricate .... *Cornus*
15.   Bud scales valvate 16
16(15). Terminal flower buds subglobose, always glabrous ... *Cornus*
16.   Terminal flower buds flask shaped, often pubescent ....
         .... *Viburnum*
17(1).   Thorns or spines present 18
17.   Thorns or spines absent 27
18(17). Bundle scars 4 or more 19
18.   Bundle scars 1–3 20
19(18). Twigs moderately slender; spur shoots common; sap milky;
         bark orange; habit arborescent .... *Maclura*
19.   Twigs stout, ≥ ½ in. (13 mm) diameter; spur shoots absent;
         bark gray-brown; habit generally small and thicket forming ..
         .... *Aralia*
20(18). Spines present 21
20.   Thorns present 25
21(20). Spines paired at each leaf scar 22
21.   Spines on spur shoots 23
22(21). Buds conspicuous, reddish brown, and hairy; broken twigs aro-
         matic .... *Zanthoxylum*
22.   Buds hidden by leaf scar; broken twigs non-aromatic . *Robinia*
23(21). Buds present on spur shoot; bark often gray 24
23.   Buds absent on spur shoot; bark often black or reddish black .
         .... *Prunus*
24(23). Twigs glabrous .... *Pyrus*
24.   Twigs pubescent .... *Malus*
25(20). Twigs exude milky sap when broken; habit typically shrubby .
         .... *Bumelia*
25.   Twigs lacking sap; habit typically arborescent 26
26(25). Buds surrounded by leaf scar, or nearly so; thorns branched ..
         .... *Gleditsia*
26.   Buds adjacent to leaf scar; thorns unbranched ..... *Crataegus*
27(17). Bundle scars 1–3 28
27.   Bundle scars 4 or more 63
28(27). Bundle scars 3 29
28.   Bundle scar 1 53

45(44). Staminate catkins present; bark white, even on small-diameter individuals .... *Betula*

45.   Staminate catkins absent; bark light or dark, but not white . 46

46(45). Buds imbedded in twig; twigs very stout; pith large, pinkish brown .... *Gymnocladus*

46.   Buds not imbedded in twig; twigs not stout; pith relatively small, not pinkish 47

47(46). Buds superposed .... *Albizia*

47.   Buds not superposed 48

48(47). Buds gray or brown, not mucilaginous when chewed; twigs fluted; pith stellate in cross section .... *Castanea*

48.   Buds dark red or green, mucilaginous when chewed; twigs round; pith round in cross section .... *Tilia*

49(43). Leaf scars raised, with 2 lines leading from the sides of their bases .... *Cercis*

49.   Leaf scars not raised and lacking lines 50

50(49). Bud scales not striated, in vertical rows; seed not enclosed in bladderlike sac 51

50.   Bud scales striated, not in vertical rows; seed enclosed in bladderlike sac .... *Ostrya*

51(50). Bud scales in 2 rows; bark furrowed, shreddy, or rough ...52

51.   Bud scales in 4 rows; bark smooth and fluted ...... *Carpinus*

52(51). Buds < ¹⁄₁₀ in. (2 mm) long .... *Planera*

52.   Buds ≥ ¹⁄₁₀ in. (3 mm) long .... *Ulmus*

53(28). Twigs and buds covered with silvery pubescence ..... *Clethra*

53.   Twigs and buds lacking silvery pubescence 54

54(53). Leaf scars lacking .... *Taxodium*

54.   Leaf scars present 55

55(54). True terminal bud present 56

55.   True terminal bud absent 59

56(55). Twigs ridged with scattered hairs; pith chambered . *Symplocos*

56.   Twigs not ridged with scattered hairs; pith not chambered ...
.... 57

57(56). Twigs glaucous, green, and spicy aromatic when cut . *Sassafras*

57.   Twigs not glaucous, not green, and not aromatic 58

58(57). Buds about ³⁄₁₀ in. (6 mm) long; bundle scar raised; pith spongy; fruit a capsule .... *Stewartia*

58.   Buds about ¹⁄₁₀ in. (3 mm) long; bundle scar not raised; pith not spongy; fruit a drupe .... *Ilex*

59(55). Pith chambered or diaphragmed 60

59.   Pith continuous 61

60(59). Leaf scar half-round; older stems glabrous; buds with 2 scales; fruit a large berry, woody calyx persists on tree . . . . . *Diospyros*

60.   Leaf scar heart shaped; older stems often silky-shreddy; buds with 2–4 scales; fruit a persistent 4-winged, nutlike drupe . . . . *Halesia*

61(59). Buds naked . . . . *Styrax*

61.   Buds with distinct scales 62

62(61). Leaves deciduous; bundle scar C shaped; fruit a persistent, long cluster of capsules; habit arborescent . . . . *Oxydendrum*

62.   Leaves tardily deciduous to evergreen; bundle scar oval; fruit a 10-seeded berry; habit shrubby . . . . *Vaccinium*

63(27). Buds naked or scales indistinct 64

63.   Buds with distinct scales 67

64(63). Leaf scars 3-lobed . . . . *Melia*

64.   Leaf scars not 3-lobed 65

65(64). Leaf scar encircling bud or nearly so 66

65.   Leaf scar subtending bud . . . . *Asimina*

66(65). Twigs with milky sap when broken; habit generally thicket forming and shrubby . . . . *Rhus*

66.   Twigs lacking milky sap when broken; habit arborescent . . . . *Cladrastis*

67(63). Stipule scars encircle twig 68

67.   Stipule scars do not encircle twig or are absent 72

68(67). Leaf scar surrounds bud; fruit a persistent multiple of achenes . . . . *Platanus*

68.   Leaf scar adjacent to bud; fruit not a multiple of achenes . . 69

69(68). Buds with numerous scales . . . . *Fagus*

69.   Buds with 2–3 scales 70

70(69). Terminal bud densely pubescent . . . . *Magnolia*

70.   Terminal bud glabrous 71

71(70). Terminal bud ≥ ½ in. (13 mm) long; fruit a conelike aggregate of follicles; bark not furrowed . . . . *Magnolia*

71.   Terminal bud ≤ ½ in. (13 mm) long; fruit a conelike aggregate of samaras; bark furrowed . . . . *Liriodendron*

72(67). Buds resinous . . . . *Sorbus*

72.   Buds not resinous 73

73(72). Buds clustered at end of twig; pith stellate in cross section . . . . *Quercus*

73.   Buds not clustered at end of twig 74

74(73). Leaf scars large, shield shaped or triangular 75

74.   Leaf scars small, narrow 78

75(74). True terminal bud present 76
75.   True terminal bud absent 77
76(75). Pith chambered . . . . *Juglans*
76.   Pith continuous . . . . *Carya*
77(75). Buds imbedded; twigs lacking offensive odor when broken; pith pinkish brown; bark black and scaly . . . . *Gymnocladus*
77.   Buds not imbedded; twigs with offensive odor when broken; pith light brown; bark light and relatively smooth . . *Ailanthus*
78(74). Bud scales 2–3 79
78.   Bud scales 4 or more . . . . *Morus*
79(78). Pith diaphragmed at nodes . . . . *Broussonetia*
79.   Pith continuous 80
80(79). Buds ovoid, mucilaginous when chewed; twigs lacking rank odor when broken; bark with long, narrow furrows; large tree at maturity . . . . *Tilia*
80.   Buds elongate, not mucilaginous when chewed; twigs with rank odor when broken; bark basically smooth; small tree at maturity
           . . . . *Cornus* (*alternifolia*)

Tree Descriptions A–Z

Abies—fir
PINACEAE—pine family

Key to *Abies*

1.   Cone scale bracts not visible in intact cone . . . *Abies balsamea*
1.   Cone scale bracts exserted beyond cone; restricted to highest elevations of southern Appalachian Mountains . . *Abies fraseri*

Abies balsamea (Linnaeus) Miller
balsam fir, balsam, Canada balsam, eastern fir

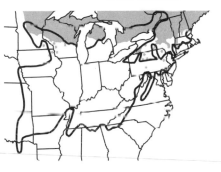

Abies balsamea

HABIT. Medium-sized tree, 40–60 ft. (12–18 m) tall, 12–18 in. (31–46 cm) in diameter, with a slender, dense, symmetrical, spirelike crown.
BARK. Thin, dull gray, smooth when young except for numerous, raised resin blisters that persist on larger stems; developing small, flat, irregular, rough ridges with age.
TWIGS. Slender, pale yellow-green, initially covered with fine pubescence, becoming light gray tinged in red; leaf (needle) scars round and flat.
BUDS. Nearly round, ⅛–¼ in. (3–6 mm) in diameter, milk-chocolate colored, covered with opaque wax.
LEAVES. Needles sessile, flat; dark green, lustrous, and grooved above; silvery-white below, with 4–8 rows of stomata (looks like 2 distinct white bands per needle); ½–1 in. (13–25 mm) long and somewhat upright and

Figure 10. *Abies balsamea* foliage

Figure 11. *Abies balsamea* cones

Figure 12. *Abies balsamea* bark, small tree

Figure 13. *Abies balsamea* bark, large tree

crowded on upper side of cone-bearing branches; twice as long or more and rather spreading and flattened (2-ranked) on branches not bearing cones, especially on heavily shaded branches; apex blunt or slightly notched; with fragrance like citrus when bruised; persisting 7–10 years. FRUIT. Erect; oblong-cylindric cone 2–4 in. (5–10 cm) long, green tinged with dark rich purple, finely hairy; cone scales break away from central cone axis upon maturity, leaving upright spikes on uppermost branches; scale fan shaped.

WOOD. Pale brown streaked with yellow, light, soft, not strong, coarse grained; used for pulpwood, crates, boxes, and knotty "pine" paneling; grown for Christmas trees and greens.

HABITAT AND RANGE. In central Appalachia only at highest elevations in West Virginia and Virginia; farther north in upper elevation, moist forests in the mountains to timberline and swamps over organic soils in the Northeast and upper Midwest.

PROPAGATION. Seed, stratify in moist medium 15–30 days at 34–41°F (1–5°C).

WILDLIFE VALUE. Oil-rich seed is eaten by chickadee, nutcracker, squirrel, and porcupine; foliage is browsed by moose and whitetail deer.

LANDSCAPE VALUE. Limited; a beautiful tree that is very tolerant of cold and shade, but is not tolerant of summer dry spells and heavy clay soils in portions of the Midwest. Zones 3–5 (6 at cooler, higher elevations.)

BEST RECOGNIZABLE FEATURES. Resin blisters on bark; milk-chocolate-colored buds covered with opaque resin; rounded leaf scars on twigs; upright cones that shatter upon maturity.

Abies fraseri (Pursh) Poiret
Fraser fir, she-balsam

HABIT. Similar to balsam fir but typically smaller, 30–50 ft. (9–15 m) tall.

BARK. Similar to balsam fir.

TWIGS. Thicker and more pubescent than balsam fir but otherwise similar.

BUDS. Similar to balsam fir.

LEAVES. Similar to balsam fir but generally not more than 1 in. long, and with 8–12 bands of stomata on lower surface, making the underside of needles appear more chalky white.

Abies fraseri

FRUIT. Oblong ovoid, dark purple, finely pubescent cone, 2½ in. (6 cm) long; yellow-green reflexed bracts exerted beyond cone scales; upright on branch.

WOOD. Pale brown, light, soft, not strong, coarse grained; used locally for construction and pulpwood; grown for Christmas trees and greens.

HABITAT AND RANGE. Moist, cool slopes at high elevations of mountains of Virginia, North Carolina, and Tennessee.

PROPAGATION. Same as for balsam fir.

WILDLIFE VALUE. Seed is eaten by red squirrel.

LANDSCAPE VALUE. Same as for balsam fir. Some Christmas tree growers believe *A. fraseri* is a superior choice to *A. balsamea*. Zones 4–7 (at higher elevations).

BEST RECOGNIZABLE FEATURES. Resin blisters on bark; milk-chocolate-

Figure 14. *Abies fraseri* foliage

Figure 16.
Abies concolor form

Figure 15. *Abies concolor* foliage

colored buds covered with opaque resin; rounded leaf scars on twigs; upright cones with exerted, reflexed bracts.

Other firs commonly planted in the regional landscape:
Abies concolor (Gordon & Glendinning) Lindley ex Hildebrand, white fir. To 80 ft. (24 m) tall in eastern landscapes, but over 200 ft. (61 m) tall and 6 ft. (2 m) in diameter in western native range; barrel-shaped crown of upright foliage that is 2½ in. (6 cm) long, flattened, evenly colored bluish white on both sides of needle; cones green, 3–5 in. (8–13 cm) long, oblong; bark dark ash-gray, very irregular with deep and narrow furrows. Native to dry montane forests of the Rockies and Sierras. Probably the most reliable fir for planting in the eastern United States. Certainly a beautiful choice, given foliage color and dense crown. Numerous varieties even more attractive. Zones 3–7.

Acer—maple
ACERACEAE—maple family

Key to *Acer*

1.   Leaves pinnately compound; new growth green (summer) or purple (winter) and covered with thick glaucous bloom . . . . *Acer negundo*

1.   Leaves simple; new growth not green or purple, or if green is not covered with thick glaucous bloom 2

2(1). Leaf margin toothed 3

2.   Leaf margin entire 6

3(2). Buds stalked; fruit ripening in fall 4

3.   Buds not stalked; fruit ripening in late spring to early summer 5

4(3). Leaves 5-lobed, margin coarsely serrate, stems slightly pubescent . . . . *Acer spicatum*

4.   Leaves 3-lobed, margin finely and doubly serrate, stems glabrous . . . . *Acer pensylvanicum*

5(3). Leaves deeply 5-lobed with narrow sinuses; seeds to 2.5 in. (6 cm) long . . . . *Acer saccharinum*

5.   Leaves 3- to 5-lobed with broad, shallow sinuses; seeds to 1 in. (2.5 cm) long . . . . *Acer rubrum*

6(2). Lobes of leaves somewhat rounded . . . . *Acer barbatum*

6.   Lobes of leaves pointed 7

7(6). Leaves generally 3-lobed; stems mottled and waxy; buds pubescent . . . . *Acer nigrum*

7.   Leaves generally 5-lobed; stems evenly brown colored; buds lacking pubescence . . . . *Acer saccharum*

Acer barbatum Michaux
Florida maple, southern sugar maple

HABIT. Medium-sized tree, 50–60 ft. (15–18 m) tall, with small, erect, spreading branches.

BARK. Thin, smooth, gray, becoming thick, dark, rough, furrowed.

TWIGS. Slender, reddish brown, glabrous, lenticellate; leaf scars U shaped with 3–7 bundle traces; pith homogeneous, white.

BUDS. Obtuse, 1/8 in. (3 mm) long, with hairy, dark chestnut-brown scales.

LEAVES. Opposite, simple, 1½–3 in. (4–8 cm) in diameter, often drooping in appearance, dark green and lustrous above, pale and pubescent (and often glaucous) below, 3–5 somewhat rounded lobes, 3- to 5-nerved; margin wavy, entire; petiole hairy, 1½–3 in. (4–8 cm) long, swollen at base; fall color yellow to scarlet.

Acer barbatum

FLOWERS. Apetalous; yellowish green, drooping corymbs in early spring; generally dioecious.

FRUIT. Glabrous, green samara to 1 in. (2.5 cm) long, paired, maturing in fall.

WOOD. Light brown, heavy, strong, coarse grained; used for furniture, interior finishing, cabinets.

HABITAT AND RANGE. Low wet woods and limestone ridges in southern United States from southeastern Virginia to eastern Oklahoma and Texas.

PROPAGATION. Seed, stratify in moist medium 60–90 days at 41°F (5°C).

WILDLIFE VALUE. Fruit has poor value; browse is fair for deer.

LANDSCAPE VALUE. Good replacement for sugar maple in South, although Florida maple is smaller and does not color as well in fall. Zones 7–9.

BEST RECOGNIZABLE FEATURES. Blue-green leaves densely hairy below; leaf petiole swollen at base; very similar to sugar maple except for above and smaller stature.

Acer negundo Linnaeus
boxelder, ashleaf maple

PLATE 1

HABIT. Medium-sized tree, 40–60 ft. (12–18 m) tall, with a short trunk and a wide, dense crown.

Acer negundo

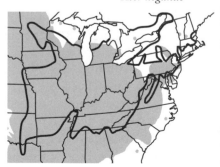

BARK. Light brown becoming grayish to greenish brown, thin, shallowly fissured with narrow, rounded ridges.

TWIGS. Moderately stout, with slight odor when scratched, bright green to deep purple, glaucous or shiny, smooth; leaf scars whitish, raised, V shaped; pith white, continuous.

Figure 17. *Acer negundo* foliage

Figure 18. *Acer negundo* flowers

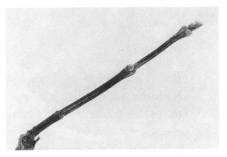

Figure 19. *Acer negundo* fruit

Figure 20. *Acer negundo* twig and buds

Figure 21. *Acer negundo* bark, small tree

Figure 22. *Acer negundo* bark, medium-sized tree

Figure 23. *Acer negundo* bark, large tree

BUDS. Terminal ⅛ in. (3 mm) long, ovoid, white, densely woolly; laterals similar but smaller, appressed, opposite.

LEAVES. Opposite, pinnately compound, 6 in. (15 cm) long, green above, pale below, with 3–7 ovate to lanceolate leaflets 2–4 in. (5–10 cm) long, each irregularly shallow lobed or notched; fall color yellow.

FLOWERS. Apetalous, yellow-green; dioecious; appearing as the leaves unfold.

FRUIT. Length 1–1½ in. (2.5–4 cm) long; reddish brown to yellow-brown; wings diverge initially, then converge near the tips; in large clusters, August through the winter.

WOOD. Creamy white, light, soft, not strong, close grained; used for low-quality furniture, interior finishing, paper pulp, cooperage, and woodenware.

HABITAT AND RANGE. Deep, moist soils from Vermont to Minnesota, south to eastern Texas, east to Florida.

PROPAGATION. Seed, stratify 60–90 days at 33°F (1°C).

WILDLIFE VALUE. Seed is fair for songbirds and small rodents.

LANDSCAPE VALUE. Little to recommend in planting this species; brittle wood, disease and insect susceptible, messy fruit, short lived; becomes a weed species. Zones 2–9.

BEST RECOGNIZABLE FEATURES. Shiny, glaucous green twig; opposite, pinnately compound leaves with 3 and 5 leaflets; V shaped (upside down) fruit in drooping clusters.

Acer nigrum Michaux f.

PLATE 2

black maple, hard maple, rock maple

HABIT. Similar to sugar maple, but 70–90 ft. (21–27 m) tall.

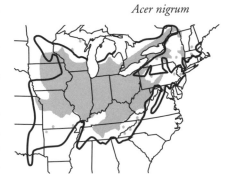

Acer nigrum

BARK. Dark gray to black, smooth when young becoming plated with age, more deeply furrowed than sugar maple.

TWIGS. Thicker than sugar maple, typically mottled, waxy, and greenish brown to orange-brown; stipule scars prominent; leaf scars V shaped; pith white, continuous.

BUDS. Similar to sugar maple, but generally larger and with more grayish pubescence.

LEAVES. Opposite, simple, 4–6 in. (10–15 cm) in diameter, dark green above, yellow-green and hairy below, 3- or 5-lobed, the lobes often curling inward to give a drooping appearance; stipules large, leafy; fall color yellow.

FLOWERS. Similar to sugar maple.

FRUIT. Similar to sugar maple.

WOOD. Brown, heavy, hard, strong, coarse grained; used for cabinets, furniture.

HABITAT AND RANGE. Moist, cool sites from Vermont to southern Minnesota, south to Missouri, east to West Virginia.

PROPAGATION. Seed, stratify 60–90 days at 36–41°F (4–5°C).

WILDLIFE VALUE. Seed is fair for songbirds and rodents.

Figure 24. *Acer nigrum* foliage

Figure 25. *Acer nigrum* fruit

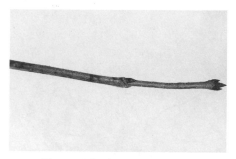

Figure 26. *Acer nigrum* twig and buds

Figure 27. *Acer nigrum* bark, medium-sized tree

Figure 28. *Acer nigrum* bark, large tree

LANDSCAPE VALUE. Has the outstanding ornamental characteristics of sugar maple, but is more tolerant of heat and drought. The cultivar 'Greencolumn' is a good street tree for the Midwest. Zones 4–8.

BEST RECOGNIZABLE FEATURES. Stipules at base of petiole; mottling of first-year twig growth; 3-lobed, somewhat "droopy" leaves.

Acer pensylvanicum Linnaeus
striped maple, moosewood

PLATES 3, 4

HABIT. Small tree or large shrub, 20–30 ft. (6–9 m) tall, with a short bole and an upright, open crown.

BARK. Bright green with white longitudinal stripes becoming reddish brown to grayish brown with age.

TWIGS. Moderately stout, brown to green with white stripes on older growth; leaf scars U shaped with 5–7 bundle scars; pith pale, continuous.

BUDS. Terminal ½ in. (13 mm) long, red, valvate, stalked, with keeled scales; laterals similar but smaller.

LEAVES. Opposite, simple, 5–7 in. (13–18 cm) long, light green above, pale below, 3-lobed; margin doubly serrate; petiole stout, grooved; fall color yellow.

Acer pensylvanicum

FLOWERS. Yellow-green, in pendulous, terminal racemes; appearing after the leaves have unfolded (but are not fully expanded).

FRUIT. Length 1–1½ in. (2.5–4 cm); light brown; wings widely divergent; September.

WOOD. Light brown, light, soft, close grained; commercially unimportant.

Figure 29. *Acer pensylvanicum* foliage

Figure 30. *Acer pensylvanicum* fruit

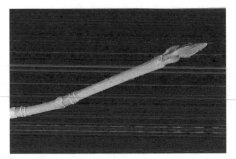

Figure 31. *Acer pensylvanicum* twig and buds

Figure 32. *Acer pensylvanicum* bark, small tree

Figure 33. *Acer pensylvanicum* bark, medium-sized tree

Figure 34. *Acer pensylvanicum* bark, large tree

HABITAT AND RANGE. Moist, cool upland sites in understories from southern Ontario to Nova Scotia, south in the Appalachian Mountains to Georgia, west to Minnesota.

PROPAGATION. Seed, stratify 90–120 days at 41°F (5°C).

WILDLIFE VALUE. Seed is fair for ruffed grouse and squirrel; browse is good for deer, rabbit, and beaver.

LANDSCAPE VALUE. Attractive small tree with unusual bark, for moist but well drained, shaded situations. Zones 3–7 (at higher elevations).

BEST RECOGNIZABLE FEATURES. Opposite, stalked, red buds; green bark (smaller stems) with white longitudinal stripes; flowers in drooping racemes; glabrous twigs.

Acer rubrum Linnaeus
red maple, scarlet maple, swamp maple

PLATES 5, 6, 7

HABIT. Medium-sized tree, 40–70 ft. (12–21 m) tall, with a long, clear bole supporting a narrow, irregular crown.

BARK. Gray, thin, and smooth when young, becoming darker colored and fissured with long, wide, divergent plates at maturity.

TWIGS. Slender, red, lenticellate, odorless when scratched (unlike silver maple); pith white, continuous.

BUDS. Terminal leaf buds ⅛–¼ in. (3–

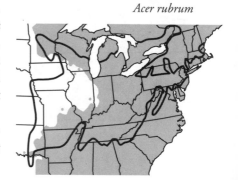

Acer rubrum

Figure 35. *Acer rubrum* foliage

Figure 36. *Acer rubrum* fruit

Figure 37. *Acer rubrum* twig and buds

Figure 38. *Acer rubrum* bark, small tree

Figure 39. *Acer rubrum* bark, medium-sized tree

Figure 40. *Acer rubrum* bark, large tree

6 mm) long, red, blunt tipped; laterals similar but smaller; flower buds globose, collateral to leaf buds, with 2–4 pairs of scales.

LEAVES. Opposite, simple, 3–6 in. (8–15 cm) in diameter, light green above, pale (or with a white bloom in *A. rubrum* var. *drummondii*) below, 3- to 5-lobed; margin serrate; fall color bright red to yellow.

FLOWERS. Bright red or yellow; 5 petals, 5–8 stamens; appearing long before the leaves in early spring.

FRUIT. Length ¾–1 in. (2–2.5 cm); red or reddish brown, double samara; wings slightly divergent (V shaped); April to May. This species and silver maple are the only native maples with fruit ripening in the spring.

WOOD. Light brown, often slightly tinged with red, very heavy, not strong, close grained; used for furniture, gunstocks, woodenware.

HABITAT AND RANGE. Very moist or very dry sites from Newfoundland to northern Minnesota, south to eastern Texas, east to southern Florida.

PROPAGATION. Fresh seed should germinate promptly in the spring; other seed, stratify 60–75 days at 41°F (5°C).

WILDLIFE VALUE. Seed is fair for songbirds, squirrel, and small rodents; browse is good for deer; buds are good for squirrel.

LANDSCAPE VALUE. Excellent medium-sized tree that tolerates wet and dry conditions. Numerous varieties available that offer more reliable intense fall color or particular form. The cultivars 'Armstrong', 'Autumn Flame', 'Bowhall', 'Karpick', 'October Glory', and 'Red Sunset' are good choices for street trees in the Midwest. Zones 3–9.

BEST RECOGNIZABLE FEATURES. Gray, scaly bark; red, lustrous twigs and red, round flower buds; fruit maturing in late spring; leaf 3- to 5-lobed, pale to white below, with serrated margin.

Acer saccharinum Linnaeus
silver maple, soft maple, white maple

PLATE 8

HABIT. Medium-sized to large tree, 60–80 ft. (18–24 m) tall, with a short bole and ascending branches supporting a spreading, round crown.

BARK. Gray, thin, smooth when young becoming shaggy with small narrow plates at maturity.

TWIGS. Slender, red to reddish brown, lenticellate, ill scented when broken; leaf scars V shaped; pith continuous.

BUDS. Terminal ⅛–¼ in. (3–6 mm)

Acer saccharinum

Figure 41. *Acer saccharinum* foliage

Figure 42. *Acer saccharinum* fruit

Figure 43. *Acer saccharinum* twig and buds

Figure 44. *Acer saccharinum* bark, all sizes

Figure 45. *Acer saccharinum* bark, medium-sized tree

Figure 46. *Acer saccharinum* bark, large tree

long, bright red, blunt or globose; laterals similar but smaller; flower buds larger, globose, collateral, with 2–4 pairs of scales.

LEAVES. Opposite, simple, 5–7 in. (13–18 cm) in diameter, pale green above, white to silvery below, deeply 5-lobed; margin serrate; fall color yellow.

FLOWERS. Red, 1–1½ in. (2.5–4 cm) long; corolla lacking; 5-lobed calyx, 3–7 stamens; appearing long before the leaves in early spring.

FRUIT. Length to 2.5 in. (6 cm); reddish brown, double samara; wings widely divergent; ripens in the spring.

WOOD. Pale brown, hard, rather brittle, easily worked, close grained; used for low-quality furniture, flooring.

HABITAT AND RANGE. Rich, moist bottomland from New Brunswick to South Dakota, south to Oklahoma, east to northern Florida.

PROPAGATION. Fresh seed germinates without pretreatment.

WILDLIFE VALUE. Seed is fair for songbirds, small rodents, and squirrel.

LANDSCAPE VALUE. Fine in its native habitat but poor choice for urban or home planting. Fast growing, brittle; messy samaras in the spring; very shallow root system; a host of insect and disease problems; and few ornamental assets. Marketed as a good choice because it grows fast and is very cheap to produce. Some cities now have ordinances against planting this and a few other species. More cities should be so discriminating, as there generally are many better species to select instead. The cultivars 'Celebration' and 'Scarlet Sentinel' are the result of cross between *A. rubrum* and *A. saccharinum*, and are recommended over *A. saccharinum*. Zones 3–9.

BEST RECOGNIZABLE FEATURES. Deeply 5-lobed leaves with rounded sinuses; leaves pale green above, silvery below; freshly broken twigs ill scented; large, brown, double samara, maturing in late spring; very large winter clusters of flower buds.

Acer saccharum Marshall   PLATES 9, 10
sugar maple, hard maple, rock maple

HABIT. Large tree, 70–90 ft. (21–27 m) tall, with a short bole and a large round or pyramidal crown.

BARK. Gray, moderately thick, smooth when young breaking into long, curved plates with age.

TWIGS. Slender, glabrous, reddish brown and lenticellate on new growth, gray-brown on old growth; leaf scars V shaped, opposite, encircling twig or nearly so, with 3 bundle scars; pith white, continuous.

BUDS. Terminal ⅛–¼ in. (3–6 mm) long, reddish brown, acute, slightly pubescent, imbricate; laterals smaller, opposite, with 4–8 pairs of imbricate scales; collateral flower buds absent.

Acer saccharum

LEAVES. Green above, pale below, 3–5 in. (8–13 cm) in diameter, 5-lobed, rarely 3-lobed; margin not serrate; fall color outstanding combination of orange and red.

FLOWERS. Apetalous, bright yellow; in long, pendulous stalks; with emerging leaves, about 2–3 weeks after red maple flowers.

Figure 47. *Acer saccharum* foliage

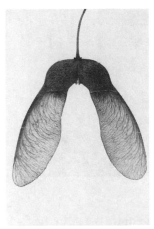

Figure 48. *Acer saccharum* fruit

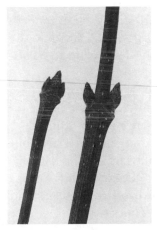

Figure 49. *Acer saccharum* twigs and buds

Figure 50. *Acer saccharum* form

Figure 51.
*Acer
saccharum*
form,
winter

Figure 52.
*Acer
saccharum*
bark, small
tree

Figure 53. *Acer saccharum* bark, large tree

FRUIT. Length 1–1½ in. (2.5–4 cm); double samara; reddish to yellowish brown; wings parallel or slightly divergent; August to October.

WOOD. Light brown tinged with red, heavy, hard, strong, close grained; used for furniture, fuel, interior finishing, cabinets.

HABITAT AND RANGE. Cool, moist soils from Newfoundland to Manitoba, south to northeast Texas, east to Alabama.

PROPAGATION. Seed, stratify 60–90 days at 36–41°F (4–5°C).

WILDLIFE VALUE. Fruit is poor but eaten by squirrel; browse is fair for deer; buds, especially when they are expanding, are good for squirrel.

LANDSCAPE VALUE. One of our most attractive, large, native trees but does not reach potential on hot, dry sites. The cultivars 'Bonfire', 'Commemoration', 'Goldspire', 'Green Mountain', 'Legacy', and 'Seneca Chief' are good choices for street trees where urban stresses (e.g., road salt, heat, compaction, drought) are not severe. Zones 4–8.

BEST RECOGNIZABLE FEATURES. Evenly colored reddish brown twigs with pale lenticels; petiole without stipules; leaf usually 5-lobed, margin not serrated; sharp-pointed buds.

COMMENT. Our main source of maple syrup.

Acer spicatum Lamarck
mountain maple, moose maple

PLATE 11

Acer spicatum

HABIT. Shrub to small tree, 20–30 ft. (6–9 m) tall, with a short bole.

BARK. Brown to reddish brown and thin, becoming slightly furrowed or warty with age (without the white longitudinal streaks of striped maple).

TWIGS. Slender, grayish pubescent especially near apex, purplish red after the first year; pith white, continuous.

BUDS. Terminal ⅛ in. (3 mm) long, valvate, acute, stalked, with bright red scales, tomentose; laterals smaller, glabrous or pubescent.

LEAVES. Opposite, simple, 2¼–4½ in. (6–11 cm) long, with 3 short lobes, coarsely toothed; fall color orange or red.

FLOWERS. Pale yellow flowers in terminal, erect panicle; late spring to early summer.

FRUIT. Double samara; bright red or yellow when mature, becoming brown; wings somewhat divergent, ½ in. (13 mm) long.

WOOD. Light brown tinged with red, light, soft, close grained; commercially unimportant.

HABITAT AND RANGE. Moist, rocky hillsides under the canopy, from

Figure 54. *Acer spicatum* foliage

Figure 55. *Acer spicatum* fruit

Figure 56. *Acer spicatum* twig and buds

Figure 57. *Acer spicatum* bark, small tree

Figure 58. *Acer spicatum* bark, larger tree

Newfoundland, Labrador, Manitoba, and Saskatchewan, south to New England, along the Appalachian Mountains to northern Georgia.

PROPAGATION. Seed, stratify 90–120 days at 41°F (5°C).

WILDLIFE VALUE. Seed is fair for songbirds, small rodents, and squirrel; browse is good for deer.

LANDSCAPE VALUE. Suitable only on cool, moist to wet, shaded sites where low, dense cover is wanted. Zones 2–7 (at high elevations).

BEST RECOGNIZABLE FEATURES. Stalked, tomentose, red buds; no longitudinal streaks in bark; flowers in terminal, erect racemes; finely pubescent twigs.

Other maples in the Central Hardwood Forests:

Acer leucoderme Small, chalk maple. A large shrub or small tree to 40 ft. (12 m) tall; characteristics similar to sugar maple, except that stature is smaller, wings of paired samaras are more divergent, and bark is smooth, chalky white. Outstanding scarlet fall color and ability to tolerate fairly dry soil suggest that this species deserves consideration in South where sugar maple does not tolerate heat. Native to southeastern United States and occurs in Central Hardwood Forests in western Arkansas. Zones 5–9.

Acer leucoderme

Other maples commonly planted in the regional landscape:
Acer campestre Linnaeus, hedge maple. To 40 ft. (12 m) tall; rounded crown of leaves similar in shape to *A. saccharum,* but smaller and with

Figure 59. *Acer campestre* foliage

Figure 60. *Acer ginnala* foliage

Figure 61. *Acer palmatum* foliage

Figure 62. *Acer platanoides* foliage

Figure 63. *Acer platanoides* fruit

Figure 64. *Acer platanoides* twigs and buds

Figure 65. *Acer platanoides* bark

Figure 66. *Acer pseudoplatanus* foliage

rounded lobes, and the broken leaf petiole exudes a milky sap. Very hardy and pest-free compared to most maples. Native to Europe and Asia. The cultivar 'Queen Elizabeth' is a good street tree in the Midwest. Zones 5–8.

Acer ginnala Maximowicz, Amur maple. To 20 ft. (6 m) tall; small tree or large multistemmed shrub with long, narrow, dark green foliage that turns yellow to red in autumn. Native to China and Japan. Zones 2–8.

Acer palmatum Thunberg, Japanese maple. To 20 ft. (6 m) tall; generally a small, very handsome, widespreading tree. Native to China and Japan. Numerous varieties of many foliage colors and texture. Zones 5–8.

Acer platanoides Linnaeus, Norway maple. To 50 ft. (15 m) tall; bark with interlacing pattern (ashlike), leaves usually dark green and turning yellow in autumn, broken petiole exudes milky sap. Much overused in the landscape, particularly the varieties with maroon-colored foliage.

Native to Europe. The cultivars 'Emerald Lustre' and 'Emerald Queen' are good street trees in the Midwest. Zones 3–7.

Acer pseudoplatanus Linnaeus, sycamore maple. To 60 ft. (18 m) tall; bark reddish brown to grayish brown, flaking off into small rectangular plates; foliage dark green to purplish. Native to Europe. Zones 4–7.

Aesculus—buckeye
HIPPOCASTANACEAE—buckeye family

Key to *Aesculus*

1. Individuals generally single stemmed, becoming large trees; flowers lacking red coloration 2
1. Individuals generally shrublike; flowers red or partially red . . 3
2(1). Stems with fetid odor; stamens exserted beyond petals; fruit husk prickly; bark corky and irregular . . . . *Aesculus glabra*
2. Stems without fetid odor; stamens shorter than petals; fruit husk smooth; bark platy and scaly . . . . *Aesculus octandra*
3(1). Habit often thicket-forming; flowers red . . . . . . *Aesculus pavia*
3. Habit not thicket-forming; flowers yellow and red . . . . *Aesculus sylvatica*

Aesculus glabra Willdenow
Ohio buckeye, fetid buckeye, stinking buckeye

PLATE 12

HABIT. Large tree, 40–60 ft. (12–18 m) tall, with a short bole, stout and some what pendulous branches, and an oblong, rounded crown.

BARK. Ash-gray, with corky warts, rougher and more furrowed than yellow buckeye, may feel spongy when pressed into, with fetid odor when cut.

TWIGS. Stout, round, reddish brown to ash-gray, new growth hairy becoming smooth with age; sap with fetid

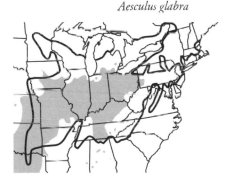

Aesculus glabra

(skunklike) odor; leaf scars large; pith white, continuous; ends of branches curve upwards.

Figure 67. *Aesculus glabra* foliage

Figure 68. *Aesculus glabra* fruit

Figure 69. *Aesculus glabra* twig and bud

Figure 70. *Aesculus glabra* bark, medium-sized tree

Figure 71. *Aesculus glabra* bark, large tree

BUDS. Terminal ⅔ in. (17 mm) long; laterals smaller, reddish brown, with strongly keeled scales and hairy margin, opposite, nonresinous.

LEAVES. Opposite, palmately compound, 8–14 in. (20–36 cm) long, dark green and smooth above, pale below, with 5–7 elliptic to obovate leaflets 5–7 in. (13–18 cm) long, with fetid odor; margin serrate; rachis 4–6 in. (10–15 cm) long, smooth, stout; emerging very early each spring and dropping in late summer to early autumn; fall color yellow to orange.

FLOWERS. Creamy yellow; borne in erect clusters, 5–7 in. (13–18 cm) long; stamens longer than petals (unlike yellow buckeye); very showy; April to May.

FRUIT. Capsule, 1–2 in. (2.5–5 cm) in diameter; husk prickly, leathery orange-brown; seed smooth, mahogany-brown, with a large, gray spot ("buck's eye"); September to October.

WOOD. Pale brown to nearly white, soft, weak, close grained; used for pulpwood and furniture.

HABITAT AND RANGE. Moist, rich soils from Pennsylvania west to southeastern Nebraska, south to Oklahoma, east to Tennessee.

PROPAGATION. Seed, stratify 60–120 days at 33–41°F (1–5°C).

WILDLIFE VALUE. Fruit has little value, but is eaten by fox and gray squirrel.

LANDSCAPE VALUE. Somewhat messy (brittle wood, fruit) and susceptible to disease, particularly leaf spots; nevertheless, the flowers are very attractive. Needs a moist but well-drained soil for best results. Zones 3–7.

BEST RECOGNIZABLE FEATURES. Opposite, palmately compound leaf (5 leaflets); twigs with fetid odor when scratched; prickly husk splits to expose large, shiny, rounded seeds; opposite buds, with keeled scales.

Aesculus octandra Marshall
yellow buckeye, sweet buckeye

PLATE 13

HABIT. Similar to Ohio buckeye, but taller, 60–90 ft. (18–27 m) tall.

BARK. Gray-brown or dark brown, slightly furrowed and covered by large, thin scales; more scaly than Ohio buckeye.

TWIGS. Similar to Ohio buckeye, but without fetid odor.

BUDS. Terminal ⅔ in. (17 mm) long; laterals smaller, brown, not strongly keeled, opposite.

Aesculus octandra

Figure 72.
Aesculus
octandra
foliage

Figure 73.
Aesculus
octandra
flowers

Figure 74. *Aesculus octandra* fruit

Figure 75.
Aesculus
octandra
twigs and
buds

Figure 76.
Aesculus
octandra
bark, small
tree

Figure 77.
Aesculus
octandra
bark,
medium-
sized tree

Figure 78. *Aesculus octandra* bark, large tree

LEAVES. Similar to Ohio buckeye, but without fetid odor.
FLOWERS. Similar to Ohio buckeye, but stamens shorter than petals.
FRUIT. Capsule, 1–2 in. (2.5–5 cm) in diameter, light brown, pear shaped; husk leathery, not prickly; seed similar to Ohio buckeye.
WOOD. Creamy white, soft, close grained; used for pulpwood, handicrafts.
HABITAT AND RANGE. Rich, moist sites from southeastern Pennsylvania to southern Illinois, south to northern Georgia and east to West Virginia.
PROPAGATION. Seed, stratify 60–120 days at 33–41°F (1–5°C).
WILDLIFE VALUE. Fruit has little value, but is eaten by fox squirrel.
LANDSCAPE VALUE. Like Ohio buckeye has beautiful flowers, but tree can be messy and is rather coarse in texture. Attractive foliage is orange-yellow-brown in autumn. Requires a moist but well-drained soil for best results. Zones 3–8.
BEST RECOGNIZABLE FEATURES. Opposite, palmately compound leaves; smooth fruit husk; thin, rough, scaly bark; keeled bud scales; twigs without fetid odor when crushed.

Aesculus pavia Linnaeus   PLATE 14
red buckeye, scarlet buckeye

HABIT. Large shrub to small tree, to 30 ft. (9 m) tall, often thicket-forming, round topped.
BARK. Smooth, brown gray to light gray.
TWIGS. Stout, olive brown, lenticellate; leaf scars large, triangular, with V-shaped bundle scars in 3 groups; pith homogeneous, white, somewhat 6-sided.

BUDS. Terminal ⅓–½ in. (8–13 mm) long, with overlapping bud scales, ovoid, brown, glabrous; laterals smaller.

LEAVES. Opposite, palmately compound, with 5 oblong-obovate, acuminate leaflets 3–6 in. (8–15 cm) long, lustrous, glabrous, dark green above, pale yellow-green below, often with tufts of axillary hairs; petiole slender, 4–7 in. (10–18 cm) long.

Aesculus pavia

FLOWERS. Red, in narrow panicles 4–8 in. (10–20 cm) long, in midspring; stamens exerted; very showy.

FRUIT. Spineless, subglobose, light brown, capsule about 2 in. (5 cm) in diameter, splitting along 2–3 lines, containing 1–2 shiny, dark chestnut-brown seeds 1 in. (2.5 cm) in diameter.

Figure 79. *Aesculus pavia* foliage

Figure 80. *Aesculus pavia* flowers

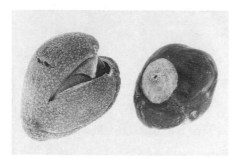

Figure 81. *Aesculus pavia* fruit

Figure 82. *Aesculus pavia* twig and buds

Figure 83.
Aesculus
pavia bark,
small tree

Figure 84.
Aesculus
pavia bark,
larger tree

WOOD. Pale brown, light, soft, close grained.

HABITAT AND RANGE. Bottomlands and moist, wooded uplands of the southeastern United States from southeastern North Carolina to south central Texas.

PROPAGATION. Seed, stratify in moist medium 120 days at 41°F (5°C) or sow outside in autumn at about 1 in. (2.5 cm) depth.

WILDLIFE VALUE. Fruit has little value, but is eaten by fox squirrel.

LANDSCAPE VALUE. Beautiful, upright clusters of dark red flowers. Good choice for moist, well-drained soils in sun or shade, especially in informal borders. Zones 4–8.

BEST RECOGNIZABLE FEATURES. Upright clusters of dark red flowers; dark chestnut-brown seed covered by spineless husk; shrubby appearance, often thicket-forming.

Aesculus sylvatica Bartram   PLATE 15
painted buckeye, dwarf buckeye, Georgia buckeye

HABIT. Large shrub or small tree, to 20 ft. (6 m) tall, with erect and spreading branches, round topped.

BARK. Thin, dark brown, becoming scaly.

TWIGS. Stout, glabrous, gray-brown, lenticellate; leaf scars shield shaped, very pronounced; pith homogeneous, white.

BUDS. Length ⅓–½ in. (8–13 mm), with light reddish brown scales that are short pointed at apex.

LEAVES. Opposite, palmately compound, with 5 ovate to obovate, acuminate leaflets 4–6 in. (10–15 cm) long, with stout orange-colored midrib, yellow-green above, green below; petiole 4½–6 in. (11–15 cm) long.

FLOWERS. Variable in color from red on upper side to pale yellow on lower side to all red or all yellow, in broad panicles in early spring; very showy.

FRUIT. Globose, about 1 in. (2.5 cm) diameter, with thin, light brown, covering; seed, globose, dark chestnut-brown, usually single.

Aesculus sylvatica

WOOD. Pale brown, light, soft, close grained.

HABITAT AND RANGE. Central North Carolina, into northern South Carolina and Georgia, northeastern Alabama, and eastern Tennessee.

PROPAGATION. Seed, stratify in moist medium 120 days at 41°F (5°C) or sow outside in autumn at about 1 in. (2.5 cm) depth.

WILDLIFE VALUE. Fruit is poor.

Figure 85. *Aesculus ×carnea* flowers

Figure 86. *Aesculus hippocastanum* foliage

Figure 87. *Aesculus hippocastanum* flowers

Figure 88. *Aesculus hippocastanum* fruit

Figure 89. *Aesculus hippocastanum* twig and buds

Figure 90. *Aesculus parviflora* foliage

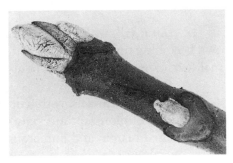

Figure 91. *Aesculus parviflora* twig and buds

LANDSCAPE VALUE. Excellent choice for moist soil in partial shade. Zones 6–9.

BEST RECOGNIZABLE FEATURES. Flowers yellow or sometimes tinged with red; smooth fruit husk, typically encasing one dark brown seed; shrubby form.

Other buckeyes commonly planted in the regional landscape:

Aesculus ×carnea Hayne, red horsechestnut. Small tree, to 40 ft. (12 m) tall; palmately compound, lustrous, dark green leaves with 5 (sometimes 7) leaflets; large, resinous buds; fruit husk slightly prickly, flowers in panicles to 10 in. (25 cm) long, generally red. Resulted from a cross between *A. pavia* and *A. hippocastanum*. The cultivar 'Briotii' is a good street tree in the Midwest. Zones 5–7.

Aesculus hippocastanum Linnaeus, horsechestnut. To 70 ft. (21 m) tall; large, widespreading tree with 7 leaflets; large, resinous, sticky buds; a very prickly fruit husk; creamy white panicles of flowers in early May. Native to Greece and Albania. Zones 3–7.

Aesculus parviflora Walter, bottlebrush buckeye. To 10 ft. (3 m) tall; a widespreading, multistemmed shrub with distinct, upright habit. Flowers in the summer on white panicles 8–12 in. (20–31 cm) long; very shade tolerant. Native to Alabama, Georgia. Zones 4–8.

Ailanthus—ailanthus
SIMAROUBACEAE—quassia family

Ailanthus altissima (Miller) Swingle
ailanthus, tree-of-heaven

HABIT. Medium-sized tree, 40–60 ft. (12–18 m) tall, with a clear bole, large, ascending branches, and a crown becoming round with age.

BARK. Gray, thin, smooth or with shallow, interlacing ridges and light-colored fissures.

TWIGS. Stout, tan to reddish with prominent, raised lenticels, with fetid odor when broken; annual growth to 6 ft. (2 m) or more (sprouts vigorously); leaf scars large, heart shaped, with raised margin and numerous bundle scars; pith large, light brown.

BUDS. Terminal absent; laterals ⅛ in. (3 mm) in diameter, brown, smooth or lightly hairy, partially imbedded in twig with 2–4 exposed scales.

LEAVES. Alternate, pinnately compound, 1–3 ft. (0.3–1 m) long, green and smooth above, pale below, with 13–41 lanceolate leaflets 3–5 in. (8–13 cm) long, each with 2–4 gland-tipped teeth at the base; ill scented when bruised; fall color yellowish green.

FLOWERS. Dioecious; males with very unpleasant odor; June to July.

FRUIT. Samara, 1–1½ in. (2.5–4 cm) long, light brown; oblong, twisted; one seeded; in large clusters; September to October, persisting into winter.

WOOD. Light brown, light, soft, close grained; used for fuel, rough construction.

HABITAT AND RANGE. Variety of sites, common in urban areas; native to China, naturalized in United States via England, now throughout eastern United States.

PROPAGATION. Seed, stratify 30–60 days at 33–41°F (1–5°C).

WILDLIFE VALUE. Not significant to any native wildlife species.

LANDSCAPE VALUE. Nearly indestructible, somewhat tropical-looking tree, which has the potential to become quite a weed problem. Plantings should be limited to severe sites as this species spreads rapidly. Male flow-

Figure 92. *Ailanthus altissima* foliage

Figure 93. *Ailanthus altissima* fruit

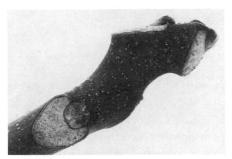

Figure 94. *Ailanthus altissima* twig and buds

Figure 95. *Ailanthus altissima* bark, medium-sized tree

Figure 96. *Ailanthus altissima* bark, large tree

ers have a very offensive odor, and female trees produce many offspring; both sexes root sprout vigorously. Zones 4–8.

BEST RECOGNIZABLE FEATURES. Alternate, compound leaves, base of leaflets with glands; twigs with fetid odor when broken; gray, relatively smooth bark even on large trees; fruit a twisted samara, turning brown.

Albizia—silktree
MIMOSACEAE—mimosa family

Albizia julibrissin Durazzini
silktree, mimosa, albizia

PLATE 16

HABIT. Small tree, to 20 ft. (6 m) tall, with widely spreading branches on a short trunk, resulting in a broad, flat-topped crown.

BARK. Gray-brown, with large, conspicuous lenticels, otherwise smooth.

TWIGS. Moderately stout, often angled, zigzag, gray-green, with pea odor when broken, glabrous; lenticels large and raised; leaf scars large, raised, 3-lobed with prominent shiny, dark margin and 3 bundle scars; pith homogeneous, white, large.

BUDS. Terminal absent; laterals ¹⁄₁₆ in. (2 mm) long, brown, globose, superposed with 2–3 scales, slightly hairy.

LEAVES. Alternate, bipinnately compound, 6–20 in. (15–51 cm) long, with 5–12 pairs of side axes, each axis consisting of 15–30 pairs of

Figure 97. *Albizia julibrissin* foliage and flowers

Figure 98. *Albizia julibrissin* bark, medium-sized tree

oblong, pale green leaflets about ½ in. (13 mm) long, closing along rachis at night.

FLOWERS. Crowded in round head; long stamens that are white at base and pink to red at ends are arranged such that flower has appearance of pink pin cushion; very showy; late spring to summer.

FRUIT. Length 5–8 in. (13–20 cm); flat, oblong, yellow-brown legume.

HABITAT AND RANGE. Native from Persia to China, commonly planted and escaped through Midwest and South.

PROPAGATION. Seed, scarify by soaking 30 minutes in sulfuric acid; collect root cuttings in spring.

WILDLIFE VALUE. Not significant to any native wildlife species.

LANDSCAPE VALUE. Graceful tree with attractive, unusual flowers but is short lived due to disease (mimosa wilt) and insect problems. Zones 6–9.

BEST RECOGNIZABLE FEATURES. Bipinnately compound leaves; pink, pin-cushion-like flowers; fruit a long, flat legume.

Alnus—alder
BETULACEAE—birch family

Alnus serrulata (Aiton) Willdenow
hazel alder, common alder, tag alder

PLATE 17

HABIT. Multistemmed shrub to straggly tree, to 20 ft. (6 m) tall, wide-spreading.

BARK. Dark gray to brown, smooth, similar to American hornbeam, with lenticels.

TWIGS. Slender, circular, olive brown to gray-brown, usually pale woolly, lenticellate; leaf scars raised, triangular to half-round, with 3 bundle scars; pith continuous, triangular in cross section, greenish brown.

Alnus serrulata

BUDS. Terminal absent; laterals stalked, with 2 (or rarely 3) valvate scales.

LEAVES. Alternate, simple, 2–4½ in. (5–11 cm) long, ovate to obovate, pinnately veined, finely toothed, gummy and aromatic when immature, dull green above, light green below; fall color reddish brown.

Figure 99. *Alnus serrulata* foliage and fruit

Figure 100. *Alnus serrulata* bark, small tree

Figure 101. *Alnus serrulata* bark, larger tree

FLOWERS. Male in drooping catkins 1½–3 in. (4–8 cm) long; female in "cones" ¼ in. (6 mm) long; opening in early spring.

FRUIT. Conelike structure, ⅝ in. (16 mm) long; black, woody, short stalked; matures in autumn, persisting in winter along with catkins; seeds, tiny, flat nutlets.

WOOD. Light brown, light, soft, close grained; commercially unimportant.

HABITAT AND RANGE. Along streams from Nova Scotia to Oklahoma, Florida, and Louisiana.

PROPAGATION. Fresh seed germinates without pretreatment; other seed, stratify 120–180 days at 35–41°F (4–5°C).

WILDLIFE VALUE. Tree provides good cover for woodcock and deer; browse is good for deer and rabbit.

LANDSCAPE VALUE. Excellent choice for dense, low cover on wet soils;

could play important role in constructing wetlands since it is a nitrogen fixer. Zones 4–9.

BEST RECOGNIZABLE FEATURES. Shrubby habit, near streams or other wet areas; woody, conelike fruit; stalked, valvate buds; catkins present in autumn and winter.

Other alders in the Central Hardwood Forests:

Alnus rugosa (Du Roi) Sprengel, speckled alder. Low, clump-forming, shrub; bark gray to brown, covered with horizontally arranged orange-brown lenticels; leaves 2–4 in. (5–10 cm) long, pale green or glaucous below, 9–12 pairs of lateral veins, doubly serrate; twig with triangular pith in cross section; flowers very early in spring before the leaves appear; fruit about ½ in. (13 mm) in diameter, conelike, persisting into winter. Offering little ornamental value, except near water where soils support relatively few other woody species. Grows in wet soils of swamps, bottomlands, and lake margins throughout northern United States into Canada. Zones 3–6.

Alnus rugosa

Other alders commonly planted in the regional landscape:

Alnus glutinosa (Linnaeus) Gaertner, black or European alder. To 60 ft. (18 m) tall; very rapid grower in youth, 2–3 ft. (0.6–1 m) per year; important species in land reclamation since it is a nitrogen fixer. Native to Europe and Asia. Zones 3–7.

Figure 102. *Alnus rugosa* foliage

Figure 103. *Alnus rugosa* twigs and buds

Figure 104.
Alnus rugosa bark, large stem

Figure 105. *Alnus glutinosa* foliage

Amelanchier—serviceberry
ROSACEAE—rose family

Amelanchier arborea (Michaux f.) Fernald   PLATE 18
downy serviceberry, serviceberry, shadbush, shadblow

HABIT. Multistemmed shrub or small to medium-sized tree, 30–50 ft. (9–15 m) tall, with a round crown and fine branchlets.

BARK. Smooth, light gray with very thin longitudinal fissures, often with a reddish cast, with age developing large, dark fissures from the base of the trunk upwards and eventually becoming scaly.

Amelanchier arborea

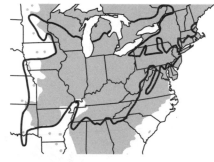

TWIGS. Slender, reddish brown to grayish brown, with numerous lenticels, often covered with a gray film, usually smooth or slightly hairy, with slight odor of bitter almonds; pith continuous, white, slightly angled.

BUDS. Length ½ in. (13 mm); greenish yellow tinged with reddish brown, conical, many scaled, imbricate; acute laterals, usually appressed or recurved toward the twig.

LEAVES. Alternate, 1½–4 in. (4–10 cm) long, obovate to elliptic or ob-

Figure 106. *Amelanchier arborea* foliage

Figure 107. *Amelanchier arborea* flowers

Figure 108. *Amelanchier arborea* fruit

Figure 109. *Amelanchier arborea* twig and buds

Figure 110. *Amelanchier arborea* bark, small tree

Figure 111. *Amelanchier arborea* bark, large tree

long, dull light green above; pale and sometimes hairy below; petiole hairy or smooth; margin toothed; leaf base heart shaped; fall color orange-red to yellow.

FLOWERS. White, ½–¾ in. (13–19 mm) in diameter; very showy; appearing before or with the leaves in early spring.

FRUIT. Red, maturing to purple or nearly black, ⅓–½ in. (8–13 mm) in diameter; glaucous; variable taste, sometimes dry; June to July.

WOOD. Reddish brown; heavy, hard, close grained; used for fuel, tool handles.

HABITAT AND RANGE. Swamps and along riverbanks to sandy ridges and limestone cliffs from New Brunswick west to Ontario and Minnesota, south to Nebraska and Texas, east to Florida.

PROPAGATION. Seed, stratify 90–120 days at 33–41°F (1–5°C).

WILDLIFE VALUE. Fruit is good for grouse, songbirds, squirrel, and small rodents; bark and leaves are good for beaver and deer.

LANDSCAPE VALUE. Excellent small ornamental tree with a profusion of spring flowers, good fall color, and attractive bark. Naturally tolerates dry to wet conditions. Many varieties exist. Zones 4–9.

BEST RECOGNIZABLE FEATURES. Smooth light gray bark; recurved greenish to reddish brown buds; twigs with slight odor of bitter almonds when scratched.

COMMENT. Allegheny serviceberry, *Amelanchier arborea* var. *laevis,* can be distinguished from downy serviceberry by the following characteristics: seldom over 30 ft. (9 m) tall; sweet, succulent blue-black fruit; smooth petioles, pedicels, and peduncles of flowers; bronze-purple color of unfolding smooth leaves; ciliate buds with white hairs; and sparse lenticels, smooth twigs.

Other serviceberries in the Central Hardwood Forests:

Amelanchier sanguinea (Pursh) de Candolle, roundleaf serviceberry. Large shrub to small tree with one or more main stems, to 20 ft. (6 m) tall; leaves to nearly 3 in. (8 cm) long, elliptic to nearly circular, coarsely serrate margin; twigs initially reddish and slender; flowers with 5 white petals, appearing in early spring before the leaves; fruit pomelike, blackish, sweet, juicy, edible. Rocky slopes and streambanks, Canada to New York, Nebraska, and Indiana. Zone 4.

Amelanchier sanguinea

Aralia—devils-walkingstick
ARALIACEAE—ginseng family

Aralia spinosa Linnaeus
devils-walkingstick, Hercules-club

PLATE 19

HABIT. Small tree or large shrub, 10–20 ft. (3–6 m) tall, with stout branches forming a flat-topped outline, frequently in dense thickets.

BARK. Gray-brown, thin, fissured, spiny; inner bark bright yellow.

TWIGS. Very stout, gray to yellowish brown, smooth, heavily spined, club-like; leaf scars nearly encircling twigs, with numerous bundle scars in a single row; pith large, white, continuous.

Aralia spinosa

BUDS. Terminal ½ in. (13 mm) long; laterals ¹⁄₁₆–¼ in. (2–6 cm) long, brownish gray, appressed, single, triangular or conical, with few scales.

LEAVES. Alternate, 2½–3½ ft. (0.8–1.1 m) long, green above, whitish below, bipinnately compound; leaflets ovate, 2–3 in. (5–8 cm) long, 13 on each rachis; fall color yellow.

FLOWERS. White, large flat clusters; very showy; July.

FRUIT. Drupe, ¼ in. (6 mm) wide; black, angled borne on red inflorescence; late September.

Figure 112. *Aralia spinosa* form and foliage

Figure 113. *Aralia spinosa* foliage and flowers

Figure 114. *Aralia spinosa* twig and bud

Figure 115. *Aralia spinosa* stem, young

Figure 116. *Aralia spinosa* stem, large

WOOD. Commercially unimportant.

HABITAT AND RANGE. Moist woodlands from New Jersey to Iowa, south to Texas, east to Florida.

PROPAGATION. Seed, stratify 60–120 days at 33–41°F (1–5°C).

WILDLIFE VALUE. Fruit is good for songbirds, ruffed grouse, and mice.

LANDSCAPE VALUE. Unusual, thicket-forming, coarse textured, short, widespreading ornamental. Should do well on dry soils. Zones 4–9.

BEST RECOGNIZABLE FEATURES. Large bipinnately compound leaf; stout stems covered with numerous, thick spines; usually in clumps (root suckers).

Asimina—pawpaw
ANNONACEAE—custard-apple family

Asimina triloba (Linnaeus) Dunal
PLATES 20, 21
pawpaw

HABIT. Small tree to large shrub, 20–30 ft. (6–9 m) tall, with a slender bole; crown dense, round in the forest, pyramidal in the open.

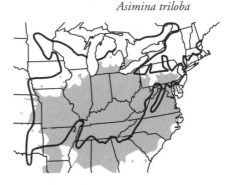

Asimina triloba

BARK. Dark brown to gray, mottled with ash-gray blotches, thin, smooth except for blisterlike outgrowths, shallowly fissured with age.

TWIGS. Slender, light brown to dark brown, reddish hairy, ill scented when bruised; leaf scars crescent shaped; pith initially white with green diaphragms, becoming brown and chambered.

BUDS. Terminal ½ in. (13 mm) long; laterals ⅛ in. (3 mm) long, reddish brown, hairy, naked; flower buds globose; leaf buds elongated, slender.

LEAVES. Alternate, 10–12 in. (25–31 cm) long, light green above, pale below, smooth, obovate-oblong, with fragrance of green bell pepper when crushed; margin entire; apex short pointed; fall color yellow.

FLOWERS. Deep red-purple; 2 in. (5 cm) in diameter; solitary; greenish yellow before mature; April to May; showy.

FRUIT. Berry 3–5 in. (8–13 cm) long, glabrous, greenish yellow becoming brown-spotted when ripe; seeds 1 in. (2.5 cm), dark brown, flattened; flesh edible with a banana-like taste and custardlike texture; October.

Figure 117. *Asimina triloba* foliage

Figure 118. *Asimina triloba* fruit

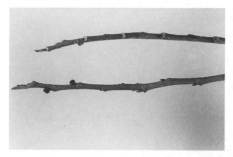

Figure 119. *Asimina triloba* twigs and buds

Figure 120. *Asimina triloba* bark, small tree

Figure 121. *Asimina triloba* bark, larger tree

WOOD. Light yellow shaded with green, light, soft, weak, spongy, coarse grained; commercially unimportant.

HABITAT AND RANGE. Moist woodlands from New York to Florida, west to eastern Texas, north to Nebraska.

PROPAGATION. Seed, stratify 60 days at 33–41°F (1–5°C).

WILDLIFE VALUE. Fruit is fair for opossum, mice, raccoon, and people.

LANDSCAPE VALUE. Exceptional, small ornamental tree for rich, moist soil; fruit is a delicious bonus. Zones 5–8.

BEST RECOGNIZABLE FEATURES. Foliage with green pepper smell when crushed; naked, dark, silky-hairy buds; smooth, gray-brown blotched bark; often thicket-forming.

Betula—birch
BETULACEAE—birch family

Key to *Betula*

1. Cut twigs and bark with wintergreen odor; fruit held upright 2
1. Cut twigs and bark without wintergreen odor; fruit pendent 3
2(1). Twigs glabrous; bark with blackish or dark gray plates . . . . *Betula lenta*
2. Twigs pubescent; bark golden and exfoliating . . . . *Betula alleghaniensis*
3(1). Fruit matures in early summer; bark cinnamon colored and exfoliating; naturally occurs in wet habitats . . . . . *Betula nigra*
3. Fruit matures in autumn; bark white 4
4(3). Leaves triangular; staminate catkins typically solitary; bark white but not exfoliating; habit typically multistemmed . . . . *Betula populifolia*
4. Leaves ovate; staminate catkins typically in groups of 2 and/or 3; bark white and exfoliating into broad, papery strips; habit typically single stemmed . . . . *Betula papyrifera*

Betula alleghaniensis Britton
yellow birch

PLATE 22

HABIT. Large tree, 70–100 ft. (21–31 m) tall, with a short, clear bole, a round crown, and drooping branches.
BARK. Smooth and bronze becoming bronze-yellow, papery, peeling; reddish brown and plated with age; young stems lenticellate.
TWIGS. Slender, yellow-green to dark brown, similar to sweet birch except hairy; wintergreen fragrance less conspicuous than sweet birch; pith green, continuous.

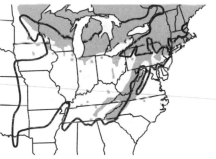

Betula alleghaniensis

BUDS. Similar to sweet birch, but less sharp and the laterals are appressed to the twig; may be hairy.

Figure 122. *Betula alleghaniensis* foliage

Figure 123. *Betula alleghaniensis* flowers

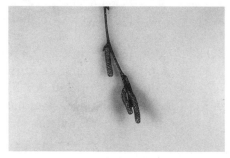

Figure 124. *Betula alleghaniensis* fruit

Figure 125. *Betula alleghaniensis* staminate flower buds

Figure 126. *Betula alleghaniensis* twigs and buds

Figure 127. *Betula alleghaniensis* bark, small tree

Figure 128. *Betula alleghaniensis* bark, medium-sized tree

Figure 129. *Betula alleghaniensis* bark, large tree

Figure 130. *Betula alleghaniensis* stilt roots

LEAVES. On older twigs often in pairs, appearing whorled, 3–5 in. (8–13 cm) long, ovate to oblong-ovate, dull dark green above, pale yellow-green below; leaf base rounded or wedge shaped; margin doubly serrate; petiole hairy; fall color yellow.

FLOWERS. Catkins; May.

FRUIT. Similar to sweet birch, but broader and longer; both species, borne upright.

WOOD. Light brown tinged with red, heavy, hard, very strong, close grained; used for flooring, furniture, fuel, boxes.

HABITAT AND RANGE. Cool, moist uplands from Manitoba to Newfoundland, south to northeastern Georgia in the Appalachian Mountains, west to Iowa.

PROPAGATION. Fresh seed should be sown but not covered with media; cold stratification 80–90 days at 41°F (5°C) may improve germination.

WILDLIFE VALUE. Fruit is fair for songbirds; browse is good for deer.

LANDSCAPE VALUE. Large handsome tree for cool, moist soils. Zones 3–7 (at higher elevations).

BEST RECOGNIZABLE FEATURES. Finely pubescent twigs with wintergreen odor and taste when crushed; bronze-gray bark on larger trees; leaves often appear in pairs on spur shoots; upright fruit.

Betula lenta Linnaeus
sweet birch, black birch, cherry birch

HABIT. Medium-sized to large tree, 50–80 ft. (15–24 m) tall, with a long, clear bole supporting a spherical crown.

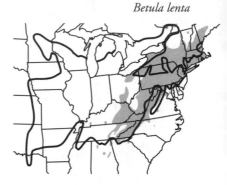

Betula lenta

BARK. Reddish brown to black, smooth with lenticels when young, becoming brownish black to ash-gray, scaly with age; aromatic when cut.

TWIGS. Slender, glabrous bright reddish brown, becoming brown to nearly black, lustrous, smooth, zigzag, with short spur shoots each bearing 2 leaves; strong wintergreen smell and taste; pith continuous, greenish white to brown.

BUDS. Terminal usually absent; laterals ¼ in. (6 mm) long, reddish brown, conical, mostly glabrous, sharp pointed, divergent, on spur shoots.

LEAVES. Alternate, 2–5 in. (5–13 cm) long, ovate to ovate-oblong,

Figure 131. *Betula lenta* foliage

Figure 132. *Betula lenta* flowers, male

Figure 133. *Betula lenta* twig and buds

Figure 134.
Betula lenta
fruit

Figure 135.
Betula lenta
bark, small
tree

Figure 136.
Betula lenta
bark,
medium-
sized tree

Figure 137. *Betula lenta* bark, large tree

smooth and shiny above, typically in pairs on spur shoots; base heart shaped; margin doubly serrate; tufts of hair in axils of veins on underside; petiole hairy; fall color yellow.

FLOWERS. Catkins, ½–1 in. (13–25 mm) long; pinkish brown; April.

FRUIT. Length 1¼ in. (3 cm); aggregate of winged nutlets erect (borne upright); wings hairless or nearly so.

WOOD. Reddish brown, hard, close grained; used for cabinets, furniture, plywood, pulpwood.

HABITAT AND RANGE. Deep, moist soils or dry ridgetops in the Appalachian Mountains from Maine to northern Alabama and from southern Michigan to New Jersey.

PROPAGATION. Seed, stratify 30–60 days at 33–41°F (1–5°C); seed needs light to germinate.

WILDLIFE VALUE. Fruit is fair for songbirds and mice; browse is good for deer.

LANDSCAPE VALUE. Handsome tree that tolerates drier soils. Zones 3–7 (at high elevations).

BEST RECOGNIZABLE FEATURES. Glabrous twigs with wintergreen odor and taste when crushed; cherrylike bark; upright fruit.

Betula nigra Linnaeus
river birch, red birch

PLATE 23

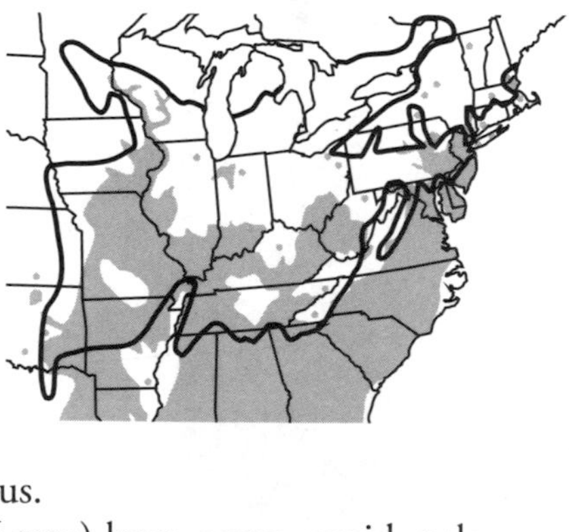

HABIT. Large tree, to 80 ft. (24 m) tall; irregular crown.

Betula nigra

BARK. Dark reddish brown when very young, becoming gray to dark brown and distinctly ridged and scaly, exfoliating into thin, papery "sheets," exposing a light pinkish tan, gray-brown, or cinnamon-brown inner bark.

TWIGS. New growth tomentose, gradually turning glabrous; dark red, slender, lustrous, dull reddish brown in the second year, later exfoliating; pith continuous.

BUDS. Terminal absent; laterals ¼ in. (6 mm) long, acute, ovoid, pale tomentose in summer, only slightly so in winter, bright chestnut-brown, frequently with hook at tip (unlike yellow birch and sweet birch).

LEAVES. Alternate, simple, 1½–3 in. (4–8 cm) long, somewhat triangular shape, shiny and dark green above, whitish below; base wedge shaped; margin doubly serrate; fall color dull yellow.

Figure 138. *Betula nigra* foliage

Figure 139. *Betula nigra* flowers, male

Figure 140. *Betula nigra* fruit

Figure 141. *Betula nigra* twigs and buds

Figure 142. *Betula nigra* bark, small stem

Figure 143. *Betula nigra* bark, small tree

Figure 144. *Betula nigra* bark, large tree

FLOWERS. Staminate aments clustered; April.

FRUIT. Ripens in May to June (unlike the other native birches that ripen in late summer to early autumn); barrel shaped, pubescent; 1½ in. (4 cm) long, ½ in. (13 mm) wide; erect, stout tomentose peduncles.

WOOD. Light brown, light, somewhat hard, strong, close grained; used in furniture, woodenware.

HABITAT AND RANGE. Low elevations along streams and wet areas from Massachusetts to Florida, west to Minnesota and Kansas.

PROPAGATION. Seed, sow when collected in the spring; softwood cuttings.

WILDLIFE VALUE. Fruit is fair for songbirds and mice; browse is good for deer.

LANDSCAPE VALUE. The best birch for midwestern and southern landscapes since it is not susceptible, as are the white bark birches, to bronze birch borers. Does not do very well on excessively dry sites. The cultivar 'Heritage' is highly recommended by Dirr (1990). Zones 4–9.

BEST RECOGNIZABLE FEATURES. Reddish brown to cinnamon-brown exfoliating bark; triangular leaf; fruit ripening in spring; found along bodies of flowing water.

Betula papyrifera Marshall
PLATE 24

paper birch, canoe birch, white birch

HABIT. Medium-sized tree, to 70 ft. (21 m) tall, with a narrow, open crown of short pendulous branches.

BARK. Very thin, smooth, dark orange-brown when young, lustrous, and lenticellate on very young stems, becoming chalky to creamy white, with

papery strips; black and deeply furrowed at base of old trees.

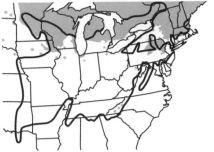

Betula papyrifera

TWIGS. Light green, becoming dull red
by the first winter, then covered with
horizontal lenticels; spur shoots numerous on older twigs; leaf scars half-
elliptic with 3 bundle traces.

BUDS. Terminal absent; laterals obovoid, acute, about ¼ in. (6 mm) long,
dark chestnut-brown, glabrous, slightly
resinous.

LEAVES. Alternate, simple, 2–4 in. (5–10 cm) long, ovate, dull dark green;
lower surface covered with minute, black glands; margin coarsely and
doubly serrate; apex acute; base rounded or obtuse; petiole slender, black-
glandular; alternate on long shoots produced in current year, in whorls
on spur shoots; fall color light clear yellow.

FLOWERS. Staminate flowers (catkins) "preformed" (i.e., visible throughout autumn and winter preceding the spring), slender, pendent, borne in
groups of 2 and/or 3; pistillate flowers (catkins) visible only during spring
flowering period.

FRUIT. A cylindrical, pendent, strobile about 1½ in. (4 cm) long, holding
very small (¹⁄₁₆ in. (2 mm) long) winged, ellipsoidal nut.

WOOD. Light brown tinged with red, light, strong, hard, tough, very close
grained; used for veneer, specialty items, pulpwood.

HABITAT AND RANGE. Moist upland soils and burned or cutover lands in
the northern and northeastern United States and throughout Canada.

PROPAGATION. Fresh seed germinates without pretreatment, but needs
light to germinate; stratify seed in moist medium 60–90 days at 41°F
(5°C).

WILDLIFE VALUE. Seed is eaten by small birds and rodents; buds are eaten
by grouse; twigs are eaten by moose and deer; and inner bark is eaten by
beaver.

LANDSCAPE VALUE. Use in warmer areas must be tempered with knowl
edge that bronze birch borer typically kills older specimens, especially
those that have been stressed by drought or nearby construction; otherwise a handsome accent tree, especially in combination with evergreen
background. One of cold hardiest trees in North America. Zones 2–6 (7,
at high elevations).

BEST RECOGNIZABLE FEATURES. Thin, white bark; flowers are catkins,
opening in early spring; cylindric, pendent strobilus.

COMMENT. Mountain paper birch (*Betula papyrifera* var. *cordifolia*, syn-
onym *B. cordifolia*) can be distinguished from paper birch by the fol-

Figure 145. *Betula papyrifera* foliage

Figure 146. *Betula papyrifera* flowers, male

Figure 147. *Betula papyrifera* twig and buds

Figure 148. *Betula papyrifera* bark, small stem

Figure 149. *Betula papyrifera* bark, medium-sized tree

Figure 150. *Betula papyrifera* bark, large tree

lowing characteristics: a smaller stature; heart-shaped leaf; often dark reddish brown bark (although may be chalky white); and distribution restricted to elevations over 5000 ft. (1524 m) in North Carolina and to isolated areas around Lake Superior.

Betula populifolia Marshall
gray birch, white birch, oldfield birch

HABIT. The smallest of our native arborescent birches, to 30 ft. (9 m) tall, with a conical or narrowly pyramidal crown over many stems, branches ascending.

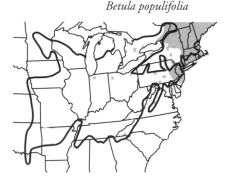

Betula populifolia

BARK. Thin, dull chalky-white, smooth, not exfoliating, becoming black and roughed by fissures on oldest trunks; dark, triangular patches (chevrons) below branches along the bole.

TWIGS. Slender, reddish brown or grayish, covered with warty resinous exudations; lenticels horizontally elongated and raised; pith homogenous, greenish white to brown.

BUDS. Terminal absent; laterals ⅕ in. (5 mm) long, ovoid, pointed, brownish, divergent, somewhat resinous, with imbricate scales and finely downy on margin.

LEAVES. Deciduous, alternate, simple, 2–3 in. (5- 8 cm) long, triangular, shiny and dark green above, paler below; apex long pointed (attenuate); base truncate (wedge shaped); margin coarsely or doubly serrate; petiole to 1 in. (2.5 cm) long, dotted with black glands; fall color pale yellow.

FLOWERS. Staminate catkin borne singly (rarely in pairs), terminally.

FRUIT. Slender aggregate (strobile) of small, winged nutlets; scales and nutlets hairy; about 1 in. (2.5 cm) long; seed small, oval, winged.

WOOD. Light brown, light, soft, not strong, not durable, close grained; used mostly for fuel and locally for spools, pulpwood, barrel hoops.

HABITAT AND RANGE. Early colonizer of badly degraded lands, dry barren uplands, and abandoned agricultural fields; also margins of swamps and ponds; from Nova Scotia and Ontario to Delaware.

PROPAGATION. Seed, stratify 60–90 days at 33–41°F (1–5°C).

WILDLIFE VALUE. Fruit is good for grouse and songbirds; browse is good for deer.

LANDSCAPE VALUE. Fine texture, somewhat pendulous form, valuable ornamental feature in white bark, resistant to the bronze birch borer;

Figure 151. *Betula populifolia* foliage

Figure 152. *Betula populifolia* flowers, male

Figure 153. *Betula populifolia* fruit

Figure 154. *Betula populifolia* twig and buds

Figure 155. *Betula populifolia* bark, small tree

Figure 156. *Betula populifolia* bark, medium-sized tree

Figure 157. *Betula populifolia* bark, large tree

however, does poorly on high pH soils, is very susceptible to leaf miner, and is fairly short lived. Very important species for reclamation of derelict lands. Zones 3–6.

BEST RECOGNIZABLE FEATURES. Single, terminal staminate catkin; triangular-shaped leaf; black dots on petiole; warty twigs; nonexfoliating, dull, chalky-white bark; multistemmed.

Other birches commonly planted in the regional landscape:
Betula pendula Roth, European white birch. Pyramidal, somewhat pendulous tree, to 50 ft. (15 m) tall; bark thin and exfoliating less than paper birch; lower trunk becomes black with age. Bronze birch borer leads to the early demise of this species in Midwest and South. Native to Europe and northern Asia. Zones 2–6.

Figure 158. *Betula pendula* foliage

Figure 159. *Betula pendula* fruit

Broussonetia—paper-mulberry
MORACEAE—mulberry family

Broussonetia papyrifera (Linnaeus) Ventenat
paper-mulberry

HABIT. Medium-sized tree, to 50 ft. (15 m) tall, with widespreading branches; root sprouts common.

BARK. Smooth to fissured, yellowish brown to gray-brown, thin.

TWIGS. Moderately stout, round, gray-green, with large orange lenticels, zigzag, hairy when young, exuding milky sap when cut; leaf scars large, round, and raised with a sunken center; pith very large and white, interrupted at the nodes by very thin green diaphragms.

Figure 160. *Broussonetia papyrifera* foliage

Figure 161. *Broussonetia papyrifera* foliage

Figure 162. *Broussonetia papyrifera* bark, small stem

Figure 163. *Broussonetia papyrifera* bark, large stem

BUDS. Terminal absent; laterals conical, solitary, sessile, with 1–2 visible striate scales.

LEAVES. Deciduous, alternate or opposite, simple, 3–8 in. (8–20 cm) long, ovate, entire to deeply 3- to 5-lobed, velvety hairy above and below; margin coarsely serrate.

FLOWERS. Dioecious; males in yellowish catkins to 3 in. (8 cm) long, females in clusters ½ in. (13 mm) in diameter; April to May.

FRUIT. Globose aggregate of drupes, ¾ in. (19 mm) in diameter; red; maturing in late summer.

WOOD. Commercially unimportant.

HABITAT AND RANGE. Native to China and Japan; found naturalized throughout eastern United States.

PROPAGATION. Softwood cuttings collected in midsummer.

WILDLIFE VALUE. Little value to native wildlife species.

LANDSCAPE VALUE. Not especially attractive but tolerates worst urban conditions. Zones 6–10.

BEST RECOGNIZABLE FEATURES. Pith interrupted at nodes by very thin green diaphragm; velvety hairy, variably shaped leaves; thin yellowish brown to gray-brown bark.

Bumelia—bumelia
SAPOTACEAE—sapodilla family

Key to *Bumelia*

1.   Lower surface of leaves villous . . . . *Bumelia lanuginosa*

1   Lower surface of leaves glabrous . . . . *Bumelia lycioides*

Bumelia lanuginosa (Michaux) Persoon
gum bumelia, black haw, chittimwood, ironwood, coma

HABIT. Shrub or small tree, to 50 ft. (15 m) tall, with a narrow crown.

BARK. To ½ in. (13 mm) thick, deeply fissured into dark gray-brown ridges.

TWIGS. Slender, red-gray, initially covered with dense rufous tomentum, may be armed with reddish straight or curved thorns; leaf scars small, semi-orbicular, with 2 vascular bundle scars; sap milky or gummy.

BUDS. About ⅛ in. (3 mm) long, woolly, obtuse.

LEAVES. Alternate, simple, often clustered in false whorls (spurs), 1–4 in. (2.5–10 cm) long, 1 in. (2.5 cm) wide, oblanceolate to obovate or elliptic; margin entire; apex rounded or notched; conspicuous reticulate veins on both surfaces; young leaves villous with white to rufous hairs; mature leaves dark, lustrous green above and villous below; petiole ½ in. (13 mm) long, villous.

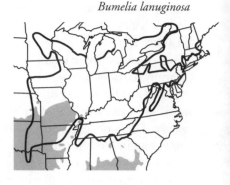

Bumelia lanuginosa

FLOWERS. Small, ⅛ in. (3 mm) wide, numerous in umbels, pedicels ½ in. (13 mm) long, hairy to subglabrous; May to July.

FRUIT. Drupelike berry; ½ in. (13 mm) long; purplish black, ovoid; flesh thick; seed ¼ in. (6 mm) long.

WOOD. Yellowish brown, weak, ring-porous, close grained; has been used in eastern Texas for cabinets.

HABITAT AND RANGE. Sandy soils of uplands and dry bottomlands, from Florida to Texas and north to Arkansas, southern Missouri, southern Indiana, and southern Virginia.

PROPAGATION. Seed, stratify in moist medium 60 days at 41°F (5°C).

WILDLIFE VALUE. Fruit is eaten by songbirds.

LANDSCAPE VALUE. Excellent small tree, especially for hot, dry sites. Zones 5–8.

BEST RECOGNIZABLE FEATURES. Gummy sap; leaves villous below; spur shoot common.

Bumelia lycioides Gaertner f.
buckthorn bumelia, buckthorn, ironwood

HABIT. Small tree or large shrub, 10–20 ft. (3–6 m) tall, with an open crown.

BARK. Thin, light reddish brown, smooth or with thin scales.

TWIGS. Slender, often armed with stout curved spines to ¾ in. (19 mm) long, black-purple; sap somewhat milky; spur shoots common; pith homogeneous, white, often striped brown.

BUDS. Minute, glabrous, hemispherical, consisting of about 4 scales, embedded.

Bumelia lycioides

LEAVES. Deciduous, alternate on new growth, clustered on spurs of older twigs, 3–6 in. (8–15 cm) long, elliptic or oblanceolate; margin recurved, entire.

FLOWERS. Bell shaped, ⅛ in. (3 mm) in diameter, white, in axillary clusters (umbels); July.

FRUIT. Length ½ in. (13 mm); black, oval; bittersweet pulp; one large seed; October.

WOOD. Light brown or yellow heartwood, lighter colored sapwood, heavy, hard, not strong, close grained; commercially unimportant.

HABITAT AND RANGE. Swamp and stream borders from southeastern Virginia south to northern Florida, west to southeastern Texas and north to southern Indiana.

PROPAGATION. Seed, stratify 60 days at 41°F (5°C); or scarify by soaking 20 minutes in sulfuric acid, then stratify 120–150 days at 35–45°F (4–8°C).

WILDLIFE VALUE. Fruit is fair for songbirds.

LANDSCAPE VALUE. Attractive small tree, especially for naturalized settings. Zone 5.

BEST RECOGNIZABLE FEATURES. Spur growth and stout curved spines; white flower clusters in July; black oblong fruit; glabrous leaves.

Carpinus—hornbeam
BETULACEAE—birch family

Carpinus caroliniana Walter
PLATE 25

American hornbeam, blue-beech, musclewood, ironwood

HABIT. Small tree or shrub, 25–30 ft. (8–9 m) tall, single or multistemmed, with a wide, flat crown.

BARK. Dark bluish gray, thin, smooth, fluted (musclelike) longitudinally with age.

TWIGS. Slender, dark reddish brown becoming gray, zigzag, lenticellate, seldom pubescent; pith pale, continuous.

BUDS. Alternate terminal absent; laterals of 2 sizes, ¹⁄₁₆–¼ in. (2–6 mm) long,

Carpinus caroliniana

Figure 164. *Carpinus caroliniana* foliage

Figure 165. *Carpinus caroliniana* fruit

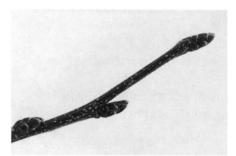

Figure 166. *Carpinus caroliniana* twig and buds

Figure 167. *Carpinus caroliniana* bark, small tree

Figure 168. *Carpinus caroliniana* bark, medium-sized tree

reddish brown, greenish at the base, sharp pointed, appressed to the twig; lower scales aligned, somewhat hairy on the margin.

LEAVES. Alternate, simple, 1–3 in. (2.5–8 cm) long, ovate to oblong, smooth and green above, pale and hairy below; margin doubly serrate; veins unbranched to the margin.

FLOWERS. Catkins; early spring.

FRUIT. Ribbed nut, ¼ in. (6 mm) long; borne at base of a 3-lobed bract arranged in a spikelike cluster 3–6 in. (8–15 cm) long; October.

WOOD. Light brown, hard, strong, close grained; used for tool handles.

HABITAT AND RANGE. Moist to dry soils, usually in the understory from Nova Scotia to Florida, west to Texas, north to western Ontario.

PROPAGATION. Seed, stratify 60 days at 68°F (20°C), then 60 days at 42°F (5°C).

WILDLIFE VALUE. Fruit has little value, but is eaten by squirrel.

LANDSCAPE VALUE. Tough, small tree suited for deep shade; unusual sinewy bark. Zones 3–9.

BEST RECOGNIZABLE FEATURES. Fruit in loose, pendulous clusters; smooth, fluted bark; leaf surface smooth, margin doubly serrate.

COMMENT. This is the only genus in Betulaceae (*Alnus, Betula, Carpinus, Corylus, Ostrya*) without preformed male flowers (staminate catkins) conspicuous in the winter.

Other hornbeams commonly planted in the regional landscape:
Carpinus betulus Linnaeus, European hornbeam. Medium-sized, broad tree to 60 ft. (18 m) tall; similar to American hornbeam but with thicker leaves and deeper venation; also found in variety of rather dense, upright forms (e.g., 'Columnaris', 'Fastigiata', 'Pyramidalis'). The predominant

Figure 169. *Carpinus betulus* foliage

Figure 170. *Carpinus betulus* bark, large tree

Carpinus species in cultivation, and justifiably so since it is superior in appearance. Zones 4–7.

Carya—hickory
JUGLANDACEAE—walnut family

Key to *Carya*

1.   Terminal bud long, consisting of 4–6 valvate scales and appearing naked; fruit husk winged along sutures 2
1.   Terminal bud ovoid, consisting of 6 or more imbricate scales; fruit not winged 4
2(1).   Buds bright yellow colored; bark interlacing with thin ridges and shallow furrows . . . . *Carya cordiformis*
2.   Buds yellow-brown; bark loose 3
3(2).   Terminal bud ≤ 0.3 in. (6 mm) long; nut flattened . . . .
        . . . . *Carya aquatica*
3.   Terminal bud about 0.5 in. (13 mm) long; nut ellipsoidal . . .
        . . . . *Carya cordiformis*
4(1).   Bark loose, breaking into long, broad strips; outer bud scales loose but persistent 5
4.   Bark tight; outer bud scales appressed or often breaking away .
        6
5(4).   Leaflets usually 5; stems dark reddish brown; upland habitats .
        . . . . *Carya ovata*
5.   Leaflets usually 7; stems light tan; poorly drained soils . . . .
        . . . . *Carya laciniosa*
6(4).   Rachis densely tomentose; terminal bud ≥ 0.5 in. (13 mm) long
        . . . . *Carya tomentosa*
6.   Rachis not tomentose; terminal bud < 0.5 in. (13 mm) long . 7
7(6).   Buds covered with silver or yellow scales 8
7.   Buds lacking silver or yellow scales 9
8(7).   Bud scales nearly glabrous, dotted with silvery scales; fruit husk hairy and dotted with silvery scales . . . . *Carya pallida*
8.   Bud scales red hairy, dotted with scales; fruit husk not dotted with silvery scales . . . . *Carya texana*
9(7).   Leaflets usually 5; sutures typically split only partially to base of nut . . . . *Carya glabra*
9.   Leaflets usually 7; sutures typically split to base of nut . . . .
        . . . . *Carya ovalis*

Carya aquatica (Michaux f.) Nuttall
water hickory, swamp hickory, bitter pecan

HABIT. Large tree, 70–100 ft. (21–31 m) tall, with a long, clear bole, buttressed base, and a narrow crown.

BARK. Light brown to gray, thick fissured, very scaly; inner bark reddish.

TWIGS. Slender to moderately stout, brown, lenticellate; similar to sweet pecan; pith continuous, nearly round, pale to brown (as in all hickories).

BUDS. Length ¼–½ in. (6–13 mm); yellow-brown covered with yellow scurfy pubescence.

Carya aquatica

LEAVES. Alternate, 9–15 in. (23–38 cm) long, green and smooth above, pale and lightly hairy below, with 9–17 scythe-shaped and curved leaflets 2–5 in. (5–13 cm) long, each with a long, sharp-pointed apex; margin serrate.

FLOWERS. Catkins, in separate sexes on same tree (as in all hickories).

FRUIT. Dark brown, 1–1½ in. (2.5–4 cm) in diameter, flattened with a thin, 4-winged husk (with bright yellow scales); seed bitter, inedible; October.

WOOD. Dark brown, heavy, strong, rather brittle, close grained; used for fuel, fencing; considered inferior to other hickories.

HABITAT AND RANGE. Floodplain soils from southern Virginia to Florida, west to eastern Texas, north to southern Illinois.

PROPAGATION. Seed, stratify 60–150 days at 33–41°F (1–5°C).

Figure 171. *Carya aquatica* foliage

Figure 172. *Carya aquatica* bark, medium-sized tree

Figure 173. *Carya aquatica* bark, large tree

WILDLIFE VALUE. Fruit is fair for wood duck, mallard, squirrel, and small mammals.

LANDSCAPE VALUE. Very tolerant of flooded soils, otherwise little else to recommend. Zones 6–7.

BEST RECOGNIZABLE FEATURES. Leaflets pubescent below; winged husk splits to expose flattened nut; scaly bark; found in bottomlands.

COMMENT. This species hybridizes freely with sweet pecan, producing *Carya* × *leconte*, which has intermediate botanical characteristics and site preferences.

Carya cordiformis (Wangenheim) K. Koch   PLATE 26
bitternut hickory, bitternut, pignut

HABIT. Medium-sized to large tree, 60–80 ft. (18–24 m) tall, with a long, clear bole and an oblong, spreading crown.

BARK. Slate-gray to light gray-brown, smooth becoming shallowly fissured with tight, interlacing ridges.

TWIGS. Gray-brown to green-brown, lenticellate, moderately stout; pith brownish white.

BUDS. Terminal ½ in. (13 mm) long, slender, bright sulfur-yellow, valvate; laterals ¼ in. (6 mm) long.

LEAVES. Alternate, 6–10 in. (15–25 cm) long, green and shiny above,

Carya cordiformis

Figure 174. *Carya cordiformis* foliage

Figure 175. *Carya cordiformis* fruit

Figure 176. *Carya cordiformis* twig and buds

Figure 177. *Carya cordiformis* bark, small tree

Figure 178. *Carya cordiformis* bark, medium-sized tree

Figure 179. *Carya cordiformis* bark, large tree

pale and lightly hairy below, with 7–11 ovate to lanceolate and sessile leaflets 2–6 in. (5–15 cm) long; rachis slender, lightly hairy; fall color yellow.

FLOWERS. Catkins, in separate sexes on same tree.

FRUIT. Light yellow-green, 1 in. (2.5 cm) in diameter, with a thin, 4-winged husk (splitting at the sutures); September to November.

WOOD. Dark brown, heavy, very hard, strong, tough, close grained; used for fuel, fence posts, tool handles.

HABITAT AND RANGE. Moist, deep soils along streams from Maine to Minnesota, south to Texas, east to Florida.

PROPAGATION. Seed, stratify 60–150 days at 33–41°F (1–5°C).

WILDLIFE VALUE. Fruit is good for squirrel, mice, and deer.

LANDSCAPE VALUE. Good, large shade tree for moist sites, although can be messy in autumn as fruit drops. Zones 4–9.

BEST RECOGNIZABLE FEATURES. Valvate terminal bud bright sulfur-yellow; subglobose nut covered by husk winged above middle; bitter seed; bark with long, narrow, flat, interlacing ridges.

Carya glabra (Miller) Sweet
pignut hickory, pignut, sweet pignut

PLATE 27

HABIT. Medium-sized tree, 60–70 ft. (18–21 m) tall, with a narrow, oblong crown usually supported by a long, clear symmetrical bole as in most hickories.

BARK. Light to dark gray, deeply furrowed at maturity with narrow, interlacing ridges.

TWIGS. Moderate, reddish brown, smooth, with pale lenticels; pith continuous.

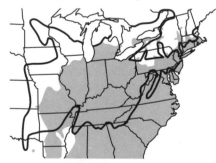

Carya glabra, including *C. ovalis*

BUDS. Length ¼–½ in. (6–13 mm); inner scales tan or grayish, exposed by the winter dropping of glabrous, reddish brown outer scales; rounded with a sharp apex.

LEAVES. Alternate, pinnately compound, 6–12 in. (15–31 cm) long, green and shiny above, pale below, with 5 or rarely 7 ovate-lanceolate leaflets 3–6 in. (8–15 cm) long; rachis smooth; fall color yellow.

FLOWERS. Catkins, in separate sexes on same tree.

FRUIT. Spherical to pear shaped, 1½ in. (4 cm) in diameter, with a thin husk usually splitting only to ¾ length of the nut and exposing an

Figure 180. *Carya glabra* foliage

Figure 181. *Carya glabra* fruit

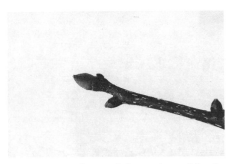

Figure 182. *Carya glabra* twig and buds

Figure 183. *Carya glabra* bark, medium-sized tree

Figure 184. *Carya glabra* bark, large tree

unridged, compressed nut; seed sweet to bitter; September to October.
WOOD. Light or dark brown; heavy, hard, strong, tough; used for fuel, tool handles, fence posts.

HABITAT AND RANGE. Upland forests and dry ridges from New Hampshire to northeastern Kansas, south to Arkansas, east to northwestern Florida.

PROPAGATION. Seed, stratify 90–150 days at 33–40°F (1–5°C).

WILDLIFE VALUE. Fruit is good for turkey, squirrel, small rodents, raccoon, and deer.

LANDSCAPE VALUE. Good shade tree with outstanding fall color, well suited to dry sites. Fruit can be messy in autumn. Zones 4–9.

BEST RECOGNIZABLE FEATURES. Interlacing ridges of bark; typically 5 leaflets; fruit husk splits to ¾ the length of nut; moderately slender, glabrous twigs.

Carya illinoensis (Wangenheim) K. Koch
pecan, sweet pecan

HABIT. Large tree, 100–140 ft. (31–43 m) tall, with a clear bole and buttressed base; crown pyramidal and narrow in the forest, spreading in the open.

Carya illinoensis

BARK. Light brown to gray, thick, narrow fissures with scaly ridges.

TWIGS. Stout, reddish brown to grayish brown, lightly hairy, lenticellate; leaf scars large with many bundle scars; pith continuous.

BUDS. Terminal ½ in. (13 mm) long, yellowish brown with a powdery (scurfy) pubescence, valvate, alternate; laterals smaller, divergent.

LEAVES. Alternate, pinnately compound, 12–20 in. (31–51 cm) long, yellowish green and smooth above, pale and lightly hairy below, with 9–17 oblong-lanceolate leaflets 4–8 in. (10–20 cm) long, curved; margin serrate.

FLOWERS. Catkins, in separate sexes on same tree.

FRUIT. Nut, 1½–2 in. (4–5 cm) in diameter; reddish brown; typically in clusters of 3–12; thin shelled, edible; enclosed in a thin, 4-winged (to the base) husk; September to October.

WOOD. Light brown tinged with red, heavy, hard, not strong, brittle, coarse grained; used for furniture, interior finishing, fuel, tool handles.

Figure 185. *Carya illinoensis* foliage

Figure 186. *Carya illinoensis* fruit

Figure 187. *Carya illinoensis* bark, small tree

Figure 188. *Carya illinoensis* bark, medium-sized tree

Figure 189. *Carya illinoensis* bark, large tree

HABITAT AND RANGE. Rich, moist soils from Indiana south to Louisiana, west to southern Texas, north to Iowa.

PROPAGATION. Seed, stratify 60–150 days at 33–41°F (1–5°C).

WILDLIFE VALUE. Fruit is excellent for squirrel, raccoon, and deer.

LANDSCAPE VALUE. Numerous varieties are planted in the lower Midwest and Southeast for their fruit. Zones 5–9.

BEST RECOGNIZABLE FEATURES. Scurfy, yellowish brown, valvate terminal bud; bark with scaly ridges; elongated, 4-winged, thin husk; delicious seed covered by thin shell.

Carya laciniosa (Michaux f.) Loudon
shellbark hickory, big shagbark hickory, kingnut

HABIT. Large tree, 80–100 ft. (24–31 m) tall, with a short bole, a large oblong crown, and stout branches.

BARK. Slate-gray, smooth becoming broken into longitudinal narrow, straight plates when 4–8 in. (10–20 cm) in diameter.

TWIGS. Light orange-brown, hairy, with orange lenticels, stout; leaf scars large, triangular.

Carya laciniosa

BUDS. Terminal ¾ in. (19 mm) long, brown with 3–5 loose-fitting scales; outer bud scales persistent; laterals ½ in. (13 mm) long, divergent from the twig.

LEAVES. Alternate, pinnately compound, 12–24 in. (31–61 cm) long, dark green above, pale yellow-green and hairy below, with 5–9 (usually 7) sessile, oblong-lanceolate leaflets 2–8 in. (5–20 cm) long; rachis stout, hairy.

FLOWERS. Catkins, in separate sexes on same tree.

FRUIT. Light brown, to 2½ in. (6 cm) in diameter, with a thick, 4- or 6-ribbed husk that splits easily along the ribs at maturity; often pointed at both ends; seed sweet; August to October.

WOOD. Dark brown, very heavy, hard, strong, tough, close grained; used for tool handles, agricultural implements, athletic goods, interior finishing, fuel.

HABITAT AND RANGE. Bottomland and moist upland sites from New York to Georgia, west to Oklahoma, north to Iowa.

PROPAGATION. Seed, stratify 60–150 days at 33°F (1°C).

WILDLIFE VALUE. Fruit is good for squirrel.

Figure 190. *Carya laciniosa* foliage

Figure 191. *Carya laciniosa* fruit

Figure 192. *Carya laciniosa* twig and buds

Figure 193. *Carya laciniosa* bark, medium-sized tree

Figure 194. *Carya laciniosa* bark, large tree

LANDSCAPE VALUE. Attractive large shade tree for wet soils, although fruit can be messy (but seeds are sweet). Zones 5–8.

BEST RECOGNIZABLE FEATURES. Usually 7 leaflets; large subglobose husk with 4–6 sections; wet to moist sites; stout, light colored, glabrous twigs with orange lenticels.

Carya ovalis (Wangenheim) Sargent PLATE 28
red hickory, sweet pignut hickory

HABIT. Medium-sized to large tree, 70–100 ft. (21–31 m) tall, with cylindrical to pyramidal crown, upright spreading upper branches, and drooping lower branches.

BARK. Gray, similar to pignut hickory on younger trees, becoming somewhat shaggy on older trees.

TWIGS. Slender, reddish brown, usually smooth with small lenticels; pith continuous.

Figure 195. *Carya ovalis* foliage

Figure 196. *Carya ovalis* flowers

Figure 197. *Carya ovalis* fruit

Figure 198. *Carya ovalis* bark, medium-sized tree

BUDS. Length ¼–½ in. (6–13 mm); inner scales tan or grayish, woolly, below reddish brown outer scales that drop early; somewhat rounded with sharp apex.

LEAVES. Alternate, pinnately compound, 8–12 in. (20–31 cm) long, green and shiny above, pale below, with 5–9 (usually 7) ovate-lanceolate leaflets; rachis smooth or lightly hairy in the spring; fall color deep yellow.

FLOWERS. Catkins, in separate sexes on same tree.

FRUIT. Length 1–1¼ in. (2.5–3 cm); spherical to usually ellipsoidal; husk thin and splitting tardily to the base exposing a nut 4-ribbed above the center, seed sweet; September to October.

WOOD. Light or dark brown, heavy, hard, tough, flexible; used for tool handles, fuel.

HABITAT AND RANGE. A variety of mixed hardwood sites but has best growth on cool, moist soils from New Hampshire to Wisconsin, south to Arkansas, east to Georgia (see distribution map for *C. glabra*).

PROPAGATION. Seed, stratify 90–120 days at 33–40°F (1–4°C).

WILDLIFE VALUE. Fruit is excellent for turkey, squirrel, small rodents, raccoon, and deer.

LANDSCAPE VALUE. Attractive large tree with beautiful golden fall color, well suited for dry soils. Zones 4–9.

BEST RECOGNIZABLE FEATURES. Fruit husk splits entirely to base; somewhat shaggy bark on older individuals; typically 7 leaflets.

COMMENT. Some taxonomists consider this species *C. glabra* var. *odorata*. In the forest, distinct pignut hickory and red hickory can be encountered. Most specimens in this complex, however, are often very difficult to separate. Realizing that much hybridization occurs between the two species, one may be more comfortable recognizing only *C. glabra*.

Carya ovata (Miller) K. Koch   PLATE 29
shagbark hickory, scalybark hickory, shellbark hickory

HABIT. Medium-sized to large tree, 60–90 ft. (18–27 m) tall, with a long, clear bole, and a short, open crown.

BARK. Slate-gray, smooth becoming broken into longitudinal, curved, rough plates when 4–8 in. (10–20 cm) in diameter.

TWIGS. Dark reddish brown with orange lenticels, slight pubescence on newest growth, stout; leaf scars heart shaped.

BUDS. Terminal ¾–1 in. (19–25 mm) long, brown, with 5–8 loose-fitting scales; tips of scales divergent; laterals ½ in. (13 mm) long, divergent; outer bud scales persistent.

LEAVES. Alternate, pinnately compound, 8–16 in. (20–41 cm) long, green and smooth to lightly hairy above, pale and hairy below, usually with 5 (or sometimes 7) elliptic to oblong-lanceolate leaflets 3–7 in. (8–18 cm) long; rachis stout, usually hairy; fall color golden-brown.

Carya ovata

FLOWERS. Catkins, in separate sexes on same tree.

FRUIT. Brown to brown-black; 2 in. (5 cm) in diameter; thick, 4-ribbed husk; often rounded at the base; meat is sweet, light brown; August to October.

WOOD. Light brown, heavy, very hard, strong, tough, flexible, close grained; used for tool handles, agricultural implements, athletic goods, interior finishing, fuel.

HABITAT AND RANGE. Upland and bottomland sites from southern Maine to Iowa, south to eastern Texas, east to northern Georgia.

Figure 199. *Carya ovata* foliage

Figure 200. *Carya ovata* flowers

Figure 201. *Carya ovata* fruit

Figure 202. *Carya ovata* twig and buds

Figure 203. *Carya ovata* bark, large tree

PROPAGATION. Seed, stratify 60–150 days at 33–41°F (1–5°C).
WILDLIFE VALUE. Fruit is excellent for squirrel, mice, and deer.
LANDSCAPE VALUE. Beautiful large tree with excellent fall color, well suited for dry sites. Zones 4–8.
BEST RECOGNIZABLE FEATURES. Usually 5 leaflets; subglobose, 4-sectioned husk; bark broken into long shaggy plates; dark colored twigs with orange lenticels; generally dry upland sites.

Carya pallida (Ashe) Engler & Graebner
sand hickory, pale hickory

HABIT. Medium-sized to large tree, 40–100 ft. (12–31 m) tall, with stout, erect upper branches and somewhat pendulous lower branches forming a dense crown.

BARK. Dark gray to black with diamond-shaped ridges similar to *C. glabra* but rougher.

TWIGS. Similar to *C. glabra* except covered by minute yellowish or silvery scales.

BUDS. Similar to *C. glabra* except covered by minute yellowish or silvery scales.

Carya pallida

LEAVES. Alternate, pinnately compound, 7–15 in. (18–38 cm) long, with 7 (rarely to 9) lanceolate, long tapered, resinous, fragrant, finely serrate leaflets attached to hairy, scaly rachis and covered by minute yellowish or

Figure 204. *Carya pallida* foliage

silvery scales in spring, turning light green and lustrous above, pale and somewhat pubescent below.

FLOWERS. Catkins, in separate sexes on same tree.

FRUIT. Nearly globose, 1 in. (2.5) in diameter, hairy, covered with yellow scales, often depressed at apex; husk splitting to base; nut thin shelled, angular, edible; seed sweet.

WOOD. Brown, heavy, hard; used for tool handles, fuel.

HABITAT AND RANGE. Dry, sandy or rocky soils from coast of Virginia and North Carolina through northern South Carolina and northern Georgia into Tennessee, Alabama, and Mississippi.

PROPAGATION. Seed, stratify in moist medium 30–150 days at 33–40°F (1–4°C).

WILDLIFE VALUE. Nuts are fair for squirrel, rodents, and larger birds.

LANDSCAPE VALUE. As is true for all hickories, difficult to transplant because of large taproots and offering few unique characteristics to the landscape while being rather messy; however, worth maintaining in natural stands or planting on dry sites. Zones 5–7.

BEST RECOGNIZABLE FEATURES. Typically 7 leaflets; rachis hairy, fragrant, resinous, and covered by minute silvery scales; fruit husk thin, hairy, and covered with minute silvery scales.

Carya texana Buckley
black hickory

HABIT. Medium-sized tree, to 50 ft. (15 m) tall, with branches ascending or spreading to form a narrow, round-topped crown.

BARK. Reddish brown to blackish, deeply furrowed, about ¾ in. (19 mm) thick with rough, platelike scales.

TWIGS. Slender, less than ¼ in. (6 mm) in diameter; present growth densely covered with rusty hairs, older growth glabrous and grayish brown.

BUDS. Terminal ¼–½ in. (6–13 mm) long; scales with tufts of red hairs at apex, scurfy; laterals much smaller, multiple, superposed.

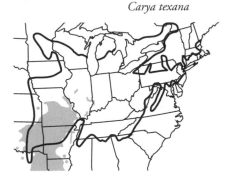

Carya texana

LEAVES. Alternate, pinnately compound, 8–12 in. (20–31 cm) long, with 5–7 (usually 7) leaflets to 5 in. (13 cm) long and 1½ in. (4 cm) wide, subsessile or short stalked, dark green and glabrous above, yellow-green and covered with red pubescence below; rachis slender; difficult to distinguish from stalked leaflets of *C. illinoensis*.

FLOWERS. Catkins, in separate sexes on same tree.

FRUIT. Globose, 1½ in. (4 cm) long; dark-brown, covered with yellow scales; husk thin, splitting to base along sutures; nut compressed at both ends, with bright reddish brown, very bitter kernel.

WOOD. Strong, close grained.

HABITAT AND RANGE. Dry, sterile, sandy or rocky soils, or heavy clays; from Louisiana and eastern Texas north to southern Indiana, southern Illinois, southern Missouri, and eastern Oklahoma; occurs as occasional tree in mixed forests.

PROPAGATION. Seed, stratify in moist medium 30–150 days at 33–40°F (1–4°C).

WILDLIFE VALUE. Nuts are fair for squirrel, rodents, and larger birds.

LANDSCAPE VALUE. Tolerates the driest soils.

BEST RECOGNIZABLE FEATURES. Usually 7 leaflets; rusty pubescence on leaves, twigs, and buds; globose nut.

Carya tomentosa (Poiret) Nuttall
mockernut hickory, white hickory, mockernut

HABIT. Medium-sized to large tree, 50–90 ft. (15–27 m) tall, with an open, round crown and branchlets either erect or turned upwards.

BARK. Young stems very tight and steel-blue, becoming blue-gray to light gray, often with rich chocolate color beneath the surface; shallowly fissured with interlacing ridges, rough but not shaggy.

TWIGS. Very stout, brown to dark gray with pale lenticels, initially tomentose becoming slightly pubescent; pith continuous.

BUDS. Length ½–¾ in. (13–19 mm), dark reddish brown; terminal egg shaped, yellow to tan, silky; outer bud scales falling early (deciduous).

LEAVES. Pinnately compound, 8–20 in. (20–51 cm) long, with 7–9 oblong-lanceolate leaflets 2–8 in. (5–20 cm) long, yellow-green above, pale and hairy beneath; rachis hairy and stout; fall color yellow.

FRUIT. Nut, 4-angled with globular husk that splits nearly to the base, ⅛–¼ in. (3–6 mm) thick; strongly fragrant; small, dark, sweet kernel; September to October.

WOOD. Dark brown, heavy, hard, strong, coarse grained; used for tool handles, fuel, fence posts.

Carya tomentosa

HABITAT AND RANGE. Dry upland forests from southern New Hampshire to southern Michigan, south to eastern Texas and northern Florida.

Figure 205. *Carya tomentosa* foliage

Figure 206. *Carya tomentosa* fruit

Figure 207. *Carya tomentosa* twig and buds

Figure 208. *Carya tomentosa* bark, small tree

Figure 209. *Carya tomentosa* bark, medium-sized tree

Figure 210. *Carya tomentosa* bark, large tree

PROPAGATION. Seed, stratify 90–150 days at 33–40°F (1–4°C).

WILDLIFE VALUE. Fruit is excellent for turkey, squirrel, small rodent, raccoon, and deer.

LANDSCAPE VALUE. Large, attractive shade tree with beautiful fall color and well suited for dry soils. Fruit can be messy. Zones 4–9.

BEST RECOGNIZABLE FEATURES. Stout, tomentose leaf rachis; silky-hairy egg-shaped winter buds, with outer bud scales deciduous; tight bark with interlacing ridges and shallow furrows; dry upland sites.

Castanea—chestnut
FAGACEAE—beech family

Key to *Castanea*

1.   Leaves glabrous below; fruit with 2–3 nuts .. *Castanea dentata*
1.   Leaves pubescent below; fruit with solitary nut 2
2(1).   Leaves whitish hairy below; young twigs covered with thick pubescence . . . . *Castanea pumila*
2.   Leaves less hairy below; young twigs glabrous or finely pubescent . . . . *Castanea ozarkensis*

Castanea dentata (Marshall) Borkhausen
American chestnut, chestnut

PLATE 30

HABIT. Once a large tree, to 120 ft. (37 m) tall, with a long, clear bole and a dense, widespreading crown. Because of chestnut blight (see Comment below) this species has been reduced mostly to small stump sprouts that rarely become over a few inches in diameter.

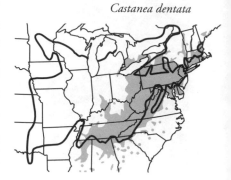

Castanea dentata

BARK. Light gray, smooth, becoming distinctly ridged, furrowed, and thickened with age.

TWIGS. Moderately stout, somewhat angled, lenticellate, light yellow-green often tinged with red, becoming olive green and glabrous, zigzag; pith continuous, white, stellate.

BUDS. Terminal usually absent; laterals ¼ in. (6 mm) long, ovoid, obliquely sessile with only 2–3 visible imbricate scales, gray to dark brown.

LEAVES. Alternate, simple, 5–9 in. (13–23 cm) long, leathery, oblong-lanceolate, coarsely toothed; apex long pointed.

FLOWERS. Catkins; June.

FRUIT. Usually 2–3 flattened nuts per fruit; nuts 1 in. (2.5 cm) wide, surrounded by leathery involucre 2 in. (5 cm) in diameter and covered with stiff, needle-sharp, many-branched glabrous spines; seed edible, very sweet. Few American chestnuts reach fruiting age today.

WOOD. Reddish brown, light, soft, once one of the major timber species throughout eastern United States, so rot resistant that chestnuts that have been dead for over 50 years are still being infrequently harvested.

HABITAT AND RANGE. A wide range of well-drained soils from southern Maine to Michigan, south to Mississippi and Alabama.

PROPAGATION. Seed (difficult to find), stratify in moist medium 60–90 days at 33–41°F (1–5°C).

WILDLIFE VALUE. Once one of the most important wildlife plants in eastern United States; today nuts are rare.

LANDSCAPE VALUE. Keep if naturally occurring. If nut crop is wanted, look for disease-resistant Chinese chestnut and hybrids.

BEST RECOGNIZABLE FEATURES. Spiny, leathery fruit husk with glabrous spines; coarsely toothed leaves with long-pointed apex; 2 to 3 glabrous bud scales; glabrous twigs; generally occurs as small multiple sprouts on drier sites.

Figure 211. *Castanea dentata* foliage

Figure 212. *Castanea dentata* fruit

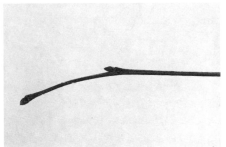

Figure 213. *Castanea dentata* twig and buds

Figure 214. *Castanea dentata* bark, small stem, with chestnut blight

Figure 215. *Castanea dentata* log

COMMENT. At one time this species was a dominant tree in forests throughout eastern United States; now usually found as a stump sprout attaining a diameter of a few inches because of chestnut blight. The fungus that causes this disease was introduced in this country around 1906. A few decades later, most of the chestnuts were killed. Some large boles still remain because of the species' extremely decay resistant wood.

Castanea ozarkensis Ashe
Ozark chinkapin, Ozark chestnut

HABIT. Apparently susceptible to chestnut blight, which has reduced this species to a shrubby stump sprouter.

Castanea ozarkensis

BARK. Gray-brown, smooth, becoming furrowed into scaly plates.
TWIGS. Gray, slender, initially hairy becoming glabrous.
BUDS. Similar to *Castanea pumila*.
LEAVES. Alternate, simple, 6–10 in. (15–25 cm) long, narrow-oblong or lanceolate, bristle tipped, yellow-green above, pale and finely hairy below.
FLOWERS. Unisexual or bisexual aments, 3–6 in. (8–15 cm) long; in summer.
FRUIT. One rounded to ovate dark brown nut per fruit; each fruit 1 in. (2.5 cm) in diameter; spines of bur hairy; seed sweet.
HABITAT AND RANGE. Acidic soils on dry rocky uplands and ravines.
PROPAGATION. Seed, stratify in moist medium 60–90 days at 33–41°F (1–5°C).
WILDLIFE VALUE. Nuts are good for whitetail deer, squirrel, and chipmunk.
BEST RECOGNIZABLE FEATURES. Shrubby habit; leaves bristle tipped along marginal teeth, pubescent below; spines on bur pubescent; fruit containing only one rounded nut.

Castanea pumila Miller
Allegheny chinkapin

HABIT. Large shrub or round-topped tree, to 20 ft. (6 m) tall, often multistemmed and thicket-forming (through stolons); apparently resistant to chestnut blight.

BARK. Reddish brown, slightly furrowed, with loose and platy ridges.

TWIGS. Slender, orange-brown, glabrous, shiny.

BUDS. Terminal usually absent; laterals ⅛ in. (3 mm) long, ovoid, red, scurfy-pubescent.

LEAVES. Alternate, simple, 3–5 in. (8–13 cm) long, oblong-elliptic, coarsely serrate, bright yellow-green above, velvety white-hairy below, thick, firm;

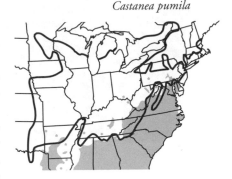

Castanea pumila

apex acute; base unequal or wedge shaped; margin coarsely serrate with rigid teeth; fall color dull yellow.

FLOWERS. Unisexual or bisexual aments, 3–6 in. (8–15 cm) long, in summer.

FRUIT. One ovoid, shiny, dark brown nut ¾ in (19 mm long) per fruit; each fruit 1 in. (2.5 cm) in diameter; spines of bur needle-sharp, very dense, clustered, hairy; apex silvery-white pubescent; seed sweet.

WOOD. Dark brown, light, hard, strong, coarse grained; used locally for poles, posts, crossties.

HABITAT AND RANGE. Dry sandy and rocky uplands from southern Pennsylvania east to New Jersey, and south to western Florida; in the Gulf states, and through Arkansas to Oklahoma and Missouri.

PROPAGATION. Seed, stratify in moist medium 60–90 days at 33–41°F (1–5°C).

WILDLIFE VALUE. Nuts are source of food for many small game animals; tree provides excellent cover.

LANDSCAPE VALUE. Could be used in sunny, dry areas in front of wooded areas to encourage wildlife. Zones 5–9.

BEST RECOGNIZABLE FEATURES. Lower surface of leaf pubescent and leaf

Figure 216. *Castanea pumila* foliage and flowers

Figure 217. *Castanea pumila* fruit

Figure 218. *Castanea mollissima* foliage and fruit

apex blunt; spines of bur pubescent; fruit containing only one rounded nut.

Other chestnuts commonly planted in the regional landscape:
Castanea mollissima Blume, Chinese chestnut. Tree to 50 ft. (15 m) tall with widespreading crown, popular since chestnut blight has prevented the planting of our native chestnut; habit is open and low-branching, making the species undesirable for timber production. Differs from American chestnut in that twigs, spines on husk, and undersides of leaves are tomentose. Though the nuts supposedly are not as sweet and flavorful as American chestnut, they still provide an excellent food source for wildlife and people. These nuts are often available annually each autumn at selected food markets. Hybrids, with Chinese chestnut as one parent, produce bigger crops of sweeter nuts. Native to Korea and China. Zones 4–8.

Catalpa—catalpa
BIGNONIACEAE—bignonia family

Key to *Catalpa*

1. Flowers with numerous purple spots; bark scaly . . . . *Catalpa bignonioides*
1. Flowers with few purple spots; bark furrowed . . . . *Catalpa speciosa*

Catalpa bignonioides Walter
southern catalpa, catawba, Indian-bean, cigartree

HABIT. Tree smaller than northern catalpa, 30–40 ft. (9–12 m) tall, with broadly rounded crown, and short, crooked branches.

Catalpa bignonioides

BARK. Light brown to reddish gray, thin, scaly.

TWIGS. Stout, pale orange to brownish gray, brittle, finely hairy, lenticellate; leaf scars raised, craterlike with depressed center, and with bundle scars in a closed ring; pith large, white, continuous.

BUDS. Terminal absent; laterals very small, globose, reddish brown, hairy with about 6 brown, loosely overlapping, pointed scales.

LEAVES. Opposite or whorled, 5–8 in. (13–20 cm) long, green and smooth above, pale and hairy below, heart shaped; ill scented when crushed; margin entire.

FLOWERS. White with yellow and purple spots; 2 in. long; in clusters 8–10 in. (20–25 cm) long; June.

FRUIT. Capsule, to 20 in. (51 cm) long, about ⅜ in. (10 mm) in diameter; separates into 2 halves in spring releasing tufted, papery, unfringed seeds, with pointed wings; autumn.

WOOD. Pale brown, light, soft, coarse grained; used for fence posts, railroad ties.

HABITAT AND RANGE. Moist sites and old fields; naturalized from New England to Michigan, south to Texas, east to Florida.

PROPAGATION. Seed germinates when mature.

WILDLIFE VALUE. Limited wildlife value except perhaps to provide nesting sites for some birds.

LANDSCAPE VALUE. Medium-sized, coarse tree with attractive flowers but large amounts of messy fruit. Zones 5–9.

BEST RECOGNIZABLE FEATURES. Whorled (or seldom opposite) buds and leaves; leaves ill scented when crushed, large, heart shaped; long, slender, 2-parted fruit ("cigars"); white flowers with yellow and conspicuous purple spots; scaly bark.

Catalpa speciosa Warder ex Engelmann   PLATE 31
northern catalpa, hardy catalpa, cigartree, Indian-bean

HABIT. Medium-sized tree, to 60 ft. (18 m) tall, with a short bole and several large, ascending branches forming a narrow, rounded crown.

Catalpa speciosa

BARK. Reddish brown or gray, thin, with irregular ridges and deep furrows.

TWIGS. Stout, olive brown, with lenticels, smooth; leaf scars raised with many bundle scars; pith large, white.

BUDS. Terminal absent; laterals brown to black, ¹⁄₁₆ in. (2 mm) long, small, round, smooth, opposite or whorled.

LEAVES. Opposite or whorled, 6–12 in. (15–31 cm) long, green and smooth above, hairy below, heart shaped; not ill scented when crushed.

Figure 219. *Catalpa speciosa* foliage

Figure 220. *Catalpa speciosa* flowers

Figure 221. *Catalpa speciosa* fruit and foliage

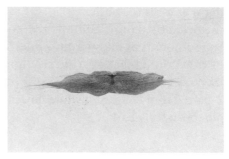

Figure 222. *Catalpa speciosa* seed

Figure 223.
*Catalpa
speciosa*
twig

Figure 224.
*Catalpa
speciosa*
form

Figure 225.
*Catalpa
speciosa*
bark,
medium-
sized tree

Figure 226.
*Catalpa
speciosa*
bark, large
tree

FLOWERS. White with yellow and occasional purple spots; 2 in. (5 cm) long; in clusters 4–8 in. (10–20 cm) long; May to early June.

FRUIT. Podlike capsule, 6–20 in. (15–51 cm) long, about ½ in. (13 mm) in diameter, slender, persistent; separates into 2 halves in spring releasing fringed, papery seeds, with rounded wings; autumn.

WOOD. Light brown, soft, weak, brittle, coarse grained; used for fence posts, interior finishing, railroad ties.

HABITAT AND RANGE. Moist bottomlands and old fields and homesites from southwestern Indiana and Illinois to southern Missouri and western Tennessee; naturalized in Virginia, West Virginia, Ohio, and Kansas, south to Texas and Louisiana.

PROPAGATION. Seed germinates when mature.

WILDLIFE VALUE. Limited wildlife value except perhaps to provide nesting sites for some birds.

LANDSCAPE VALUE. As is true for all catalpas, tends to be messy (brittle branches, much fruit), therefore should not be planted in the city; the flower display is beautiful but overall appearance of tree is coarse. Zones 4–8.

BEST RECOGNIZABLE FEATURES. Usually whorled buds and leaves; leaves not ill scented when crushed; large white spongy pith; long, 2-valved capsules (fruit) enclosing winged seeds; flowers less conspicuously colored with purple spots; ridged and furrowed bark.

Celtis—hackberry
ULMACEAE—elm family

Key to *Celtis*

1.   Leaf margin evenly toothed; mature fruit dark purple . . . . *Celtis occidentalis*
1.   Leaf margin obscurely toothed or entire; mature fruit reddish or orange-brown 2
2(1).   Leaves to 6 in. (15 cm) long; typically a medium-sized tree . . . . *Celtis laevigata*
2.   Leaves < 3 in. (8 cm) long; typically a small tree or large shrub . . . . *Celtis tenuifolia*

Celtis laevigata Willdenow
sugarberry, sugar hackberry, hackberry

HABIT. Medium-sized tree, to 80 ft. (24 m) tall, with straight or crooked bole supporting an open crown with slightly drooping branches.

BARK. Blue-gray to brown-gray, with warty projections not becoming ridge-like, like hackberry; much variation possible.

TWIGS. Similar to hackberry.

BUDS. Terminal absent; laterals 1/16–1/8 in. (2–3 mm) long, ash-brown, slightly hairy, sharp pointed, appressed.

Celtis laevigata

Figure 227. *Celtis laevigata* foliage

Figure 228. *Celtis laevigata* fruit and seed

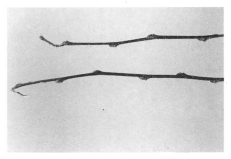

Figure 229. *Celtis laevigata* twigs and buds

Figure 230. *Celtis laevigata* bark, medium-sized tree

Figure 231. *Celtis laevigata* bark, large tree

LEAVES. Alternate, simple, 2–5 in. (5–13 cm) long; similar to common hackberry but narrower and with a longer, more pointed apex.

FLOWERS. Perfect or imperfect; appearing with or soon after the leaves in mid spring.

FRUIT. Drupe, ¼ in. (6 mm) in diameter; orange to yellowish becoming purplish black at maturity; flesh sweet; September, persisting through winter; fruit stalks about the same length as the leaf petiole.

WOOD. Pale yellow, heavy, soft, close grained; used for fence posts, furniture, rough construction.

HABITAT AND RANGE. Moist bottomlands from Virginia to Florida, west to southeastern New Mexico and southern Kansas.

PROPAGATION. Seed, stratify 60–90 days at 33–41°F (1–5°C).

WILDLIFE VALUE. Fruit is good for songbirds and mice.

LANDSCAPE VALUE. Tolerates urban conditions well; has cleaner appearance than *C. occidentalis*, therefore might be a better choice. The cultivar 'All Seasons' is a good choice for a street tree in the Midwest. Zones 5–9.

BEST RECOGNIZABLE FEATURES. Glossy, smooth, narrow leaves without sign of galls; lack of witches'-brooms throughout crown; wet sites.

Celtis occidentalis Linnaeus
common hackberry, nettletree, sugarberry

PLATE 32

HABIT. Medium-sized to large tree, 50–90 ft. (15–27 m) tall; bole long and buttressed, crown narrow and round in the forest; crown broad with low-hanging branches in the open.

BARK. Grayish brown to ash-gray, smooth on saplings, with wartlike projections along bole becoming more prominent with age and occasionally forming scales or plates; much variation.

Celtis occidentalis

TWIGS. Slender, usually shiny, zigzag, numerous, light olive brown, with lenticels; becoming brownish; wood greenish yellow when moistened; stems hairy; pith white, usually chambered.

BUDS. Terminal absent; laterals ¼ in. (6 mm) long or smaller, grayish brown, finely hairy, flattened, closely appressed, sharp pointed, triangular with about 4 visible bud scales.

LEAVES. Alternate, 2–5 in. (5–13 cm) long, ovate to oblong-ovate, smooth and lustrous above, paler below; apex short pointed to long

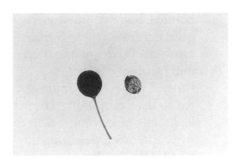

Figure 232. *Celtis occidentalis* foliage

Figure 233. *Celtis occidentalis* fruit and seed

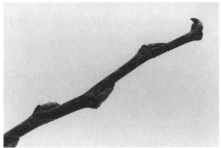

Figure 234. *Celtis occidentalis* twig and buds

Figure 235. *Celtis occidentalis* bark, small tree

Figure 236. *Celtis occidentalis* bark, very large tree

pointed; base asymmetrical; margin serrate; leaf surface often covered by galls; fall color yellow-brown.

FLOWERS. Perfect or imperfect; appearing with or soon after the leaves in mid spring.

FRUIT. Drupe, ¼–⅓ in. (6–8 mm) in diameter; orange becoming dark red to dark purple at maturity; borne on a stalk ½–1 in. (13–25 mm) long; stalk much longer than that of sugarberry; flesh sweet, datelike flavor; September, persisting through winter.

WOOD. Pale yellow, heavy, soft, close grained; used for fence posts, furniture.

HABITAT AND RANGE. Moist woodlands and roadsides from New Hampshire to North Dakota, south to Oklahoma, east to northern Georgia.

PROPAGATION. Seed, stratify 60–90 days at 33–41°F (1–5°C).

WILDLIFE VALUE. Fruit is good for songbirds and mice.

LANDSCAPE VALUE. A seemingly indestructible large tree with no outstanding ornamental characteristics. The cultivar 'Prairie Pride' is a good choice for a street tree in the Midwest. Zones 2–9.

BEST RECOGNIZABLE FEATURES. Asymmetrically oval leaf with 3 primary veins; warty bark; small, globular, dark fruit with large, stony seed; chambered pith.

Celtis tenuifolia Nuttall
Georgia hackberry, dwarf hackberry

HABIT. Large shrub to small tree, to 30 ft. (9 m) tall.

BARK. Gray, initially smooth, becoming corky or warty.

TWIGS. Very slender, zigzag, red-brown, rough pubescent; leaf scars crescent shaped, with 3 bundle traces; pith white, finely chambered at nodes.

BUDS. Terminal absent; laterals to ⅛ in. (3 mm) long, oval, pointed, grayish brown, finely hairy, appressed.

Celtis tenuifolia

LEAVES. Alternate, simple, to 2½ in. (6 cm) long, ovate, dark green and rough above; apex acute or acuminate, obliquely rounded at base; margin entire or irregularly sharply serrate; petiole longer than fruit stalks.

FLOWERS. Greenish yellow, not showy; perfect or imperfect; appearing with or soon after the leaves in mid spring.

FRUIT. Subglobose, dark orange-red, ½ in. (13 mm) in diameter; covering a ridged nutlet; stalks pubescent.

WOOD. Light yellow, heavy, close grained; used locally for fence posts.

HABITAT AND RANGE. Dry, rocky soils widely scattered throughout Midwest and Southwest.

PROPAGATION. Seed, stratify in moist medium 60–90 days at 33–41°F (1–5°C).

WILDLIFE VALUE. Fruit is good for game birds, raccoon, skunk, and squirrel.

LANDSCAPE VALUE. Tolerates most soil conditions; plant in full sun in front of wooded areas to encourage wildlife visits to fruit. Zone 5.

BEST RECOGNIZABLE FEATURES. Ovate, roughened leaves about 2 in. (5 cm) long; dark, orange-red fruit; small stature, even at maturity.

Cephalanthus—buttonbush
RUBIACEAE—madder family

Cephalanthus occidentalis Linnaeus   PLATE 33
buttonbush

HABIT. Large shrub or small tree, to 20 ft. (6 m) tall, with spreading crown and often multistemmed.

BARK. Thin, gray to brown, becoming shallowly fissured with age.

TWIGS. Slender to stout depending on growth rate, dark reddish brown, pale lenticels; leaf scars raised, crescent shaped, with C-shaped bundle scars; pith green, spongy.

Cephalanthus occidentalis

BUDS. Terminal absent; twig tip usually dies back after first frost; laterals scaly but imbedded in twig, small, conical.

LEAVES. Opposite or whorled, 3–6 in. (8–15 cm) long, 2–3 in. (5–8 cm) wide, ovate to elliptic-lanceolate, shiny above, sparsely hairy below; margin entire, wavy.

FLOWERS. Spherical heads, 1–1½ in. (2.5–4 cm) in diameter, on slender stalks 2–3 in. (5–8 cm) long; 1–3 heads per cluster; white, fragrant, showy.

FRUIT. Spherical heads of brownish achenes, about 1 in. (2.5 cm) in diameter; persisting into winter.

Figure 237. *Cephalanthus occidentalis* foliage

Figure 238. *Cephalanthus occidentalis* flower

Figure 239. *Cephalanthus occidentalis* fruit

Figure 240. *Cephalanthus occidentalis* bark, small stem

Figure 241. *Cephalanthus occidentalis* bark, large stem

WOOD. Light brown, soft; commercially unimportant.

HABITAT AND RANGE. Swamps, stream margins, and pond edges in full sunlight, from southeastern Canada to Florida, across Midwest to California and Mexico.

PROPAGATION. Seed germinates without pretreatment; softwood and hardwood cuttings root easily.

WILDLIFE VALUE. Seed may be eaten by waterfowl; tree provides important cover for many species in wetlands and may be browsed by beaver and deer.

LANDSCAPE VALUE. Attractive choice for very wet soils due to unusual flowers in late summer and glossy leaves; does not tolerate dry conditions. Zones 5–10.

BEST RECOGNIZABLE FEATURES. Opposite and whorled leaves often on same plant; persistent spherical fruit; very wet sites.

Cercis—redbud
CAESALPINIACEAE—caesalpinia family

Cercis canadensis Linnaeus
eastern redbud, Judas-tree, redbud

PLATE 34

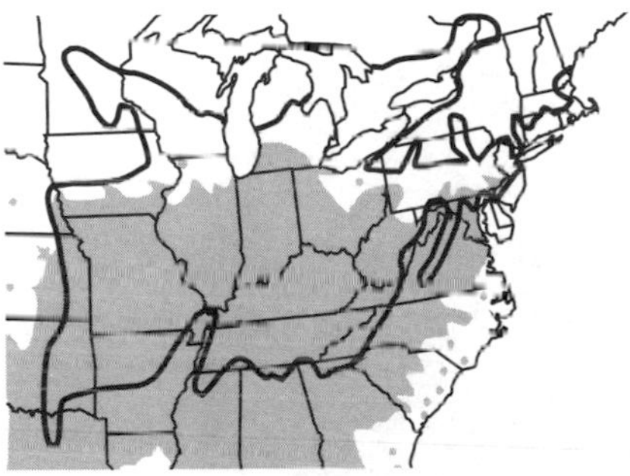

HABIT. Small tree, to 20 ft. (6 m) tall, with low branches and a broad crown of ascending branches.

BARK. Brown, thin, and smooth, becoming darker and scaly with age; inner bark orange and visible on large trunks.

TWIGS. Slender, dark reddish purple to dark brown, smooth, zigzag, shiny with light lenticels; pith continuous, white often with reddish streaks.

Cercis canadensis

BUDS. Terminal absent; laterals 1/16 in. (2 mm) long, dark purplish, blunt, appressed, with 2 scales on leaf buds, 8 scales on preformed flower buds; flower buds stalked, keeled, conspicuous each autumn on twigs older than the previous year's growth.

LEAVES. Alternate, 3–5 in. (8–13 cm) long, green above and below, heart shaped; margin entire; petiole swollen at both ends; fall color yellow.

Figure 242.
*Cercis
canadensis*
foliage

Figure 243. *Cercis canadensis* flowers

Figure 244.
*Cercis
canadensis*
fruit and
seeds

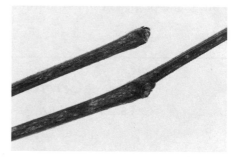

Figure 245. *Cercis canadensis* twigs and buds

Figure 246.
*Cercis
canadensis*
bark,
medium-
sized tree

Figure 247.
*Cercis
canadensis*
bark, large
tree

FLOWERS. Rose-pink; in clusters on branches and trunk, before tree leafs out; very showy in mass; April.

FRUIT. Length 2–3 in. (5–8 cm); flat, pod; October.

WOOD. Dark reddish brown, heavy, hard, close grained; commercially unimportant.

HABITAT AND RANGE. Forest understories and old fields from Connecticut west to Iowa, south to Texas, east to Florida.

PROPAGATION. Same as for yellowwood.

WILDLIFE VALUE. Limited value except to provide some cover and nesting sites.

LANDSCAPE VALUE. Ornamental features include clusters of pink flowers, heart-shaped leaf turning yellow in autumn, and broad form. Cultivars have white flowers (e.g., *C. canadensis* 'Alba') or various shades of pink flowers, and deeper shades of foliage color. Zones 4–9.

BEST RECOGNIZABLE FEATURES. Heart shaped, symmetrical leaf with swollen petiole base; pink flowers in early spring; persistent pods.

Other redbuds commonly planted in the regional landscape:
Cercis chinensis Bunge, Chinese redbud. Occasionally planted; shrubby in appearance; flowers rosy-purple. Most characteristics resemble eastern redbud, although flowers are slightly larger. Zones 6–7.

Chionanthus—fringetree
OLEACEAE—olive family

Chionanthus virginicus Linnaeus
fringetree

PLATE 35

HABIT. Small tree or shrub, 20–30 ft. (6–9 m) tall, with spreading branches, often wider than tall.

BARK. Gray, thin, scaly on older individuals.

TWIGS. Moderate to stout, green to buff-brown, with corky lenticels, thickened below the nodes, 4-angled, hairy or smooth; leaf scars opposite, with single, compound, V-shaped bundle scar; pith white, continuous.

BUDS. Terminal ½ in. (13 mm) long, green or brown, angled, with keeled scales; laterals ¹⁄₁₆–⅛ in. (2–3 mm) long, opposite to subopposite, may be superposed.

LEAVES. Opposite (to subopposite), simple, 4–6 in. (10–15 cm) long, narrow oblong to obovate-oblong, semileathery, shiny above, pale beneath; margin entire; apex short pointed to long pointed; base wedge shaped; fall color yellow.

FLOWERS. Fragrant, white; in 4–6 in. (10–15 cm) long, loose, pendent clusters; very showy; May.

FRUIT. Drupe, ½–⅗ in. (13–15 mm) long; dark blue with a whitish bloom; large stone; September.

Chionanthus virginicus

WOOD. Light brown, heavy, hard, close grained; commercially unimportant.

HABITAT AND RANGE. Moist sites from southern Pennsylvania south to Florida, west to Texas, and north to southern Missouri.

Figure 248. *Chionanthus virginicus* foliage

Figure 249. *Chionanthus virginicus* foliage and flowers

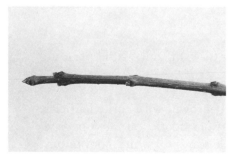

Figure 250. *Chionanthus virginicus* twig and buds

Figure 251. *Chionanthus virginicus* bark, small stem

Figure 252. *Chionanthus virginicus* bark, large stem

PROPAGATION. Seed, stratify 90–150 days at 68/86°F (20/30°C) night/ day, then 30–90 days at 33–41°F (1–5°C).

WILDLIFE VALUE. Fruit is fair for songbirds.

LANDSCAPE VALUE. Exceptional, native woody species, with attractive masses of white flowers, yellow fall color, large blue fruit. Unfortunately, a much neglected species with great potential for use in the landscape. Zones 3–9.

BEST RECOGNIZABLE FEATURES. Fruit appears like a grape in loose clusters; shrub with opposite, semi-leathery leaves; white flowers in open, drooping clusters.

Cladrastis—yellowwood
FABACEAE—bean or pea family

Cladrastis kentukea (Dumond de Courset) Rudd
yellowwood, virgilia   PLATE 36

HABIT. Medium-sized tree, 30–60 ft. (9–18 m) tall, with a short bole and a broad, open, rounded crown.

BARK. Gray, smooth, thin.

TWIGS. Slender, glabrous, reddish brown to grayish brown, with odor and taste of dried peas, zigzag, brittle, often with a grayish bloom; pith continuous, white, round.

BUDS. Terminal absent; laterals ¹⁄₁₆–¹⁄₈ in. (2–3 mm) long, pyramidal, golden-brown, hairy; usually 2–4 superposed buds that resemble just one; surrounded by leaf scars (and covered by the base of the leaf petiole in the summer).

Cladrastis kentukea

LEAVES. Alternate, odd pinnately compound, 8–12 in. (20–31 cm) long, green above, pale below, usually with 7–9 elliptic to ovate leaflets; terminal to 4 in. (10 cm) long, others smaller; hollow base of petiole encloses the bud.

FLOWERS. White; long, drooping clusters; very showy; May.

FRUIT. Length 2½–3½ in. (6–9 cm); light brown, flat pod; 4–6 seeds per pod; October, persisting into winter.

WOOD. Bright yellow to light brown; heavy, hard, strong, close grained; used for fuel, gunstocks.

Figure 253. *Cladrastis kentukea* foliage

Figure 254. *Cladrastis kentukea* flowers

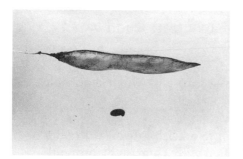

Figure 255. *Cladrastis kentukea* fruit and seed

Figure 256. *Cladrastis kentukea* twig and bud

Figure 257. *Cladrastis kentukea* bark, large tree

HABITAT AND RANGE. Rich, moist slopes from western North Carolina to central Tennessee, northern Alabama, Kentucky, southern Illinois, and southern Indiana.

PROPAGATION. Seed, scarify by soaking 30–60 minutes in sulfuric acid and rinsing thoroughly with water, or by mechanically filing the seed coat, then stratify 60–90 days at 33–41°F (1–5°C).

WILDLIFE VALUE. Limited value except to provide some cover and nesting sites.

LANDSCAPE VALUE. Excellent, medium-sized shade tree with wide-spreading crown, a profusion of graceful flowers, and beautiful fall color. One of our rarest native trees. Zones 4–8.

BEST RECOGNIZABLE FEATURES. Persistent pods; U-shaped leaf scar; smooth, light gray bark; petiole of leaf enclosing bud; bright yellow wood.

Clethra—clethra
CLETHRACEAE—pepperbush family

Clethra acuminata Michaux
cinnamon clethra

PLATE 37

HABIT. Shrub or treelike, 6–10 ft. (2–3 m) tall, with upright spreading branches.

BARK. Polished cinnamon color spotted with lighter areas, exfoliating on larger stems.

TWIGS. Slender with star-shaped hairs, vigorous growth, very deep red; pith continuous, relatively large.

BUDS. Length 1/16 in. (2 mm), solitary, sessile, loosely scaled.

LEAVES. Alternate, 3–6 in. (8–15 cm) long, ovate-elliptic to elliptic-oblong, dark green and smooth above; pale and hairy below; apex sharp pointed; petiole 1/2–1 in. (13–25 mm) long, hairy.

FLOWERS. Length 3–8 in. (8–20 cm); solitary racemes composed of white, fragrant flowers; July.

Clethra acuminata

Figure 258. *Clethra acuminata* foliage

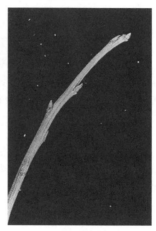

Figure 259. *Clethra acuminata* twig and buds

Figure 260. *Clethra acuminata* bark

FRUIT. Gray-brown, dry dehiscent; borne in a persistent, nodding raceme.

WOOD. Commercially unimportant.

HABITAT AND RANGE. Moist sites in the Appalachian Mountains in Kentucky, West Virginia, Georgia, Tennessee, Virginia, and North Carolina.

PROPAGATION. Fresh seed germinates without pretreatment; cuttings taken in summer root readily, and rooting may be hastened with a hormone dip.

WILDLIFE VALUE. Fruit is poor for wildlife species.

LANDSCAPE VALUE. Small tree adapted to shade and dry soils, blooms in summer, has unusual exfoliating bark. Zones 5–8.

BEST RECOGNIZABLE FEATURES. Cinnamon-colored bark; white racemes of flowers in late summer; persistent fruit in form of nodding raceme.

Cornus—dogwood
CORNACEAE—dogwood family

Key to *Cornus*

1.	Leaves slightly alternate	*Cornus alternifolia*
1.	Leaves opposite	2
2(1).	Habit typically single-stemmed tree; 4 large white bracts surround flowers; fruit a red drupe	*Cornus florida*
2.	Habit typically shrubby; flowers lacking large bracts; fruit a blue or white drupe	3
3(2).	Stems relatively stout, bright green or red	*Cornus stolonifera*
3.	Stems slender, gray or brown	4
4(3).	Fruit white	5
4.	Fruit blue	6
5(4).	Leaves scabrous and hairy above, hairy below; fruit sometimes light blue	*Cornus drummondii*
5.	Leaves glabrous above and below; fruit lacking blue tint	*Cornus racemosa*
6(4).	Stems yellowish green in summer, pinkish purple in winter	*Cornus rugosa*
6.	Stems dark maroon	*Cornus stricta*

Cornus alternifolia Linnaeus
alternate-leaf dogwood, pagoda dogwood

PLATE 38

HABIT. Low, spreading tree or large shrub, 15–20 ft. (5–6 m) tall, with distinct horizontal branching and numerous short, upright slender branchlets, resulting in a tiered effect.

BARK. Thin, dark reddish brown, smooth when young, becoming broken into irregular narrow ridges.

TWIGS. Slender, glabrous, shiny, somewhat glaucous, green to reddish or purplish green, with a rank odor when bruised; pith white, continuous.

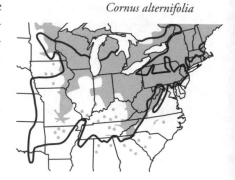

Cornus alternifolia

Figure 261. *Cornus alternifolia* foliage

Figure 262. *Cornus alternifolia* flowers

Figure 263. *Cornus alternifolia* twig and buds

Figure 264. *Cornus alternifolia* bark, small and medium-sized stems

BUDS. Flower bud terminal, valvate, ¼ in. (6 mm) long, purplish, glabrous at base, pubescent towards tip; vegetative buds alternate, very small, valvate, finely hairy; both with 2–3 overlapping scales.

LEAVES. Mostly alternate, clustered toward the end of the twigs, 2–5 in. (5–13 cm) long, elliptic-ovate, glabrous above (or nearly so), with about 6 pairs of primary veins visible; margin incurved; fall color reddish purple.

FLOWERS. Cream colored; arranged on cymes 1½–2½ in. (4–6 cm) in diameter; very fragrant, May.

FRUIT. In loose, spreading, red-stemmed clusters; ripening in early autumn; consisting of subglobose, glaucous, bluish black drupes; ⅓ in. (8 mm) in diameter; flesh thin, bitter.

WOOD. Brown tinged with red, heavy, hard, close grained; commercially unimportant.

HABITAT AND RANGE. Rich woodlands and along streams and creeks, in well-drained soil from New Brunswick to Minnesota, south to Georgia and Alabama.

PROPAGATION. Seed, stratify 60 days at 68/86°F (20/30°C) night/day, then 60 days at 41°F (5°C).

WILDLIFE VALUE. Fruit is fair for songbirds and small mammals; browse is good for deer.

LANDSCAPE VALUE. Unique for its form, especially in the winter; "flowers" do not compare ornamentally with flowering dogwood. The fall color (shades of purple, maroon, red) can be outstanding, although some authors have observed mediocre color. More tolerant of colder portions of Midwest and Northeast than flowering dogwood. Zones 3–9.

BEST RECOGNIZABLE FEATURES. Tiered branches; smooth, shiny, bright green to purple twigs; purplish black clusters of fruit; small, cream-colored flowers in flat clusters 2 in. (5 cm) in diameter.

Cornus drummondii C. A. Meyer
roughleaf dogwood, swamp dogwood

HABIT. Small tree or large shrub, 10–30 ft. (3–9 m) tall, with a short bole and an open, spreading crown.

BARK. Grayish to reddish brown, thin, fissured.

TWIGS. Slender, reddish brown to green, finely hairy on new growth; without rank odor when bruised; pith brown, continuous.

BUDS. Length ⅛ in. (3 mm), slender,

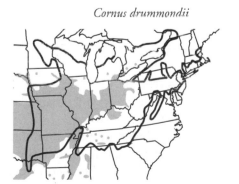

Cornus drummondii

Figure 265. *Cornus drummondii* foliage

grayish brown to gray, hairy, sharp pointed, opposite, with 2–3 overlapping visible scales.

LEAVES. Opposite, 2–4 in. (5–10 cm) long, elliptic-ovate, rough and hairy and green above, hairy and pale below; margin entire.

FLOWERS. White, ¼ in. (6 mm) in diameter, in flat-topped clusters 2–3 in. (5–8 cm) wide; May.

FRUIT. Drupe, ¼ in. (6 mm) in diameter; white; borne on red stalks; August to October.

WOOD. Brown, heavy, hard, close grained; used for tool handles.

HABITAT AND RANGE. Moist bottomlands to dry uplands from southern Ontario south to Louisiana, west to central Texas, north to South Dakota.

PROPAGATION. Seed, stratify at 60 days at 68/86°F (20/30°C) night/day, then 60 days at 41°F (5°C).

WILDLIFE VALUE. Fruit is excellent for songbirds, grouse, turkey, small mammals, squirrel, raccoon, and opossum; browse is excellent for rabbit and deer.

LANDSCAPE VALUE. Excellent shrub to attract wildlife, for wet to dry sites. Zone 4.

BEST RECOGNIZABLE FEATURES. Brown pith; clusters of white fruit on red stalks; leaf surface rough above, hairy below.

Cornus florida Linnaeus   PLATE 39
flowering dogwood, dogwood, cornel

HABIT. Rarely a shrub, generally a small understory tree, 15–30 ft. (5–9 m) tall, usually wider than tall, with distinct low, upturned branches and a flat-topped crown.

BARK. Light gray and smooth becoming scaly and grayish brown, eventually developing distinct small blocks ("alligator hide" appearance).

TWIGS. Slender but thicker than gray dogwood, upper side deep red to purple especially in the winter, underside greenish; slightly glaucous, pubescent when young becoming glabrous, upturned at the ends; leaf scars nearly encircling twig; pith continuous, pale. BUDS. Flower bud preformed, terminal, light gray, subglobose (buttonlike), stalked, valvate, covered by 2 large silky, appressed, pubescent scales; vegetative buds opposite, small (often covered by a raised leaf scar that nearly encircles the twig), valvate, slender, purple.

Cornus florida

LEAVES. Opposite, 2½–5 in. (6–13 cm) long, elliptic, shiny green above, conspicuously veined; veins with abundant latex; margin slightly wavy, appearing entire; fall color bright red.

FLOWERS. Very small and in a head, rather inconspicuous flowers; surrounded by 4 large, white (sometimes pink), petal-like bracts 1½–2 in. (4–5 cm) long that are very showy; April to May.

Figure 266. *Cornus florida* foliage

Figure 267. *Cornus florida* flowers

Figure 268. *Cornus florida* fruit

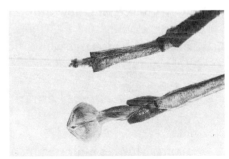

Figure 269. *Cornus florida* twigs and buds

Figure 270. *Cornus florida* bark, large tree

FRUIT. Drupe, glossy red, ¼–½ in. (6–13 mm) in diameter; 2–4 in a tight cluster; highly decorative; early autumn.

WOOD. Brown to green or red tinged, heavy, hard, strong, close grained; used for turnery, machine bearings, wheel hubs, tool handles; not large enough to be used for lumber.

HABITAT AND RANGE. Rich, well-drained soils in the understory from Massachusetts to Florida, west to Ontario, Texas, and Mexico.

PROPAGATION. Seed, stratify 120–150 days at 33–41°F (1–5°C).

WILDLIFE VALUE. Fruit is excellent for songbirds, grouse, turkey, small mammals, squirrel, raccoon, and opossum; browse is excellent for rabbit and deer.

LANDSCAPE VALUE. One of only a few native tree species with ornamental attributes all year long. Should be planted on moist but well-drained soils in light shade, otherwise may be short lived. Could never be overplanted. Numerous varieties available, selected for larger flower bracts, pink or red bracts, fragrant flowers, colored foliage (variegated), various forms, and even yellow fruit. Zones 5–9.

BEST RECOGNIZABLE FEATURES. Bright red fruit; large, buttonlike terminal flower buds; large white "flowers"; "alligator hide" bark.

Cornus racemosa Lamarck
gray dogwood

PLATES 40, 41

HABIT. Mostly a multistemmed shrub, occasionally a small tree, to 12 ft. (4 m) tall, with a short bole and an open, spreading crown.

BARK. Grayish, smooth becoming irregularly patchy and slightly scaly.

TWIGS. Slender, light reddish brown to orange becoming gray; or gray-brown not upturned conspicuously as in flowering dogwood and more slender; pith small, white or brown.

Cornus racemosa

BUDS. Terminal valvate, light to dark brown, appearing withered; laterals very small, nearly hidden by leaf scar.

LEAVES. Opposite, 2–4 in. (5–10 cm) long, ovate to lanceolate, dull green; principal leaf veins tend to parallel leaf margin.

FLOWERS. White; in terminal cymes 2 in. (5 cm) long; late spring.

FRUIT. Drupe, white, ¼ in. (6 mm) in diameter, attached to the bright red inflorescence, persisting through winter.

WOOD. Commercially unimportant.

HABITAT AND RANGE. Along moist streambanks from Maine to Ontario and Minnesota, south to Georgia and Nebraska.

PROPAGATION. Seed, stratify 60 days at 68/86°F (20/30°C) night/day, then 120 days at 41°F (5°C).

WILDLIFE VALUE. Fruit is excellent for songbirds, grouse, turkey, small mammals, squirrel, raccoon, and opossum; browse is good for deer.

LANDSCAPE VALUE. Excellent, dense, low shrub to attract wildlife. Aggressively spreads over an area through root sprouts. Zone 4.

BEST RECOGNIZABLE FEATURES. Clusters of white fruit on red stalks; multistemmed habit; "withered" terminal bud in winter.

Figure 271. *Cornus racemosa* foliage

Figure 272. *Cornus racemosa* twig and buds

Cornus rugosa Lamarck
roundleaf dogwood

HABIT. Shrub or small slender tree, to 10 ft. (3 m) tall.

Cornus rugosa

BARK. Greenish to gray, warty.

TWIGS. Slender, green to reddish brown (pink in winter), streaked with dark purple; pith white.

BUDS. Small, oblong, hairy at apex, nearly sessile.

LEAVES. Opposite, simple, broadly ovate, very densely woolly below, with 6–8 pairs of lateral veins; margin entire.

FLOWERS. Small, white, in dense, flat-topped clusters.

FRUIT. Globose, pale blue (rarely greenish white), in flat clusters.

HABITAT AND RANGE. Dry woods from Quebec to Manitoba, south to West Virginia, Illinois, and Iowa.

PROPAGATION. Seed, stratify in moist medium 60–150 days at 68/86°F (20/30°C) night/day, then 90–120 days at 41°F (5°C).

Figure 273. *Cornus rugosa* foliage

Figure 275. *Cornus rugosa* bark, small stem

Figure 274. *Cornus rugosa* flower

WILDLIFE VALUE. Fruit is excellent for songbirds, grouse, turkey, small mammals, squirrel, raccoon, and opossum; browse is excellent for rabbit and deer.

LANDSCAPE VALUE. Excellent shrub to attract wildlife; tolerates very dry soils. Zone 3.

BEST RECOGNIZABLE FEATURES. Opposite, very broad leaves with 6–8 pairs of veins; green or reddish brown twigs streaked with dark purple.

Cornus stolonifera Michaux
red-osier dogwood, kinnikinnik, red dogwood

HABIT. Typically a thicket-forming, large shrub; rarely a small tree, to 10 ft. (3 m) tall.

BARK. Smooth or slightly furrowed, gray or brown.

TWIGS. Moderately stout (relative to other dogwoods), purplish red, glabrous; pith homogeneous, white, large.

BUDS. Flower buds terminal, valvate, white-hairy; vegetative buds valvate, pressed against twig.

Cornus stolonifera

LEAVES. Opposite, simple, 2–5 in. (5–13 cm) long, elliptic to ovate, dull green above, glaucous beneath and covered with fine hairs; apex acute; base rounded; margin entire; about 5 main pairs of veins evident.

FLOWERS. White, ¼ in. (6 mm) in diameter, in flat cluster about 2 in. (5 cm) wide.

FRUIT. Drupe, white, globose, less than ½ in. (13 mm) in diameter; maturing in late summer.

Figure 276. *Cornus stolonifera* foliage

Figure 277. *Cornus stolonifera* fruit

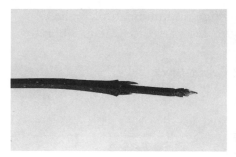

Figure 278. *Cornus stolonifera* twig and buds

Figure 279. *Cornus stolonifera* bark, large stem

HABITAT AND RANGE. Moist to wet soils in open from Newfoundland to Manitoba, south to Virginia, Kentucky, and Nebraska.

PROPAGATION. Seed, stratify in moist medium 60–90 days at 41°F (5°C); hardwood cuttings taken and placed out in late winter root readily.

WILDLIFE VALUE. Fruit is eaten by many birds including ruffed grouse and bobwhite quail; twigs and foliage are browsed by whitetail deer, cottontail, snowshoe hare, and moose.

LANDSCAPE VALUE. Excellent in large masses where bright red stems provide some color in otherwise dreary winter landscape. Zones 2–8.

BEST RECOGNIZABLE FEATURES. Moderately stout (for dogwoods), reddish twigs; white pith; white fruit; thicket-forming habit.

Cornus stricta Lamarck
stiffcornel dogwood

HABIT. Large shrub with stiff, upright branches and flat-topped crown, or small tree to 20 ft. (6 m) tall.

BARK. Gray, smooth when young, developing shallow furrows with age.

TWIGS. Slender, upright, glabrous although hairy towards apex, brown or gray; pith white.

BUDS. Very small, ovoid, sharp pointed, reddish brown, pubescent.

LEAVES. Opposite, simple, 1½–4 in. (4–10 cm) long, lanceolate to ovate, dark green and glabrous and smooth

Cornus stricta

above, whitish green below; apex pointed; base rounded or broadly tapered; margin entire.

FLOWERS. White to yellowish, very small, not attractive alone but occur in loose, open clusters.

FRUIT. Drupe, ¼ in. (6 mm) in diameter, dark blue to purple, in open clusters.

WOOD. White, hard, fine grained.

HABITAT AND RANGE. Wet soils from eastern Virginia to central Florida, west to Louisiana, north to southeastern Missouri and central Indiana.

PROPAGATION. Seed, stratify in moist medium 90 days at 68/86°F (20/30°C) night/day, then 90 days at 41°F (5°C).

WILDLIFE VALUE. Fruit is eaten by quail, catbird, mockingbird, robin, and brown thrasher.

LANDSCAPE VALUE. Not particularly showy but grows in the wettest soils; good for attracting birds. Zone 6.

BEST RECOGNIZABLE FEATURES. Stiff, upright branches; shrubby habit; leaves resemble flowering dogwood but are smaller; open clusters of flowers and fruit.

Other dogwoods commonly planted in the regional landscape:
Cornus kousa Hance, Kousa dogwood. Small, bushy tree to 20 ft. (6 m)

Figure 280. *Cornus kousa* flowers

Figure 281. *Cornus mas* foliage

Figure 282. *Cornus mas* flowers

tall; flower bracts 2 in. (5 cm) long, white, tapered pointed compared to *C. florida*, open in late spring to early summer; bark exfoliating to expose a variety of browns and greens; fruit resembles a raspberry. Perhaps the best of all dogwoods, native or exotic. Numerous varieties sold. Zones 5–8.

Cornus mas Linnaeus, Cornelian cherry dogwood. Large multistemmed shrub or small tree to 20 ft. (6 m) tall; yellowish flowers without large white bracts, nevertheless showy in February to March; bark attractive, exfoliating, flaky; fruit a bright red cherrylike drupe, ripening in July. Zones 4–8.

Cotinus—smoketree
ANACARDIACEAE—sumac family

Cotinus obovatus Rafinesque
American smoketree, smoketree

PLATE 42

HABIT. Large shrub or small tree, to 30 ft. (9 m) tall, with a short bole and many widespreading, arching or slightly pendulous branches.

Cotinus obovatus

BARK. Very thin, light gray to grayish brown, broken into thin, oblong scales.

TWIGS. Slender, glabrous, shiny, bright green or red-brown to purple, white lenticels prominent and corky; leaf scars prominent, crescent shaped or 3-lobed, with generally 3 (to 7) bundle scars, and with distinct wrinkles; pith continuous, whitish or golden-brown, oval in cross section; sap resinous and aromatic (fruity).

BUDS. Terminal ¼ in. (6 mm) long, acute, having 4 visible, dark brown scales; laterals smaller, often clustered near end of twig.

LEAVES. Alternate, simple, 4–6 in. (10–15 cm) long, obovate or elliptic, dark green above; paler below and hairy on principal veins; margin entire, slightly wavy, commonly curled under; apex notched or rounded; base obtuse or gradually tapering; petiole stout, about 1 in. (2.5 cm) long; fall color orange to scarlet.

FLOWERS. Greenish yellow; dioecious; in terminal, slender, long-branched panicles to 6 in. (15 cm) long; in late April to early May.

Figure 283. *Cotinus obovatus* foliage

Figure 284. *Cotinus obovatus* flowers

Figure 285. *Cotinus obovatus* twig

Figure 286. *Cotinus obovatus* bark, large stem

FRUIT. Dry, obliquely oblong, somewhat compressed drupe; seed kidney shaped, very small.

WOOD. Bright clear deep orange, light, soft, rather coarse grained, very durable in contact with soil; used in past, when more abundant, for fencing.

HABITAT AND RANGE. Dry, limy uplands and ravines in widely scattered, rather isolated areas of western Kentucky, south central Tennessee, northern Alabama, southern Missouri, northern Arkansas, eastern Oklahoma, and south central Texas.

PROPAGATION. Seed (difficult), scarify by soaking 30–60 minutes in sulfuric acid, then stratify in moist medium 90 days at 41°F (5°C); cuttings also difficult.

WILDLIFE VALUE. Little value except to provide cover and nesting sites for some wildlife species.

Figure 287. *Cotinus coggygria* foliage

Figure 288. *Cotinus coggygria* flowers

LANDSCAPE VALUE. Underutilized, naturally rare tree that has unusual floral display (male trees more attractive), with outstanding fall color and handsome bark. Especially well adapted to dry soils. Zones 4–8.

BEST RECOGNIZABLE FEATURES. Dark green oblong leaf with long petiole and apex often notched; flowers with smoky hue as fruit ripens; very limited in nature, typically on limestone-derived soils.

Other smoketrees commonly planted in the regional landscape:
Cotinus coggygria Scopoli, smokebush. A large, wide, multistemmed shrub to 12 ft. (4 m) tall; leaves alternate, simple, bluish green, oval to obovate, to 3½ in. (9 cm) long, rounded or notched at apex, aromatic when crushed; buds small, sharp pointed, dark reddish brown, aromatic; twig stout, brown or purplish, glaucous, glabrous, fragrant when crushed; pith orange-brown; flower clusters to 8 in. (20 cm) long and showy through summer. Native from southern Europe to central China. Zones 5–8.

Crataegus—hawthorn
ROSACEAE—rose family

Crataegus spp. Linnaeus
hawthorn

PLATES 43, 44, 45, 46

HABIT. Generally a small deciduous tree, to 30 ft. (9 m) tall, occasionally a shrub, varying in shape from widespreading to columnar, open to dense.

BARK. Brown to gray, usually becoming scaly or broken into small ridges on older specimens.

TWIGS. Usually orange, brown, or reddish brown to gray, round, slender, more or less zigzag, moderate or stout, armed at some nodes with sharp, stiff thorns ½–6 in. (1–15 cm) long; pith white or pale, continuous.

BUDS. Small, globular, reddish, with imbricate scales, generally glabrous.

LEAVES. Deciduous, alternate, simple, 1–4 in. (2.5–10 cm) long, stipulate, variable in shape, toothed or lobed at the margin.

FLOWERS. White, typically very showy, borne in large numbers either terminally or axillary; clusters, with or before leaf maturity; April to June.

FRUIT. Small pomes in cymes, usually scarlet or orange; shiny or dull; ripening in autumn, persisting into winter; highly decorative for most species.

WOOD. Red-brown, heavy, hard, tough, close grained; used for tool handles, mallets; commercially unimportant.

HABITAT AND RANGE. A variety of sites, from Newfoundland to northern Mexico and throughout western United States.

PROPAGATION. Most seeds respond to warm stratification 120 days at 68/86°F (20/30°C) night/day, then cold stratification 120 days at 41°F (5°C). Horticultural selections are budded onto seedling understock.

WILDLIFE VALUE. Fruit is excellent for songbirds, grouse, turkey, deer, and squirrel.

LANDSCAPE VALUE. Profusion of late spring flowers, red or orange berries, manageable size, and lack of any serious pests. *Crataegus phaenopyrum* and *C. viridis* are regarded as best choices for landscape use. Zones (generally) 3–6+ (depends on species).

BEST RECOGNIZABLE FEATURES. Thorns, with single bud at base; red to orange clusters of applelike (but small) fruit; white clusters of flowers in spring.

COMMENT. Some taxonomists have estimated that less than 50 species of hawthorns occur in North America, while others believe there are hundreds of species. There may be more than 20 species in the Central Hardwood Forests, of which the 4 described below are sold by nurseries.

Hawthorns in the Central Hardwood Forests:

Crataegus crus-galli Linnaeus, cockspur hawthorn. Leaves glossy dark green, obovate to oblong-obovate, to 4 in. (10 cm) long; fruit brick-red, to ½ in. (13 mm) in diameter; thorns 2–3 in. (5–8 cm) long. Zones 3–7.

Crataegus mollis (Torrey & A. Gray) Scheele, downy hawthorn. Leaves broad, ovate, to 4 in. (10 cm) long; flowers 1 in. (2.5 cm) in diameter, white; fruit scarlet or crimson, ½–1 in. (13–25 mm) in diameter. Zones 3–6.

Crataegus phaenopyrum (Linnaeus f.) Medicus, Washington hawthorn. Leaves broad to triangular-ovate, to 3 in. (8 cm) long, dark green and shiny above; flowers abundant, white, ½ in. (13 mm) in diameter; fruit shiny, reddish orange, ¼ in. (6 mm) in diameter. Zones 3–8.

Crataegus viridis Linnaeus, green hawthorn. Leaves oblong-ovate to elliptic, to 3½ in. (9 cm) long; flowers showy, white, ¾ in. (19 mm) in diameter; fruit bright red, to ⅓ in. (8 mm) in diameter. The cultivar 'Winter King' is an exceptional hawthorn. Zones 4–7.

Other hawthorns commonly planted in the regional landscape:

Crataegus laevigata (Poiret) de Candolle, English hawthorn. Leaves deep dark green, broad-ovate or obovate, with rounded lobes; fruit scarlet, to ½ in. (13 mm) long. Native to Europe and northern Africa. Numerous varieties available, some with pink or red flowers. 'Crimson Cloud' is a good choice for street planting in the Midwest. Zones 4–7.

Crataegus × *lavallei* Hérincq. A cross between *C. crus-galli* and *C. stipula-*

Figure 289. *Crataegus phaenopyrum* foliage and fruit

Figure 290. *Crataegus* sp. twigs and buds

Figure 291. *Crataegus* sp. bark, small stem

Figure 292. *Crataegus* sp. bark, large stem

ceae; leaves dark green, pubescent below; fruit very large, red-orange. Zones 4–7.

Crataegus monogyna Jacquin, single seed hawthorn. Leaves broad-ovate, deeply 3- to 7-lobed; fruit red, ⅜ in. (10 mm) in diameter, one seeded. Native to Europe, northern Africa, western Asia. Varieties available. Zones 4–7.

Crataegus 'Vaughn'. A cross between *C. crus-galli* and *C. phaenopyrum*. Well suited for urban planting. Zones 4–7.

Diospyros—persimmon
EBENACEAE—ebony family

Diospyros virginiana Linnaeus
persimmon, simmon, possumwood, persimmon

HABIT. Medium-sized tree, 40–60 ft. (12–18 m) tall, with a short bole and a low, wide, rounded crown.

Diospyros virginiana

BARK. Dark gray to black, to 1 in. (2.5 cm) thick, checkered when young, developing deep dark orange fissures and thick, square blocks, odorless when cut (unlike sassafras), exhibiting a rippling of deep purple and deep red layers.

TWIGS. Slender, moderate gray to reddish brown, with orange lenticels, zigzag; leaf scars raised with single, prominent bundle scar; pith white, diaphragmed or continuous.

BUDS. Terminal absent; laterals ⅛ in. (3 mm) long, ovoid, acute, closely appressed, reddish black, smooth, solitary, with 2 overlapping, lustrous scales.

LEAVES. Alternate, simple, 4–6 in. (10–15 cm) long, ovate to elliptic, leathery, dark green and smooth above, pale below; margin entire; base rounded; young leaves with translucent veins; fall color yellow-green.

FLOWERS. Small, about ½ in. (13 mm) long, urn shaped; generally dioecious; May to June.

FRUIT. Berry, 1–1½ in. (2.5–4 cm) wide; stalks persistent; pale orange at maturity, sweet, delicious when ripe; 1–8 large purple seeds; October.

Figure 293. *Diospyros virginiana* foliage

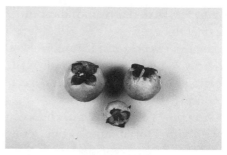

Figure 294. *Diospyros virginiana* fruit

Figure 295. *Diospyros virginiana* twig and buds

Figure 296. *Diospyros virginiana* bark, medium-sized tree

Figure 297. *Diospyros virginiana* bark, large tree

WOOD. Black heartwood, dark brown sapwood, hard, heavy; used for golf club heads, shuttles, billiard cues, brush handles.

HABITAT AND RANGE. Dry to moist sites in forests, old fields, and fence-rows from Connecticut to Iowa and eastern Kansas, south to eastern Texas, east to Florida.

PROPAGATION. Seed, stratify 60–90 days at 47–50°F (8–10°C).

WILDLIFE VALUE. Fruit is excellent for songbirds, turkey, quail, small rodents, opossum, skunk, raccoon, fox, and deer.

LANDSCAPE VALUE. Tolerates dry to wet sites, and typically forms large thickets through root sprouting. Numerous varieties available, selected for fruit characteristics. Zones 4–9.

BEST RECOGNIZABLE FEATURES. Large fruit, glaucous orange at maturity; "alligator hide" bark; 2 bud scales, upper overlapping lower one.

Euonymus—burningbush
CELASTRACEAE—bittersweet family

Euonymus atropurpureus Jacquin
eastern burningbush, eastern wahoo, wahoo, strawberry-bush

HABIT. Larger shrub or small tree, to 20 ft. (6 m) tall, with spreading, irregular branches.

BARK. Thin, smooth, green when young becoming ash-gray.

TWIGS. Slender, 4-sided, glabrous, initially green becoming gray after a few years, prominent lenticels; leaf scars half-round and slightly raised, whitish, prominent against the green stems; pith green, spongy.

Euonymus atropurpureus

BUDS. Length ⅛ in. (3 mm), acute, with 3–5 pairs of sharp pointed, appressed, glabrous, narrow scales.

LEAVES. Opposite, simple, 2–4 in. (5–10 cm) long, elliptic, acuminate, finely toothed.

FLOWERS. In divergently branched cymes; June to July.

FRUIT. Capsule, ½ in. (13 mm) in diameter; deeply 4-lobed; purple, opening to expose a scarlet aril surrounding a brown seed; maturing in early autumn, persisting into winter.

Figure 298. *Euonymus atropurpureus* foliage

Figure 299. *Euonymus atro-purpureus* fruit

Figure 300. *Euonymus atro-purpureus* bark, small stem

Figure 301. *Euonymus atro-purpureus* bark, large stem

WOOD. White tinged with orange, heavy, hard, very close grained; commercially unimportant.

HABITAT AND RANGE. Borders of woods in rich soil from New York to Florida, west to Minnesota, Nebraska, Oklahoma, and Texas.

PROPAGATION. Seed, stratify 90 days at 75°F (24°C), then 90–120 days at 41°F (5°C).

WILDLIFE VALUE. Fruit is fair for songbirds; browse is excellent for deer.

LANDSCAPE VALUE. Interesting in fruit, otherwise adds little to landscape. Zones 4–9.

BEST RECOGNIZABLE FEATURES. Bright green twigs; white leaf scar; bright orange-scarlet fruit.

Other burningbushes commonly planted in the regional landscape: *Euonymus alatus* (Thunberg) Siebold, winged euonymus. To 20 ft. (6

m) tall. The common *Euonymus* species planted for its brilliant red fall color. Ideally suited to mass planting and foundations. Leaves and fruit smaller than *E. atropurpureus*; form much bushier. Zones 4–8.

Fagus—beech
FAGACEAE—beech family

Fagus grandifolia Ehrhart
American beech, beech

PLATE 47

HABIT. Medium-sized to large tree, 60–80 ft. (18–24 m) tall, with a long bole supporting a wide, spreading crown; bole frequently with persistent, small branches.

Fagus grandifolia

BARK. Steel-gray, thin, smooth.

TWIGS. Slender, reddish brown to silvery-gray, smooth, zigzag; stipule scars encircling twig; spur twigs numerous; pith continuous.

BUDS. Length ¾–1 in. (19–25 mm), yellowish to reddish brown, shiny, narrow, made up of 10–24 visible scales, sharp pointed, divergent from the twig at a 45° angle.

LEAVES. Alternate, simple, 3–5 in. (8–13 cm) long, ovate-oblong, glossy dark green above, yellow-green below, leathery ("sun" leaves) to wax-papery ("shade" leaves) in texture, persisting into winter, unlobed, coarsely toothed, pinnately veined; fall color yellow or brown.

FLOWERS. Monoecious; male flowers in a rounded head, female flowers spikes of 2–4 flowers; April to early May.

FRUIT. Triangular nut, ½–¾ in. (13–19 mm) in diameter, reddish brown; enclosed in a light brown, 4-valved, prickly husk (involucre) 1–1½ in. (2.5–4 cm) long; October.

WOOD. Reddish brown, heavy hard, strong, close grained; used for fuel, furniture, tool handles.

HABITAT AND RANGE. Cool, moist sites from Nova Scotia to Ontario, south to eastern Texas, east to northern Florida.

PROPAGATION. Seed, stratify 90 days at 41°F (5°C).

WILDLIFE VALUE. Fruit is excellent for songbirds, turkey, ruffed grouse, squirrel, mice, and deer.

Figure 302. *Fagus grandifolia* foliage

Figure 303. *Fagus grandifolia* fruit

Figure 304. *Fagus grandifolia* twig and bud

Figure 305. *Fagus grandifolia* bark, small tree

Figure 306. *Fagus grandifolia* bark, medium-sized tree

Figure 307. *Fagus grandifolia* bark, large tree

Figure 308. *Fagus grandifolia* bark, large tree

LANDSCAPE VALUE. Beautiful tree that should be maintained where it exists; requires moist but well-drained soils. Beech bark disease in the northeastern portion of this species' range has caused tremendous mortality of many majestic individuals. Zones 3–9.

BEST RECOGNIZABLE FEATURES. Smooth blue-gray bark; long-pointed buds; prickly fruit with triangular seeds.

Other beeches commonly planted in the regional landscape:
Fagus sylvatica Linnaeus, European beech. Tree large, commonly to 60 ft. (18 m) tall, very important forest and ornamental tree in Europe, exhibiting much variation in foliage color, texture, and general form; leaves undulate, not coarsely serrate as in American beech; fruit husks larger and pubescent. Much more commonly planted than the native species, often as one of numerous varieties. Not susceptible to the beech bark disease. Zones 4–7.

Figure 309. *Fagus sylvatica* foliage

Figure 310. *Fagus sylvatica* fruit

Forestiera—swamp-privet
OLEACEAE—olive family

Forestiera acuminata (Michaux) Poiret
swamp-privet, common adelia, whitewood

HABIT. Small tree or large shrub, 10–30 ft. (3–9 m) tall, with a slender, leaning trunk and a short, irregular crown.
BARK. Dark brown, thin, smooth, lenticellate, slightly warty.
TWIGS. Slender, light brown, warty, lenticellate, may appear thorny; leaf scars small with single, U-shaped bundle scar; pith pale brown, continuous.
BUDS. Terminal 1/16 in. (2 mm) long, green, globose, with many scales; laterals 1/32 in. (<1 mm) long, opposite.

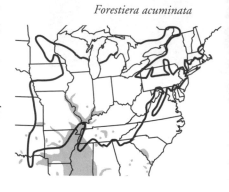

Forestiera acuminata

LEAVES. Opposite, simple, 2–4 in. (5–10 cm) long, yellowish green, diamond shaped, smooth above, pale below; margin slightly serrate, mostly above middle.
FLOWERS. Minute, yellow or greenish yellow; dioecious; borne in loose clusters of 3 flowers; without petals; April.
FRUIT. Drupe, 3/8–5/8 in. (10–16 mm) in diameter, ovoid, purple, dry; stone ridged; August.

Figure 311. *Forestiera acuminata* foliage

Figure 312. *Forestiera acuminata* bark, medium-sized stem

WOOD. Commercially unimportant.

HABITAT AND RANGE. Floodplain forests from South Carolina to northern Florida, west to eastern Texas, north to central Illinois.

PROPAGATION. Layering; softwood or hardwood cuttings; fresh seed might germinate without pretreatment.

WILDLIFE VALUE. Fruit is good for wood duck, mallard, songbirds, and small mammals.

LANDSCAPE VALUE. Good small tree or large shrub for wet soils to attract wildlife. Zone 5.

BEST RECOGNIZABLE FEATURES. Somewhat warty bark; black drupes.

Fraxinus—ash
OLEACEAE—olive family

Key to *Fraxinus*

1. Leaflets sessile; terminal bud often stalked; bark corky . . . . *Fraxinus nigra*
1. Leaflets stalked; terminal bud not stalked; bark ridged and furrowed 2
2(1). Stems 4-angled . . . . *Fraxinus quadrangulata*
2. Stems round 3
3(2). Leaflets, rachis, and twigs densely pubescent . . . . *Fraxinus profunda*
3. Leaflets, rachis, and twigs glabrous or lightly pubescent 4
4(3). Leaflets often glaucous below, margins of leaflets serrated only from apex to midpoint; leaf scars notched . *Fraxinus americana*
4 Leaflets not glaucous below, margins of leaflets serrated from apex to base; leaf scars not notched . . . *Fraxinus pennsylvanica*

Fraxinus americana Linnaeus
PLATES 48, 49
white ash, ash, Biltmore ash

HABIT. Large tree, 80–90 ft. (24–27 m) tall, with a long, clear, straight bole and ascending branches supporting a round or pyramidal crown.

BARK. Gray-brown, thick, deeply furrowed with sharp, interlacing ridges that are cork-colored when cut.

TWIGS. Stout, gray or brown or greenish brown, lenticellate; leaf scars usually notched at the bud and usually at a sharp angle to the twigs; pith white, continuous. Biltmore ash, a variety, has densely hairy twigs.

BUDS. Terminal ¼ in. (6 mm) long, grayish brown to brown, appearing powdery, with 4–6 scales, appressed, imbricate; laterals similar, but smaller, opposite.

LEAVES. Pinnately compound, 8–12 in. (20–31 cm) long, green above, grayish white and lightly hairy below, with 5–11 (usually 7) ovate to ovate-lance-olate leaflets 2–5 in. (5–13 cm) long, stalked on the rachis; rachis smooth; apex short pointed to long pointed; base rounded or tapered; margin, at least below middle of leaflet, entire; fall color purple or yellow.

FLOWERS. Apetalous, dioecious, in panicles; appearing before or with the leaves in April.

Fraxinus americana

Figure 313. *Fraxinus americana* foliage

Figure 314. *Fraxinus americana* flowers, male

Figure 315. *Fraxinus americana* flowers, female

Figure 316. *Fraxinus americana* fruit

Figure 317. *Fraxinus americana* twigs and buds

Figure 318. *Fraxinus americana* bark, small tree

Figure 319. *Fraxinus americana* bark, large tree

FRUIT. Length 1–2 in. (2.5–5 cm); yellowish tan; samara with wing partially surrounding the seed; borne in clusters.

WOOD. Brown, heavy, hard, strong, tough, close grained; used for tool handles, furniture, interior finishing, baseball bats.

HABITAT AND RANGE. Moist to dry uplands from Nova Scotia to southern Minnesota, south to eastern Texas, east to Florida.

PROPAGATION. Seed, stratify 30 days at 58/86°F (14/30°C) night/day, then 60 days at 41°F (5°C).

WILDLIFE VALUE. Seed is fair for quail, songbirds, and rodents.

LANDSCAPE VALUE. Beautiful large shade tree, especially in autumn. Numerous varieties available, selected for foliage (especially fall color) or form. 'Autumn Applause', 'Autumn Purple', 'Champaign County', and 'Rosehill' are good cultivars for urban plantings. Zones 3–9.

BEST RECOGNIZABLE FEATURES. Oar-shaped fruit; buds inset in leaf scar, in U-shaped depression; knobby and warty twig; leaflets whitish below; diamond-shaped bark.

Fraxinus nigra Marshall
black ash, swamp ash, basket ash, hoop ash

HABIT. Medium-sized tree, 40–70 ft. (12–21 m) tall, with upright branches that form a narrow, open crown.

Fraxinus nigra

BARK. Corky, irregular, reddish brown to gray, scaly soft ridges, flaky when rubbed, with shallow fissures.

TWIGS. Moderately stout, light orange-brown to gray, lenticellate, rounded, becoming glabrous; leaf scars nearly circular or elliptic; pith homogenous, white.

BUDS. Terminal ¼ in. (6 mm) long, dark brown to black, ovoid, sharp pointed; laterals nearly rounded, rather blunt, appressed, last pair at end of twig set below terminal bud.

LEAVES. Opposite, pinnately compound, 10–16 in. (25–41 cm) long, with 7–11 leaflets, dark green above and paler below, broadly lance shaped; apex sharp pointed; margin finely serrate; lateral leaflets sessile; petiole grooved; fall color brown-yellow.

FLOWERS. Perfect or dioecious; purplish, in panicles 4–5 in. (10–13 cm) long; appearing before the leaves in April.

FRUIT. Samara, broad-oblong, 1–1½ in. (2.5–4 cm) long, angled at apex and blunt at base; in open panicles 8–10 in. (20–25 cm) long.

WOOD. Dark brown, heavy, somewhat soft, not strong, tough, durable,

Figure 320. *Fraxinus nigra* foliage

Figure 321. *Fraxinus nigra* fruit

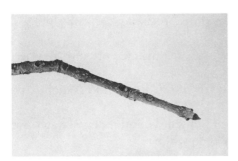

Figure 322. *Fraxinus nigra* twig and buds

Figure 323. *Fraxinus nigra* bark, small tree

Figure 324. *Fraxinus nigra* bark, medium-sized tree

Figure 325. *Fraxinus nigra* bark, large tree

Figure 326. *Fraxinus nigra* bark, large tree

coarse grained; used for interior finish, cabinets, fences, barrel hoops, baskets, woven chair bottoms.

HABITAT. Cold, wet soils of swamps, bogs, streamsides; often with American elm.

PROPAGATION. Seed, stratify 60 days at 58/86°F (14/30°C) night/day, then 90 days at 41°F (5°C).

WILDLIFE VALUE. Seed is fair for quail, songbirds, and rodents; waterfowl utilize this species more commonly than white ash.

LANDSCAPE VALUE. Little value relative to other species in this genus, except in northern areas in wet soils. Zones 2–5.

BEST RECOGNIZABLE FEATURES. Sessile leaflets; stalked terminal bud; corky bark, ridges roughly diamond shaped; cold, wet habitat.

Fraxinus pennsylvanica Marshall green ash, swamp ash, red ash

PLATES 50, 51, 52

HABIT. Similar to white ash, but 60–80 ft. (18–24 m) tall.

BARK. Similar to white ash (but perhaps more tightly interlacing).

TWIGS. Stout, gray to gray-brown, lightly hairy; leaf scars not usually notched near the bud, angle of leaf scars to stem not sharp.

BUDS. Similar to white ash except can be covered with rusty hairs.

Fraxinus pennsylvanica

LEAVES. Pinnately compound, 6–10 in. (15–25 cm) long, yellow-green above, pale and very hairy below, with 5–9 (usually 7) ovate to oblong-lanceolate leaflets 1–6 in. (2.5–15 cm) long, stalked; rachis lightly hairy, often grooved; margin serrate along entire length; fall color yellow.

FLOWERS. Apetalous, dioecious, in panicles; appearing after the leaves have begun to unfold in April.

FRUIT. Length ½ in. (13 mm); yellow-brown; samara with wing enclosing only the tip of the seed; borne in clusters around the twig.

WOOD. Light brown; heavy, hard, rather strong, brittle, coarse grained; usually marketed as white ash.

HABITAT AND RANGE. Wet sites along streambanks from Nova Scotia to Manitoba, south to Kansas, west to Georgia.

PROPAGATION. Same as for white ash.

WILDLIFE VALUE. Seed is fair for quail, songbirds, and rodents.

Figure 327. *Fraxinus pennsylvanica* foliage

Figure 328. *Fraxinus pennsylvanica* fruit

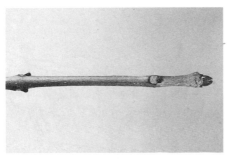

Figure 329. *Fraxinus pennsylvanica* twig and buds

Figure 330. *Fraxinus pennsylvanica* bark, medium-sized tree

Figure 331. *Fraxinus pennsylvanica* bark, large tree

LANDSCAPE VALUE. Tolerates wide range of soil conditions and is an attractive tree although overplanted. Numerous varieties available, selected for form and foliage. The cultivars 'Marshall Seedless', 'Patmore', 'Summit', and 'Urbanite' are good choices for urban plantings. Zones 3–9.

BEST RECOGNIZABLE FEATURES. Diamond-shaped bark; slender fruit; bud set above leaf scar, leaf scars nearly straight across at top; margin of leaflet serrated above and below the middle; wet soils.

Fraxinus profunda (Bush) Bush
pumpkin ash, red ash

HABIT. Similar to green ash.
BARK. Brown to gray-brown, otherwise similar to green ash.
TWIGS. Similar to green ash except more densely hairy.
BUDS. Similar to green ash.
LEAVES. Opposite, compound, 8–16 in. (20–41 cm) long; similar to green ash except much more densely hairy below, usually with 7–9 oblong-lanceolate or ovate leaflets 3–7 in. (8–18 cm) long.
FLOWERS. Dioecious, in panicles; April.
FRUIT. Length 2–3 in. (5–8 cm); yellow-green; not flattened; wing almost completely enclosing the seed.

Fraxinus profunda

Figure 332. *Fraxinus profunda* foliage

Figure 333. *Fraxinus profunda* bark, small stem

Figure 334. *Fraxinus profunda* bark, medium-sized stem

Figure 335. *Fraxinus profunda* bark, large stem

WOOD. Brown, heavy, hard, strong, close grained; used for boxes, paper, fuel.

HABITAT AND RANGE. Floodplain soils along the Atlantic and Gulf coastal plains from Maryland to Louisiana and north in the Mississippi Valley to southwestern Ohio.

PROPAGATION. Seed, stratify 60–90 days at 41°F (5°C).

WILDLIFE VALUE. Seed is good for wood duck, songbirds, and small rodents.

LANDSCAPE VALUE. Large tree for wet (flooded) sites. Zones 5–9.

BEST RECOGNIZABLE FEATURES. Densely hairy twigs; pinnately compound leaflets, pubescent below; wet sites.

Fraxinus quadrangulata Michaux
blue ash

HABIT. Medium-sized to large tree, 60–80 ft. (18–24 m) tall, with a short bole and deep, round crown; dead branches persist on the bole.

BARK. Bluish gray to brown-gray, thick-furrowed with interlacing ridges, becoming scaly, then shaggy with age.

TWIGS. Stout, light green to gray, lenticellate, square in cross section on new growth (4-angled), lightly hairy or smooth; leaf scars notched at bud; pith continuous; sap turns bluish when exposed to air.

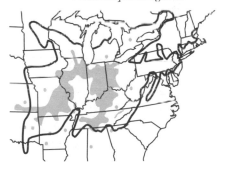

Fraxinus quadrangulata

Figure 336. *Fraxinus quadrangulata* foliage

Figure 337. *Fraxinus quadrangulata* fruit

Figure 338. *Fraxinus quadrangulata* twig and buds

Figure 339. *Fraxinus quadrangulata* bark, medium-sized tree

Figure 340. *Fraxinus quadrangulata* bark, large tree

BUDS. Terminal ¼ in. (6 mm) long, gray to reddish brown, hairy; laterals similar but smaller.

LEAVES. Pinnately compound, 8–12 in. (20–31 cm) long, yellow-green and smooth above, pale and hairy below, with 7–11 ovate to lanceolate leaflets 3–5 in. (8–13 cm) long, stalked; margin serrate; rachis slender; fall color pale yellow.

FLOWERS. Perfect, in panicles; appearing before the leaves unfold in April.

FRUIT. Length 1–2 in. (2.5–5 cm); dark green to gray; samara, wing completely enclosing flattened seed.

WOOD. Light yellow streaked with brown, heavy, hard, rather brittle, close grained; used for flooring. The inner bark produces a blue dye when macerated in water.

HABITAT AND RANGE. Dry upland sites from Ontario to Iowa, south Oklahoma, east to central Tennessee.

PROPAGATION. Seed, stratify 30 days at 68/86°F (20/30°C) night/day, then 60 days at 41°F (5°C).

WILDLIFE VALUE. Seed is fair for quail, songbirds, and rodents.

LANDSCAPE VALUE. Good, large shade tree for dry sites. Zones 4–7.

BEST RECOGNIZABLE FEATURES. Very broad fruit; young twigs 4-sided; shaggy, ridged bark.

Other ashes commonly planted in the regional landscape:
Fraxinus excelsior Linnaeus, European ash. Large tree to 80 ft. (24 m) tall; easy to recognize because of its black buds. Native to Europe and Asia Minor and long in cultivation. The cultivar 'Hessei' does not have compound leaves, but the twigs, buds, and form are unmistakenly that of an ash. Zones 5–7.
Fraxinus holotricha Koehne 'Moraine', moraine ash. Round-headed, attractive street tree to 40 ft. (12 m) tall, typically with whorled leaves and buds. Native to eastern Balkan peninsula. Zone 5.

Gleditsia—honeylocust
CAESALPINIACEAE—caesalpinia family

Key to *Gleditsia*

1. Legume 12–18 in. (31–46 cm) long; dry–wet sites and extensively planted .... *Gleditsia triacanthos*
1. Legume to 2 in. (5 cm) long; poorly drained sites and not planted .... *Gleditsia aquatica*

Gleditsia aquatica Marshall
waterlocust

HABIT. Medium-sized tree, 40–60 ft. (12–18 m) tall, with a clear bole and an irregular, spreading crown.

BARK. Grayish brown, scaly or plated, with slender short-branched thorns on the surface; similar to honeylocust.

TWIGS. Brown, moderately stout, zigzag, with slender short-branched thorns each 2–4 in. (5–10 cm) long; similar to honeylocust.

BUDS. Similar to honeylocust.

LEAVES. Pinnate or bipinnate, 4–8 in. (10–20 cm) long, dark green

Gleditsia aquatica

Figure 341. *Gleditsia aquatica* foliage

Figure 342. *Gleditsia aquatica* bark, small tree

Figure 343. *Gleditsia aquatica* bark, medium-sized tree

Figure 344. *Gleditsia aquatica* bark, large tree

above, yellow-green below, with oblong-lanceolate leaflets ½–1 in. (13–25 cm) long; smaller and with fewer leaflets than honeylocust.

FLOWERS. Similar to honeylocust.

FRUIT. Legume, 1–2 in. (2.5–5 cm) long; shiny brown with 1 or rarely 2–3 seeds without pulp between seeds; October.

WOOD. Rich, bright brown tinged with red, heavy, very hard, strong, coarse grained; used for rough construction, fence posts.

HABITAT AND RANGE. Floodplain forests from South Carolina to central Florida, west to Texas, north to southern Illinois.

PROPAGATION. Seed, soak in concentrated sulfuric acid for 1–2 hours, rinse thoroughly with water, then sow promptly.

WILDLIFE VALUE. Fruit is good for squirrel, rabbit, and deer.

LANDSCAPE VALUE. Has potential as large tree for wet (flooded) sites. Zone 6.

BEST RECOGNIZABLE FEATURES. Short-branched thorns; wet sites; pinnate or/and bipinnately compound leaves; short legume pod containing up to 3 seeds.

Gleditsia triacanthos Linnaeus
honeylocust, sweet-locust, thorny-locust

PLATE 53

HABIT. Medium-sized to large tree, 60–80 ft. (18–24 m) tall, with a short bole, 6–20 ft. (2–6 m) tall, stout ascending limbs, spreading, pendulous branches, and rounded, flat crown.

BARK. Smooth and greenish to grayish brown, becoming dark brown to blackish, broken into long, narrow peeling, scaly ridges separated by deep furrows and curling from the trunk; thorns normally abundant, becoming less conspicuous with age.

Gleditsia triacanthos

TWIGS. Slender, reddish to greenish brown, lustrous, often mottled or streaked, smooth, zigzag, with enlarged nodes; thorns 2–4 in. (5–10 cm) long, straight branched, persistent, normally abundant except on the thornless *G. triacanthos* var. *inermis;* pith continuous, white.

BUDS. Terminal absent; laterals very small, sunken, grayish green, 1–5 per node, naked or with scales, smooth, superposed, may be covered by the leaf scar.

LEAVES. Pinnately and doubly pinnately compound, often on the same

Figure 345. *Gleditsia triacanthos* foliage, pinnately compound

Figure 346. *Gleditsia triacanthos* foliage, bipinnately compound

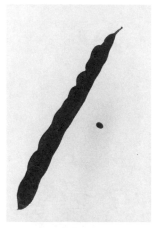

Figure 347. *Gleditsia triacanthos* fruit and seed

Figure 348. *Gleditsia triacanthos* twig

Figure 349. *Gleditsia triacanthos* bark, small tree

Figure 350. *Gleditsia triacanthos* thorns

Figure 351. *Gleditsia triacanthos* bark, medium-sized tree

leaf, 6–10 in. (15–25 cm) long, dark green above, yellowish green below; leaflets oblong-lanceolate ½–1½ in. (1.3–4 cm) long; fall color yellow.
FLOWERS. In a raceme 2–3 in. (5–8 cm) long; greenish, fragrant; May.
FRUIT. Leathery pod; 8–15 in. (20–38 cm) long; reddish brown, black, or dark purple; straplike, twisted; with 6–12 brown, flattened, hard seeds surrounded by pulp; September to October.
WOOD. Reddish brown, heavy, strong, durable, coarse grained; used for fence posts, fuel, rough construction.
HABITAT AND RANGE. Moist to dry sites, especially common on limestone soils, from Pennsylvania to southeastern South Dakota, south to eastern Texas, east to Alabama.
PROPAGATION. Seed, scarify by soaking in sulfuric acid 1 hour and rinsing thoroughly with water, or by mechanically filing the seed coat to allow water inside; no stratification needed.
WILDLIFE VALUE. Fruit is good for bobwhite quail, rabbit, squirrel, small mammals, and deer; young stems are browsed by rabbit; flowers are visited by bees.
LANDSCAPE VALUE. Nice form and foliage but overplanted partly as a replacement for dead American elm. Landscape diversity should be sought whenever possible to avoid future disasters similar to the death of American elms. The typical thorned honeylocust has beautiful, light texture but nasty thorns; however, many thornless varieties have been chosen based on form and leaf color. The cultivars 'Halka', 'Imperial', 'Moraine', 'Shademaster', and 'Skyline' are good choices for urban plantings. Zones 3–9.
BEST RECOGNIZABLE FEATURES. Pinnately and bipinnately compound leaves; 3-branched thorn; large legume pod; platy rough bark.

Gymnocladus–coffeetree
CAESALPINIACEAE—caesalpinia family

Gymnocladus dioicus (Linnaeus) K. Koch
Kentucky coffeetree, coffeetree

HABIT. Medium-sized to large tree, 50–100 ft. (15–31 m) tall, with "dead" appearance in the deciduous condition, and a narrow, rounded crown; bole short in the open, long in the forest.

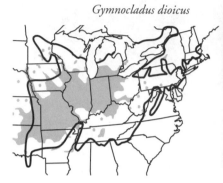

Gymnocladus dioicus

BARK. Gray to gray-brown with scaly ridges that curl away on one edge from the bole; inner bark red-orange.

TWIGS. Very stout, often contorted, grayish brown often with a mottled appearance; leaf scars large, irregularly heart shaped, with 3–5 raised bundle scars; pith salmon-pink and large.

BUDS. Terminal absent; laterals ⅛–¼ in. (3–6 mm) round, partially sunken, bronze; downy, surrounded by incurved hairy rim of bark, occasionally 2 superposed buds; scales indistinct.

LEAVES. Bipinnately compound except at the base of the main rachis where pinnately compound, 1–3 ft. (0.3–1 m) long, dull green and smooth above and below; leaflets 1–3 in. (2.5–8 cm) long, ovate, glabrous; fall color yellow.

FLOWERS. White to purplish, in large panicles, dioecious; late May to early June.

Figure 352. *Gymnocladus dioicus* foliage

Figure 353. *Gymnocladus dioicus* fruit

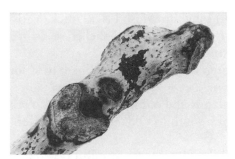

Figure 354. *Gymnocladus dioicus* twig and buds

Figure 355. *Gymnocladus dioicus* form, winter

Figure 356. *Gymnocladus dioicus* bark, small tree

Figure 357. *Gymnocladus dioicus* bark, medium-sized tree

Figure 358. *Gymnocladus dioicus* bark, large tree

FRUIT. Length 4–10 in. (10–25 cm) long, brownish black, thick, leathery pod with 3–5 blackish, ¾ in. (19 mm) long, hard-shelled seeds in a sweet, sticky, pulp; October, persisting through winter.

WOOD. Reddish brown, heavy, strong, durable, coarse grained; used for fence posts, fuel, rough construction.

HABITAT AND RANGE. Rich bottomlands and old fields from New York and Pennsylvania west to Minnesota, south to Oklahoma, east to Kentucky and Tennessee.

PROPAGATION. Seed, scarify by soaking 60 minutes in sulfuric acid and rinsing thoroughly with water, or by mechanically filing the seed coat, or by soaking seed in hot water.

WILDLIFE VALUE. Little wildlife value, although deer eat the fruit and the tree provides nesting and hiding places.

LANDSCAPE VALUE. Handsome shade tree with a unique coarse appearance and unusual bark, particularly interesting in the winter; can become messy in autumn and root suckers freely; grows under wide range of soil conditions. Zones 3–8.

BEST RECOGNIZABLE FEATURES. Large bipinnately compound leaves; persistent leathery fruit pods; coarse, "dead" appearance in winter; large orange pith; stout stems.

Halesia—silverbell
STYRACACEAE—snowbell family

Halesia carolina Linnaeus
Carolina silverbell, snowdrop-tree

PLATE 54

HABIT. Small tree, 20–40 ft. (6–12 m) tall, with a short trunk divided near ground level into several stems.

BARK. Reddish brown with distinctive chalky-white streaks, slightly ridged, separating into thin, closely appressed scales.

TWIGS. Slender, somewhat zigzag, densely hairy initially, becoming nearly glabrous, orange-brown to reddish brown; stem becoming stringy after

Halesia carolina

Figure 359. *Halesia carolina* foliage

Figure 360. *Halesia carolina* flowers

Figure 361. *Halesia carolina* fruit

Figure 362. *Halesia carolina* bark, small stem

Figure 363. *Halesia carolina* bark, medium-sized tree

first year; leaf scars heart shaped with single bundle scar; pith white, chambered or spongy.

BUDS. Terminal absent; laterals ⅛ in. (3 mm) long, ovoid, with 2–4 broad, red, pointed, hairy scales, often superposed and slightly stalked.

LEAVES. Alternate, 2–4 in. (5–10 cm) long, ovate to elliptic, dark green and glabrous above, pubescent below; margin finely serrate; fall color yellow.

FLOWERS. White (rarely pinkish white) bell shaped; ½ in. (13 mm) long, in small clusters along 1-year-old growth; early spring.

FRUIT. Length 1½ in. (4 cm); oblong, 4-winged; green changing to brown; maturing in late summer, persisting through autumn.

WOOD. Light brown, light, soft, close grained.

HABITAT AND RANGE. Wooded slopes and streambanks from West Virginia to Florida west to eastern Texas.

PROPAGATION. Seed, stratify 120 days at 75°F (24°C), then 90 days at 33°F (1°C).

WILDLIFE VALUE. Little wildlife value except to provide a nesting or hiding place.

LANDSCAPE VALUE. Surprisingly underused given its beautiful white flowers, nice habit, and form; grows best on rich, moist, well-drained sites. Zones 4–8.

BEST RECOGNIZABLE FEATURES. White, bell-shaped flowers; chambered pith; woody, 4-winged fruit.

Hamamelis—witch-hazel
HAMAMELIDACEAE—witch-hazel family

Hamamelis virginiana Linnaeus   PLATE 55
witch-hazel

HABIT. Small tree or more frequently a large shrub, 15–30 ft. (5–9 m) tall, with a spreading, irregular crown.

BARK. Light brown to dark gray, thin, mottled; inner bark purplish.

TWIGS. Slender, yellowish brown to gray with brownish or rusty pubescence on new growth, becoming smooth, zigzag; pith pale green, continuous.

BUDS. Terminal ¼–½ in. (6–13 mm) long, yellow-brown, pubescent, naked, long, slender; laterals smaller, stalked; flower buds globose, curved.

LEAVES. Alternate, 4–6 in. (10–15 cm) long, ovate to elliptic, dark green above, pale and hairy below; margin wavy; fall color yellow.

FLOWERS. Yellow; straplike petals and sepals; October to November.

FRUIT. Length ¼ in. (6 mm); brown, woody, 2-seeded capsule; explosively ejects shiny black seeds in the summer after flowering the previous autumn.

WOOD. Light brown, heavy, hard, close grained; commercially unimportant.

Hamamelis virginiana

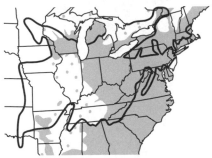

HABITAT AND RANGE. A variety of sites from southern Quebec to Minnesota, south to Missouri, east to northern Georgia.

PROPAGATION. Seed (difficult and germination rate is low), stratify 60 days at 68/86°F (20/30°C) night/day, then 90 days at 41°F (5°C).

WILDLIFE VALUE. Foliage and stems are browsed by deer.

Figure 364. *Hamamelis virginiana* foliage

Figure 365. *Hamamelis virginiana* flowers

Figure 366. *Hamamelis virginiana* fruit and seed

Figure 367. *Hamamelis virginiana* twig and buds

Figure 368. *Hamamelis virginiana* bark, various size stems

LANDSCAPE VALUE. Interesting large shrub that flowers during an otherwise bleak period in the landscape; grows in very dry soils. Zones 3–8. BEST RECOGNIZABLE FEATURES. Leaf with wavy-toothed margin; yellow fall flower with 4 straplike petals; fruit a persistent, woody pod; multistemmed shrub or small tree.

Ilex—holly
AQUIFOLIACEAE—holly family

Key to *Ilex*

1. Leaves evergreen, margin tipped with very sharp prickles .... *Ilex opaca*
1. Leaves deciduous, margin lacking prickles 2
2(1). Main leaf veins visible on underside of leaf; buds generally globose .... *Ilex verticillata*
2. Main leaf veins not visible on underside of leaf; buds generally pointed 3
3(2). Largest leaves ≥ 4 in. (10 cm) long, apex of leaf long pointed . ... *Ilex montana*
3. Largest leaves < 4 in. (10 cm) long, apex of leaf short pointed 4
4(3). Leaf margin typically undulate .... *Ilex decidua*
4. Leaf margin basically flat .... *Ilex ambigua*

Ilex ambigua (Michaux) Torrey
Carolina holly, sand holly

HABIT. Large shrub or sometimes a
small tree, to 20 ft. (6 m) tall.
BARK. Smooth to scaly, dark brown to
blackish.
TWIGS. Slender, dark reddish brown,
glabrous to very hairy.
BUDS. Sharp pointed; scales keeled.
LEAVES. Alternate, simple, 1–4 in.
(2.5–10 cm) long, elliptic or lanceolate, dull green above, pale below; apex
pointed; base tapering or rounded;
margin finely crenate.

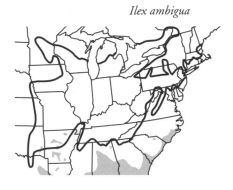

Ilex ambigua

FLOWERS. White, ¼ in. (6 mm) in diameter; dioecious.
FRUIT. Berrylike, ¼ in. (6 mm) in diameter, elliptic to subglobose, red at
maturity; seeds, 4 per fruit, deeply furrowed.
HABITAT AND RANGE. Moist, well-drained soils of upland forests from
North Carolina to central Florida, west to eastern Texas and southeast-
ern Oklahoma.
PROPAGATION. Seed, store in moist medium 90–150 days at 68/86°F
(20/30°C) night/day, then 90 days at 33–41°F (1–5°C).
WILDLIFE VALUE. Fruit attracts birds.
LANDSCAPE VALUE. Attractive small tree for dry sites.
BEST RECOGNIZABLE FEATURES. Leaf apex pointed but not long tapering;
elliptic, red fruit; absent from mountains of region.

Ilex decidua Walter
PLATE 56
possumhaw, winterberry, swamp holly, deciduous holly

HABIT. Small, low-branching tree or tall
shrub, 20–30 ft. (6–9 m) tall, with several stems and an irregular, open crown.
BARK. Light brown to gray, smooth or
somewhat warty.
TWIGS. Slender, silvery-gray, smooth or
slightly hairy; spur shoots common;
leaf scars small with single bundle scar.
BUDS. Small, ⅟32–⅟16 in. (1–2 mm) long,
light gray, rounded, with ovate scales.

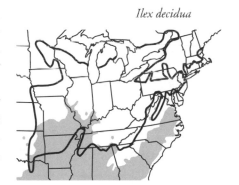

Ilex decidua

Figure 369. *Ilex decidua* foliage

Figure 370.
Ilex decidua
bark, small
stem

Figure 371. *Ilex decidua* bark, large stem

LEAVES. Alternate, but may appear whorled on spur shoots, 1½–3 in. (4–8 cm) long, obovate to obovate-oblong, shiny green above, dull and lightly hairy below; margin with rounded teeth.

FLOWERS. Green to white; ½ in. (13 mm) wide; 5 petals; dioecious; March to May.

FRUIT. Drupe, ¼ in. (6 mm) in diameter, red or reddish orange; 1–3 per spur shoot; persistent, nutlets ribbed only on back; September to October.

WOOD. Creamy white, heavy, hard, close grained; commercially unimportant.

HABITAT AND RANGE. Bottomlands from Maryland west to eastern Kansas, south to Texas, east to Florida.

PROPAGATION. Seed, stratify 90–150 days at 68/86°F (20/30°C) night/day, then 60–120 days at 33–41°F (1–5°C); cuttings are also effective.

WILDLIFE VALUE. Fruit is excellent for songbirds, bobwhite quail, wild turkey, and mice; browse is good for deer.

LANDSCAPE VALUE. Good small tree to attract wildlife; especially suited for wet sites. Numerous varieties available, selected for beautiful fruit display. Zones 5–9.

BEST RECOGNIZABLE FEATURES. Bright red fruit through the winter; deciduous; wet sites.

Ilex montana Torrey & Gray
mountain winterberry, mountain holly

PLATE 57

Ilex montana

HABIT. Shrub or small tree, to 30 ft. (9 m) tall.

BARK. Thin, light brown to gray, roughened by numerous lenticels.

TWIGS. Slender, olive green to reddish brown, glabrous, enlarged at the nodes.

BUDS. Length ⅛ in. (3 mm), broad-ovoid, light brown, appressed, keeled, sharp pointed, with finely hairy scales.

LEAVES. Deciduous, 2–5 in. (5–13 cm) long, ½–2½ in. (1.3–6 cm) wide, elliptic-ovate, light green above, pale below, with prominent midrib and veins (unlike possumhaw) and marginal, glandular, incurved teeth; fall color yellow.

FRUIT. Nutlet, ½ in. (13 mm) in diameter; bright scarlet; narrowed at the ends, prominently ribbed on the back and sides.

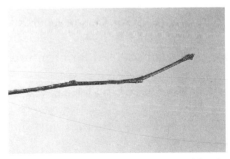

Figure 372. *Ilex montana* twig and buds

Figure 373. *Ilex montana* bark, small stem

WOOD. Creamy white, heavy, hard, close grained; commercially unimportant.

HABITAT AND RANGE. Moist woods from southern New England south in the Appalachian Mountains to Georgia and Alabama.

PROPAGATION. Softwood cuttings.

WILDLIFE VALUE. Fruit is excellent for grouse, songbirds, squirrel, small rodents, and raccoon; browse is good for deer.

LANDSCAPE VALUE. Excellent small tree to attract wildlife; for rich, moist, well-drained sites. Zone 5.

BEST RECOGNIZABLE FEATURES. Bright red fruit throughout winter; deciduous; mesic forests in mountains.

Ilex opaca Aiton
American holly, holly

PLATE 58

HABIT. Medium-sized tree, 30–50 ft. (9–15 m) tall; pyramidal in the open, irregular in the forest.

BARK. Gray, thin, smooth or with small, wartlike projections.

TWIGS. Stout, light brown with small lenticels, smooth; pith continuous.

BUDS. Length 1/32–1/16 in. (1–2 mm); gray, downy, with 2–4 scales.

LEAVES. Evergreen, 2–4 in. (5–10 cm) long, elliptic to elliptic-lanceolate, dark green and shiny above, pale green below, thick, leathery, with large spine-tipped teeth.

Ilex opaca

FLOWERS. Small, greenish white, dioecious; May to June.

FRUIT. Drupe, 1/4 in. (6 mm) in diameter, dull red; late October, persisting through winter.

WOOD. White to pale brown, weak, close grained; used for furniture, cabinets, novelties.

HABITAT AND RANGE. Moist sites from Massachusetts to Florida, west to Texas, north to Missouri.

PROPAGATION. Seed, difficult; cuttings, from female trees (for fruit) and treat with a hormone dip.

WILDLIFE VALUE. Fruit is good for songbirds, bobwhite quail, and wild turkey, but is toxic to some species.

LANDSCAPE VALUE. Attractive year round, particularly in winter when red fruit is evident (female trees only) against dense, leathery, evergreen

Figure 374. *Ilex opaca* foliage, immature fruit

Figure 375. *Ilex opaca* mature fruit

Figure 376. *Ilex opaca* bark, small stems

Figure 377. *Ilex opaca* bark, medium-sized tree

Figure 378. *Ilex opaca* bark, large tree

foliage; tolerates shade well. Hundreds of varieties have been named; many are superior in ornamental attributes compared to the species. Zones 5–9.

BEST RECOGNIZABLE FEATURES. Evergreen, prickly foliage; bright red fruit throughout winter; relatively smooth, dull gray bark.

Ilex verticillata (Linnaeus) Gray
winterberry, black-alder

PLATE 59

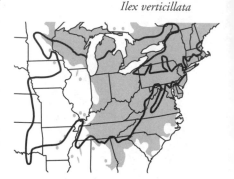

Ilex verticillata

HABIT. Large thicket-forming shrub of twisted main stems supporting many fine twigs and forming a rounded top; occasionally a slender, small tree, to 12 ft. (4 m) tall.

BARK. Thin, smooth, greenish gray becoming dark gray and roughened.

TWIGS. Very slender, olive brown to purplish brown, lenticellate, usually glabrous; leaf scars very small, half-elliptic, with 2 small blackish projections on either side; pith white and appearing chambered.

BUDS. Length ¹⁄₁₆ in. (2 mm), globose, brown, with overlapping scales, superposed.

LEAVES. Alternate, simple, 1½–3 in. (4–8 cm) long, elliptic to oblanceolate, leathery (especially when out in full sun), dark green above; apex sharp pointed; base wedge shaped; margin serrate or doubly serrate; veins pubescent below; petiole purplish.

FLOWERS. Dioecious; very small but in clusters of 6 or more for males, fewer in cluster for females.

FRUIT. Bright red drupe, ¼ in. (6 mm) in diameter, ripening in late summer, persisting into winter.

HABITAT AND RANGE. Swamps from Nova Scotia to western Ontario, west to Wisconsin, south to Florida, and west to Missouri.

PROPAGATION. Seed (difficult), stratify in moist medium 90 days at 41°F (5°C); softwood cuttings root easily with a hormone dip.

WILDLIFE VALUE. Fruit is eaten by many birds, including brown thrasher, robin, mockingbird, catbird, and bluebird; twigs, leaves, and fruit are occasionally eaten by whitetail deer.

LANDSCAPE VALUE. Female specimens in fruit are outstanding in autumn and winter, but should be planted in wet to moist soils for success; need at least one male plant nearby to pollinate females. Zones 3–9.

Figure 379. *Ilex verticillata* foliage and fruit

Figure 381. *Ilex verticillata* bark, medium-sized stem

Figure 380. *Ilex verticillata* twig and buds

BEST RECOGNIZABLE FEATURES. Very slender twigs; very small buds; often thicket-forming; bright red fruit; wet soils.

Juglans—walnut
JUGLANDACEAE—walnut family

Key to *Juglans*

1.   Terminal leaflet typically present; rachis sticky tomentose; fruit ellipsoidal and sticky; thick pubescence above leaf scar; pith dark colored; bark ash-gray . . . . *Juglans cinerea*

1.   Terminal leaflet often absent; rachis sparingly pubescent and not sticky; fruit round and not sticky; area above leaf scars glabrous; pith light colored; bark brown . . . . *Juglans nigra*

Juglans cinerea Linnaeus
butternut, white walnut, oilnut

PLATE 60

HABIT. Medium-sized tree, 40–60 ft. (12–18 m) tall, with a short bole dividing into several ascending limbs that form a rounded, symmetrical crown.
BARK. Ash-gray, smooth when young becoming brownish gray with broad, flat ridges and deep furrows; ridges chocolate-colored when cut.
TWIGS. Stout, brown to grayish brown, hairy on new growth, bitter-tasting, and coloring saliva yellow; leaf scars 3-lobed with hairy upper cushion resembling a monkey's face; pith large, chambered, chocolate-brown.
BUDS. Terminal ½–¾ in. (13–19 mm) long; laterals ¼ in. (6 mm) long, superposed, grayish white, downy, conical.

Juglans cinerea

Figure 382. *Juglans cinerea* foliage

Figure 383. *Juglans cinerea* flowers

Figure 384. *Juglans cinerea* fruit and seed

Figure 385. *Juglans cinerea* twig and buds

Figure 386.
Juglans cinerea bark, small tree

Figure 387. *Juglans cinerea* bark, medium-sized tree

Figure 388. *Juglans cinerea* bark, large tree

LEAVES. Pinnately compound, 1–2½ ft. (0.3–0.8 m) long, green, hairy above and below, with 11–17 oblong-lanceolate leaflets 2–4 in. (5–10 cm) long; margin serrate; rachis hairy, sticky; terminal leaflet usually present; fall color yellow or brown.

FLOWERS. Monoecious; male flowers in aments, female flowers in spike of 2–8 flowers; late May to early June.

FRUIT. Nut, with a sharply corrugated 4-ribbed shell, 2 in. (5 cm) long, elliptic, yellowish green, leathery, thick, resinous; husk hairy, indehiscent; seed oily, sweet, edible.

WOOD. Pale brown, light, soft, coarse grained; used for furniture, interior finishing.

HABITAT AND RANGE. Bottomlands, moist uplands, old fields from New Brunswick to southern Ontario and southeastern Minnesota, south to northern Arkansas, east to northern Georgia and western South Carolina.

PROPAGATION. Seed, stratify 90–120 days at 33–41°F (1–5°C).

WILDLIFE VALUE. Seed is eaten by mice and squirrel.

LANDSCAPE VALUE. Messy tree, but worth maintaining where it naturally occurs. Thick, hard shell covers delicious seed. Zones 3–7.

BEST RECOGNIZABLE FEATURES. Plant parts with a distinct odor; compound leaf with stalked terminal leaflet and hairy rachis; corrugated, ellipsoid nut; light gray bark, chocolate-colored ridges when cut; dark brown chambered pith.

Juglans nigra Linnaeus
PLATES 61, 62
black walnut, eastern black walnut, American walnut

HABIT. Large tree, 70–100 ft. (21–31 m) tall, with a clear bole; bole long and crown narrow in the forest, bole short and crown spreading in the open.

BARK. Gray-brown becoming brownish black, deeply fissured with age, sharp or rounded ridges forming on larger trees; ridges chocolate-colored when cut.

TWIGS. Stout, gray and downy or reddish brown and smooth, with orange lenticels; bitter-tasting and coloring saliva yellow; leaf scars 3-lobed, without hairy upper cushion as in butternut; pith buff-brown, chambered.

BUDS. Terminal ⅓ in. (8 mm) long (shorter than *J. cinerea*); laterals ¼ in. (6 mm) long, grayish white, hairy, often superposed.

LEAVES. Pinnately compound, 1–2 ft. (0.3–0.6 m) long, green and hairy above and below, with an odor, with 15–25 ovate-oblong to ovate-lanceolate leaflets 3–3½ in. (8–9 cm) long; margin serrate; rachis relatively

Figure 389. *Juglans nigra* foliage

Figure 390. *Juglans nigra* fruit and seed

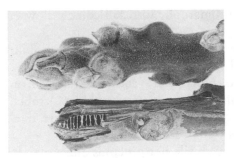

Figure 391. *Juglans nigra* twigs and buds

Figure 392. *Juglans nigra* bole

Figure 393. *Juglans nigra* bark, small tree

Figure 394. *Juglans nigra* bark, medium-sized tree

Figure 395. *Juglans nigra* bark, large tree

glabrous; terminal leaflet often prematurely lost; fall color yellow or brown.

FLOWERS. Monoecious; male flowers in aments, female flowers in spike of 2–8 flowers; late May to early June.

FRUIT. Nut, 1½–2½ in. (4–6 cm) in diameter, yellowish green, corrugated, globular; husk thick, succulent; seed oily, sweet, edible; October.

WOOD. Dark brown, heavy, hard, coarse grained; used for furniture, interior finishing, cabinets, gunstocks.

HABITAT AND RANGE. Deep, moist, fertile bottomlands and uplands, roadsides, old fields from Massachusetts to southern Minnesota and southeastern South Dakota, south to eastern Texas, east to northwestern Florida and Georgia.

PROPAGATION. Seed, stratify 90–120 days at 33–41°F (1–5°C).

WILDLIFE VALUE. Seed is eaten by squirrel and mice.

LANDSCAPE VALUE. Best left in the woods or plantations, because it is very messy (rachis, leaflets, nuts). Wood has exceptional economic value. Zones 4–9.

BEST RECOGNIZABLE FEATURES. Plant parts with a distinct odor; corrugated globose nut; terminal leaflet poorly developed or absent, rachis smooth; dark brown, deeply furrowed bark, chocolate-colored ridges when cut; light brown chambered pith.

Other walnuts commonly planted in the regional landscape:

Juglans regia Linnaeus, English or Persian walnut. Low-branching tree to 60 ft. (18 m) with very broad crown; resembles butternut but has fewer leaflets (5–9), margin of leaflet is entire, plant parts are not resinous-sticky, and pith is brown. Generally planted as a fruit tree. Varieties have been selected for thinner shells and greater cold tolerance. This is the walnut that is widely available in food stores, especially through the winter. It is also an attractive shade tree, having more refined characteristics than native walnuts. Native from southeastern Europe to the Himalayas and China. Zone 5.

Figure 396. *Juglans regia* foliage

Juniperus—juniper
CUPRESSACEAE—cypress family

Juniperus virginiana Linnaeus
eastern redcedar, red juniper, savin

PLATE 63

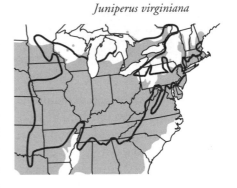

Juniperus virginiana

HABIT. Medium-sized tree, 40–50 ft. (12–15 m) tall, with a dense crown; oval or pyramidal when young, becoming rounded with age.

BARK. Tan to reddish brown, thin, fibrous, shreddy.

LEAVES. Bluish green to yellow-brown, aromatic, paired on a 4-angled stem; dimorphic with scalelike (adult foliage), ¹⁄₁₆ in. (2 mm) long, triangular, and needlelike (juvenile foliage), ⅛–¾ in. (3–19 mm) long, in pairs.

FRUIT. Cone ¼–⅓ in. (6–8 mm) in diameter, ripening the first year, bluish with a whitish bloom, berrylike, containing 1 or 2 seeds; flesh sweet, resinous, with odor of gin; usually dioecious.

WOOD. Pink-red, light, durable, fragrant, close grained; used for furniture, fence posts, fuel, interior paneling.

HABITAT AND RANGE. Old fields, dry shallow soils, and cliffs from New Brunswick west to North Dakota, south to Texas, east to Florida.

Figure 397. *Juniperus virginiana* foliage and fruit

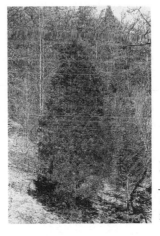

Figure 398. *Juniperus virginiana* form

Figure 399. *Juniperus virginiana* bark, medium-sized tree

Figure 400. *Juniperus virginiana* bark, large tree

PROPAGATION. Seed, requires 2 years before germination; cuttings effective.
WILDLIFE VALUE. Seed is good for songbirds and mice; browse is good for deer; tree provides good cover for deer and rabbit.
LANDSCAPE VALUE. Tolerates terrible sites as long as they are sunny and not wet. Beautiful in mass plantings. Numerous varieties available, selected for form, foliage, color, and fruit display. Zones 2–9.
BEST RECOGNIZABLE FEATURES. Dimorphic foliage (awl shaped, scale-like); glaucous, bluish berrylike cone; reddish brown, fibrous bark; fragrant, reddish heartwood.

Other junipers and "cedars" commonly planted in the regional landscape:
Juniperus chinensis Linnaeus, Chinese juniper. Numerous varieties, differing mostly by form (many are shrubs) and foliage color, are common in home and urban landscapes. Juvenile foliage generally in whorls of 3 (or in opposite pairs). Zones 3–7.
Juniperus scopulorum Sargent, Rocky Mountain juniper. Numerous varieties, differing mostly by form (many are shrubs) and foliage color, are common in home and urban landscapes. Seed ripens in second year. Zones 3–7.
Chamaecyparis thyoides (Linnaeus) Britton, Sterns, & Poggenburg, Atlantic white-cedar. Evergreen tree to 50–90 ft. (15–27 m) tall, occurring in wet soils along the coast from Maine to Florida and Mississippi; foliage bluish green, scaly with whitish *x*s on the undersurface; bark shreddy and thin; cones tiny, ¼ in. (6 mm) in diameter, with 6 scales; wood is very durable. Attractive tree that would do well in the wettest of soils. A few varieties have been selected based on more compact form. Widely planted as an ornamental. Zones 3–8.

Figure 401.
*Juniperus
chinensis*
foliage

Figure 402. *Chamaecyparis
thyoides* foliage

Kalmia—mountain-laurel
ERICACEAE—heath family

Kalmia latifolia Linnaeus
mountain-laurel, laurel

PLATE 64

HABIT. Generally a shrub, forming impenetrable thickets; occasionally a small tree, reaching 30 ft. (9 m) tall; consisting of twisted large branches forming a round topped, compact head.

BARK. Thin, papery, long dark brown scales tinged in red.

TWIGS. Slender, glabrous, green tinged with red to reddish brown, very shiny; leaf scars half-round to shield shaped, with single bundle scar; pith homogenous, green or brown.

Kalmia latifolia

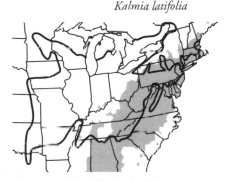

BUDS. Flower buds to 1 in. (2.5 cm) long, clustered at tips of twigs, covered with glandular white hairs; leaf buds ovate, acute, small, with 2 green outer scales.

LEAVES. Alternate or sometimes in groups of 2 or 3, simple, 3–4 in. (8–10 cm) long, oblong, thick, leathery, dull dark green above, light yellow-green below; apex acute, often sharp pointed; base wedge shaped; margin

Figure 403. *Kalmia latifolia* foliage

Figure 405. *Kalmia latifolia* bark, large stem

Figure 404. *Kalmia latifolia* fruit and foliage

entire; petiole stout, ½ in. (13 mm) long; leaves begin to fall in their second season.

FLOWERS. Wheel shaped or saucerlike, white, rose or deep pink, about 1 in. (2.5 cm) in diameter, in large open cluster; opening early April in South to late June in North.

FRUIT. Capsule, ¼ in. (6 mm) in diameter, 5-celled, globular, crowned with persistent style, persisting into following year; seeds minute, oblong, light brown.

WOOD. Brown tinged with red, heavy, hard, strong, rather brittle, close grained; burls are used to make pipes.

HABITAT AND RANGE. Hillsides and mountain slopes, often in impenetrable thickets in the open or forming dense understory in deciduous forests, from New Brunswick to northern shores of Lake Erie, south through New England, the Appalachian Mountains, the Piedmont plateau, and adjacent areas to western Florida and Louisiana.

PROPAGATION. Seed, sow on peat under lights; cuttings, very difficult to root.

WILDLIFE VALUE. Tree provides excellent cover for grouse and turkey; leaves are eaten by whitetail deer but are poisonous to livestock and people.

LANDSCAPE VALUE. Beautiful plant year round; requires acidic, moist, well-drained, cool (well-mulched) soil; well worth pampering. Varieties vary mostly in flower color (e.g., deeper shades of pink to near red, at least in bud). Zones 4–9.

BEST RECOGNIZABLE FEATURES. Evergreen, leathery leaves; round white or pinkish flowers in clusters; typically forms dense stands.

Larix—larch
PINACEAE—pine family

Larix laricina (Du Roi) K. Koch
eastern larch, American larch, tamarack

Larix laricina

HABIT. Medium-sized tree, 40–80 ft. (12–24 m) tall, with a straight bole and an open crown.

BARK. Thin, scaly, reddish brown to grayish brown.

TWIGS. Stout, reddish brown, with many small spur shoots each with spirally arranged needle scars in winter.

BUDS. Small, globose, with loose scales.

LEAVES. Clustered spirally in spur shoots, or alternately arranged at twig tips, 1–1½ in. (2.5–4 cm) long, 3-sided, light bluish green turning golden-yellow before falling in autumn.

FRUIT. Cone ½–1 in. (1.3–2.5 cm) long, red, turning brown with age, upright, without a stalk; scales rounded, stiff.

WOOD. Light brown, durable; used for framing, crossties, pulpwood.

HABITAT AND RANGE. Often in wet or saturated soils but may be found on drier sites, in New England, New York, and south of the Great Lakes.

PROPAGATION. Seed, stratify 30–60 days at 41°F (5°C), though much seed germinates without pretreatment.

WILDLIFE VALUE. Seed may be eaten by songbirds; foliage is browsed by deer.

LANDSCAPE VALUE. Nice texture and color in summer, outstanding late

Figure 406. *Larix laricina* foliage

Figure 407. *Larix laricina* cones and twig

Figure 408. *Larix laricina* bark, medium-sized tree

Figure 409. *Larix laricina* bark, large tree

fall color, tolerates wet soils. Well-suited for cold, poorly drained areas. Does not tolerate hot, dry conditions. Zones 1–5.

BEST RECOGNIZABLE FEATURES. Deciduous needles on spur shoots; tight scaly bark; open, conical crown; small, upright cones.

Other larches commonly planted in the regional landscape:
Larix decidua Miller, European larch. Medium-sized tree to 70 ft. (21 m) tall, with broadly pyramidal crown; needles to 1¼ in. (3 cm) long, light to deep green, turning yellow in autumn before falling; twigs yellowish or straw colored, having numerous spur shoots; cones upright, pubescent, ovoid, to 1½ in. (4 cm) long, with scales that extend straight out from axis at 45° angle. American larch has 22 cone scales or less per cone, while European larch has 40 to 50 cone scales. Widely planted in northeastern United States for reforestation purposes and naturalizing. Native to northern and central Europe. Zones 2–6.

Figure 410. *Larix decidua* cones

Larix kaempferi (Lambert) Carrière, Japanese larch. Similar to European larch except that it has reddish brown twigs, blue-green to glaucous needles that are wider, and shorter, broader cones with strongly reflexed scales that give the cone the appearance of an open rose. Native to Japan. Zones 4–7.

Liquidambar—sweetgum
HAMAMELIDACEAE—witch-hazel family

Liquidambar styraciflua Linnaeus
PLATE 65
sweetgum, redgum

HABIT. Large tree, 80–150 ft. (24–46 m) tall, with a clear bole and pyramidal crown on good sites; appearing rougher on poor sites.

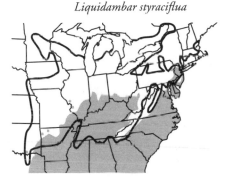

Liquidambar styraciflua

BARK. Gray to brown, deeply furrowed with long, narrow, flattened ridges.
TWIGS. Slender to moderate, reddish or yellowish brown becoming gray, aromatic, rounded or slightly angled, often with corky wings on second-year's growth, often short and spurlike; leaf scars with 3 distinct bundle scars; pith white or brown, solid, angled or star shaped.
BUDS. Terminal ¼–½ in. (6–13 mm) long, ovate to conical, reddish to yellowish brown, pointed, slightly resinous, fragrant when crushed, with 6–9 visible scales; laterals divergent, smaller.

Figure 411. *Liquidambar styraciflua* foliage

Figure 412. *Liquidambar styraciflua* fruit

Figure 413. *Liquidambar styraciflua* twig and buds

Figure 414. *Liquidambar styraciflua* bark, small tree

Figure 415. *Liquidambar styraciflua* bark, medium-sized tree

Figure 416. *Liquidambar styraciflua* bark, large tree

LEAVES. Alternate, simple, 3–5 in. (8–13 cm) in diameter, light to dark green, aromatic when crushed, star shaped, 5- or 7-lobed; margin finely serrate; fall color yellow, red, or purple.

FLOWERS. Monoecious; both types in rounded flower structures; appearing as the leaves unfold in late April to May.

FRUIT. Aggregate of capsules, 1–1½ in. (2.5–4 cm) in diameter, brown, ball-like, each capsule sharp pointed (beaked); October and persisting through winter.

WOOD. Reddish brown, heavy, hard, strong, even grained; used for flooring, furniture, interior finish, veneer, cabinets.

HABITAT AND RANGE. A variety of sites but most frequently on bottomlands from Connecticut to southern Illinois, southwest to Texas, east to Florida.

PROPAGATION. Seed, stratify 30–90 days at 33–41°F (1–5°C), or soak in water 15–20 days.

WILDLIFE VALUE. Seed is good for wood duck, quail, squirrel, and small rodents.

LANDSCAPE VALUE. Very attractive, large shade tree with beautiful fall color; fruit messy; tree does not reach potential in colder portions of region. Many varieties available, selected for better foliage, especially fall color. Has excellent potential as wetland restoration species because of its great tolerance to flooded soils. Zones 5–9.

BEST RECOGNIZABLE FEATURES. Star shaped, palmately veined leaves; persistent, spiny, globular fruit; twig with corky wings; shiny greenish black buds; leaf scar with 3 distinct vascular bundle scars.

Liriodendron—yellow-poplar
MAGNOLIACEAE—magnolia family

Liriodendron tulipifera Linnaeus
PLATE 66

yellow-poplar, tuliptree, tulip-poplar

HABIT. Large tree, 100–200 ft. (31–61 m) tall; pyramidal in the forest with a long, clear bole and a broad, oblong crown, retaining lower branches in the open.

BARK. Gray, smooth with small, white, narrow patches when young, becoming streaked with narrow, irregular lines and deeply furrowed with age; inner bark bitter.

TWIGS. Moderately slender, greenish to reddish brown, often with a whitish bloom, aromatic and very bitter; stipule scars encircling twigs that appear jointed; pith diaphragmed, white.

BUDS. Terminal ½ in. (13 mm) long, greenish to reddish brown, flattened, white dotted, with 2 valvate scales; laterals alternate, smaller; buds resemble a "duck's bill."

Liriodendron tulipifera

LEAVES. Alternate, simple, 5–7 in. (13–18 cm) long, shiny green above, pale below, tuliplike shape, 4-lobed; stipules large, persistent; fall color yellow.

FLOWERS. Tuliplike, 2 in. (5 cm) in diameter; petals light green and orange; sepals greenish white; May to June.

Figure 417. *Liriodendron tulipifera* foliage

Figure 418. *Liriodendron tulipifera* foliage and flowers

Figure 419. *Liriodendron tulipifera* fruit

Figure 420. *Liriodendron tulipifera* twig and buds

Figure 421. *Lirio-dendron tulipifera* boles

Figure 422. *Lirio-dendron tulipifera* bark, small tree

Figure 423. *Lirio-dendron tulipifera* bark medium-sized tree

Figure 424. *Lirio-dendron tulipifera* bark, large tree

Figure 425. *Liriodendron tulipifera* bark, large tree

FRUIT. Conelike aggregate of winged seeds (samaras), 2–3 in. (5–8 cm) long, yellowish brown, upright; October, persisting into winter.

WOOD. Light yellow or brown heartwood, thin creamy-white sapwood, light, soft, even grained; used for furniture, construction, fence posts, veneer, trim.

HABITAT AND RANGE. Moist, cool sites from Vermont to Michigan south to Louisiana, east to Florida.

PROPAGATION. Seed, stratify 60–90 days at 33–41°F (1–5°C).

WILDLIFE VALUE. Little wildlife value except to provide nesting and hiding places; flowers are visited by bees.

LANDSCAPE VALUE. A more stately tree does not exist; should be planted in deep, rich, moist but well-drained soils; not recommended for urban conditions, other than large parks, nor for small homes. Zones 4–9.

BEST RECOGNIZABLE FEATURES. Tuliplike leaves and flowers; twigs with stipule scars (encircling twig) and "duck-bill" bud; fruit (aggregate of samaras) persisting through winter; longitudinally furrowed light brown bark; twigs and roots aromatic when crushed.

Maclura—Osage-orange
MORACEAE—mulberry family

Maclura pomifera (Rafinesque) Schneider
Osage-orange, bodark, hedge-apple

HABIT. Medium-sized tree, to 50 ft. (15 m) tall, with a short bole and a dense, round or irregular crown.

Maclura pomifera

BARK. Ash-brown or dark orange-brown on mature trees, becoming deeply furrowed with age; inner bark orange; exposed roots bright orange.

TWIGS. Moderately stout, circular to 3-sided, buff or orange-brown, color obvious at a distance, with stout, straight, axillary spines ½-in. (13-mm) long; spur shoots present; sap milky; pith continuous, pale, round.

BUDS. Terminal absent; laterals very small, globular, consisting of 4–5 light brown scales, depressed.

Figure 426. *Maclura pomifera* foliage

Figure 427. *Maclura pomifera* fruit

Figure 428. *Maclura pomifera* twigs and buds

Figure 429. *Maclura pomifera* bark, small tree

Figure 430. *Maclura pomifera* bark, medium-sized tree

Figure 431. *Maclura pomifera* bark, large tree

LEAVES. Alternate, simple, 3–5 in. (8–13 cm) long, ovate to oblong-lance-olate, smooth, shiny; margin entire; broken petiole exudes sap; fall color yellow.

FLOWERS. Dioecious, both sexes in rounded inflorescence; June.

FRUIT. Aggregation of drupes resembling a brain, 3–5 in. (8–13 cm) in diameter, yellowish green; exuding milky, bitter sap when bruised; dioecious; September.

WOOD. Orange when cut, becoming brown when dried, heavy, hard, flexible, durable, coarse grained; used for fence posts, bows, fuel, tool handles, railroad ties.

HABITAT AND RANGE. Bottomlands, old fields, roadsides, occurring naturally in northeastern Texas, southern Arkansas, and southern Oklahoma, now naturalized throughout eastern and southern United States.

PROPAGATION. Seed, stratify 30 days at 41°F (5°C).

WILDLIFE VALUE. Little wildlife value except to provide nesting and hiding places.

LANDSCAPE VALUE. Poor choice for residential planting due to large fruit and spiny branches, but few species make a better natural fencerow; tolerates very difficult sites (e.g., hot to cold, dry to wet). Some thornless varieties are available. Zones 4–9.

BEST RECOGNIZABLE FEATURES. Yellow-orange fibrous bark; twigs with spines and spurs; grapefruit-sized fruit that exudes milky sap when bruised; glossy leaf, broken petiole exudes milky sap.

Magnolia—magnolia
MAGNOLIACEAE—magnolia family

Key to *Magnolia*

1. Leaves < 10 in. (25 cm) long; bark ridged and furrowed; habit typically single stemmed .... *Magnolia acuminata*
1. Leaves ≥ 10 in. (25 cm) long; bark generally smooth; habit often multistemmed 2
2(1). Leaves tapered at base .... *Magnolia tripetala*
2. Leaves auriculate at base 3
3(2). Leaves to 18 in. (46 cm) long; buds glabrous and purple .....
.... *Magnolia fraseri*
3. Leaves ≥ 20 in. (51 cm) long; buds covered with white pubescence .... *Magnolia macrophylla*

Magnolia acuminata Linnaeus
cucumbertree, cucumber magnolia

PLATE 67

Magnolia acuminata

HABIT. Large tree, 70–80 ft. (21–24 m) tall, with buttressed base, clear, symmetrical bole, and a short, dense, pyramidal crown.

BARK. Dark brown, thin, narrow and scaly ridges separated by longitudinal fissures.

TWIGS. Moderately stout, reddish brown, spicy odor, bitter-tasting; stipule scars encircling twig (as in all magnolias); leaf scars U shaped; pith continuous, round, large.

BUDS. Length ½–1 in. (13–25 mm), greenish white, densely hairy, naked or covered with one keeled scale.

LEAVES. Alternate, simple, 6–10 in. (15–25 cm) long, elliptic to oblong-ovate, yellow-green, smooth above, smooth or hairy below; petiole 1½–2 in. (4–5 cm) long; fall color dull yellow or brown.

FLOWERS. Petals 2–3 in. (5–8 cm) long; greenish yellow; cup shaped; May.

FRUIT. Aggregate of follicles, 2–3 in. (5–8 cm) long, green (cucumber-like), becoming red at maturity; seeds scarlet-red, hanging by white threads from open follicles; August to September.

WOOD. Light yellow-brown, light, soft, close grained; used for cabinets, flooring, furniture.

HABITAT AND RANGE. Moist soils from New York through Illinois to eastern Oklahoma, east to Georgia.

Figure 432. *Magnolia acuminata* foliage

Figure 433. *Magnolia acuminata* flower

Figure 434. *Magnolia acuminata* fruit and seed

Figure 435. *Magnolia acuminata* twig and buds

Figure 436. *Magnolia acuminata* bark, small tree

Figure 437. *Magnolia acuminata* bark, medium-sized tree

Figure 438. *Magnolia acuminata* bark, large tree

PROPAGATION. Seed, stratify 90–150 days at 33–41°F (1–5°C).
WILDLIFE VALUE. Fruit has little wildlife value; browse is fair for deer.
LANDSCAPE VALUE. Large shade tree with coarse texture; best on rich, moist but well-drained sites. Zones 3–8.
BEST RECOGNIZABLE FEATURES. Aggregate fruit resembles cone, with bright red seeds; greenish white, hairy buds; eventually a large tree (other native magnolias half this size at maturity); scaly, ridged, dark brown bark (other native magnolias with smooth, gray bark).

Magnolia fraseri Walter

PLATE 68

Fraser magnolia, mountain magnolia, umbrella-tree

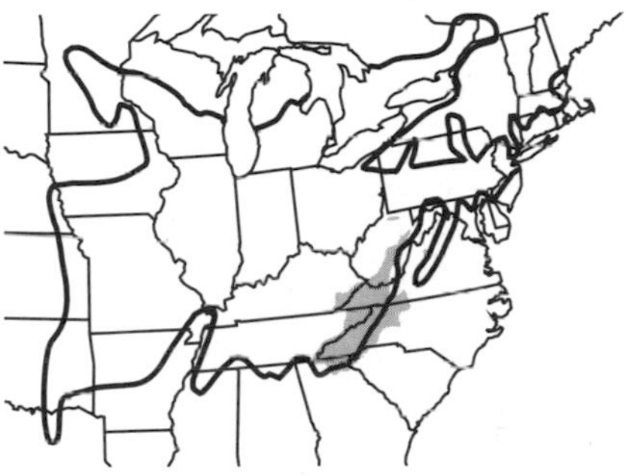

HABIT. Tree or large shrub, 30–40 ft. (9–12 m) tall, multistemmed or occasionally a single stem, with a short, spreading crown.
BARK. Light gray to dark brown, smooth becoming scaly with age, thin.
TWIGS. Stout, reddish brown with lenticels, swollen near the tip, brittle, spicy aromatic.
BUDS. Length ½–2 in. (1.3–5 cm), purple, smooth, tapered.

Magnolia fraseri

LEAVES. Alternate, simple, 10–18 in. (25–46 cm) long, oblong-obovate, bright green and smooth above, pale below; with earlike appendages at the base; petiole 2–4 in. (5–10 cm) long.
FLOWERS. Pale cream–yellow, 8–10 in. (20–25 cm) in diameter; aromatic, cup shaped; June.
FRUIT. Aggregate of follicles, 4–5 in. (10–13 cm) long, bright red, smooth, oblong; early autumn.
WOOD. Light brown, light, soft, weak, close grained; used for fuel.
HABITAT AND RANGE. Cool, moist sites on slopes and in coves in the Appalachian Mountains from Virginia and Kentucky south to Georgia and Alabama.
PROPAGATION. Seed, stratify 90–150 days at 33–41°F (1–5°C).
WILDLIFE VALUE. Little wildlife value except to provide nesting and hiding places.
LANDSCAPE VALUE. Coarse, tropical-looking tree that is suitable for large areas where soil is moist but well drained. Zones 5–8.
BEST RECOGNIZABLE FEATURES. Earlike base of leaves; smooth, purple buds; aggregate fruit; smooth, gray-brown bark.

Figure 439. *Magnolia fraseri* foliage

Figure 440. *Magnolia fraseri* fruit

Figure 441. *Magnolia fraseri* bark, small tree

Figure 442. *Magnolia fraseri* bark, large tree

Magnolia macrophylla Michaux   PLATE 69
bigleaf magnolia, silverleaf magnolia, umbrella-tree

HABIT. Tree or shrub, 30–40 ft. (9–12 m) tall, multistemmed and branching near the ground, with a round, open crown.

BARK. Gray, smooth or slightly scaly, thin.

TWIGS. Stout, gray to reddish brown, hairy on new growth, brittle, spicy aromatic.

BUDS. Length ½–2 in. (1.3–5 cm), white, densely hairy; terminal conical, blunt; laterals flattened.

LEAVES. Alternate, simple, 20–30 in. (0.5–0.8 m) long, oblong-obovate, shiny green above, white-hairy below; earlike lobes at the base.

FLOWERS. Creamy-white, 8–14 in. (20–36 cm) in diameter, fragrant; June.

FRUIT. Aggregate of follicles, 1½–3 in. (4–8 cm) long, bright rose-red, ovate.

WOOD. Light brown, close grained; used for fuel.

HABITAT AND RANGE. Moist sites in mountains, occasionally dry ridges, in scattered locations from Kentucky to Florida, west to Louisiana, north to Arkansas.

PROPAGATION. Seed, stratify 90–150 days at 33–41°F (1–5°C).

Magnolia macrophylla

WILDLIFE VALUE. Little wildlife value except to provide nesting and hiding places.

LANDSCAPE VALUE. Coarse, tropical-looking tree suitable for large areas where soil is moist but well drained. Zones 5–8.

Figure 443. *Magnolia macrophylla* foliage

Figure 444. *Magnolia macrophylla* fruit

Figure 445. *Magnolia macrophylla* twig and bud

Figure 446. *Magnolia macrophylla* bark, medium-sized tree

Figure 447. *Magnolia macrophylla* bark, large tree

BEST RECOGNIZABLE FEATURES. Earlike base of leaves; white, hairy buds; aggregate fruit; smooth, gray bark.

Magnolia tripetala Linnaeus
PLATE 70

umbrella magnolia, umbrella-tree, elkwood

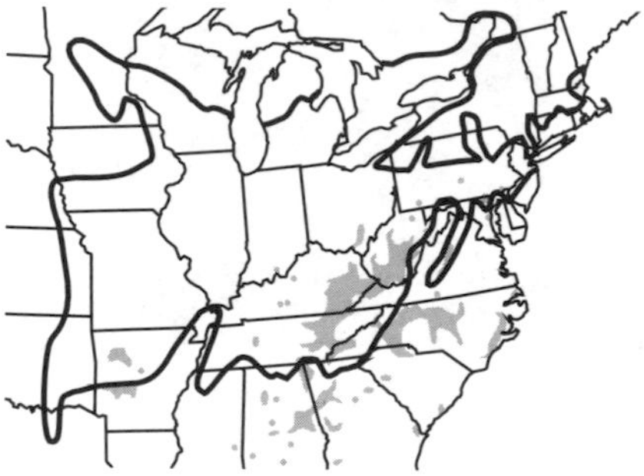

HABIT. Small tree or large shrub, 20–30 ft. (6–9 m) tall, multistemmed with stout ascending branches and a short, spreading crown.

Magnolia tripetala

BARK. Ash-gray, smooth with blister-like outgrowths, thin.

TWIGS. Stout, green becoming reddish brown with whitish bloom, smooth, spicy aromatic.

BUDS. Length ½–2 in. (1.3–5 cm), purplish with whitish bloom, glabrous, tapering, flattened.

LEAVES. Alternate, simple, 10–20 in. (25–51 cm) long, oblong-obovate, shiny green above, pale below, tapered at base, clustered at the twig tips to create "umbrella."

FLOWERS. Creamy white 7–10 in. (18–25 cm) wide, cup shaped; ill scented; May.

FRUIT. Aggregate of follicles, 2–4 in. (5–10 cm) long, rose colored at maturity, smooth.

WOOD. Light brown, light, soft, not strong, close grained; commercially unimportant.

Figure 448. *Magnolia tripetala* foliage

Figure 449. *Magnolia tripetala* fruit

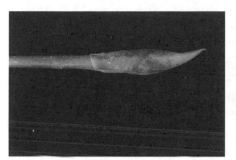

Figure 450. *Magnolia tripetala* twig and bud

Figure 451. *Magnolia tripetala* bark, small tree

Figure 452. *Magnolia tripetala* bark, large tree

HABITAT AND RANGE. Moist woodlands and streamsides in the coastal plain and Piedmont from Virginia to Georgia; infrequent in the Appalachian Mountains.

PROPAGATION. Seed, stratify 90–150 days at 33–41°F (1–5°C).

WILDLIFE VALUE. Little wildlife value except to provide nesting and hiding places.

LANDSCAPE VALUE. Coarse, tropical-looking tree suitable for large areas where soil is moist but well drained. Zones 5–8.

BEST RECOGNIZABLE FEATURES. Tapered base of leaves; glabrous, purple bud; aggregate fruit; smooth, ash-gray bark.

Other magnolias commonly planted in the regional landscape:

Magnolia grandiflora Linnaeus, southern magnolia. To 80 ft. (24 m) tall; without a doubt, the most beautiful magnolia native to the United States because of its deep, glossy dark green evergreen foliage (brownish red pubescence below) and large, to 8 in. (20 cm) wide, creamy white flowers. Unfortunately, this species is not very cold hardy, although some varieties will survive in Zone 6. Native to the southern United States, from North Carolina to Florida and Texas. Zones 7–9.

Magnolia ×soulangiana Soulange-Bodin, saucer magnolia. Hybrid of Asian species. Spectacular spring blooms and light green, rather small foliage compared to our native magnolias. Blooms very early each spring. Zones 4–9.

Magnolia stellata (Siebold & Zuccarini) Maximowicz, star magnolia. Spectacular spring blooms and light green, rather small foliage compared to our native magnolias. Native of Asia. Blooms very early each spring. Zones 4–8.

Magnolia virginiana Linnaeus, sweetbay. Large shrub to medium-sized,

Figure 453. *Magnolia grandiflora* foliage

Figure 454. *Magnolia grandiflora* flower

Figure 455. *Magnolia* ×*soulangiana* foliage

Figure 456. *Magnolia* ×*soulangiana* flowers

multistemmed tree to 40 ft. tall; broadly conical crown; bark thin, smooth, gray, aromatic and bitter; leaves semievergreen (tardily deciduous in more northern locations), 3–6 in. (8–15 cm) long, glossy green above and glaucous below, elliptic, leathery, aromatic; terminal buds covered with white silky hairs; flowers 2–3 in. (5–8 cm) in diameter, solitary, fragrant, 8–12 white petals, late spring to early summer; fruit conelike aggregate of follicles, 2 in. (5 cm) long, ellipsoid, yellowish to red, seeds shiny and red. Where hardy, a beautiful patio or specimen

Figure 457. *Magnolia stellata* foliage

Figure 458. *Magnolia stellata* flowers

Figure 459. *Magnolia virginiana* foliage

tree. Common in wet soils of swamps and flatwoods in coastal United States from Massachusetts to Florida and Texas. Zones 5–9.

Malus—apple
ROSACEAE—rose family

Key to *Malus*

1.	Leaves pubescent below	*Malus ioensis*
1.	Leaves glabrous below	2
2(1).	Leaves with rounded apex, tapered base ...	*Malus angustifolia*
2.	Leaves with pointed apex, rounded base	*Malus coronaria*

Malus angustifolia (Aiton) Michaux
southern crab apple, narrow-leaf crab, wild crab

HABIT. Thicket-forming large shrub or small tree, to 30 ft. (9 m) tall, with a short bole and spreading, rounded crown.
BARK. Thin, gray, scaly, with deep longitudinal fissures.
TWIGS. Slender to stout depending on growth rate, dark reddish brown, with pale orange lenticels, hairy when young; leaf scars slender with 3 bundle scars; stipule scars tiny; pith homogenous, slightly angled.

Malus angustifolia

BUDS. Small, rounded, with 4 loose, hairy outer scales.
LEAVES. Alternate, simple, 1–3 in. (2.5–8 cm) long, ½–1 in. (13–25 mm) wide, ovate to elliptic, dull green above; margin coarsely toothed; apex blunt; base tapered.
FLOWERS. Diameter 1 in. (2.5 cm); on slender stalks 1 in. (2.5 cm) long; 5 pink or white petals, in clusters; fragrant; April to May.
FRUIT. Pome, about 1½ in. (4 cm) in diameter, yellowish green, very sour apples; August to September.
WOOD. Dark brown, hard, heavy heartwood; commercially unimportant, but has been used for specialty items.

HABITAT AND RANGE. A variety of sites from Washington, D.C., south to northern Florida, west to Louisiana and Arkansas.

PROPAGATION. Seed, stratify 60–90 days at 41°F (5°C).

WILDLIFE VALUE. Fruit is excellent high-energy food for various birds and mammals; young stems may be heavily browsed by deer.

LANDSCAPE VALUE. Attractive native species susceptible to cedar-apple rust. Zone 5.

BEST RECOGNIZABLE FEATURES. Leaves with blunt apex, tapered base; gray, scaly bark; hairy, small buds; small apple fruit.

Malus coronaria (Linnaeus) Miller
sweet crab apple

HABIT. Small tree, to 30 ft. (9 m) tall, forming dense thickets, and with low branching into several stout, spreading branches.

Malus coronaria

BARK. Light gray to dark gray, becoming longitudinally fissured, the outer layers separating into long, narrow, persistent, red-brown scales.

TWIGS. Initially tomentose, bright red-brown, occasionally lenticellate, becoming glabrous and light gray, forming stout, spurlike lateral branches that often end in a spine; pith homogenous.

BUDS. Obtuse, with 3–6 bright red scales fringed with hairs.

LEAVES. Alternate, simple, 1½–3 in. (4–8 cm) long, ovate; margin serrate; apex pointed; base rounded; fall color yellow.

FLOWERS. White tinged with rose, 1½–2 in. (4–5 cm) in diameter, with 5 petals; fragrance like violet; pink in bud; early May.

FRUIT. Pome subglobose, yellow-green, about 1½ in. (4 cm) in diameter, very acidic, on slender pedicels 1½ in. (4 cm) long.

WOOD. Light red, heavy, not strong, close grained; used for levers, fuel, tool handles, specialty items.

HABITAT AND RANGE. Along woodland openings, roadsides, and fencerows from southern Ontario to New Jersey, south to Tennessee, west to Missouri.

PROPAGATION. Seed, stratify 60–90 days at 60–65°F (16–18°C), then 60–90 days at 40–45°F (4–7°C).

WILDLIFE VALUE. Fruit is excellent for grouse, mice, opossum, deer, and raccoon; browse is good for rabbit and deer.

LANDSCAPE VALUE. Attractive native species very susceptible to cedar-apple rust. Zone 4.

BEST RECOGNIZABLE FEATURES. Leaves with pointed apex, rounded base; some buds located near tip of spurlike branches; small, yellow-green applelike fruit; light gray bark, becoming flaky and darker with age.

Malus ioensis (Wood) Britton
prairie crab apple, wild crab apple, Iowa crab, prairie crab

HABIT. Large shrub to small rounded tree, to 20 ft. (6 m) tall, with stout spreading branches and widespreading crown.

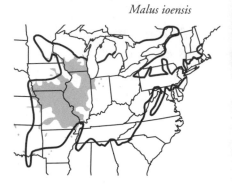

Malus ioensis

BARK. Covered with long, narrow, reddish brown, scaly ridges.

TWIGS. Initially densely hairy becoming glabrous, bright reddish brown; lateral branchlets often with spines; leaf scars narrow, curved, with 3 bundle scars; pith homogenous.

BUDS. Minute, broadly ovate, finely pubescent above middle; terminal present.

LEAVES. Alternate, simple, 2½–4 in. (6–10 cm) long, coarsely serrate, elliptic, often lobed, dark green, shiny, somewhat thickened, glabrous above, tomentose below; veins prominent; petiole slender, hairy; fall color yellow.

FLOWERS. Diameter 1–1½ in. (2.5–4 cm); 5 pink to white petals, fragrant, 3 or more flowers per cluster; sepals hairy on outside, pedicels hairy; appearing late compared to most crab apples.

FRUIT. Pome, less than 1½ in. (4 cm) in diameter, yellowish green, glaucous, hard, subglobose, long stalked, bitter.

WOOD. Light red, heavy, not strong, close grained; used for turned articles, tool handles.

HABITAT AND RANGE. Moist soils along streamsides, in prairie and forest edges.

PROPAGATION. Seed, stratify 60–90 days at 33–41°F (1–5°C); can be grafted onto various *Malus* understocks.

WILDLIFE VALUE. Fruit is excellent for grouse, mice, opossum, deer, and raccoon; browse is good for rabbit and deer.

LANDSCAPE VALUE. One of literally hundreds of crab apple species and cultivars, which is difficult to justify planting unless emphasis is on native species. Very susceptible to cedar-apple rust. Zone 2.

BEST RECOGNIZABLE FEATURES. Hairy stems; leaves hairy below; yellow-green, hard, bitter-tasting pome; hairy flower parts.

COMMENT. Bechtel crab apple (*M. ioensis* var. *plena*) can be distinguished from prairie crab apple by its rose-colored, double flowers. It is occasionally planted.

Other crab apples in the Central Hardwood Forests:

Malus bracteata Rehder, Buncombe crab. Small tree that occurs in openings or woodland edges in the center of the Central Hardwood Forests Region (i.e., Missouri, Kentucky, Tennessee, North Carolina, Georgia, and Alabama), but is not common. Leaves densely hairy below, but otherwise similar to southern crab.

Malus glabreata Rehder, Biltmore crab. Small tree that occurs in the southern Appalachian Mountains on deep, rich soils. Distinguished from the other crabs by its triangular leaves with a coarsely serrate margin, stout spines, and small, angled fruit 1–2 in. (2.5–5 cm) in diameter.

Malus glaucescens Rehder, Dunbar crab. Small tree of the southern Appalachian Mountains northward to Ohio and Pennsylvania. Similar to Biltmore crab, but leaf with white underside.

Malus lancifolia Rehder, lanceleaf crab. Leaves narrow, pointed, 2–4 in. (5–10 cm) long; fruit small, green. Similar to wild crab apple, except for pointed leaves. Scattered throughout the Central Hardwood Forests.

Other crab apples commonly planted in the regional landscape: Most are species and varieties of Asian *Malus*. In all, over 500 types exist, although "only" 100 to 200 are in the trade today. One should be cautious in selecting a crab apple because many are highly susceptible to disease. Flower colors are white, pink, carmine, red, and rose; fruit colors are

Figure 460. *Malus* sp. twig and bud

Figure 461. *Malus* sp. bark, small stem

green, yellow, orange, and red. Fruit of most crab apples makes a delicious jelly.

Melia—chinaberry
MELIACEAE—mahogany family

Melia azederach Linnaeus
chinaberry

HABIT. Medium-sized tree, reaching 40 ft. (12 m) tall, with round-headed crown of stiff coarse branches.
BARK. Ridged and furrowed, gray-brown.

Figure 462. *Melia azederach* foliage

Figure 463. *Melia azederach* fruit

Figure 464. *Melia azederach* bark, medium-sized tree

Figure 465. *Melia azederach* bark, large tree

TWIGS. Stout, usually olive green, angled, lenticellate, ill scented when crushed; leaf scars large, 3-lobed, with many bundle scars in 3 clusters; pith homogeneous, white, large, round.

BUDS. Terminal absent; laterals ¹⁄₁₆ in. (2 mm) in diameter, gray brown, globose, hairy, fleshy buds appearing naked, set in notch above leaf scar.

LEAVES. Alternate, bipinnately compound, 8–18 in. (20–46 cm) long, with numerous leaflets 1–2 in. (2.5–5.0 cm) long; leaflets shiny, rich green, lanceolate or ovate, serrate or lobed; evergreen farther south.

FLOWERS. Pale purple, fragrant, in large terminal panicles.

FRUIT. Berry, about ⅝ in. (16 mm) in diameter, yellow, fleshy, wrinkled, poisonous; persisting through winter.

WOOD. Light to reddish brown, soft, weak, brittle; used for tool handles, furniture, cabinets, cigar boxes, fuel.

HABITAT AND RANGE. Native to the Himalayas, widely planted and naturalized throughout the Southeast.

PROPAGATION. Seed germinates without pretreatment.

WILDLIFE VALUE. Fruit is eaten by catbird, robin, and mockingbird, but can be toxic to birds if too many are ingested.

LANDSCAPE VALUE. Short lived, rather messy and unkempt-looking. Zones 7–10.

BEST RECOGNIZABLE FEATURES. Round yellow fruit; bipinnately compound foliage with bitter taste and strong odor; common in waste places and along fencerows throughout the South.

Morus—mulberry
MORACEAE—mulberry family

Key to *Morus*

1. Leaves dull, dark green, very rough on upper surface; buds green, sharp-pointed, divergent from twig; bark gray and somewhat shaggy .... *Morus rubra*

1. Leaves shiny, medium green, glabrous on upper surface; buds orange, blunt, appressed on twig; bark orange-brown and deeply furrowed .... *Morus alba*

Morus alba Linnaeus
white mulberry, silkworm mulberry, Russian mulberry

HABIT. Small to medium-sized tree, 30–50 ft. (9–15 m) tall, with a short bole, a broad, round crown, and many short branchlets.

BARK. Ash-orange to light brown becoming brown with age, tight with deep, dark orange furrows and yellow-brown ridges.

TWIGS. Slender, yellowish green to brownish gray, smooth, shiny, zig-zag, sweet-tasting; leaf scars oval, slightly hollowed, with many raised bundle scars; sap white; pith continuous, white.

BUDS. Terminal absent; laterals ⅛ in. (3 mm) long, ovate, nearly as broad as long, light orange-brown to reddish brown, with margins of the 4–8 scales finely hairy, appressed, only slightly if at all darker.

LEAVES. Alternate, simple, 2–5 in. (5–13 cm) long, ovate, dark green and

Figure 466. *Morus alba* foliage

Figure 467. *Morus alba* fruit

Figure 468. *Morus alba* twig and buds

Figure 469. *Morus alba* bark, small tree

Figure 470.
Morus alba
bark,
medium-
sized tree

Figure 471.
Morus alba
bark, large
tree

smooth and shiny above, smooth below, 3- or 5-lobed, tending to be more lobed on vigorous shoots; margin serrate, entire.

FLOWERS. Small, yellowish green, in racemes or spikes; monoecious or dioecious; appearing with the leaves in April.

FRUIT. Aggregate of drupes, ½–1 in. (13–25 mm) long; white, pink or purple; sweet, edible; June to July.

WOOD. Orange-brown, light, soft, coarse grained; used for fence posts.

HABITAT AND RANGE. Old fields, roadsides throughout United States; widely planted and since naturalized; native to China.

PROPAGATION. Seed, stratify 30–90 days at 33–41°F (1–5°C).

WILDLIFE VALUE. Fruit is good for songbirds, mice, and people.

LANDSCAPE VALUE. Tough tree for difficult sites, but with few ornamental assets and very messy fruit, especially after birds eat it. Fruitless varieties are available. Zones 4–8.

BEST RECOGNIZABLE FEATURES. Shiny, slick leaf, variable in shape; tan twig with reddish brown, somewhat appressed buds; yellow-brown, non-scaly bark, with orange furrows; widespreading, open growth habit.

Morus rubra Linnaeus
red mulberry, moral

HABIT. Medium-sized tree, 50–70 ft. (15–21 m) tall, with a short bole, and a dense, broad, round crown.

BARK. Light gray, tight, slightly ridged when young, becoming brownish gray and scaly with age.

TWIGS. Slender, reddish to greenish brown, zigzag; bundle scars numerous (unlike blackgum, which has 3 bundle scars); sap milky; pith continuous.

BUDS. Length ¼ in. (6 mm), greenish to reddish brown, each scale longer than broad, 4–8 with a dark margin, divergent or less often appressed, shiny.

LEAVES. Alternate, simple, 4–6 in. (10–15 cm) long, broad-ovate to oblong-ovate, green and rough hairy above, hairy below; margin serrate, entire to 3- to 5-lobed; fall color yellow.

Morus rubra

FLOWERS. Small, yellowish green, in racemes or spikes; monoecious or dioecious; appearing with the leaves in April.

FRUIT. Aggregate of drupes, 1–1½ in. (2.5–4 cm) long, red becoming dark purple, sweet, edible; June.

WOOD. Orange-brown, light, soft, decay-resistant, coarse grained; used for fence posts, barrels.

Figure 472. *Morus rubra* foliage

Figure 473. *Morus rubra* flowers

Figure 474. *Morus rubra* bark, medium-sized tree

Figure 475. *Morus rubra* bark, large tree

HABITAT AND RANGE. Moist woodlands from Vermont to Minnesota and South Dakota, south to Texas, east to Florida.

PROPAGATION. Seed, stratify 30–90 days at 33–41°F (1–5°C).

WILDLIFE VALUE. Fruit is excellent for songbirds, ruffed grouse, turkey, squirrel, mice, raccoon, and people.

LANDSCAPE VALUE. Handsome, moderately large shade tree with dark, leathery foliage and shaggy bark; best planted on rich, moist but well-drained sites. Zones 5–9.

BEST RECOGNIZABLE FEATURES. Sandpapery-textured, dark green, dull leaves; dark green, shiny, divergent buds; zigzag twig growth; grayish bark with scaly ridges.

Nyssa—tupelo
NYSSACEAE—gum family

Key to *Nyssa*

1.   Leaves 5–7 in. (13–18 cm) long; fruit about 1 in. (2.5 cm) long and reddish purple; restricted to very wet habitats . . . .
. . . . *Nyssa aquatica*

1.   Leaves ≤ 5 in. (13 cm) long; fruit ≤ ½ in. (13 mm) long and bluish black; found on very dry to very wet sites . . . .
. . . . *Nyssa sylvatica*

Nyssa aquatica Linnaeus
water tupelo, tupelo-gum, cotton-gum, sourgum

HABIT. Large tree, 80–100 ft. (24–31 m) tall, with a strongly buttressed base, a tapering bole, and a flattened, spreading crown.

BARK. Dark brown or gray, thin, finely fissured with scaly ridges.

TWIGS. Moderately stout, reddish brown, lenticellate, glabrous in winter; leaf scars round or heart shaped, with 3 bundle scars; pith white, diaphragmed; spur shoots common.

Nyssa aquatica

Figure 476.
Nyssa
aquatica
foliage

Figure 477. *Nyssa aquatica* fruit

Figure 478.
Nyssa
aquatica
bark, small
tree

Figure 479.
Nyssa
aquatica
bark,
medium-
sized tree

Figure 480. *Nyssa aquatica* bark, large tree

BUDS. Terminal ⅛–¼ in. (3–6 mm) long, nearly globose, yellowish brown; laterals smaller, nearly imbedded in twig.

LEAVES. Deciduous, alternate, simple, 5–7 in. (13–18 cm) long, oblong-ovate, acuminate, dark green and lustrous above, pale and somewhat downy pubescent below; margin entire or irregularly toothed.

FLOWERS. Small, greenish white; appearing as the leaves unfold in March to April.

FRUIT. Similar to blackgum except larger, to 1 in. (2.5 cm) long, reddish purple; covering a distinctly ridged nutlet; on dropping stalks 3–4 in. (8–10 cm) long.

WOOD. Light brown to nearly white, light, soft, not strong, close grained, difficult to split; used for boxes, pulp, flooring, broom handles.

HABITAT AND RANGE. Floodplain soils from southern Virginia south to northern Florida, west to eastern Texas, north to southern Illinois.

PROPAGATION. Seed, stratify 60–120 days at 41°F (5°C).

WILDLIFE VALUE. Fruit is excellent for wood duck, songbirds, squirrel, raccoon, and deer.

LANDSCAPE VALUE. Grows in knee-deep (or deeper) water. Zones 6–9.

BEST RECOGNIZABLE FEATURES. Large reddish purple, glaucous fruit; wet sites; swollen base of bole; diaphragmed pith; leaves to 7 in. (18 cm) long.

Nyssa sylvatica Marshall   PLATE 71
blackgum, black tupelo, pepperidge, tupelo, sourgum

HABIT. Large tree, to 100 ft. (31 m) tall, excurrent when young, becoming irregularly round or flat topped with age.

Nyssa sylvatica

BARK. Ash-gray when young, becoming gray, brown, or black with age, thick, blocky, "alligator hide" appearance; golden-brown when cut. Blocks may be squarish or rectangular on the same tree.

TWIGS. Slender, green to reddish brown, becoming grayish; spur shoots numerous, glabrous, sharp angled, giving a broken-glass effect as one looks up the bole; leaf scars with 3 bundle scars; pith white, diaphragmed.

BUDS. Length ⅛–¼ in. (3–6 mm), ovoid, yellow-brown to red-brown, acute, with 3–5 scales, each with a dark margin, smooth or slightly downy at the tip, divergent; laterals divergent.

Figure 481.
Nyssa
sylvatica
foliage

Figure 482.
Nyssa
sylvatica
fruit and
seed

Figure 483. *Nyssa sylvatica* twig
and bud

Figure 484.
Nyssa
sylvatica
bark, small
tree

Figure 485. *Nyssa sylvatica* bark, large tree

LEAVES. Deciduous, alternate, simple, 2–5 in. (5–13 cm) long, obovate or elliptic, thick, shiny; margin entire or wavy; fall color scarlet, reddish purple, orange, or yellow.

FLOWERS. Small, greenish white; appearing as the leaves unfold in early spring.

FRUIT. Drupe, fleshy, ovoid, ⅓–½ in. (8–13 mm) long, bluish black, 2–3 per stalk, bitter, indistinctly ribbed; September.

WOOD. Yellowish brown, with twisted grain, soft, not durable; used for furniture, lumber, crates, pulpwood, gunstocks.

HABITAT AND RANGE. Variety of sites from Maine west to Michigan, south through Missouri to eastern Texas, east to Florida.

PROPAGATION. Seed, stratify 60–120 days at 41°F (5°C).

WILDLIFE VALUE. Fruit is excellent for songbirds, grouse, turkey, mice, opossum, raccoon, and deer.

LANDSCAPE VALUE. Exceptional medium-sized tree due to glossy green foliage, brilliant scarlet fall color, distinct form and texture; suitable for a range of growing conditions, including very dry or very wet. Zones 3–9.

BEST RECOGNIZABLE FEATURES. "Alligator hide" bark; small, shiny obovate leaves; twig with diaphragmed pith; bluish black drupe; brilliant scarlet fall color.

Ostrya—hophornbeam
BETULACEAE—birch family

Ostrya virginiana (Miller) K. Koch
eastern hophornbeam, American hophornbeam, ironwood, hornbeam

HABIT. Small tree, 20–30 ft (6–9 m) tall, with a short, columnar bole and a round or vaselike crown.

BARK. Reddish brown or bronze to purple, smooth (cherrylike, but young black cherry stems are darker), with conspicuous horizontal lenticels when young, becoming gray-brown, loose, shredded, and flaky with age.

TWIGS. Slender, dark reddish brown, shiny, smooth to lightly hairy, zigzag; pith white, continuous.

BUDS. Terminal absent; laterals ⅛–¼ in. (3–6 mm) long, yellowish green, smooth or lightly hairy, strongly divergent (unlike American hornbeam), usually vertically striated (hand lens helpful); staminate aments preformed.

LEAVES. Alternate, simple, 2–4 in. (5–10 cm) long, oval-lanceolate, dark green and lightly hairy above, paler and more pubescent below; margin doubly serrate; veins branch one to several times as they approach the margin; fall color yellow.

FLOWERS. Catkins, monoecious; April.

FRUIT. Nutlet ribbed, enclosed in a papery sac, aggregated into pendent, conelike clusters.

WOOD. Light brown to white, sometimes reddish, hard, durable; used for tool handles, fence posts, fuel.

HABITAT AND RANGE. From streambanks to dry rocky slopes throughout eastern United States.

Ostrya virginiana

Figure 486. *Ostrya virginiana* foliage

Figure 487. *Ostrya virginiana* flowers

Figure 488. *Ostrya virginiana* fruit

Figure 489. *Ostrya virginiana* twig, leaf buds, staminate flower buds

Figure 490.
*Ostrya
virginiana*
bark, small
tree

Figure 491.
*Ostrya
virginiana*
bark,
medium-
sized tree

Figure 492. *Ostrya virginiana* bark, large tree

PROPAGATION. Seed (difficult), stratify 60 days at 68/86°F (20/30°C) night/day, then 90–150 days at 33–41°F (1–5°C).

WILDLIFE VALUE. Limited wildlife value except to provide nesting and hiding places.

LANDSCAPE VALUE. Very sturdy small to medium-sized shade tree that tolerates very dry soils and shade; has attractive foliage and interesting bark; apparently tolerates urban conditions well. Zones 3–9.

BEST RECOGNIZABLE FEATURES. Hoplike clusters of fruit; shreddy bark; terminal preformed staminate catkins; vertically striated bud scales.

Oxydendrum—sourwood
ERICACEAE—heath family

Oxydendrum arboreum (Linnaeus) de Candolle
sourwood, sorrel-tree, lily-of-the-valley tree   PLATES 72, 73

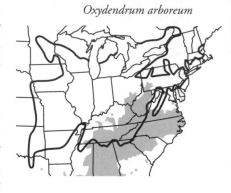

Oxydendrum arboreum

HABIT. Small to medium-sized tree, 15–50 ft. (5–15 m) tall; bole slender with a short, oblong to flat-topped crown in the forest, bole short and leaning with a broad irregular crown in the open.

BARK. Silvery-gray to gray-brown, without an odor (unlike sassafras), scaly, interlacing ridges, occasionally blocky; inner bark deep reddish orange; ridges deep reddish orange when cut.

TWIGS. Slender to moderate, bright red or olive green with lenticels, smooth or lightly hairy, shiny, zigzag, sometimes angled; leaf scars shield shaped, with a single C-shaped bundle scar; pith white, continuous.

BUDS. Terminal absent; laterals ⅛ in. (3 mm) in diameter, reddish brown, globose-conical, partially embedded, with 3–6 overlapping scales.

LEAVES. Alternate, simple, 4–7 in. (10–18 cm) long, elliptic-oblong to oblong-lanceolate, shiny dark green above, pale below; margin finely

Figure 493. *Oxyden-drum arboreum* foliage

Figure 494. *Oxydendrum arboreum* flowers

Figure 495. *Oxydendrum arboreum* fruits

Figure 496. *Oxydendrum arboreum* twig

Figure 497. *Oxydendrum arboreum* bark, small tree

Figure 498. *Oxydendrum arboreum* bark, medium-sized tree

Figure 499. *Oxydendrum arboreum* bark, large tree

toothed; petiole 1 in. (2.5 cm) long or less; sour-tasting; fall color scarlet to purple.

FLOWERS. White, urn shaped, ⅛–¼ in. (3–6 mm) long; in clusters 6–10 in. (15–25 cm) long; very showy; June to August.

FRUIT. Capsule, ½ in. (13 mm) long, brown, 5-celled, erect, dry, woody; opening September to October, persisting through winter.

WOOD. Brown, tinged with red, heavy, hard, very close grained; used for fuel, pulpwood.

HABITAT AND RANGE. Moist uplands to dry ridgetops from Pennsylvania to Indiana, south to Louisiana, east to northern Florida.

PROPAGATION. Seed, stratify 0–60 days at 41°F (1–5°C) and do not cover after sowing.

WILDLIFE VALUE. Flowers are good for honeybees; fruit is fair for song-birds and mice.

LANDSCAPE VALUE. One of the finest small ornamental trees of North America because it contributes to the landscape throughout the year, particularly in late summer and autumn; should be planted in moist but well-drained, acidic soil. Zones 5–9.

BEST RECOGNIZABLE FEATURES. Fragrant flowers, in long clusters during summer; seed capsules persisting into winter; reddish brown twigs in winter; lateral buds minute, globular; sour-tasting leaves; bark ridges deep orange-colored when cut.

Paulownia—paulownia
BIGNONIACEAE—catalpa family

Paulownia tomentosa (Thunberg) Siebold & Zuccarini ex Steudel
royal paulownia, princess-tree, empress-tree, paulownia

HABIT. Medium-sized tree, 30–60 ft. (9–18 m) tall, variable with site but with stout branches and a rounded, open crown.

BARK. Gray, thin, smooth or shallowly fissured, with interlacing ridges.

TWIGS. Stout, brittle, round, brownish green, with lip-shaped lenticels, hairy when young becoming smooth with age; leaf scars raised, with bundle scars in a ring; pith chambered or sometimes hollow between nodes, white.

BUDS. Length ¹⁄₁₆ in. (2 mm), brownish green, hairy, half-round, usually

Figure 500. *Paulownia tomentosa* foliage

Figure 501. *Paulownia tomentosa* flower buds

Figure 502. *Paulownia tomentosa* fruit

Figure 503. *Paulownia tomentosa* bark, medium-sized tree

Figure 504. *Paulownia tomentosa* bark, large tree

superposed, opposite (or rarely whorled); flower buds very conspicuous in the winter; rounded, curved downward, clustered.

LEAVES. Opposite or whorled, 6–16 in. (15–41 cm) long, smooth and green above, hairy below, may be 3-toothed or 3-lobed, heart shaped; petiole 4–8 in. (10–20 cm) long.

FLOWERS. Pale violet with dark spots and yellow stripes inside; bell shaped, 2 in. (5 cm) long; in clusters to 12 in. (31 cm) long, with fragrance like vanilla, very showy; April to early May.

FRUIT. Capsule, 1 in. (2.5 cm) long, brown, woody, ovoid, beaked, in long panicles, with many small, winged seeds; September, persisting through winter.

WOOD. Purplish brown, light, soft, with a satinlike surface, easily worked; used for tea boxes in Japan; has very high value.

HABITAT AND RANGE. Old fields, old homesites, strip mines; native to Asia but a common escapee throughout the central and southeastern United States.

PROPAGATION. Seed germinates when sown, but needs light to germinate.

WILDLIFE VALUE. Little wildlife value except to provide nesting and hiding places.

LANDSCAPE VALUE. Flowers are beautiful, but the tree is rather messy; tolerates extreme soil conditions. Zones 5–9.

BEST RECOGNIZABLE FEATURES. Persistent woody-beaked capsules; opposite or whorled large leaves; large, white, spongy, often-chambered pith; long clusters of violet flowers.

Picea—spruce
PINACEAE—pine family

Key to *Picea*

1.   Needles bluish green; twigs with capitate and acute hairs; cones blackish, about 1 in. (2.5 cm) long, and persistent on tree . . . . *Picea mariana*
1.   Needles green; twigs with acute hairs only; cones reddish, > 1 in. (2.5 cm) long, and not persistent on tree . . . . *Picea rubens*

Plate 1. *Acer negundo* (boxelder) flowers

Plate 2. *Acer nigrum* (black maple) fall color

Plate 3. *Acer pensylvanicum* (striped maple) flowers

Plate 4. *Acer pensylvanicum* (striped maple) bark

Plate 5. *Acer rubrum* (red maple) male flowers

Plate 6. *Acer rubrum* (red maple) female flowers

Plate 7. *Acer rubrum* (red maple) fall color

Plate 8. *Acer saccharinum* (silver maple) male (*lower*) and female (*upper*) flowers

Plate 9. *Acer saccharum* (sugar maple) flowers

Plate 10. *Acer saccharum* (sugar maple) fall color

Plate 12. *Aesculus glabra* (Ohio buckeye) flowers

Plate 11. *Acer spicatum* (mountain maple) flowers

Plate 13. *Aesculus octandra* (yellow buckeye) flowers

Plate 14. *Aesculus pavia* (red buckeye) flowers

Plate 15. *Aesculus sylvatica* (painted buckeye) flowers

Plate 16. *Albizia julibrissin* (silktree) flowers

Plate 17. *Alnus serrulata* (hazel alder) flowers

Plate 18. *Amelanchier arborea* (downy service-berry) fruit

Plate 19. *Aralia spinosa* (devils-walkingstick) fruit

Plate 20. *Asimina triloba*
(pawpaw) flower

Plate 21. *Asimina triloba* (pawpaw) fall color

Plate 22. *Betula alleghaniensis* (yellow birch) bark

Plate 23. *Betula nigra* (river birch) bark

Plate 24. *Betula papyrifera* (paper birch) bark

Plate 25. *Carpinus caroliniana* (American hornbeam) flowers

Plate 26. *Carya cordiformis* (bitternut hickory) bark

Plate 27. *Carya glabra* (pignut hickory) fall color

Plate 28. *Carya ovalis* (red hickory) flowers

Plate 29. *Carya ovata* (shagbark hickory) bark

Plate 30. *Castanea dentata* (American chestnut) male flowers

Plate 31. *Catalpa speciosa* (northern catalpa) flower

Plate 32. *Celtis occidentalis* (common hackberry) bark

Plate 33. *Cephalanthus occidentalis* (buttonbush) flowers

Plate 34. *Cercis canadensis* (eastern redbud) flowers

Plate 35. *Chionanthus virginicus* (fringetree) fruit

Plate 36. *Cladrastis kentukea* (yellowwood) fall color

Plate 37. *Clethra acuminata* (cinnamon clethra) bark

Plate 38. *Cornus alternifolia* (alternate-leaf dogwood) fall color

Plate 39. *Cornus florida* (flowering dogwood) fall color

Plate 40. *Cornus racemosa* (gray dogwood) flowers

Plate 41. *Cornus racemosa* (gray dogwood) fruit

Plate 42. *Cotinus obovatus* (American smoketree) fall color

Plate 44. *Crataegus crus-galli* (cockspur hawthorn) fruit

Plate 43. *Crataegus crus-galli* (cockspur hawthorn) flowers

Plate 45. *Crataegus phaenopyrum* (Washington hawthorn) flowers

Plate 47. *Fagus grandifolia* (American beech) bark

Plate 46. *Crataegus phaenopyrum* (Washington hawthorn) fruit

Plate 48. *Fraxinus americana* (white ash) fall color

Plate 49. *Fraxinus americana* (white ash) bark

Plate 50. *Fraxinus pennsylvanica* (green ash) male flowers

Plate 51. *Fraxinus pennsylvanica* (green ash) female flowers

Plate 52. *Fraxinus pennsylvanica* (green ash) fall color

Plate 53. *Gleditsia triacanthos* (honeylocust) bark

Plate 54. *Halesia carolina* (Carolina silverbell) flowers

Plate 55. *Hamamelis virginiana* (witch-hazel) flowers and fall color

Plate 56. *Ilex decidua* (possumhaw) fruit

Plate 57. *Ilex montana* (mountain winterberry) fruit

Plate 58. *Ilex opaca* (American holly) fruit

Plate 59. *Ilex verticillata* (winterberry) fruit

Plate 60. *Juglans cinerea* (butternut) bark

Plate 61. *Juglans nigra* (black walnut) flowers

Plate 62. *Juglans nigra* (black walnut) bark

Plate 63. *Juniperus virginiana* (eastern red-cedar) foliage and fruit

Plate 64. *Kalmia latifolia* (mountain-laurel) flowers

Plate 65. *Liquidambar styraciflua* (sweetgum) fall color

Plate 66. *Liriodendron tulipifera* (yellow-poplar) flowers

Plate 67. *Magnolia acuminata* (cucumbertree) fruit

Plate 68. *Magnolia fraseri* (Fraser magnolia) flowers

Plate 69. *Magnolia macrophylla* (bigleaf magnolia) flowers

Plate 70. *Magnolia tripetala* (umbrella magnolia) flowers

Plate 71. *Nyssa sylvatica* (blackgum) fall color

Plate 72. *Oxydendrum arboreum* (sourwood) flowers

Plate 73. *Oxydendrum arboreum* (sourwood) fruit and fall color

Plate 74. *Platanus occidentalis* (sycamore) bark

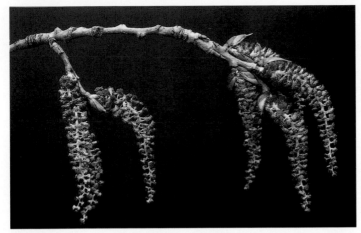

Plate 75. *Populus deltoides* (eastern cottonwood) male flowers

Plate 76. *Populus grandidentata* (bigtooth aspen) flowers

Plate 77. *Populus tremuloides* (quaking aspen) flowers

Plate 78. *Prunus americana* (American plum) flowers

Plate 80. *Prunus pensylvanica* (pin cherry) bark

Plate 79. *Prunus pensylvanica* (pin cherry) fruit

Plate 81. *Prunus pensylvanica* (pin cherry) fall color

Plate 82. *Prunus serotina* (black cherry) fruit

Plate 83. *Prunus virginiana* (chokecherry) flowers

Plate 84. *Quercus alba* (white oak) male flowers

Plate 85. *Quercus alba* (white oak) bark

Plate 86. *Quercus coccinea* (scarlet oak) fall color

Plate 87. *Quercus macrocarpa* (bur oak) bark

Plate 88. *Quercus palustris* (pin oak) form and fall color

Plate 89. *Quercus phellos* (willow oak) form

Plate 90. *Quercus prinus* (chestnut oak) bark

Plate 91. *Quercus rubra* (northern red oak) fall color

Plate 92. *Quercus rubra* (northern red oak) bark

Plate 93. *Quercus velutina* (black oak) bark

Plate 94. *Rhamnus caroliniana* (Carolina buck-thorn) fruit

Plate 95. *Rhododendron catawbiense* (Catawba rhododendron) flowers

Plate 96. *Rhododendron maximum* (rosebay rhododendron) flowers

Plate 97. *Rhus typhina* (staghorn sumac) fruit and fall color

Plate 99. *Salix discolor* (pussy willow) flowers

Plate 98. *Robinia pseudoacacia* (black locust) flowers

Plate 100. *Sambucus canadensis* (American elder) flowers

Plate 101. *Sassafras albidum* (sassafras) flowers

Plate 102. *Sassafras albidum* (sassafras) fall color

Plate 103. *Sorbus americana* (American mountain-ash) fruit

Plate 104. *Staphylea trifolia* (American bladdernut) flowers

Plate 105. *Stewartia ovata* (mountain stewartia) flowers

Plate 106. *Styrax americanus* (American snowbell) flowers

Plate 107. *Symplocos tinctoria* (sweetleaf) flowers

Plate 108. *Taxodium distichum* (baldcypress) bark

Plate 109. *Tilia americana* (American basswood) flowers

Plate 110. *Toxicodendron vernix* (poison-sumac) foliage and flowers

Plate 111. *Ulmus rubra* (slippery elm) flowers

Plate 112. *Vaccinium arboreum* (tree sparkleberry) flowers

Plate 113. *Viburnum lentago* (nannyberry) flowers

Plate 114. *Viburnum lentago* (nannyberry) fruit

Plate 115. *Viburnum prunifolium* (blackhaw) flowers

Plate 116. *Zanthoxylum americanum* (common prickly-ash) fruit

Picea mariana (Miller) Britton, Sterns & Poggenburg
black spruce, bog spruce

HABIT. Small tree, generally 20–30 ft. (6–9 m) tall but reaching 100 ft. (31 m) under optimum growing conditions, with crown generally covering only upper third of bole.

Picea mariana

BARK. Thin, gray-brown, scaly ridges.

TWIGS. Short, covered with numerous peglike projections (sterigmata) where needles were attached, with 2 types of rusty pubescence (which can be differentiated with aid of 10× hand lens)— capitate or lollipop shaped, and acute.

BUDS. Short, ovoid, acute, light reddish brown, pubescent; slender, long filaments occur with terminal bud.

LEAVES. Needles about ½ in. (13 mm) long, 4-sided, dull blue green, glaucous, blunt pointed, somewhat radially aligned on twig.

FRUIT. Cone about 1 in. (2.5 cm) long, purplish to turning brown at maturity, ovoid, on strongly incurved stalks; margin of scale erose; persisting for decades; scales stiff and round; cones produced at early age.

WOOD. Pale yellow-white, light, soft, not strong; used for pulpwood, fuel.

HABITAT AND RANGE. Restricted to bogs in southern portion of range, found on dry slopes farther north; found from Labrador to Alaska, south to Wisconsin and Michigan and in mountains of Virginia.

PROPAGATION. Seed germinates without pretreatment.

Figure 505. *Picea mariana* foliage

Figure 506. *Picea mariana* fruit

3

Figure 507.
*Picea
mariana*
form

Figure 508. *Picea mariana* bark,
medium-sized tree

WILDLIFE VALUE. Younger trees are eaten by snowshoe hare when little else is available; seed is eaten by squirrel.

LANDSCAPE VALUE. Relative to other spruces, slow growing and short lived; does not grow in most of the Central Hardwood Forests due to inadequate moisture and too warm. Zones 2–5.

BEST RECOGNIZABLE FEATURES. Two types of pubescence on twig, blunt tipped and sharp pointed; twigs with numerous peglike projections where needles were attached; blue-green, short foliage that is somewhat radially aligned on twig; persistent, relatively small cones with erose cone scales.

Picea rubens Sargent
red spruce

HABIT. Large tree, usually 70–80 ft. (21–24 m) tall, to 120 ft. (37 m); bole long, clear bole with a short conical crown in the forest, or broad conical crown covering most of bole in the open.

BARK. Irregularly shaped, gray to reddish brown scales.

TWIGS. Orange-brown, typically covered with sharp-pointed pubescence and with numerous peglike projections (sterigmata) where needles were attached.

Picea rubens

Figure 509. *Picea rubens* foliage

Figure 510. *Picea rubens* cones

Figure 511. *Picea rubens* bark, small tree

Figure 512. *Picea rubens* bark, medium-sized tree

Figure 513. *Picea rubens* bark, large tree

Figure 514. *Picea abies* cone

BUDS. Ovoid, acute, to ⅓ in. (8 mm) long, reddish brown; slender, long filaments occur with terminal bud.

LEAVES. Needles about ½ in. (13 mm) long, 4-sided, shiny, dark yellow-green; apex blunt or acute; persisting for about 5 years.

FRUIT. Cone ovoid-oblong, to 1½ in. (4 cm) long, chestnut-brown, lustrous; scales rigid, rounded; margin entire; seeds about ⅛ in. (3 mm) long, dark brown, winged.

WOOD. Pale, slightly tinged with red, light, soft, not strong, close grained; used for construction lumber, boats, musical instruments.

HABITAT AND RANGE. Well-drained uplands and mountain slopes from the southern and central Appalachian Mountains at high elevations to the northern Appalachian Mountains into Newfoundland.

PROPAGATION. Seed germinates without pretreatment.

WILDLIFE VALUE. Seed is very important to the diet of red squirrel and chipmunk, and is eaten by small seed-eating birds such as white-winged crossbill; young trees are browsed in winter by whitetail deer and rabbit.

LANDSCAPE VALUE. Not suited to hot, dry climate (relative to where it is naturally abundant) of Midwest. Zones 2–5.

BEST RECOGNIZABLE FEATURES. Twigs covered with sharp-pointed (acute) pubescence; twigs with numerous peglike projections where needles were attached; nonpersistent cones with smooth scale margin; yellow-green needles, somewhat flattened on twig.

Other spruces commonly planted in the regional landscape:

Picea abies (Linnaeus) Karsten, Norway spruce. Commonly to 80 ft. (24 m) tall in eastern United States; needles resemble red spruce but are longer; bud scales typically reflexed; twigs glabrous; cones to 7 in. (18 cm) long; side branches of foliage pendulous; widely planted in Mid-

Figure 515. *Picea pungens* foliage

Figure 516. *Picea pungens* cone

west but often has ragged appearance here; grows better in cultivation than the native spruces in the East, and has naturalized there; over 100 horticultural varieties exist. Native to northern and central Europe. Zones 2–7.

Picea pungens Engelmann, blue or Colorado spruce. Commonly 80–100 ft. (24–31 m) tall in native stands of Colorado, Utah, Wyoming, and New Mexico mountains; needles very sharp at apex, dark green or blue-green to almost silver; twigs glabrous, yellow-brown, stout; bud scales usually reflexed; cones to 4 in. (10 cm) long and golden-brown, with erose margin, flexible scales; dense, pyramidal crown. The most commonly planted spruce in the eastern United States because this species is well-adapted to growing conditions of Midwest, and some of its varieties have beautiful blue to silver foliage. Zones 2–7.

Pinus—pine
PINACEAE—pine family

Key to *Pinus*

1. Needles in groups of 2 and/or 3 2
1. Needles in groups of 5 . . . . *Pinus strobus*
2(1). Needles predominantly in groups of 3 3
2. Needles predominantly in groups of 2 4
3(2). Needles < 5 in. (13 cm) long; cones ovoid, < 3 in. (8 cm) long
. . . . *Pinus rigida*
3. Needles ≥ 5 in. (13 cm) long; cones cylindrical, generally > 3 in.
(8 cm) long . . . . *Pinus taeda*
4(2). Needles to 6 in. (15 cm) long, breaking cleanly when bent . . .
. . . . *Pinus resinosa*
4. Needles < 6 in. (15 cm) long, not breaking cleanly when bent
. . . . 5
5(4). Needles ≥ 3 in. (8 cm) long . . . . *Pinus echinata*
5. Needles < 3 in. (8 cm) long 6
6(5). Needles to > 2 in. (5 cm) long; cones cylindrical or ovoid . . . 7
6. Needles < 2 in. (5 cm) long; cones irregular in shape, < 2.5 in.
(6 cm) long . . . . *Pinus banksiana*
7(6). Needles < 2.5 in. (6 cm) long; stems lacking purplish bloom;
cones to 3.5 in. (9 cm) in diameter . . . . *Pinus pungens*
7. Needles to 3 in. (8 cm) long; stems with purplish bloom; cones
< 3 in. (8 cm) in diameter . . . . *Pinus virginiana*

Pinus banksiana Lambert
jack pine, scrub pine

HABIT. Generally a small tree, to 30 ft. (9 m) tall, reaching 80 ft. (24 m) on good sites; crown short and bushy or pyramidal in the open, narrow and often crooked in natural stands.
BARK. Blackish, with small scaly ridges.
TWIGS. Dark purple, slender, tough, flexible.
LEAVES. Needles to 1½ in. (4 cm) long, stout, flat, often twisted, yellow-green to dark green, in fascicles of 2, divergent within fascicle, persisting for 2–3 years.
FRUIT. Cones to about 2 in. (5 cm) long, oblong-conical, sessile, light

Pinus banksiana

Figure 517. *Pinus banksiana* foliage

Figure 518. *Pinus banksiana* cones

Figure 519. *Pinus banksiana* bark, small tree

Figure 520. *Pinus banksiana* bark, medium-sized tree

Figure 521. *Pinus banksiana* bark, large tree

brown, lustrous, short stalked, strongly incurved and often pointed forward along twig, persistent, usually serotinous (not opening), borne at very early age; scales thin, stiff, often irregularly developed, mostly unarmed (prickles minute and deciduous).

WOOD. Clear pale brown, light, soft, not strong, close grained; used for general construction lumber, poles, pulpwood.

HABITAT AND RANGE. Common on sandy soils and barren land in the northern United States into a large portion of Canada, to tree line.

PROPAGATION. Seed generally germinates without pretreatment, or may be stratified in moist medium for a short period at 41°F (5°C).

WILDLIFE VALUE. Seed is eaten by small mammals (e.g., red squirrel, chipmunk, white-footed mice) and seed-eating birds (e.g., goldfinch, bronzed grackle, robin); young trees are browsed by whitetail deer, snowshoe hare, and porcupine.

LANDSCAPE VALUE. Not a very pretty tree, short lived, exceptionally tolerant of infertile, dry, sandy soils; one of hardiest trees native to North America. Zones 2–6.

BEST RECOGNIZABLE FEATURES. Persistent, usually serotinous cones; short, divergent needles in fascicles of 2; pioneer on excessively drained, infertile, sandy soils.

Pinus echinata Miller
shortleaf pine, southern yellow pine

HABIT. Large tree, 80–100 ft. (24–31 m) tall, with a long, clear bole, a broad, open crown, and a deep taproot.

BARK. Blackish brown, scaly, becoming reddish brown and large plated with age; resin pockets numerous; inner bark white.

TWIGS. Slender, green, tinged with purplish bloom on new growth.

BUDS. Reddish brown, with appressed scales.

LEAVES. Needles 3–5 in. (8–13 cm) long; dark yellow-green, flexible, in fascicles of 2 (infrequently 3), frequently found tufted on the main bole; fascicle sheath persistent.

FRUIT. Cone 1½–2½ in. (4–6 cm) long, narrowly ovate, brown to brownish gray; scales thin and with small deciduous prickles which curve toward the base of the cone; often persistent.

WOOD. Reddish brown, heavy, hard, coarse grained; used for interior finishing, pulpwood, construction.

Pinus echinata

Figure 522. *Pinus echinata* foliage

Figure 523. *Pinus echinata* cones

Figure 524. *Pinus echinata* bark, small tree

Figure 525. *Pinus echinata* bark, medium-sized tree

Figure 526. *Pinus echinata* bark, large tree

HABITAT AND RANGE. Dry slopes or shallow soils from Long Island to southern Illinois to eastern Oklahoma, south to Texas, east to the Florida panhandle.

PROPAGATION. Seed, stratify 15–60 days at 33–41°F (1–5°C).

WILDLIFE VALUE. Seed is eaten by songbirds, turkey, ruffed grouse, quail, squirrel, and mice.

LANDSCAPE VALUE. Attractive tree; tolerates dry, acidic soils. Zones 6–9.

BEST RECOGNIZABLE FEATURES. Slender needles mostly in bundles of 2 (occasionally 3); short, somewhat narrow cones, weakly prickled; large rectangular plates on bark of larger individuals, with conspicuous resin pockets; often with small tufts of foliage along bole.

Pinus pungens Lambert
Table Mountain pine, hickory pine, mountain pine, prickly pine

HABIT. Medium-sized tree, to 40 ft. (12 m) tall, with stout, spreading branches forming a broad, open crown.

BARK. Reddish brown to grayish brown, thick, scaly, irregular plates.

TWIGS. Stout, somewhat brittle, initially light orange but becoming dark brown.

BUDS. Oblong, blunt, dark chestnut-brown, resinous.

LEAVES. Needles dark green, 1½–2½

Pinus pungens

Figure 527. *Pinus pungens* foliage

Figure 529. *Pinus pungens* bark, medium-sized tree

Figure 528. *Pinus pungens* cones

in. (4–6 cm) long, in fascicles (persistent) of 2 (rarely 3), stout, rigid, very sharp pointed, somewhat twisted.

FRUIT. Cone 2–3½ in. (5–9 cm) long, light brown, ovoid, symmetrical or oblique at base, sessile; scales with stout, upwardly curved spines; opening slowly, persisting for many years on tree, therefore large numbers common on any cone-producing individual.

WOOD. Pale brown, light, soft, not strong, brittle, very coarsely grained; used for fuel, charcoal.

HABITAT. Dry slopes and rocky areas of the central and southern Appalachian Mountains at moderate elevations; often with other pines or in pure stands.

PROPAGATION. Seed germinates without pretreatment.

WILDLIFE VALUE. Seed is good for songbirds, turkey, ruffed grouse, quail, squirrel, and mice.

LANDSCAPE VALUE. Coarse-textured tree with very interesting cones; worth considering on infertile, rocky, dry sites. Zone 5.

BEST RECOGNIZABLE FEATURES. Stout needles in fascicles of 2; heavily armed, persistent cones; dry, mountainous habitat at moderate elevations.

Pinus resinosa Aiton
red pine, Norway pine

HABIT. Medium-sized to large tree, 60–80 ft. (18–24 m) tall, with oval-shaped crown when young, becoming broad and somewhat symmetrical with age; one whorl of branches produced each year.

BARK. Scaly, orange-red on young trees, becoming reddish brown with thick, flat, square to rectangular scaly ridges and shallow fissures at maturity.

TWIGS. Stout, glabrous, pale brown or orange-brown.

Pinus resinosa

BUDS. About ¾ in. (19 mm) long, ovoid, sharp pointed, resinous, with thin scales fringed on margin.

LEAVES. Needles dark green (occasionally yellowish green), 5–6 in. (13–15 cm) long, slender, sharp pointed, somewhat aligned closely to stem and clustered near tip of twigs, in fascicles (persistent sheath) of 2, moderate texture, appearing tufted on older specimens, breaking cleanly when bent in half.

FRUIT. Cone about 2 in. (5 cm) long, ovoid, light brown, solitary or in pairs, nearly sessile; scales keeled, unarmed, slightly thickened at apex.

WOOD. Pale red, light, hard, very close grained; used for general construction, pulpwood, millwork, piles, masts.

HABITAT. Well-drained, sandy or dry, gravelly uplands.

PROPAGATION. Fresh seed germinates; other seed, stratify 60 days at 41°F (5°C).

WILDLIFE VALUE. Seed is good for songbirds, turkey, and mice.

Figure 530. *Pinus resinosa* foliage

Figure 531. *Pinus resinosa* cones

Figure 532. *Pinus resinosa* bark, small tree

Figure 533. *Pinus resinosa* bark, medium-sized tree

Figure 534. *Pinus resinosa* bark, large tree

LANDSCAPE VALUE. Excellent for reforestation of degraded land, windbreaks, and plantations, especially in more northern areas. Also, single specimens make a fine ornamental or shade tree. Zone 2.

BEST RECOGNIZABLE FEATURES. Medium green needles in fascicles of 2, breaking cleanly when bent; reddish brown on larger tree, with rectangular ridges; unarmed cone the shape and size of small egg.

Pinus rigida Miller
pitch pine

HABIT. Medium-sized tree, 60–70 ft. (18–21 m) tall, with a clear, symmetrical bole and a small, open crown; variable appearance with sites, being more contorted on poor sites.

BARK. Dark and scaly when young, becoming dark reddish brown with scaly plates and narrow irregular fissures; without resin pockets.

Pinus rigida

TWIGS. Stout, prominently ridged, brown to orange; epicormic shoots common on branches and the bole.

BUDS. Length ¾ in. (19 mm), conical, covered with reddish brown scales, resinous.

LEAVES. Needles 3–5 in. (8–13 cm) long, yellow-green, in fascicles of 3, stiff, twisted, arranged perpendicular to the twig, frequently found on main bole.

FRUIT. Cone 3 in. (8 cm) long, egg shaped, persistent, light brown becoming gray with age; base flat; scales thick, with persistent prickles.

WOOD. Reddish brown heartwood, yellowish sapwood, hard, durable, coarse grained; used for rough lumber, fuel, pulpwood, mine props.

Figure 535. *Pinus rigida* foliage

Figure 536. *Pinus rigida* cones

Figure 537. *Pinus rigida* bark, small tree

Figure 538. *Pinus rigida* bark, medium-sized tree

Figure 539. *Pinus rigida* bark, large tree

HABITAT AND RANGE. Dry rocky or sandy soils; often found with Virginia pine; in and near the Appalachian Mountains from Maine to Lake Ontario, south to western Kentucky and northern Georgia.
PROPAGATION. Seed germinates without pretreatment.
WILDLIFE VALUE. Seed is good for songbirds, turkey, and mice.
LANDSCAPE VALUE. Bold tree that often has a rather contorted form; tolerates a great range of site conditions, especially dry, sandy, infertile soils. Zones 4–7.
BEST RECOGNIZABLE FEATURES. Yellow-green needles in bundles of 3; egg shaped, persistent cone, heavily prickled, flat base; epicormic shoots along bole.

Pinus strobus Linnaeus
eastern white pine, white pine, northern white pine

HABIT. Large tree, more than 100 ft. (31 m) tall, with a pyramidal crown when young, becoming flattened or broadly rounded with age; branches with plumelike appearance and in whorls along bole, each whorl representing one year's growth; young trees retain dead branches on bole, which becomes long and clear with age.
BARK. Green, thin, and smooth, becoming brown to black, fissured, and rectangular blocky with age.

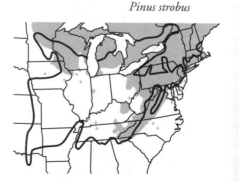

Pinus strobus

Figure 540. *Pinus strobus* foliage

Figure 541. *Pinus strobus* cones

Figure 542. *Pinus strobus* form

Figure 543. *Pinus strobus* bark, small tree

Figure 544. *Pinus strobus* bark, medium-sized tree

Figure 545. *Pinus strobus* bark, large tree

BUDS. Ovoid, sharp pointed, resinous.

TWIGS. Greenish brown the first winter, becoming glabrous.

LEAVES. Needles 3–5 in. (8–13 cm) long, slender, dark bluish green, flexible, in fascicles of 5, with white lines of stomata, persisting for 2 years; fascicle sheath deciduous.

FRUIT. Cone 6–8 in. (15–20 cm) long, pinkish brown, resinous, often curved, pendent; scales rounded, thin, without prickles.

WOOD. Light brown, light, soft, easily worked, straight grained; used for interior finishing (knotty pine), furniture, construction.

HABITAT AND RANGE. Moist upland soils from Newfoundland to Manitoba, south to Iowa, northern Illinois, and in the Appalachian Mountains to northern Georgia.

PROPAGATION. Seed, stratify 30–60 days at 33–41°F (1–5°C).

WILDLIFE VALUE. Seed is fair for songbirds, ruffed grouse, turkey, quail, and mice.

LANDSCAPE VALUE. Beautiful evergreen that is well-suited to average sites and large areas. Some interesting (e.g., dwarf, pendulous) varieties are available. Zones 3–8.

BEST RECOGNIZABLE FEATURES. Bluish green needles in fascicles of 5; deciduous fascicle sheath; slightly curved, pinkish brown cone, unarmed; bark becoming dark gray, thick and furrowed into longitudinal ridges.

Pinus taeda Linnaeus
loblolly pine

HABIT. Large tree, 90–110 ft. (27–34 m) tall, with a long, clear bole and a large, open crown.

BARK. Black and scaly when young, becoming irregularly blocky and dark brown; inner bark slate-gray; without resin pockets.

TWIGS. Slender, glabrous, brown tinged with yellow, becoming darker with age.

LEAVES. Needles 6–9 in. (15–23 m) long, fragrant, resinous, yellowish to grayish green, slender, stiff, in fascicles of 3 (rarely 2), persisting for 2 years.

Pinus taeda

FRUIT. Cone 3–6 in. (8–15 cm) long, yellowish brown, becoming gray with age, sessile, persistent, narrowly conical; scales with sharp, stout persistent prickles.

Figure 546. *Pinus taeda* foliage

Figure 547. *Pinus taeda* cone

Figure 548. *Pinus taeda* bark, small tree

Figure 549. *Pinus taeda* bark, medium-sized tree

WOOD. Yellow-brown, weak, brittle, coarse grained; used for pulpwood, construction lumber.

HABITAT AND RANGE. Found on moist sites from new Jersey to North Carolina west to Arkansas, south to southern Texas, east to Florida.

PROPAGATION. Seed, stratify 30–60 days at 33–41°F (1–5°C).

WILDLIFE VALUE. Seed is good for songbirds, turkey, bobwhite quail, and squirrel.

LANDSCAPE VALUE. Tolerates a great range of site conditions, especially dry, sandy, infertile soils, but not reliably hardy throughout much of the Central Hardwood Forests. Zones 6–9.

BEST RECOGNIZABLE FEATURES. Needles in bundles of 3, longer than pitch pine; yellowish brown cones with stout, persistent prickles; generally limited to southern portion of region and farther south.

Pinus virginiana Miller
Virginia pine, scrub pine

HABIT. Medium-sized tree, 40–60 ft. (12–18 m) tall; crown flat topped or pyramidal in the open; persistent dead branches in the forest.

BARK. Dark brown, smooth, becoming scaly with age, may be orange-brown on large limbs and upper bole.

TWIGS. With a distinct pinkish or purplish glaucous bloom on the first-year growth.

LEAVES. Needles 1½–3 in. (4–8 cm) long, yellow-green, stout, flattened, twisted, in fascicles of 2; long fascicle sheath persistent.

Pinus virginiana

Figure 550. *Pinus virginiana* foliage

Figure 551. *Pinus virginiana* cones

Figure 552. *Pinus virginiana* form

Figure 553. *Pinus virginiana* bark, small tree

Figure 554. *Pinus virginiana* bark, medium-sized tree

Figure 555. *Pinus virginiana* bark, large tree

BUDS. Sharp-pointed resinous.

FRUIT. Cone 1½–3 in. (4–8 cm) long, reddish brown, becoming gray with age (persistent); scales slender, long, with very sharp prickles; inner lip of each scale has a dark purplish band; numerous, persistent.

WOOD. Orange-brown, weak, brittle, coarse grained; used for pulpwood.

HABITAT AND RANGE. Dry, shallow soils or abandoned fields from southern New York, west to southern Indiana, south to Georgia and South Carolina.

PROPAGATION. Seed germinates without pretreatment.

WILDLIFE VALUE. Seed is fair for songbirds, turkey, quail, and mice.

LANDSCAPE VALUE. Tolerates a great range of site conditions, including the driest, most acidic, most infertile soils, but not reliably hardy throughout much of the Central Hardwood Forests. Zones 4–8.

BEST RECOGNIZABLE FEATURES. Twisted needles in bundles of 2; pinkish or purplish glaucous bloom on first-year twigs; persistent cones with sharp prickles; orange-brown bark, upper bole.

Other pines commonly planted in the regional landscape:

Pinus nigra Arnold, Austrian pine. Large tree to 60 ft. (18 m) tall, with broad crown; dark green needles 4–6 in. (10–15 cm) long, in fascicles of 2; much coarser texture than red pine, needles do not break cleanly when bent; cone typically unarmed, 2½–3½ in. (6–9 cm) long; bark develops large, gray, rectangular ridges. Native to eastern Europe. Zones 4–7.

Pinus sylvestris Linnaeus, Scotch (or Scots) pine. Often a picturesque tree, to 50 ft. (15 m) tall; needles bluish green to green (variable), twisted, 1½–3 in. (4–8 cm) long) in fascicles of 2; stems stouter and without pinkish or purplish bloom of Virginia pine; inner bark orange; upper

Figure 556. *Pinus nigra* foliage

Figure 557. *Pinus nigra* cones

Figure 558. *Pinus sylvestris* foliage

Figure 559. *Pinus sylvestris* cones

bole reddish orange; cone unarmed, 1½–2½ in. (4–6 cm) long, not persisting on tree. Widely planted in United States, especially for Christmas trees and for reforestation. Native to Europe and Asia. Zones 2–8.

Planera—water elm
ULMACEAE—elm family

Planera aquatica J. F. Gmelin
water elm, planertree

HABIT. Large shrub to small tree, to 40 ft. (12 m) tall, form similar to that of *Ulmus americana* (i.e., vaselike crown).
BARK. Light gray-brown, thin, forming shreddy scales that exfoliate and expose reddish brown inner bark.
TWIGS. Slender, slightly zigzag, new growth light reddish brown, hairy

lenticellate, becoming silvery-gray and glabrous; leaf scars circular or triangular, with 3 bundle scars; pith homogeneous.

Planera aquatica

BUDS. Terminal absent; laterals minute, about ¹⁄₁₆ in. (2 mm) long, blunt, ovoid, chestnut-brown, hairy, with imbricate scales.

LEAVES. Alternate, simple, 2–2½ in. (5–6 cm) long, dark green above, duller below, ovate; base rounded asymmetrical; margin crenate-serrate with glandular teeth; petiole short.

FLOWERS. Small, greenish yellow; appearing with the leaves

FRUIT. Drupe, ½ in. (13 mm) long, elliptic, pale brown, warty; May.

WOOD. Pale brown, light, soft, not strong, close grained; used for fence posts, fuel; commercially unimportant.

HABITAT AND RANGE. Wet soils, especially those periodically inundated, from southeastern North Carolina to northern Florida, west to eastern Texas, north to southern Illinois.

WILDLIFE VALUE. Little value except to provide nesting and hiding places.

LANDSCAPE VALUE. Has potential for rehabilitating wetlands within its natural range. Zone 7.

BEST RECOGNIZABLE FEATURES. Minute, imbricate-scaled buds; warty fruit; shreddy bark and red-brown inner bark; swampy habitat.

Figure 560. *Planera aquatica* foliage

Figure 561. *Planera aquatica* bark, medium-sized tree

Platanus—planetree
PLATANACEAE—sycamore family

Platanus occidentalis Linnaeus
PLATE 74

sycamore, American sycamore, American planetree

HABIT. Large tree, 100–170 ft. (31–52 m) tall, with a massive bole and a broad, open crown of large, crooked branches.

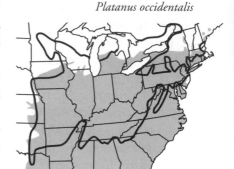

Platanus occidentalis

BARK. Reddish brown to gray when young, thin, flaky, becoming blotched with white as outer bark exfoliates.

TWIGS. Stout, yellowish brown to orange-brown, zigzag, smooth, shiny; stipule scar encircling twig; pith continuous, pale round.

BUDS. Terminal absent; laterals ¼–⅜ in. (6–10 mm) long, dark reddish brown, smooth, shiny, conical, divergent, consisting of one caplike scale, surrounded by leaf scar.

LEAVES. Alternate, simple, 5–8 in. (13–20 cm) long, green and shiny above, whitish and hairy below, triangular; teeth large, irregular; venation palmate; base of petiole encloses bud; fall color muddy brown.

FLOWERS. Monoecious; both types in separate, rounded inflorescences; appearing with the leaves in April.

FRUIT. Globose aggregate of achenes, 1 in. (2.5 cm) in diameter, each on a single brown stalk 3–6 in. (8–15 cm) long; October, persisting through winter.

WOOD. Tan or light brown, hard, strong, with twisted grain; used for crates, pulpwood, furniture, butcher blocks.

HABITAT AND RANGE. Bottomlands and waste places from Maine to southern Wisconsin and eastern Nebraska, south to eastern Texas, east to northern Florida.

PROPAGATION. Seed germinates when mature, sow preferably in spring.

WILDLIFE VALUE. Seed is eaten by some songbirds; dens are used by woodpecker, squirrel, and raccoon.

LANDSCAPE VALUE. Very large, messy tree that has several serious pests, especially anthracnose disease; however, maintain where it naturally occurs; has great potential use in wetland rehabilitation. Zones 4–9.

Figure 562. *Platanus occidentalis* foliage

Figure 563. *Platanus occidentalis* fruit

Figure 564. *Platanus occidentalis* twigs and buds

Figure 565. *Platanus occidentalis* bark, small tree

Figure 566. *Platanus occidentalis* bark, medium-sized tree

Figure 567. *Platanus occidentalis* bark, large tree

BEST RECOGNIZABLE FEATURES. Scaly, mottled bark; fruit balls persisting into winter, borne singly; palmately veined, lobed leaf with hollow petiole that encloses a one-scaled bud.

Other sycamores commonly planted in the regional landscape: *Platanus* ×*acerifolia* 'Bloodgood', London planetree. A cultivar of a hybrid between *P. occidentalis* and *P. orientalis* (Oriental planetree). Good resistance to anthracnose disease, which has caused a great decline in many native sycamores; tolerates very difficult growing conditions including the worst that a city can offer. Both this hybrid and our native species have been much overplanted. Zones 4–8.

Populus—poplar
SALICACEAE—willow family

Key to *Populus*

1.	Lower surface of leaf, petiole, and stems densely white tomentose . . . . *Populus alba*	
1.	Lower surface of leaf, petiole, and stems not tomentose 2	
2(1).	Petiole rounded 3	
2.	Petiole flattened 5	
3(2).	Leaves white below and typically with orange blotches; buds resinous and very aromatic; mostly northern in distribution . 4	
3.	Leaves evenly pale below; buds slightly resinous but not aromatic; mostly southern in distribution . . . *Populus heterophylla*	
4(3).	Leaves with rounded base . . . . *Populus balsamifera*	
4.	Leaves with cordate base . . . . *Populus* ×*gileadensis*	
5(2).	Leaves triangular; bud often > 0.5 in. (13 mm) long . . . . *Populus deltoides*	
5.	Leaves rounded or ovate; bud typically ≤ 0.5 in. (13 mm) long 6	
6(5).	Leaves rounded; leaf margin with small teeth; buds glabrous . . . . *Populus tremuloides*	
6.	Leaves ovate; leaf margin with big teeth; buds tomentose . . . . *Populus grandidentata*	

Figure 568.
Platanus
×*acerifolia*
foliage

Figure 569.
Platanus
×*acerifolia*
fruit

Populus alba Linnaeus
white poplar, silver poplar

HABIT. Medium-sized tree, 60–80 ft. (18–24 m) tall, with an oblong to irregularly rounded crown on a short bole.

BARK. White-gray, smooth becoming shallowly furrowed and very dark gray to black with age.

TWIGS. Greenish gray, white-hairy, slender; pith brown, stellate in cross section.

BUDS. Length ¼–⅓ in. (6–8 mm), light brown, often covered with thick white hair, acute, appressed to the twig.

LEAVES. Alternate, simple, 2–4 in. (5–10 cm) long, 3- to 5-lobed, leathery, dark green above, covered with thick white hairs below; petiole white-hairy; fall color reddish.

FLOWERS. Catkins, 1–3 in. (2.5–8 cm) long; dioecious.

FRUIT. Capsule, ¼ in. (6 mm) long, 3- to 4-valved, dehiscent, releasing cottony seeds in spring.

HABITAT AND RANGE. Moist roadsides and old fields in United States and southern Canada. Native to Europe and Asia, but naturalized in the Central Hardwood Forests.

PROPAGATION. Cuttings; seed germinates when mature.

WOOD. Pale brown, light, soft, readily warping; not used commercially.

WILDLIFE VALUE. Little wildlife value except to provide nesting and hiding places.

LANDSCAPE VALUE. As is true for all *Populus* species, is short lived and has brittle wood, many insect and disease problems, and few ornamental

Figure 570. *Populus alba* foliage

Figure 571. *Populus alba* bark, medium-sized tree

Figure 572. *Populus alba* bark, large tree

assets. This species is fine for a park or other large area, but is not without these problems. Zones 3–8.

BEST RECOGNIZABLE FEATURES. Leaf surface white tomentose below, dark green above; densely white-hairy twigs; white-gray bark becoming very dark with age;

Populus balsamifera Linnaeus

balsam poplar, balm, balm-of-Gilead, tacamahac, cottonwood

HABIT. Large tree, to 100 ft. (31 m) tall, with narrow, open head; typically in large clumps because species root suckers like quaking aspen.

BARK. Light brown tinged with red when young, roughed by dark diamond-shaped openings that eventually develop into deep furrows separating thick gray ridges.

TWIGS. Reddish brown to dark orange, moderately stout, lustrous, glabrous or pubescent; lenticels oblong, bright orange.

Populus balsamifera

BUDS. Terminal ovoid, long pointed, about 1 in. (2.5 cm) long, saturated with yellow, sticky resin having strong odor of balsam; laterals smaller, appressed, or divergent near apex.

LEAVES. Alternate, simple, 3–6 in. (8–15 cm) long, ovate-lanceolate, acuminate, glabrous, deep dark green and lustrous above, pale green or glaucous and usually with orange-brown blotches below; base cordate or rounded; margin finely crenate-serrate with glandular teeth; petiole slender, round, 1½ in. (4 cm) long.

FLOWERS. Catkins, 4–5 in. (10–13 cm) long.

Figure 573. *Populus balsamifera* foliage

Figure 574. *Populus balsamifera* twig and buds

Figure 575. *Populus balsamifera* bark, small stem

Figure 576. *Populus balsamifera* bark, medium-sized stem

FRUIT. Capsule, ovoid-oblong, 2-valved, light brown, about ⅓ in. (8 mm) long.

WOOD. Light reddish brown, light, soft, weak, close grained; used for veneer strips (for fruit baskets), paper pulp, excelsior, boxes, crates.

HABITAT AND RANGE. Moist to wet soils of northern United States, throughout Canada and Alaska to tree line.

PROPAGATION. Seed, collect fresh, do not cover with medium, and keep medium wet; stem cuttings, collect and stick in ground outside in March; root cuttings, collect in late winter and grow indoors.

WILDLIFE VALUE. Buds and twigs are eaten by grouse and several song-birds; twigs and foliage are browsed by deer and moose; buds, bark, and leaves are eaten by beaver, rabbit, snowshoe hare, and porcupine.

LANDSCAPE VALUE. Short lived and requires cool, moist conditions; could be used to provide heavy shade in park or other large areas. Zone 2.

BEST RECOGNIZABLE FEATURES. Fragrant, resinous, long-pointed buds; leaf underside white with orange blotches; upper bole smooth and olive green; lower bole on older trees deeply ridged and furrowed.

Populus deltoides Bartram ex Marshall   PLATE 75
eastern cottonwood, cottonwood

HABIT. Large tree, 150–200 ft. (46–61 m) tall, with a clear, straight bole supporting an oblong or irregular crown.
BARK. Smooth and yellow-green when young, becoming brown to ash-brown to gray, corky, thick, deeply furrowed, with sharp, interlacing ridges at maturity.
TWIGS. Stout, often angular, yellowish brown, glabrous, lenticellate, with branch scars; leaf scars triangular, with

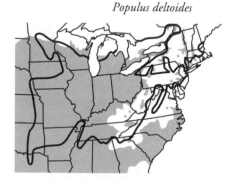

Populus deltoides

3 bundle scars; pith white (unlike swamp cottonwood), continuous, star shaped in cross section.

BUDS. Terminal ½–¾ in. (13–19 mm) long, many scaled, yellow-green, pointed, resinous, shiny; laterals similar but smaller, divergent.

LEAVES. Alternate, simple, 3–6 in. (8–15 cm) in diameter, shiny green above, pale below, triangular; apex pointed; margin serrate; petiole 3–4 in. (8–10 cm) long, flattened (unlike swamp cottonwood); fall color yellow.

FLOWERS. Dioecious; catkins in very early spring.

FRUIT. Capsule, ¼ in. (6 mm) long, 2- to 4-valved, green, borne on cat-

Figure 577. *Populus deltoides* foliage

Figure 578.
Populus deltoides fruit

Figure 579. *Populus deltoides* twig and buds

Figure 580.
Populus deltoides bark, medium-sized tree

Figure 581.
Populus deltoides bark, large tree

Figure 582.
Populus deltoides bole, large tree

kins 6–10 in. (15–25 cm) long, producing many small, cottony seeds in late spring to early summer (female trees only).

WOOD. Light, soft, readily warping; used for pulpwood, fuel.

HABITAT AND RANGE. Floodplain soils and sand dunes, from southern Quebec to Alberta, south to western Texas, east to Florida; absent from the Appalachian Mountains.

PROPAGATION. Fresh seed germinates without pretreatment; cuttings root easily.

WILDLIFE VALUE. Twigs are good for browse; fruit is poor.

LANDSCAPE VALUE. Often regarded as the fastest growing tree species native to United States; trade-off for fast growth is a short-lived, brittle, messy tree; excellent though for seasonally flooded or otherwise wet soils and has a role in wetland rehabilitation, in full sun. Zones 2–9.

BEST RECOGNIZABLE FEATURES. Resinous, shiny buds; angled twigs, white pith; deeply furrowed gray bark on older trees; large triangular leaf scar with 3 conspicuous bundle scars.

Populus ×*gileadensis* Rouleau
balm-of-Gilead

HABIT. Medium-sized to large tree, 60–90 ft. (18–27 m) tall, with a long, clear bole, an open crown, and stout spreading branches.

BARK. Gray-brown, smooth to slightly warty, lenticellate.

TWIGS. Gray-brown to brown, slender, pubescent; leaf scars with 3 bundle scars.

BUDS. Length ⅓–½ in. (8–13 mm), brown, resinous, sticky, fragrant when crushed.

LEAVES. Alternate, simple, 3–6 in. (8–15 cm) long, heart shaped, dark green and shiny above, pale and hairy below, fragrant.

FLOWERS. Pistillate catkins to 6 in. (15 cm) long; staminate flowers never recorded.

FRUIT. Absent; spreads by root sprouts.

WOOD. Commercially unimportant.

HABITAT AND RANGE. Widely planted and escaped to roadsides, old homesites throughout the Northeast.

PROPAGATION. Cuttings, only the pistillate tree is known in cultivation.

WILDLIFE VALUE. Little wildlife value except to provide nesting and hiding places.

LANDSCAPE VALUE. Short lived and requires cool, moist conditions; could be used to provide heavy shade in park or other large areas. Zone 2.

BEST RECOGNIZABLE FEATURES. Leaf surface shiny above, hairy below;

Figure 583. *Populus* ×*gileadensis* foliage

Figure 584. *Populus* ×*gileadensis* twig and buds

Figure 585. *Populus* ×*gileadensis* bark, medium-sized tree

resinous, sticky, fragrant buds; often in thickets, resulting from root sprouts; heart-shaped leaf.

COMMENT. Thought to be either a hybrid with *P. deltoides* or a clone of *P. balsamifera* var. *subcordata*. Its place of origin is not known, but it may be from North America. Widely planted throughout eastern United States.

Populus grandidentata Michaux   PLATE 76
bigtooth aspen, largetooth aspen, poplar, popple

HABIT. Medium-sized tree, 50–70 ft. (15–21 m) tall, with a clear bole, ascending branches, and an oblong or irregular crown.

BARK. Gray, smooth, thin, tight, and with conspicuous small, diamond-shaped patterns when young, becoming grayish green and fissured with age; very dark at base of old trees.

TWIGS. Slender, brown to brownish gray, hairy on new growth becoming glabrous; pith star shaped, continuous.

BUDS. Length ¼–½ in. (6–13 mm), light green above, grayish green below, smooth; margin with large, rounded teeth; petiole flattened.

LEAVES. Alternate, simple, 3–4 in. (8–10 cm) long, broadly ovate, dark green above, grayish green below, smooth; margin with large, rounded teeth; petiole flattened; fall color pale yellow to orange.

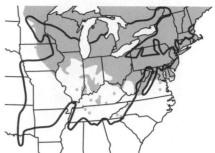

Populus grandidentata

Figure 586. *Populus grandidentata* foliage

Figure 587. *Populus grandidentata* fruit

Figure 588. *Populus grandidentata* twig and buds

Figure 589. *Populus grandidentata* bole

Figure 590.
*Populus
grandi-
dentata*
bark, small
tree

Figure 591.
*Populus
grandi-
dentata*
bark,
medium-
sized tree

FLOWERS. Dioecious, in catkins; appearing before the leaves in early
spring.
FRUIT. Capsule, ¼–½ in. (6–13 mm) long, borne on a catkin 4–6 in.
(10–15 cm) long; May.
WOOD. Light brown, light, soft; used for pulpwood.
HABITAT AND RANGE. Streambanks to exposed, dry hillsides from New
Brunswick to Minnesota, south to Iowa, Illinois, and Kentucky, east to
Virginia.
PROPAGATION. Fresh seed should be sown but not covered with media.
WILDLIFE VALUE. Buds are excellent for ruffed grouse; foliage is browsed
by deer and rabbit.
LANDSCAPE VALUE. Tolerates very dry soils. As is true for other poplars/
aspens, is very limited although an excellent choice for rehabilitating
land. Zones 3–5.
BEST RECOGNIZABLE FEATURES. Buds hairy towards tip; leaves with
coarse, rounded teeth; grayish green bark and diamond-shaped pattern
on younger stems.

Populus heterophylla Linnaeus
swamp cottonwood, swamp poplar, black cottonwood

HABIT. Large tree, 70–90 ft. (21–27 m) tall, with a long, clear bole and an
open, oblong crown.
BARK. Brown, deeply furrowed, with flattened, interlacing ridges, somewhat scaly.
TWIGS. Gray-brown, moderately stout, lenticellate, whitish tomentose;

leaf scars triangular, with 3 bundle scars; pith orange, star shaped in cross section.

BUDS. Terminal ½–¾ in. (13–19 mm) long, stout, reddish brown, acute, slightly resinous; laterals smaller.

LEAVES. Alternate, simple, 4–8 in. (10–20 cm) long, broadly ovate, dark green above, pale tomentose below; teeth fine, curved; base heart shaped; petiole slender, circular or oval in cross section.

FLOWERS. Catkins, 1–3 in. (2.5–8 cm) long; dioecious.

FRUIT. Capsule, egg shaped, about ½ in. (13 mm) long, on catkins 4–6-in. (10–15 cm) long; releases cottony seed in spring.

Populus heterophylla

Figure 592. *Populus heterophylla* foliage

Figure 593. *Populus heterophylla* bark, medium-sized tree

Figure 594. *Populus heterophylla* bark, large tree

WOOD. Dull brown, light, soft, moderately weak; used for pulpwood, fuel, interior finishing, containers.

HABITAT AND RANGE. Bottomland swamps from Connecticut to Florida, west to Louisiana, north to southern Illinois and Ohio along the Ohio River.

PROPAGATION. Fresh seed germinates without pretreatment; cuttings root easily.

WILDLIFE VALUE. Twigs are good browse.

LANDSCAPE VALUE. Fast-growing species native to the United States, short-lived, brittle, messy tree; tolerates even wetter (flooded) conditions than eastern cottonwood and has a role in wetland rehabilitation, in full sun. Zone 5.

BEST RECOGNIZABLE FEATURES. Leaf surface pale tomentose below; leaf base heart shaped; petiole rounded; orange pith, star shaped in cross section.

Populus tremuloides Michaux
quaking aspen, trembling aspen, golden aspen

PLATE 77

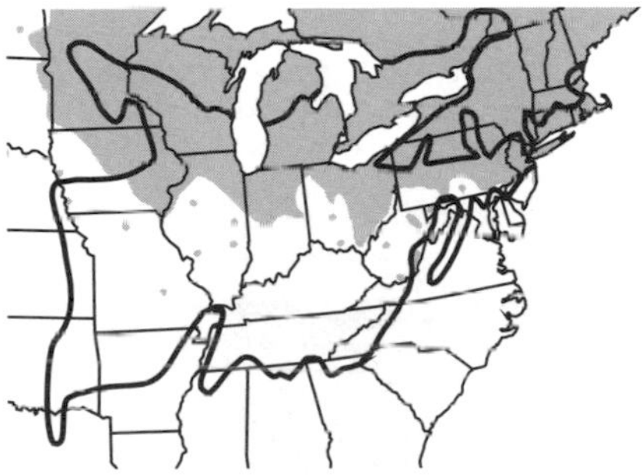

HABIT. Medium-sized tree, to 70 ft. (21 m) tall, with a narrow, short crown and a long, clear bole.

BARK. Light gray to white, becoming furrowed and dark brown to black with age; black limb scars persistent.

TWIGS. Slender, brown, shiny; leaf scars ovoid, with 3 bundle scars; pith homogenous, angled, star shaped in cross section.

BUDS. Terminal reddish brown, small, shiny, conical, sharp pointed; laterals incurved.

Populus tremuloides

LEAVES. Alternate, simple, 1–3 in. (2.5–8 cm) long, nearly round, shiny dark green above, pale below; margin crenate-serrate; petiole 1–3 in. (2.5–8 cm) long, flattened; fall color bright yellow.

FLOWERS. Catkins, 1–2 in. (2.5–5 cm) long; dioecious; March to April.

FRUIT. Capsule, ¼–½ in. (6–13 mm) long, releasing many tiny, cotton-tipped seeds in May to June.

WOOD. Dark brown heartwood, light brown sapwood, light, soft; used for pulpwood, boxes, matches, particleboard.

HABITAT AND RANGE. Recolonizes disturbed sites (especially old burns) in boreal forests from Alaska to Newfoundland, south to the northern

Figure 595. *Populus tremuloides* foliage

Figure 596. *Populus tremuloides* flowers

Figure 597. *Populus tremuloides* twig and buds

Figure 598. *Populus tremuloides* bark, small tree

Figure 599. *Populus tremuloides* bark, medium-sized tree

Appalachian Mountains, Lake states, and down Rocky Mountains to New Mexico.

PROPAGATION. Fresh seed should be sown but not covered with media.

WILDLIFE VALUE. Excellent winter browse for deer, beaver, rabbit, and hare; buds are an important winter food for ruffed grouse in the northern edge of the Central Hardwood Forests, but less important in the South.

LANDSCAPE VALUE. Tolerates very dry soils, is more tolerant of cold than bigtooth aspen. As is true for other poplars/aspens, is very limited although an excellent choice for rehabilitating land. Zones 1–6.

BEST RECOGNIZABLE FEATURES. Round leaves with small teeth and flattened petiole; white to gray bark with persistent branch scars; small, sharp-tipped, shiny buds.

Prunus—cherry
ROSACEAE—rose family

Key to *Prunus*

1.	Stems with spur shoots or spine-tipped branchlets; fruit ≥ 0.4 in. (10 mm) long; stone flattened 2	
1.	Stems lacking spur shoots or spine-tipped branchlets; fruit < 0.4 in. (10 mm) long; stone rounded 3	
2(1).	Leaves obovate to oblong, petiole ≥ 0.3 in. (9 mm) long; fruit red to yellow . . . . *Prunus americana*	
2.	Leaves lanceolate, petiole < 0.3 in. (9 mm) long; fruit dark purple . . . . *Prunus alleghaniensis*	
3(1).	Flowers in racemes; fruit blackish at maturity; bark generally blackish 4	
3.	Flowers in umbel-like clusters; fruit red at maturity; bark generally reddish black . . . . *Prunus pensylvanica*	
4(3).	Leaves often with thick, rufous tomentum along midrib on lower surface; buds greenish; bark shiny, with horizontal lenticels; habit generally arborescent . . . . *Prunus serotina*	
4.	Leaves lacking rufous tomentum along midrib on lower surface; buds grayish brown; bark dull, with irregular-shaped lenticels; habit generally shrublike and thicket-forming . . . . *Prunus virginiana*	

Prunus alleghaniensis Marshall
Allegheny plum, sloe plum, sloe, Allegheny sloe

HABIT. Shrub to small tree, to 20 ft. (6 m) tall, with many erect rigid branches; thicket-forming.

BARK. Dark brown to gray, with thin scaly ridges and shallow fissures.

Prunus alleghaniensis

TWIGS. Dark reddish brown to black, glabrous, shiny, unarmed or sometimes having short, spinelike lateral branchlets; pith homogenous.

BUDS. Terminal absent (terminal present for "cherries"); laterals small, reddish, pointed or blunt at apex.

LEAVES. Alternate, simple, 2–3½ in. (5–9 cm) long, narrowly elliptic, with 2 dotlike glands at base of blade, slightly thickened, dark green above, and paler and often hairy below; apex sharp pointed; base truncate; margin crenate-serrate; petiole hairy.

FLOWERS. Profuse; about ½ in. (13 mm) in diameter, consists of 5 rounded pinkish petals; 2–4 flowers on each slender stalk.

FRUIT. Drupe, about ½ in. (13 mm) in diameter, dark red to blackish, glaucous; flesh yellow, sour; stone large; used for preserves, jellies, and jams.

WOOD. Brown tinged with red, heavy, hard, closed grained.

HABITAT. Woodland edges in moist soils and dry rock mountain slopes.

PROPAGATION. Seed, stratify 90 days at 41°F (5°C).

WILDLIFE VALUE. Fruit is good for many birds and mammals.

LANDSCAPE VALUE. Although its showy flowers and attractive fruit make it worthy of consideration, many other ornamental species and cultivars of *Prunus* exist and are more widely planted; perhaps this one should be used more. Zone 5.

BEST RECOGNIZABLE FEATURES. Axillary "terminal" bud; thicket-forming habit; profuse, pinkish flowers; sour, blackish fruit.

Prunus americana Marshall   PLATE 78
American plum, red plum, wild plum

HABIT. Spreading and low-branching small tree, to 30 ft. (9 m) tall, with slender, somewhat pendulous branches.

BARK. Dark brown, tinged with red, the outer layer separating into long, thin, scaly, persistent plates.

TWIGS. Initially green to light orange-brown, becoming darker and tinged with red, slender to moderate, conspicuously lenticellate, odorless (unlike black cherry), forming slender, spine-like branchlets (spurs) after first year.
BUDS. Length ⅛–¼ in. (3–6 mm), acute, chestnut-brown.
LEAVES. Alternate, simple, 2½–4 in. (6–10 cm) long, elliptic; similar to black cherry but broader, stouter, and without midrib pubescence; petiole with minute glands (typical of genus).
FLOWERS. Ill scented; 1 in. (2.5 cm) in diameter; white to cream color; appearing before or with the unfolding leaves.

Prunus americana

Figure 600. *Prunus americana* foliage

Figure 601. *Prunus americana* fruit

Figure 602. *Prunus americana* bark, small tree

Figure 603. *Prunus americana* bark, medium-sized tree

Figure 604. *Prunus americana* bark, large tree

FRUIT. Drupe, subglobose, 1 in. (2.5 cm) in diameter, thick skin, turning from green to orange to bright red; pulp juicy, acidic; late summer.

WOOD. Dark rich brown tinged with red, heavy, hard, strong, close grained; commercially unimportant.

HABITAT AND RANGE. A variety of sites, particularly along open woodsides or roads and fencerows, often on very dry soils from Maine to Florida, west to Colorado, north to southern Canada.

PROPAGATION. Seed, stratify 90–120 days at 33–41°F (1–5°C).

WILDLIFE VALUE. Fruit is good for songbirds, grouse, and squirrel.

LANDSCAPE VALUE. Good choice to attract wildlife; well-suited to dry soils. Zone 3.

BEST RECOGNIZABLE FEATURES. Spinelike branches; thin, platy dark bark; plum fruit; often in thickets.

Prunus pensylvanica Linnaeus f.
pin cherry, fire cherry, bird cherry

PLATES 79, 80, 81

HABIT. Generally a small tree, to 30–40 ft. (9–12 m) tall, with a very narrow, round-topped or irregular crown; shrubby towards northern portion of range.

BARK. Thin, smooth, shiny, bright red-brown with prominent horizontal lenticels.

TWIGS. Slender, glabrous, shiny, bright red, with pale orange raised lenticels,

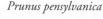

Prunus pensylvanica

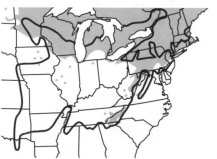

Figure 605. *Prunus pensylvanica* foliage

Figure 606. *Prunus pensylvanica* flowers

Figure 607. *Prunus pensylvanica* bark, small tree

Figure 608. *Prunus pensylvanica* bark, medium-sized tree

Figure 609. *Prunus pensylvanica* bark, large tree

developing short and thick spurlike branches in second year; with very bitter almond smell when bruised, and taste; leaf scars crescent shaped, with 3 bundle scars; pith continuous, brown.

BUDS. Small, ovoid, dull pointed, bright red-brown, clustered near end of twig.

LEAVES. Alternate, simple, 3½–4½ in. (9–11 cm) long, oblong-lanceolate, acuminate; bright green, lustrous, glabrous above; paler below; margin finely serrate with incurved teeth often tipped with minute glands; petiole slender, to 1 in. (2.5 cm) long, and often glandular above the middle; aromatic but bitter-tasting; fall color bright clear yellow to red.

FLOWERS. White, ½ in. (13 mm) in diameter, on slender stalks about 1 in. (2.5 cm) long and arranged in open cluster composed of 4–5 flowers; appearing when leaves are half-grown; in early May, later farther north.

FRUIT. Drupe, globose, ¼ in. (6 mm) in diameter, bright red; flesh very sour, thin; seed stonelike, oblong, ridged; ripening in summer.

WOOD. Light brown, light, soft, close grained; used for fuel.

HABITAT AND RANGE. Moist sites following disturbance across the northern edge of the Central Hardwood region east to New England and south into the central Appalachian Mountains.

PROPAGATION. Seed, stratify in moist medium 90 days at 33°F (1°C).

WILDLIFE VALUE. Many birds (e.g., ruffed grouse, ring-necked pheasant, evening and rose-breasted grosbeak, robin, starling, brown thrasher, thrush, cedar waxwing, red-headed woodpecker) and mammals (e.g., fox, rabbit, squirrel, chipmunks) eat the fruit; twigs and leaves are browsed by whitetail deer and moose.

LANDSCAPE VALUE. Beautiful bark when small diameter, attractive fruit display, and often with fiery fall color; surprisingly never planted; excellent for land rehabilitation. Zones 2–5.

BEST RECOGNIZABLE FEATURES. Bright red-brown bark; open clusters of small red "cherries"; small buds clustered near end of twig; twigs with bitter almond taste; brown pith.

Prunus serotina Ehrhart
black cherry, wild cherry

PLATE 82

HABIT. Medium-sized to large tree, 50–80 ft. (15–24 m) tall, with somewhat pendulous branches; bole long, clear with a narrow, oblong crown in the forest.

BARK. Olive brown to reddish brown, smooth, thin, with horizontal lenticels when young; black, thick scales with recurved edges with age.

TWIGS. Slender, reddish or olive brown with a grayish bloom and many small, pale lenticels, extremely bitter almond taste and smell upon scratching; pith continuous.

BUDS. Length ¼ in. (6 mm), yellowish green to reddish brown, sharp pointed, shiny, smooth.

LEAVES. Alternate, simple, 2–5 in. (5–13 cm) long, oblong-ovate to lanceolate, dark green above, pale below; dense reddish brown hairs typically along midrib on underside; margin serrate; petiole with small glands near leaf base; fall color yellow or reddish.

FLOWERS. White, with 5 petals, in racemes 4–6 in. (10–15 cm) long; May.

FRUIT. Drupe, ⅜ in. (10 mm) in diameter, red, becoming black, edible with strong wine flavor; August to September.

Figure 610. *Prunus serotina* foliage

Figure 611. *Prunus serotina* flowers

Figure 612. *Prunus serotina* fruit

Figure 613. *Prunus serotina* twig and buds

Figure 614.
*Prunus
serotina*
form,
summer

Figure 615.
*Prunus
serotina*
bark, small
tree

Figure 616.
*Prunus
serotina*
bark,
medium-
sized tree

Figure 617.
*Prunus
serotina*
bark,
medium-
sized tree

Figure 618. *Prunus serotina* bark, large tree

WOOD. Light reddish brown, hard, strong, close grained; used for cabinet interior finishing, furniture, veneer.

HABITAT AND RANGE. Moist woodlands, old fields, roadsides from Nova Scotia to southern Ontario, southern Minnesota, south to eastern Texas, east to central Florida.

PROPAGATION. Seed, stratify 90–120 days at 33–41°F (1–5°C).

WILDLIFE VALUE. Fruit is excellent for songbirds, ruffed grouse, and mice.

LANDSCAPE VALUE. Although flowers are attractive, they are typically too high up in tree to appreciate and they lead to a very messy (but delicious) fruit in late summer; best left in natural situations. Zones 3–9.

BEST RECOGNIZABLE FEATURES. Black bark with irregular plates; reddish brown twigs with bitter taste and smell; leaf underside often pubescent along midrib; fruit color changes from red to black; fruit is a drupe.

Prunus virginiana Linnaeus
chokecherry, eastern chokecherry

PLATE 83

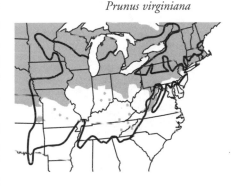

Prunus virginiana

HABIT. Thicket-forming tall shrub to small bushy tree, 15–20 ft. (5–6 m) tall, with slender horizontal branches.

BARK. Dark red-brown, becoming darker gray, irregularly fissured into small, broad plates superficially scaly, strongly ill scented.

TWIGS. Slender, brittle, smooth, pale green to bright red or gray-brown with dull lenticels, with a strong skunk/almond (fetid) odor when broken; pith continuous.

BUDS. Length ¼–½ in. (6–13 mm), ovoid, acute, pale chestnut-brown, glabrous.

LEAVES. Alternate, simple, 1½–4 in. (4–10 cm) long, broad-elliptic to obovate, dark green and shiny above, light green and sometimes hairy below; margin toothed; petiole with minute glands; fall color yellow.

FLOWERS. White, in terminal racemes 3–6 in. (8–15 cm) long; appearing after leaf emergence.

FRUIT. Drupe, ⅓ in. (8 mm) in diameter, bright scarlet to wine-red, dark lustrous, succulent, astringent; flesh covering a hard, singly sutured stone.

WOOD. Light brown, heavy, hard, not strong, close grained; commercially unimportant.

HABITAT AND RANGE. Fencerows, along highways, streambanks, moist

Figure 619. *Prunus virginiana* foliage

Figure 620. *Prunus virginiana* flowers

Figure 621. *Prunus virginiana* fruit

Figure 622. *Prunus virginiana* twig and buds

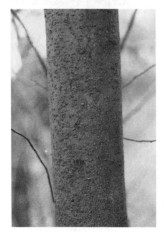

Figure 623. *Prunus virginiana* bark, medium-sized stem

sites from Newfoundland to British Columbia, south to southern California, New Mexico, Kansas, Illinois, Maryland, and southern mountains to Georgia.

PROPAGATION. Seed, stratify 120–160 days at 37–41°F (3–5°C).

WILDLIFE VALUE. Fruit is excellent for grouse, quail, turkey, songbirds, opossum, raccoon, skunk, squirrel, and small rodents; foliage is browsed by deer.

LANDSCAPE VALUE. Good, thicket-forming shrub to attract wildlife. The cultivar 'Shubert' has good potential as a small, short-service (10–20 years) street tree. Zone 2.

BEST RECOGNIZABLE FEATURES. Twigs with fetid odor when broken; bushy habit and thicket-forming; dull gray bark with diamond-shaped lenticels.

Other plums in the Central Hardwood Forests:

Prunus angustifolia Marshall, Chickasaw plum. An uncommon species found locally on disturbed sites across the southern part of the region, from New Jersey to Kansas. Usually a small tree < 20 ft. (6 m) tall or large shrub; leaves small, 1–2½ in. (2.5–6 cm) long, with leaf margin toothed and curled up toward the midrib; petioles red; fruit small, ¼–½ in. (6–13 mm) in diameter, with red or yellow skin. Zone 5.

Prunus angustifolia

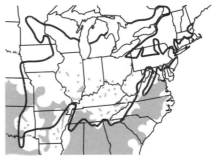

Prunus hortulana Bailey, Hortulan plum. Small tree to 20 ft. (6 m) tall; leaves 3–6 in. (8–15 cm) long, finely toothed, with an elongated tip; petioles red or orange; fruit red (occasionally yellow), 1–2 in. (2.5–5 cm) in diameter. Found on moist sites primarily along streams in Missouri, Illinois, and Indiana. Zone 5.

Prunus hortulana

Prunus mexicana Watson, Mexican plum. Found in the western part of the region, from Ohio to Kansas on a variety of sites. Small tree < 20 ft. (6 m) tall; leaves short 2–4 in. (5–10 cm) long, broad, 1–2 in. (2.5–5 cm) wide, with a doubly toothed margin; twigs short, thornlike spur shoots; fruit ½–1 in. (13–25 mm) in diameter, red or purple. Zone 5.

Prunus munsoniana Wight & Hedrick, wildgoose plum. Small tree or large shrub < 20 ft. (6 m) tall; leaves 2–4 in. (5–10 cm) long, narrow, with an elongated tip and finely toothed leaf margin; fruit small, ½–¾ in. (13–19 mm) in diameter, red. Usually restricted to moist slopes in openings and found scattered from Ohio and Kentucky west to eastern Kansas. Zone 5.

Prunus nigra Aiton, Canada plum. Small tree to 20 ft. (6 m) tall; leaves very similar to wildgoose plum, except that they have a doubly toothed margin; fruit 1–2 in. (2.5–5 cm) in diameter, red or yellowish red. Found on a variety of sites scattered from southern Canada, through New England to Ohio, Illinois, and Indiana. Zone 2.

Other cherries and plums commonly planted in the regional landscape: Most *Prunus* that are planted are cultivars of European or Asian species and are chosen because of their generally small to medium stature and beautiful spring flowers. All have round flowers (usually white or pink) with 5 petals (except double flowering types) and many stamens, a fruit that is a drupe, and glandular petioles. Consult your local nursery for selections in your area.

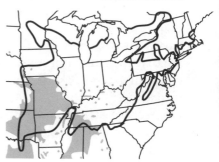

Prunus mexicana

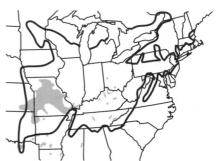

Prunus munsoniana

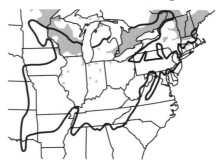

Prunus nigra

Ptelea—hoptree
RUTACEAE—citrus family

Ptelea trifoliata Linnaeus
common hoptree, wafer-ash, hoptree

HABIT. Low, spreading shrub or small tree, to 20 ft. (6 m) tall, with a rounded crown.

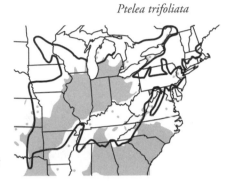

Ptelea trifoliata

BARK. Thin, bitter, ill scented, brown, roughened by wartlike growths, becoming scaly with age.

TWIGS. Slender to moderately stout, light brown becoming dark brown, lustrous with raised, elongated lenticels, with a rank odor when bruised; leaf scars alternate, U shaped, with 3 bundle scars; pith continuous, white, large.

BUDS. Terminal absent; laterals small, silvery to white, hairy, depressed, nearly round, often superposed.

LEAVES. Alternate, palmately compound, 4–7 in. (10–18 cm) long, with 3 leaflets 2–4 in. (5–10 cm) long, ovate to elliptic-oblong, dark green and shiny above, pale and sometimes hairy below, glandular dotted; with fragrance like lemon when crushed; fall color yellow.

FLOWERS. Small, greenish white; in cymes; appearing in early spring.

FRUIT. Samara, 1 in. (2.5 cm) in diameter, yellowish; thin, indehiscent, flat, with broad veiny wings, borne in clusters; persisting into winter.

WOOD. Yellow-brown, heavy, hard, close grained; commercially unimportant.

HABITAT AND RANGE. Rocky slopes from Connecticut and New York to southern Ontario, central Michigan, and eastern Kansas, south to Texas, east to northern Florida.

PROPAGATION. Seed, stratify 90–120 days at 33–41°F (1–5°C).

WILDLIFE VALUE. Little wildlife value except to provide nesting and hiding places.

LANDSCAPE VALUE. Small, seldom planted tree that tolerates wide range of soil conditions; no single outstanding feature. Zones 3–9.

BEST RECOGNIZABLE FEATURES. Horseshoe-shaped leaf scar encircling bud; waferlike fruit; twigs and leaves fragrant when crushed.

Figure 624.
Ptelea
trifoliata
foliage

Figure 625. *Ptelea trifoliata* flowers

Figure 626. *Ptelea trifoliata* fruit

Figure 627.
Ptelea
trifoliata
twig and
buds

Figure 628.
Ptelea
trifoliata
bark, small
stem

Figure 629.
Ptelea
trifoliata
bark, large
stem

Pyrus—pear
<small>ROSACEAE—rose family</small>

Pyrus communis Linnaeus
pear

HABIT. Medium-sized tree, to 40 ft. (12 m) tall, with a narrow crown.
BARK. Smooth becoming scaly, gray-brown, with flat-topped ridges.
TWIGS. Glabrous, of 2 types—long and short (or spur shoots)—with spines often at end of stout spur shoots.
BUDS. Terminal ⅓ in. (8 mm) long, conical, sharp pointed, smooth or slightly hairy; laterals smaller.
LEAVES. Alternate, or crowded on spur shoots, simple, 1½–3 in. (4–8 cm) long, broadly ovate to elliptic, shiny dark green.
FLOWERS. White, 1¼ in. (3 cm) in diameter, in long-stalked clusters; appearing in early spring as the leaves unfold.

Figure 630. *Pyrus communis* foliage

Figure 632. *Pyrus communis* bark, medium-sized tree

Figure 631. *Pyrus communis* flowers

FRUIT. Pome, 2½–4 in. (6–10 cm) long, with green to brown skin; pulp thick, juicy, sweet, edible.

WOOD. Reddish brown, hard, fine grained; used for carving, rules, drawing instruments.

HABITAT AND RANGE. Native to Europe and western Asia, a common escape throughout eastern United States.

PROPAGATION. Seed, stratify in moist medium 90 days at 33°F (1°C).

WILDLIFE VALUE. Fruit is eaten by deer, cattle, and people.

LANDSCAPE VALUE. Best left in orchard setting. Zones 4–8.

BEST RECOGNIZABLE FEATURES. Spur shoots often spine tipped; flowers with 5 white petals, in early spring; fruit a pear.

Other pears commonly planted in the regional landscape:

Pyrus calleryana Decaisne, callery pear. Medium-sized tree typically with ovate-shaped crown; has beautiful display of white flowers in early spring, glossy foliage, beautiful fall color, and very small fruit. Thornless varieties with better overall characteristics include 'Aristocrat', 'Autumn Blaze', 'Bradford', 'Chanticleer', and 'Redspire'. Zones 5–7.

Quercus—oak
FAGACEAE—beech family

Several subgenera of *Quercus* are recognized; the two included in the Central Hardwood Forests are *Erythrobalanus*, the "red oaks," and *Quercus* (or *Leucobalanus*), the "white oaks." *Erythrobalanus* is characterized by inner surface of nut shell woolly; nut bitter; lobes of leaves tipped by bristle(s); immature acorns present on some twigs in the winter; acorns require cold, moist stratification for germination; and acorn cap scales relatively thin. *Quercus* (or *Leucobalanus*) is characterized by inner surface of nut shell smooth; nut "sweet" (relative to red oaks); lobes of leaves not bristle tipped; no immature acorns present during the winter months; acorns germinate without pretreatment; and acorn cap scales relatively thickened ("knobby").

Key to *Quercus*

1. Leaves with bristle tips 9
1. Leaves lacking bristles 2
2(1). Branchlets corky; acorn cap highly fringed along margin and nearly enclosing nut . . . . *Quercus macrocarpa*
2. Branchlets not corky; acorn cap not fringed 3
3(2). Leaves strongly or weakly cruciform shaped 4
3. Leaves not cruciform shaped, glabrous or slightly pubescent below 5
4(3). Leaves distinctly cruciform shaped, tomentose below; typically found in dry habitats . . . . *Quercus stellata*
4. Leaves irregularly cruciform shaped, only pale below; found in wet soils . . . . *Quercus lyrata*
5(3). Leaf margin 7- to 9-lobed, with deep to shallow sinuses . . . . *Quercus alba*
5. Leaf margin crenate, dentate, coarsely toothed, or shallowly lobed 6
6(5). Leaves often white below, margin coarsely toothed or shallowly lobed; peduncle of acorn cap ≥ 1.5 in. (4 cm) long; bark on large branches often exfoliating into papery strips . . *Quercus bicolor*
6. Leaves green or pale below, margin crenate or dentate; peduncle of acorn cap < 1.5 in. (4 cm) long; bark on large branches not exfoliating 7
7(6). Margin of leaf gland tipped; buds glabrous or sparingly pubescent; bark on mature trees flaky, irregularly furrowed 8
7. Margin of leaf lacking glands; buds silky-hairy; bark on mature trees with thick ridges and very deep furrows . . *Quercus prinus*
8. Margin of leaf deeply crenate to coarsely dentate; bud scales reddish brown; acorn ≤ 1 in. (2.5 cm) long; found on poorly drained soils . . . . *Quercus michauxii*
8. Margin of leaf coarsely serrate; bud scales with gray margin; acorn > 1 in. (2.5 cm) long; found on well-drained soils . . . . *Quercus muehlenbergii*
9(1). Leaves not lobed or are spatulate or 3-lobed 10
9. Leaves distinctly lobed 14
10(9). Leaves 3-lobed 11
10. Leaves not 3-lobed 12
11(10). Leaf base rounded; buds often > 0.3 in. (6 mm) long; bark black and very blocky . . . . *Quercus marilandica*
11. Leaf base wedge shaped; buds ≤ 0.3 in. (6 mm) long; bark grayish black and with scaly ridges . . . . *Quercus nigra*

12(10).   Leaves highly variable in shape; buds strongly angled, hairy . .
. . . . *Quercus nigra*

12.   Leaves linear to linear-lanceolate; buds ovoid, glabrous or sparingly pubescent 13

13(12).   Leaves < 0.8 in. (19 mm) wide, glabrous; acorn to 0.5 in. (13
mm) long . . . . *Quercus phellos*

13.   Leaves ≥ 0.8 in. (19 mm) wide, pubescent below; acorn ≥ 0.5
in. (13 mm) long . . . . *Quercus imbricaria*

14(9).   Habit shrubby and often thicket-forming; typically < 20 ft. (6
m) tall at maturity . . . . *Quercus ilicifolia*

14.   Habit arborescent and not thicket-forming; much taller than
20 ft. (6 m) at maturity 15

15(14).   Lobes of leaves extending half-way to midrib or less 16

15.   Lobes of leaves extending more than half-way to midrib . . 17

16(15).   Buds glabrous and somewhat rounded; acorn cap covers only
upper ¼ of nut; bark gray with long ridges; inner bark reddish
brown . . . . *Quercus rubra*

16.   Buds tomentose and angled; acorn cap covers about ½ of nut;
bark black with short rectangular or square ridges; inner bark
yellow or orange . . . . *Quercus velutina*

17(15).   Buds pubescent, at least entire upper half 18

17.   Buds glabrous 21

18(17).   Twigs hairy; buds red; acorns ≤ 0.5 in. (13 mm) long 19

18.   Twigs glabrous; buds gray or orange-brown; acorns 0.5–1 in.
(13–25 mm) long 20

19(18).   Margins of lobes somewhat ascending; bark rough but not scaly;
generally in upland habitats . . . . *Quercus falcata*

19.   Margins of lobes nearly at right angles to midrib; bark with scaly
ridges; often in poorly drained habitats . . . .
. . . . *Quercus falcata* var. *pagodifolia*

20(18).   Sinuses of leaves oval or U shaped; buds angled, tomentose from
apex to base; scales on margin of acorn cap somewhat loose;
inner bark yellow or orange . . . . *Quercus velutina*

20.   Sinuses of leaves C shaped; buds somewhat rounded, hairy only
on upper half; scales on margin of acorn cap not loose; inner
bark reddish brown . . . . *Quercus coccinea*

21(17).   Buds straw-colored 22

21.   Buds reddish brown 23

22(21).   Acorn cap relatively deep (encloses ⅓–½ of nut); bark remaining smooth . . . . *Quercus nuttallii*

22.   Acorn cap shallow; bark developing scaly ridges . . . .
. . . . *Quercus shumardii*

23(21). Nut hemispherical, to 0.5 in. (13 mm) long; acorn cap shallow; occurs typically in poorly drained habitats .. *Quercus palustris*

23. Nut ellipsoidal, ≥ 0.5 in. (13 mm) long; acorn cap encloses ⅓– ½ of nut; occurs typically in dry habitats . *Quercus ellipsoidalis*

Quercus alba Linnaeus
white oak
subgenus *Quercus*

PLATES 84, 85

HABIT. Large tree, 80–100 ft. (24–31 m) tall, pyramidal in youth becoming upright and rounded with wide, spreading branches; clean straight bole in the forest, branched lower in the open.

Quercus alba

BARK. Light ash-gray with age, often broken into small, vertically arranged blocks, scaly, becoming irregularly plated and/or deeply fissured with narrow rectangular ridges. Not as flaky as chinkapin oak. On older trees, bark on upper bole is plated, that on lower bole ridged and furrowed.

TWIGS. Slender to moderately stout, reddish brown or purplish brown, angled, often covered with whitish bloom, lenticellate; pith star shaped in cross section, continuous (as in all oaks).

BUDS. Length ⅛–³⁄₁₆ in. (3–5 mm), reddish brown to purplish brown, broadly ovate or rounded, blunt, smooth rarely hairy, usually with a polished appearance, clustered at tip of twig (as in all oaks).

LEAVES. Alternate, simple, 5–9 in. (13–23 cm) long, obovate to oblong-

Figure 633. *Quercus alba* foliage

Figure 634. *Quercus alba* flowers and emerging foliage

Figure 636. *Quercus alba* twig and buds

Figure 635. *Quercus alba* acorn

Figure 637. *Quercus alba* bark, medium-sized tree

Figure 638. *Quercus alba* bark, large tree, upper bole

Figure 639. *Quercus alba* bark, very large tree

obovate, dark green to blue-green above, pale and often glaucous below, glabrous, 7- to 9-lobed, margin entire; sinus depth variable; fall color red or brown.

FLOWERS. Catkins, monoecious.

FRUIT. Acorn, ½–¾ in. (13–19 mm) long, lower ¼ of nut enclosed by a light chestnut-brown, bowl shaped, shallow cup; cup scales knobby, weakly fused, minutely hairy; acorn cap often with conspicuous stalk (peduncle) to 1 in. (2.5 cm) long; inner surface of nut smooth (as in all "white oaks"); September to October.

WOOD. Pale brown, heavy, hard, durable, strong, coarse grained; used for interior finishing, veneer, cabinets, general construction, fence posts, fuel, tight cooperage (e.g., whiskey barrels).

HABITAT AND RANGE. Upland forests from Maine to Minnesota, south to eastern Texas, east to northern Florida.

PROPAGATION. Mature acorns germinate upon sowing, no stratification necessary (as for most "white oaks").

WILDLIFE VALUE. Fruit is excellent for songbirds, squirrel, raccoon, and deer.

LANDSCAPE VALUE. One of our most beautiful, large, native shade trees, but slow growing, slow to establish, and not readily available; definitely worth leaving in natural stands; tolerates a wide range of site conditions, except do not disturb soil if already established. Zones 3–9.

BEST RECOGNIZABLE FEATURES. Deeply lobed bluish green leaves, whitened below; gray bark, ridged lower on tree, platy above; star-shaped pith in cross section (all oaks); glabrous, reddish, rounded buds; knobby acorn cap.

Quercus bicolor Willdenow
swamp white oak
subgenus *Quercus*

HABIT. Medium-sized tree, 60–70 ft. (18–21 m) tall, with an open, rounded or irregular crown.

BARK. Light brown and loosely plated, becoming dark brown and deeply fissured with age; larger branches may exfoliate (unlike overcup oak or bur oak).

TWIGS. Moderately stout, reddish brown becoming purple or straw colored.

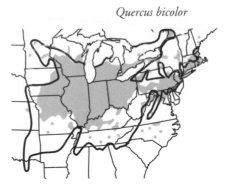

Quercus bicolor

Figure 640. *Quercus bicolor* foliage

Figure 641. *Quercus bicolor* acorns

Figure 642. *Quercus bicolor* twig and buds

Figure 643. *Quercus bicolor* bark, small tree

Figure 644. *Quercus bicolor* bark, medium-sized tree

Figure 645. *Quercus bicolor* bark, large tree

BUDS. Length ⅛ in. (3 mm), yellowish brown to reddish brown, globose, glabrous to softly hairy.

LEAVES. Alternate, simple, 4–7 in. (10–18 cm) long, oblong-obovate to obovate; dark green, shiny, smooth above; whitish, often hairy below; margin with large, rounded teeth, extremely variable lobes; fall color yellow-brown to red-purple.

FLOWERS. Catkins, monoecious.

FRUIT. Acorn, 1 in. (2.5 cm) long, with stalk (peduncle) 1–4-in. (2.5–10 cm) long, ⅓ of nut enclosed by a bowl-shaped, slightly fringed cup; nut ovoid, light brown, pubescent at apex; seed white, relatively sweet.

WOOD. Pale brown, hard, heavy, strong; used for interior finishing, cabinets, fuel, fence posts.

HABITAT AND RANGE. Moist bottomlands or upland wet depressions from central Maine south to North Carolina, west to Oklahoma, north to Minnesota.

PROPAGATION. Seed germinates when mature.

WILDLIFE VALUE. Fruit is excellent for duck, turkey, songbirds, squirrel, mice, and deer.

LANDSCAPE VALUE. Naturally found only on wet soils, but very drought-tolerant once established; should not be planted in soils with high pH (i.e., basic or alkaline soils), which lead to iron chlorosis and poor health; a very handsome shade tree. Zones 3–8.

BEST RECOGNIZABLE FEATURES. Long stalk on acorn cap; bark on branches usually exfoliating; on wet sites; variable leaf shape.

Quercus coccinea Muenchhausen
scarlet oak
subgenus *Erythrobalanus*

PLATE 86

HABIT. Medium-sized tree, to 70 ft. (21 m) tall, with an open, narrow crown, more rounded than pin oak; dead branches persistent on lower bole; tree base may be swollen, enlarged.

BARK. Light green-brown and smooth when young, becoming black, scaly, and shallowly fissured with age; inner bark red or pinkish and not bitter-tasting.

TWIGS. Slender, light brown to dull reddish brown, smooth.

Quercus coccinea

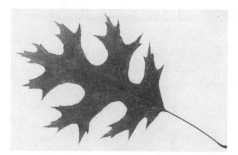

Figure 646. *Quercus coccinea* foliage

Figure 647. *Quercus coccinea* flowers

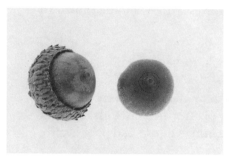

Figure 648. *Quercus coccinea* acorns

Figure 649. *Quercus coccinea* twig and buds

Figure 650. *Quercus coccinea* bark, small tree

Figure 651. *Quercus coccinea* bark, medium-sized tree

BUDS. Length ⅛–¼ in. (3–6 mm) long, dark reddish brown with whitish gray hairs near the tip, blunt, not strongly angled.

LEAVES. Alternate, simple, 4–7 in. (10–18 cm) long, oblong to elliptic, shiny and dark green above, pale below, 5- to 7-lobed, bristle tipped; sinuses C shaped and nearly to midrib (unlike pin oak); fall color scarlet.

FLOWERS. Catkins, monoecious.

FRUIT. Acorn, ½–1 in. (13–25 mm) long, sessile or nearly so, reddish brown, occasionally with concentric rings near the tip; cup deep, bowl shaped; cup scales thick, tight, shiny, smooth; seed white, bitter.

WOOD. Pale brown, heavy, hard, coarse grained; used for fuel, fence posts, general construction.

HABITAT AND RANGE. Dry slopes or ridges from Maine to southern Ontario, south to Oklahoma, east to Georgia.

PROPAGATION. Seed, stratify 30–45 days at 33–41°F (1–5°C).

WILDLIFE VALUE. Fruit is excellent for songbirds, squirrel, mice, raccoon, and deer.

LANDSCAPE VALUE. Good alternative (although without the pyramidal form) to pin oak (*Q. palustris*), especially for drier sites; fall color often brilliant scarlet. Zones 4–9.

BEST RECOGNIZABLE FEATURES. Acorn cup unfringed, covers ½–⅔ of nut; gray-white hairs on upper half of bud; C-shaped leaf sinuses; dry sites.

Quercus ellipsoidalis E. J. Hill
northern pin oak, upland pin oak, Hill's oak
subgenus *Erythrobalanus*

HABIT. Small to medium-sized tree, to 60 ft. (18 m) tall, with branches much divided and drooping, persistent on trunk; resembling *Q. palustris* and *Q. coccinea.*

BARK. Smooth or only shallowly furrowed, gray; inner bark light yellow.

TWIGS. Slender, reddish brown, pubescent but later becoming glabrous.

BUDS. Length ¼ in. (6 mm), ovoid, sharp pointed or blunt, slightly angu-

Quercus ellipsoidalis

lar, reddish brown and shiny; outer scales ciliate along margin.

LEAVES. Alternate, simple, 3–5 in. (8–15 cm) long, elliptic to elliptic-oblong, shiny above, glabrous except for tufts of hairs in axils of veins

Figure 652. *Quercus ellipsoidalis* acorn

beneath; lateral lobes 2–3 pairs, bristle tipped, separated by rounded or elliptic sinuses, extending half-way or more to midrib; petiole 1–2 in. (2.5–5 cm) long; fall color yellow or pale brown blotched with purple.

FLOWERS. Catkins, monoecious.

FRUIT. Acorn, to 1 in. (2.5 cm) long, elliptic, shaped like a top, ⅓–½ of nut covered by an ash-gray, slightly pubescent cup; cup scales tightly appressed; seed yellowish, bitter.

WOOD. Reddish brown, heavy, hard, strong, coarse grained; same uses as for northern red oak.

HABITAT AND RANGE. On well-drained, upland, sandy or clayey soils, from southern Michigan to Minnesota and northern Missouri.

PROPAGATION. Seed, stratify 30–45 days at 33–41°F (1–5°C).

WILDLIFE VALUE. Fruit is excellent for songbirds, squirrel, mice, raccoon, and deer.

LANDSCAPE VALUE. Rarely planted, but would tolerate the driest soils once established. Zone 4.

BEST RECOGNIZABLE FEATURES. Light yellow inner bark; rounded or elliptic sinuses; elliptic to broadly ovate acorn with finely hairy cap; lower branches drooping.

Quercus falcata Michaux var. *falcata*
southern red oak, Spanish oak, red oak
subgenus *Erythrobalanus*

HABIT. Large tree, 70–80 ft. (21–24 m) tall, with open, rounded crown and spreading branches.

BARK. Dark brown to nearly black, smooth when young, becoming deeply fissured and scaly; may resemble scarlet oak.

TWIGS. Moderately stout, orange-brown to dark red, rust-colored pubescence first year, then smooth.

BUDS. Terminal ¼ in. (6 mm) long, red, sharp pointed, hairy; laterals smaller.

LEAVES. Alternate, simple, 5–9 in. (13–23 cm) long, obovate to ovate, dark green and smooth above, yellow to gray pubescence below, 3- to 7-lobed, with sinuses nearly to midrib, highly variable, bristle tipped; terminal lobe longer than laterals; base U shaped; often has drooping appearance.

FLOWERS. Catkins, monoecious.

Quercus falcata var. *falcata*

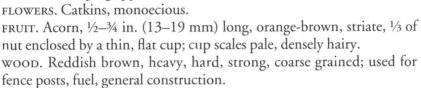

FRUIT. Acorn, ½–¾ in. (13–19 mm) long, orange-brown, striate, ⅓ of nut enclosed by a thin, flat cup; cup scales pale, densely hairy.

WOOD. Reddish brown, heavy, hard, strong, coarse grained; used for fence posts, fuel, general construction.

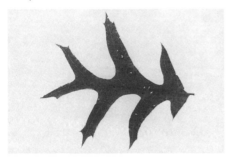

Figure 653. *Quercus falcata* var. *falcata* foliage

Figure 654. *Quercus falcata* var. *falcata* foliage

Figure 655. *Quercus falcata* var. *falcata* foliage

Figure 656. *Quercus falcata* var. *falcata* acorn

Figure 657. *Quercus falcata* var. *falcata* bark, small tree

Figure 658. *Quercus falcata* var. *falcata* bark, medium-sized tree

Figure 659. *Quercus falcata* var. *falcata* bark, large tree

HABITAT AND RANGE. Dry uplands, rarely bottomlands from New Jersey south to Florida, west to Texas, northeast to southern Indiana and Ohio.
PROPAGATION. Seed, stratify 30–90 days at 33–41°F (1–5°C).
WILDLIFE VALUE. Fruit is excellent for songbirds, turkey, squirrel, mice, raccoon, and deer.
LANDSCAPE VALUE. Handsome, long-lived large shade tree that is very well-suited to the driest sites. Zones 7–9.
BEST RECOGNIZABLE FEATURES. Hairy, sharp-pointed, red buds; small acorn with hairy cap; pale leaf, hairy below, with U-shaped base; dry upland sites.

Quercus falcata var. *pagodifolia* Elliott
cherrybark oak
subgenus *Erythrobalanus*

HABIT. Large tree, 80–100 ft. (24–31 m) tall, with an open, rounded crown and a straight bole free of branches; weakly pyramidal when young.

BARK. Light gray and smooth, becoming gray to black and scaly with age; similar to black cherry.

TWIGS. Moderately stout, lightly fluted, orange and hairy, becoming dark red and smooth.

Quercus falcata var. *pagodifolia*

BUDS. Length ⅛–¼ in. (3–6 mm), reddish brown to blood red, sharp pointed; scales hairy, with dark margin.

LEAVES. Similar to southern red oak, except with a tapered or broadly wedge-shaped base and more uniform lobing; margins of lobes perpendicular to the midrib; persisting through winter.

FLOWERS. Catkins, monoecious.

FRUIT. Acorn, ½ in. (13 mm) long, light orange-brown, shaped like a top, ⅓ of nut enclosed by a thin, flat cup; cup scales hairy.

WOOD. Reddish brown; heavy, hard, coarse grained; used for fence posts, fuel, general construction, veneer.

HABITAT AND RANGE. Bottomlands and moist uplands from coastal New Jersey south to Florida, west to eastern Texas, north in the Mississippi Valley to southern Indiana.

Figure 660. *Quercus falcata* var. *pagodifolia* foliage

Figure 661. *Quercus falcata* var. *pagodifolia* acorn

Figure 662. *Quercus falcata* var. *pagodifolia* bark, small tree

Figure 663. *Quercus falcata* var. *pagodifolia* bark, medium-sized tree

Figure 664. *Quercus falcata* var. *pagodifolia* bole, large tree

PROPAGATION. Seed, stratify 60–120 days at 33–41°F (1–5°C).
WILDLIFE VALUE. Fruit is excellent for songbirds, turkey, squirrel, mice, and deer.
LANDSCAPE VALUE. Good large shade tree for very wet soils. Zones 7–9.
BEST RECOGNIZABLE FEATURES. Bark resembles black cherry on older individuals; bottomland and moist upland sites; deep red, pointed buds.

Quercus ilicifolia Wangenheim
bear oak, scrub oak
subgenus *Erythrobalanus*

HABIT. Small tree or large shrub, to 20 ft. (6 m) tall, with a short crown, often with multiple, twisted stems.

BARK. Dark gray to black, tight, thin, becoming fissured and scaly with age.
TWIGS. Slender, brown, shiny, short; leaf scars ovoid, with multiple bundle scars; pith homogenous, angled.
BUDS. Small, rounded, shiny, blunt.
LEAVES. Alternate, simple, 2–4 in. (5–10 cm) long, with usually 5 short lobes ending in bristle-tipped teeth, dark green above, gray to white and hairy below, persisting through winter.

Quercus ilicifolia

FLOWERS. Catkins, 1–2 in. (2.5–5 cm) long; April to May.
FRUIT. Acorn, about ½ in. (13 mm) in diameter, rounded, in clusters, brown striped; deep cap with loose scales on edge; September to October.
WOOD. Dark brown, hard; commercially unimportant.
HABITAT AND RANGE. Dry, shallow soils or disturbed sites (especially after fire), in the northern Appalachian Mountains to peaks in North Carolina.

Figure 665. *Quercus ilicifolia* foliage

Figure 666. *Quercus ilicifolia* flowers

Figure 667. *Quercus ilicifolia* acorns

Figure 668. *Quercus ilicifolia* twig and buds

Figure 669.
*Quercus
ilicifolia*
bark, small
stem

Figure 670.
*Quercus
ilicifolia*
bark,
medium-
sized stem

PROPAGATION. Seed, stratify 60–120 days at 33–41°F (1–5°C).
WILDLIFE VALUE. Winter fruit is good for deer, bear, grouse, and hare.
LANDSCAPE VALUE. Good low, shrubby tree to attract wildlife, particularly
on infertile, dry soils. Zone 5.
BEST RECOGNIZABLE FEATURES. Twisted, scrubby form; 5-lobed, persis-
tent leaves, with densely hairy lower surface; small, persistent acorns.

Quercus imbricaria Michaux
shingle oak, laurel oak
subgenus *Erythrobalanus*

HABIT. Medium-sized tree, 50–70 ft.
(15–21 m) tall, with a rounded or
oblong crown, many branches, and a
straight, columnar bole.
BARK. Dark grayish brown, fissured
between wide plates.
TWIGS. Slender, dark greenish to reddish brown to gray-brown, smooth,
shiny, remaining on lower portion of
the bole.
BUDS. Length ⅛ in. (3 mm), brown,

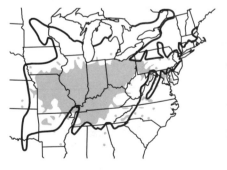

Quercus imbricaria

smooth or may be hairy, ovoid, pointed; scales often dark margined.
LEAVES. Alternate, simple, 4–6 in. (10–15 cm) long, oblong or lanceolate;
thick, shiny, dark green, and smooth above; pale green and hairy below;
margin entire, revolute; apex with single bristle; persisting into winter;
fall color yellow or reddish brown.

Figure 671. *Quercus imbricaria* foliage

Figure 672. *Quercus imbricaria* acorn

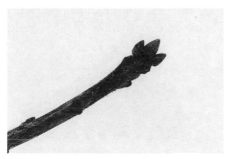

Figure 673. *Quercus imbricaria* twig and buds

Figure 674. *Quercus imbricaria* bark, small tree

Figure 675. *Quercus imbricaria* bark, medium-sized tree

FLOWERS. Catkins, monoecious.

FRUIT. Acorn, ⅝ in. (16 mm) long, dark brown, less than ½ of nut enclosed by a reddish brown, hairy, thin, bowl-shaped cup.

WOOD. Light reddish brown; coarse grained, hard, heavy; used for shingles, general construction.

HABITAT AND RANGE. Moist uplands and creeksides from New Jersey west to Wisconsin, Iowa, Nebraska, and Kansas, east from Arkansas to South Carolina.

PROPAGATION. Seed, stratify 30–60 days at 33–40°F (1–4°C).

WILDLIFE VALUE. Fruit is excellent for duck, squirrel, mice, and deer.

LANDSCAPE VALUE. Beautiful, large shade tree that has been greatly underutilized; tolerates most conditions as long as they are not extreme. Zones 4–8.

BEST RECOGNIZABLE FEATURES. Shiny, leathery, elliptic leaf tipped with single bristle; small acorn with bowl-shaped cup; shallow-fissured bark; persistent leaves into winter.

Quercus lyrata Walter
overcup oak, swamp post oak
subgenus *Quercus*

HABIT. Medium-sized tree, 60–80 ft. (18–24 m) tall, with an irregular crown, twisted branches, and a buttressed base.

BARK. Gray-brown, irregularly ridged with flat, square scaly plates; may have spiral appearance on bole.

Quercus lyrata

TWIGS. Moderately stout, angled, dull gray-brown, glabrous to slightly hairy.

BUDS. About ⅛ in. (3 mm) long, pale brown, ovoid, woolly; stipular appendages may be present near the twig tip.

LEAVES. Alternate, simple, 5–8 in. (13–20 cm) long; leathery, narrowly oblong to obovate, dark green above, green or silvery-white below, 5- to 9-lobed; sinuses irregular; petiole orange-yellow; fall color yellow, brown, or reddish.

FLOWERS. Catkins, monoecious.

FRUIT. Acorn, ¾–1 in. (19–25 mm) long, pale brown, almost entire nut enclosed by a hairy, warty cup with a ragged rim.

WOOD. Dark brown, heavy, hard, strong; used for interior finishing, cabinets, fuel, fence posts.

Figure 676. *Quercus lyrata* foliage

Figure 677. *Quercus lyrata* acorn

Figure 678. *Quercus lyrata* twig and buds

Figure 679. *Quercus lyrata* bark, medium-sized tree

Figure 680. *Quercus lyrata* bark, large tree

HABITAT AND RANGE. Poorly drained, clay sites in bottomlands and swamps on the coastal plain from New Jersey to Florida, west to eastern Texas, north in the Mississippi Valley to southern Indiana.

PROPAGATION. Seed germinates when mature.

WILDLIFE VALUE. Fruit is excellent for squirrel, mice, and deer.

LANDSCAPE VALUE. Native of flooded sites, but tolerates drier conditions; a very handsome shade tree that could be very useful in wetland rehabilitation. Zones 5–9.

BEST RECOGNIZABLE FEATURES. Irregular sinuses of leaf; acorn cap nearly enclosing nut and with ragged rim; bottomland sites.

Quercus macrocarpa Michaux
PLATE 87
bur oak, blue oak, mossycup oak
subgenus *Quercus*

HABIT. Large tree, 70–80 ft. (21–24 m) tall, weakly pyramidal to oval in youth, developing a massive trunk and broad crown of stout branches that create an overall coarse appearance.

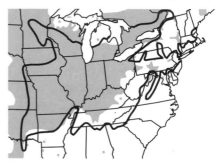

Quercus macrocarpa

BARK. Dark grayish brown, rough with deep furrows and prominent ridges, more vertically ridged and darker brown than white oak; may appear similar to swamp white oak except branches do not exfoliate.

TWIGS. Stout, yellowish brown to brown-gray, densely hairy the first year, typically developing corky ridges after the first year.

BUDS. Length ⅛–¼ in. (3–6 mm), broadly conical, yellowish gray; scales hairy and imbricate, densely hairy; stipular appendages may be found among clustered buds.

LEAVES. Alternate, simple, 4–10 in. (10–25 cm) long, obovate to oblong-obovate, 5- to 9-lobed, the center 2 sinuses reaching nearly to midrib; dark green, shiny, smooth above; pale, hairy beneath; fall color brown or yellow.

FLOWERS. Catkins, monoecious.

FRUIT. Acorn, ¾–2 in. (2–5 cm) long, to ¾ of nut enclosed by a fringed, bowl-shaped cup; tip hairy.

WOOD. Brown, heavy, hard, durable, close grained; used for cabinets, ship building, fence posts, fuel, tight cooperage.

HABITAT AND RANGE. Dry ridges to upland depressions and bottomlands

Figure 681. *Quercus macrocarpa* foliage

Figure 682. *Quercus macrocarpa* acorn

Figure 683. *Quercus macrocarpa* twig and buds

Figure 684. *Quercus macrocarpa* branches

Figure 685. *Quercus macrocarpa* bark, medium-sized tree

Figure 686. *Quercus macrocarpa* bark, large tree

from Vermont to North Dakota, south to Texas, east to Arkansas, Tennessee, and Maryland.

PROPAGATION. Seed, stratify 30–60 days at 33–41°F (1–5°C).

WILDLIFE VALUE. Fruit is good for turkey, squirrel, mice, and deer.

LANDSCAPE VALUE. Large, widespreading, long-lived tree that tolerates wet to dry conditions; has a very coarse texture, making it more suitable for large open areas. Zones 2–8.

BEST RECOGNIZABLE FEATURES. Large acorn with mossy fringed cup; leaf divided into 2 parts; corky winged projections along branches; very coarse winter appearance.

Quercus marilandica Muenchhausen
blackjack oak, blackjack, jack oak
subgenus *Erythrobalanus*

HABIT. Small tree, 20–40 ft. (6–12 m) tall; crown spreading and dense in the open, irregular in the forest.

BARK. Dark brown to black, rough with broad, squarish scaly plates.

TWIGS. Stout, red to gray-brown, lenticellate, initially with scurfy hairy, becoming less so.

BUDS. Length to ⅓ in. (8 mm), red-brown to gray, woolly, rarely conical, more often angled.

Quercus marilandica

LEAVES. Alternate, simple, 3–6 in. (8–15 cm) long, broad ovate; shiny, dark green, smooth above; tan, hairy below; 3-lobed, with shallow sinuses; base rounded; lobes bristle tipped.

FLOWERS. Catkins, monoecious.

FRUIT. Acorn, ¾ in. (19 mm) long, elliptic, often striate, ½ of nut enclosed by a top-shaped cup; cup scales reddish brown, loose, hairy; seed yellow.

WOOD. Dark brown, heavy, hard, strong; used for charcoal, fuel.

HABITAT AND RANGE. Dry, infertile soils from southern New York and New Jersey west to Iowa, south to Texas, east to Florida.

PROPAGATION. Seed, stratify 60–120 days at 33–41°F (1–5°C).

WILDLIFE VALUE. Fruit is excellent for squirrel, mice, and deer.

LANDSCAPE VALUE. Interesting appearance, especially in winter (short height, stout branches, irregular branching, almost black bark); tolerates the driest soils; maintain it where it naturally occurs. Zones 6–9.

Figure 687. *Quercus marilandica* foliage

Figure 688.
*Quercus
marilandica*
acorn

Figure 689.
*Quercus
marilandica*
bark, small
tree

Figure 690.
*Quercus
marilandica*
bark,
medium-
sized tree

Figure 691. *Quercus marilandica* bark, large tree

BEST RECOGNIZABLE FEATURES. Woolly, usually angled buds; blackish, rough bark; dry, infertile sites; shiny, 3-lobed leaf, underside hairy.

Quercus michauxii Nuttall
swamp chestnut oak, basket oak, cow oak
subgenus *Quercus*

HABIT. Large tree, to 100 ft. (31 m) tall, with a wide, rounded crown.

Quercus michauxii

BARK. Light gray or tan, narrowly ridged to plated, scaly with age; resembles white oak; inner bark red.

TWIGS. Moderately stout, dark green and hairy becoming reddish brown and smooth.

BUDS. To ¼ in. (6 mm) long, reddish brown, finely hairy; tip rounded.

LEAVES. Alternate, simple, 5–8 in. (13–20 cm) long, wider above middle, dark green above, whitish and slightly hairy below; margin with large, rounded or sometimes sharp teeth, or just wavy; fall color brown or dark red.

FLOWERS. Catkins, monoecious.

FRUIT. Acorn, 1–1½ in. (2.5–4 cm) long, ovoid, ⅓ of nut enclosed by a deep, thick, bowl shaped, fringed cup; cup scales wedge shaped, hairy; seed sweet.

WOOD. Light brown, heavy, hard, strong, coarse grained; used for general construction, fuel, fence posts, baskets.

Figure 692. *Quercus michauxii* foliage

Figure 693. *Quercus michauxii* acorn

Figure 694.
*Quercus
michauxii*
bark, small
tree

Figure 695.
*Quercus
michauxii*
bark,
medium-
sized tree

Figure 696. *Quercus michauxii* bark, large tree

HABITAT AND RANGE. Bottomlands and moist uplands on the coastal plain from New Jersey to central Florida, west to eastern Texas, north in the Mississippi Valley to central Illinois and Indiana.

PROPAGATION. Seed germinates when mature.

WILDLIFE VALUE. Fruit is good for squirrel, mice, and deer.

LANDSCAPE VALUE. Well-suited to wet soils. Zone 5.

BEST RECOGNIZABLE FEATURES. Silvery-white and densely velvety-hairy leaf underside; light gray scaly bark with age; on flooded soils.

Quercus muehlenbergii Engelmann
chinkapin oak, chestnut oak, rock oak
subgenus *Quercus*

HABIT. Large tree, 70–80 ft. (21–24 m) tall, with a weakly rounded crown becoming irregular and wide with age, a buttressed base, and fine textured.

Quercus muehlenbergii

BARK. Ash-gray, may appear greenish due to moss in bark crevices, becoming shallowly fissured and broken into irregular, squarish scales; rough, more flaky than white oak but without the large plates on upper bole as in white oak.

TWIGS. Slender, yellowish to reddish to straw-brown, initially hairy becoming smooth, lenticellate.

BUDS. Length 3/16 in. (5 mm) long, orange-brown, sharp pointed, smooth; scales with gray margin.

LEAVES. Alternate, simple, 4–6 in. (10–15 cm) long, oblong-lanceolate to obovate, bright green above, pale pubescent below; margin with large, gland-tipped teeth (not bristle tipped); fall color brown or red.

FLOWERS. Catkins, monoecious.

FRUIT. Acorn, 3/5–4/5 in. (15–20 mm) long, ovoid, dark brown to black, 1/3 of nut enclosed by a thin, woolly, chestnut-brown cup; cup scales small, appressed.

WOOD. Brown, heavy, strong, durable, close grained; used for fence posts, fuel, railroad ties.

Figure 697. *Quercus muehlenbergii* foliage

Figure 698. *Quercus muehlenbergii* acorn

Figure 699. *Quercus muehlenbergii* bark, small tree

Figure 700. *Quercus muehlenbergii* bark, large tree

Figure 701. *Quercus muehlenbergii* bark, very large tree

HABITAT AND RANGE. Dry slopes from Vermont to southern Minnesota, south to eastern Nebraska and eastern Texas, east to northern Florida.
PROPAGATION. Seed germinates when mature.
WILDLIFE VALUE. Fruit is excellent for ruffed grouse, turkey, squirrel, mice, and deer.
LANDSCAPE VALUE. Beautiful shade tree that tolerates dry, nonacidic soils. Zones 5–7.
BEST RECOGNIZABLE FEATURES. Dark green shiny leaves with gland-tipped teeth; dense crown; bark resembles white oak, more easily flaked off with hand.

Quercus nigra Linnaeus
water oak
subgenus *Erythrobalanus*

HABIT. Medium-sized to large tree, 50–80 ft. (15–24 m) tall, with a rounded, symmetrical crown and ascending branches.

BARK. Smooth and gray when young, becoming rough, scaly ridged, and gray-brown.

TWIGS. Slender, reddish brown, smooth.

BUDS. Length ¼ in. (6 mm), reddish brown, sharp pointed, angled, hairy.

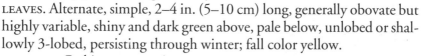

Quercus nigra

LEAVES. Alternate, simple, 2–4 in. (5–10 cm) long, generally obovate but highly variable, shiny and dark green above, pale below, unlobed or shallowly 3-lobed, persisting through winter; fall color yellow.

FLOWERS. Catkins, monoecious.

FRUIT. Acorn, ½ in. (13 mm) long, globose, dark brown, often striate, nut enclosed at base by a thin, reddish brown, hairy, saucer-shaped cup.

WOOD. Light brown, heavy, strong; used for fuel, rough construction.

HABITAT AND RANGE. Moist bottomlands from New Jersey to central Florida Gulf coastal plain, west to eastern Texas, north in the Mississippi Valley to southeastern Missouri.

PROPAGATION. Seed, stratify 30–60 days at 33–41°F (1–5°C).

WILDLIFE VALUE. Fruit is excellent for duck, songbirds, turkey, squirrel, mice, and deer.

Figure 702. *Quercus nigra* foliage

Figure 703. *Quercus nigra* acorn

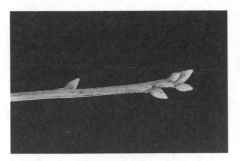

Figure 704. *Quercus nigra* twig and buds

Figure 705. *Quercus nigra* bark, small tree

Figure 706. *Quercus nigra* bark, medium-sized tree

Figure 707. *Quercus nigra* bark, large tree

LANDSCAPE VALUE. Widely planted as shade tree in South; tolerates wet soils. Zones 6–9.

BEST RECOGNIZABLE FEATURES. Glossy, variably lobed or unlobed leaves; small acorn barely enclosed by thin cup; bottomland sites.

Quercus nuttallii Palmer
Nuttall oak, red oak, pin oak
subgenus *Erythrobalanus*

HABIT. Generally a medium-sized to large tree, to 80 ft. (24 m) tall, strongly buttressed at maturity.

BARK. Dark, scaly ridges with age; similar to pin oak.

TWIGS. Moderately slender, glabrous, olive green to red-brown and turning gray.

Quercus nuttallii

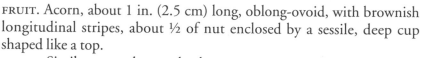

BUDS. Terminal about ¼ in. (6 mm) long, ovoid, slightly angled, straw-colored, glabrous or slightly downy; laterals smaller.

LEAVES. Alternate, simple, 4–8 in. (10–20 cm) long, dull green, glabrous (except below), tufts of hairs in axils of main veins; sinuses deep, rounded; 5- to 7- (rarely 9-) lobed, bristle tipped.

FLOWERS. Catkins, monoecious.

FRUIT. Acorn, about 1 in. (2.5 cm) long, oblong-ovoid, with brownish longitudinal stripes, about ½ of nut enclosed by a sessile, deep cup shaped like a top.

WOOD. Similar to northern red oak.

HABITAT AND RANGE. Common on wet soils of floodplains from west central Alabama west to Louisiana, north to southeastern Missouri.

PROPAGATION. Seed, stratify in moist medium 90 days at 41°F (5°C).

WILDLIFE VALUE. Excellent producer of mast for squirrel, deer, and turkey.

LANDSCAPE VALUE. Large, attractive tree for wet soils. Zone 5.

BEST RECOGNIZABLE FEATURES. Resembles scarlet oak but found in wet bottomland soils; leaves with deep sinuses; acorn cup toplike and encloses about ½ of nut.

Figure 708. *Quercus nuttallii* foliage

Figure 709. *Quercus nuttallii* acorns

Quercus palustris Muenchhausen
pin oak, swamp oak
subgenus *Erythrobalanus*

PLATE 88

HABIT. Medium-sized to large tree, 60–80 ft. (18–24 m) tall, strongly excurrent, becoming irregularly open with age, slowly loses lower branches leaving pinlike stubs.

Quercus palustris

BARK. Greenish gray to light red-brown when young, becoming grayish brown with age, thin, smooth, developing shallow furrows.

TWIGS. Slender, reddish to grayish brown, smooth, shiny, numerous, persistent; slender branches with many short spurlike twigs.

BUDS. Length ⅛ in. (3 mm), reddish brown, sharp pointed, smooth (similar to northern red oak but smaller).

LEAVES. Alternate, simple, 3–5 in. (8–13 cm) long, elliptic to elliptic-oblong, shiny and dark green above, paler below, 5-lobed; sinuses narrow, irregular, and nearly to midrib; edges divergent; persisting into winter (unlike northern red oak); fall color red or brown.

FLOWERS. Catkins, monoecious.

FRUIT. Acorn, ½ in. (13 mm) long, often striate, nearly hemispherical, nut enclosed at base by a flat, thin, saucerlike cup.

WOOD. Pale brown, heavy, hard, coarse grained, used for general construction, fuel, fence posts.

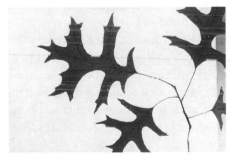

Figure 710. *Quercus palustris* foliage

Figure 711. *Quercus palustris* acorn

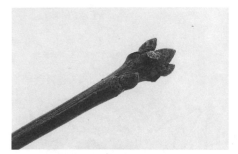

Figure 712. *Quercus palustris* twig and buds

Figure 713. *Quercus palustris* form, winter

Figure 714. *Quercus palustris* bark, small tree

Figure 715. *Quercus palustris* bark, medium-sized tree

HABITAT AND RANGE. Wet clay soils from Massachusetts west to southeastern Iowa, south to northern Oklahoma, east to northern Virginia.
PROPAGATION. Seed, stratify 30–45 days at 33–41°F (1–5°C).
WILDLIFE VALUE. Fruit is excellent for duck, squirrel, mice, and deer.
LANDSCAPE VALUE. Widely recognized as excellent shade tree and perhaps too often planted when other oak species may be better suited to particular conditions. Unfortunately, few native oak species are grown by nurseries because many are simply difficult to produce and transplant. Should not be planted in soils with high pH (i.e., basic or alkaline soils), which lead to iron chlorosis and poor health. Zones 4–8.
BEST RECOGNIZABLE FEATURES. Leaves with deep sinuses, persisting through winter; small acorn with shallow cup; smooth bark; stubby pinlike persistent branches.

Quercus phellos Linnaeus
willow oak
subgenus *Erythrobalanus*

PLATE 89

HABIT. Medium-sized to large tree, 60–80 ft. (18–24 m) tall, with a dense crown, pyramidal becoming spherical with age; bole clear in the forest.

Quercus phellos

BARK. Steel-gray to reddish brown and smooth when young, darkening with age and becoming shallowly fissured and scaly.

TWIGS. Slender, reddish brown, smooth, shiny, spurlike.

BUDS. To ¼ in. (6 mm) long, chestnut-brown, pointed, slightly if ever angled; scales sometimes ciliate.

LEAVES. Alternate, simple, 2–4 in. (5–10 cm) long, elliptic to lance shaped, thick, shiny, medium to dark green above, paler below; margin entire or wavy; terminal bristle tipped; persisting into winter; fall color pale yellow.

FLOWERS. Catkins, monoecious.

FRUIT. Acorn, about ½ in. (13 mm) long, subglobose, brown with bands of blackish brown (striated), slightly pubescent, ¼ of nut enclosed by a thin, saucerlike, usually short-stalked cup.

WOOD. Pale reddish brown, heavy, moderately soft, strong, coarse grained; used for general construction.

HABITAT AND RANGE. Rich bottomlands from New York to southern Illinois and eastern Oklahoma, south to Texas, east to Florida.

Figure 716. *Quercus phellos* foliage

Figure 717. *Quercus phellos* acorn

Figure 718.
Quercus
phellos
bark, small
tree

Figure 719.
Quercus
phellos
bark,
medium-
sized tree

Figure 720. *Quercus phellos* bark, large tree

PROPAGATION. Seed, stratify 30–90 days at 33–41°F (1–5°C).

WILDLIFE VALUE. Fruit is excellent for duck, songbirds, turkey, squirrel, mice, and deer.

LANDSCAPE VALUE. Where cold hardy, one of the most beautiful native oaks because of its texture (from slender leaves and twigs) and form. Zones 5–9.

BEST RECOGNIZABLE FEATURES. Willowlike leaf with terminal bristle; small acorn with thin saucerlike cup and yellow kernel; smooth, gray bark; fine-textured appearance.

Quercus prinus Linnaeus
chestnut oak, rock chestnut oak, rock oak
subgenus *Quercus*

PLATE 90

HABIT. Medium-sized tree, 50–70 ft. (15–21 m) tall, with a rounded, dense, broad crown.

Quercus prinus

BARK. Dark reddish brown becoming gray, coarse and deeply furrowed with thick, narrow ridges; inner bark red.

TWIGS. Moderately stout, light orange-brown to reddish brown, lenticellate, smooth.

BUDS. Length ¼ in. (6 mm), light chestnut-brown, ovate, sharp pointed, silky-hairy.

LEAVES. Alternate, simple, 4–8 in. (10–20 cm) long, obovate to obovate-oblong; shiny, dark, yellow-green, smooth above; pale green, hairy below; margin wavy, with large, rounded teeth; petiole yellow; fall color yellow-brown.

FLOWERS. Catkins, monoecious.

FRUIT. Acorn, 1–1½ in. (2.5–4 cm) long, short stalked, dark brown, ½ or less of nut enclosed by a thin, bowl-shaped cup; cup scales knobby; inner margin of cup curls away from nut (unlike white oak); seed sweet.

WOOD. Brown, heavy, hard, strong, close grained; used for fence posts, railroad ties, tannin extract, fuel.

HABITAT AND RANGE. Dry, rocky slopes or ridges from Maine to southern Illinois, south to Mississippi and Georgia.

PROPAGATION. Seed germinates when mature.

WILDLIFE VALUE. Fruit is excellent for songbirds, ruffed grouse, turkey, squirrel, mice, raccoon, and deer.

Figure 721. *Quercus prinus* foliage

Figure 722. *Quercus prinus* acorn

Figure 723. *Quercus prinus* twig and buds

Figure 724. *Quercus prinus* bark, small tree

Figure 725. *Quercus prinus* bark, large tree

LANDSCAPE VALUE. Beautiful shade tree that is well-suited to very dry soils. Zones 4–8.

BEST RECOGNIZABLE FEATURES. Leaves with coarse rounded teeth; dark, roughly fissured, nonscaly bark; orange-brown twigs with cluster of sharp-pointed, orange, silky-hairy buds; smooth, glossy acorn with thin bowl-shaped cup.

Quercus rubra Linnaeus
northern red oak, red oak
subgenus *Erythrobalanus*

PLATES 91, 92

HABIT. Medium-sized tree, 60–70 ft. (18–21 m) tall, with a rounded, symmetrical crown.

BARK. Greenish brown to gray when young, becoming brown to black, breaking into wide, flat, top ridges and deep black furrows ("ski tracks"), separated by shallow fissures; inner bark pinkish or sandy-colored and not bitter like black oak.

TWIGS. Moderately stout, reddish to greenish brown, smooth.

BUDS. Length ¼–⅓ in. (6–8 mm), dark reddish brown, shiny and smooth or rarely gray and slightly hairy, round in cross section, acute, with many imbricate scales.

Quercus rubra

LEAVES. Alternate, simple, 5–9 in. (13–23 cm) long, oval to obovate; shiny, dark green above, dull green below; 7- to 11-lobed, bristle tipped; sinuses ½ (or less) distance to the midrib; fall color red.

Figure 726. *Quercus rubra* foliage

Figure 727. *Quercus rubra* flowers

Figure 728. *Quercus rubra* acorns

Figure 729. *Quercus rubra* twig and buds

Figure 730. *Quercus rubra* bark, small tree

Figure 731. *Quercus rubra* bark, medium-sized tree

Figure 732. *Quercus rubra* upper bole, large tree

FRUIT. Acorn, ¾–1½ in. (2–4 cm) long, globose to ovoid (barrel shaped); inner surface hairy (as in all "red oaks"); nut enclosed at base by a flat, thick, shallow saucerlike cup; cup scales reddish brown, shiny.

WOOD. Light brown, heavy, hard, coarse grained; used for interior finishing, veneer, furniture, flooring, fuel, fence posts.

HABITAT AND RANGE. Moist, upland forests from Maine west to Minnesota, south to Arkansas, east through Alabama to North Carolina; absent from Gulf and south Atlantic coastal plain.

PROPAGATION. Seed, stratify 30–45 days at 33–38°F (1–3°C).

WILDLIFE VALUE. Fruit is excellent for ruffed grouse, turkey, songbirds, squirrel, mice, raccoon, and deer.

LANDSCAPE VALUE. Few other species are superior as a large shade tree on average sites (avoid extreme site conditions). Zones 4–8.

BEST RECOGNIZABLE FEATURES. Shiny, dark green leaves with red midribs, lobes with bristle tips; shiny flat-topped ridges of bark; variable acorns with flat and shallow cups; buds usually glabrous.

Quercus shumardii Buckley
Shumard oak
subgenus *Erythrobalanus*

HABIT. Medium-sized to large tree, 60–80 ft. (18–24 m) tall, with a broad, open crown of stout branches.
BARK. Dark gray to black, smooth when young breaking into thick, flat, scaly ridges; ridges prominent at the base (unlike northern red oak).
TWIGS. Moderately stout, olive green, reddish or grayish brown, smooth, shiny.

Quercus shumardii

BUDS. Length ¼–⅓ in. (6–8 mm), straw-colored or grayish (unlike pin or northern red oak), sharp pointed, angled, smooth, rarely downy hairy (unlike scarlet oak).
LEAVES. Alternate, simple, 4–7 in. (10–18 cm) long, obovate to elliptic; shiny and dark green above, paler below, leathery, 7- to 9-lobed, bristle tipped; sinuses nearly to midrib, thumb shaped; fall color brown or red.
FLOWERS. Catkins, monoecious.
FRUIT. Acorn, ¾–1¼ in. (2–3 cm) long, grayish brown, dull, oblong, tapering at the tip; cup shallow, bowl shaped; cup scales smooth or rarely hairy.
WOOD. Light brown, light, strong, durable; used for interior finishing, furniture.
HABITAT AND RANGE. Bottomlands, streambanks, and moist uplands from Florida and Texas north to Maryland, Pennsylvania, Indiana, central Illinois, eastern Iowa, and southeastern Kansas.
PROPAGATION. Seed, stratify 60–90 days at 33–41°F (1–5°C).
WILDLIFE VALUE. Fruit is excellent for songbirds, ruffed grouse, turkey, squirrel, mice, and deer.
LANDSCAPE VALUE. Good alternative to northern red oak because it seems to tolerate wetter and drier soils while having otherwise similar features. Zones 5–9.
BEST RECOGNIZABLE FEATURES. Leaf with thumb-shaped sinuses; bark with gray scaly ridges and deep, very dark furrows; thick shallow saucer-shaped cup; straw-colored buds.

Figure 733. *Quercus shumardii* foliage

Figure 734. *Quercus shumardii* acorns

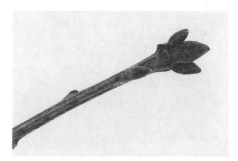

Figure 735. *Quercus shumardii* twig and buds

Figure 736. *Quercus shumardii* form, winter

Figure 737. *Quercus shumardii* bark, small tree

Figure 738. *Quercus shumardii* bark, large tree

Quercus stellata Wangenheim
post oak, iron oak
subgenus *Quercus*

HABIT. Medium-sized to large tree, 40–80 ft. (12–24 m) tall, with a dense, broad, rounded crown or with contorted branches and irregular crown; poorer form than white oak, even remaining shrubby.

Quercus stellata

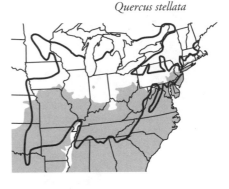

BARK. Reddish brown to gray, fissured into broad, scaly ridges, deeper fissures than white oak, often with a slight twisting appearance along the length of the bole.

TWIGS. Stout, gray to orange-brown, hairy, lenticellate.

BUDS. Length ⅛–¼ in. (3–6 mm), reddish brown, ovoid to subglobose, downy hairy to glabrous.

LEAVES. Alternate, simple, 4–6 in. (10–15 cm) long, obovate; shiny, dark green, rough above; tan, densely hairy below; typically with 5 major lobes, middle lobes squarish; petiole pubescent; fall color golden-brown to brown.

FLOWERS. Catkins, monoecious.

FRUIT. Acorn, ¾ in. (19 mm) long, ovoid, hairy at tip, ⅓ of nut enclosed by a bowl-shaped cup; cup scales thick, less knobby than white oak, tightly appressed, hairy.

WOOD. Brown, heavy, hard, close grained; used for fence posts, fuel, general construction.

Figure 739. *Quercus stellata* foliage

Figure 740. *Quercus stellata* acorn

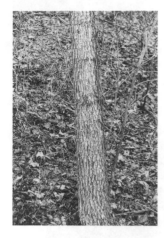

Figure 741.
*Quercus
stellata*
bark, small
tree

Figure 742.
*Quercus
stellata*
bark,
medium-
sized tree

Figure 743. *Quercus stellata* bark, large tree

HABITAT AND RANGE. Dry, sandy sites from southern New England to northern Florida, west to central Texas, north to Iowa.

PROPAGATION. Seed germinates when mature.

WILDLIFE VALUE. Fruit is excellent for songbirds, turkey, squirrel, mice, raccoon, and deer.

LANDSCAPE VALUE. As for all oaks, certainly worth maintaining where it naturally occurs; as for many oaks, rarely available and slow to establish; tolerates the driest sites. Zones 5–9.

BEST RECOGNIZABLE FEATURES. Cross-shaped leaves, densely hairy below; subtle twisting of bark around bole of older individuals; dry sites.

Quercus velutina Lamarck
black oak
subgenus *Erythrobalanus*

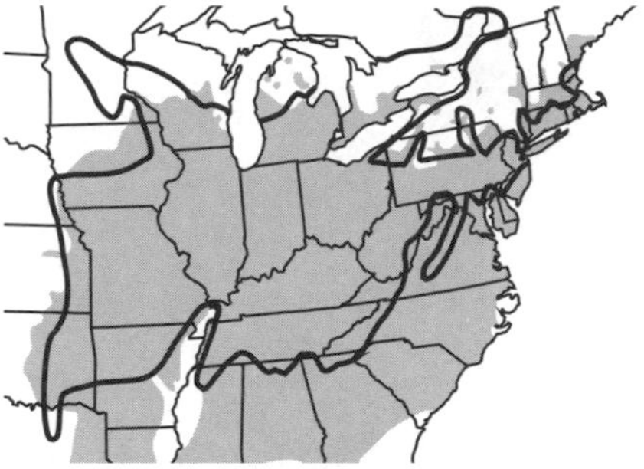

PLATE 93

HABIT. Medium-sized tree, 50–60 ft. (15–18 m) tall, with an irregular crown and often a leaning bole.

BARK. Black, deeply furrowed with horizontal fissures forming thick, scaly, blocky ridges; inner bark yellow to orange and bitter-tasting.

TWIGS. Stout, reddish brown, mottled with gray, lightly fluted, smooth, bitter-tasting.

Quercus velutina

BUDS. Length ¼–½ in. (6–13 mm) long, yellowish gray to dirty white pubescence, conical, strongly angled in cross section.

LEAVES. Alternate, simple, 5–9 in. (13–23 cm) long, oblong-ovate to obovate; shiny, dark green, smooth above; yellow-green, often hairy below; 5- to 7-lobed, bristle tipped; sinus depth variable, shallow where leaves heavily shaded, very deep where leaves get full sunlight; fall color yellow-brown or dull red.

FLOWERS. Catkins, monoecious.

FRUIT. Acorn, ½–¾ in. (13–19 mm) long, elliptic, striate, ¼–⅓ of nut enclosed by a deep, bowl-shaped cup; cup scales dull brown, hairy, free at the cup margin and thus forming a fringe; seed yellow, bitter.

WOOD. Reddish brown, heavy, hard, coarse grained; used for general construction, fuel, fence posts.

HABITAT AND RANGE. Moist uplands to dry ridges from Maine west to south central Minnesota, south to eastern Texas, east to northern Florida.

Figure 744. *Quercus velutina* foliage

Figure 745. *Quercus velutina* acorn

Figure 746. *Quercus velutina* twig and buds

Figure 747. *Quercus velutina* bark, small tree

Figure 748. *Quercus velutina* bark, large tree

PROPAGATION. Seed, stratify 30–45 days at 33–41°F (1–5°C).

WILDLIFE VALUE. Fruit is excellent for songbirds, ruffed grouse, turkey, squirrel, mice, raccoon, and deer.

LANDSCAPE VALUE. As for all oaks, certainly worth maintaining where it naturally occurs; as for many oaks, rarely available and slow to establish; tolerates the driest sites. Zones 3–9.

BEST RECOGNIZABLE FEATURES. Leaves with 5–7 bristle-tipped lobes; sinus depth highly variable; bark on old stems black with blocky ridges; buds pointed, angled, and hairy; inner bark orange or yellow and bitter-tasting.

Other oaks commonly planted in the regional landscape:
Quercus acutissima Carruthers, sawtooth oak. To 40 ft. (12 m) tall; leaves glossy dark green, long, thin, with bristlelike teeth. The general form is

Figure 749. *Quercus acutissima* foliage

low branching and very broad. Cultivated because it is an important source of mast to wildlife. Native to Japan, China, Korea, and the Himalayas. Zones 6–9.

Quercus robur Linnaeus, English oak. To 70 ft. (21 m) tall; leaves resemble a miniature white oak but the acorn is attached to tree by a peduncle 1–3 in. (2.5–8 cm) long. The upright columnar cultivar 'Fastigiata' is planted most frequently. Unlike our native white oak, the foliage of English oak often develops a serious problem of powdery mildew. Native to Europe, northern Africa, and western Asia. Zones 4–8.

Figure 750. *Quercus robur* foliage

Figure 751. *Quercus robur* acorn

Rhamnus—buckthorn
RHAMNACEAE—buckthorn family

Rhamnus caroliniana Walter
Carolina buckthorn

PLATE 94

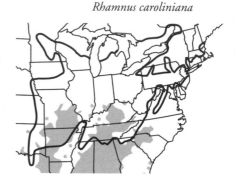

Rhamnus caroliniana

HABIT. Large shrub to small thornless tree, to 30 ft. (9 m) tall, with a spreading crown.

BARK. Thin, ash-gray, often with dark blotches, smooth to shallowly furrowed.

TWIGS. Slender, reddish brown, becoming gray, glabrous or with glaucous gloom, angled, lenticellate, ill scented when crushed; leaf scars with 3 distinct bundle scars; pith round, white, continuous.

BUDS. Terminal ¼ in. (6 mm) long, elongated, naked, covered with dense hair; laterals similar, ovoid.

LEAVES. Deciduous, alternate, simple, 2½–6 in. (6–15 cm) long, oblong, dark yellow-green and shiny above, pale below; margin finely toothed; distinct parallel veins from midrib; petiole pubescent; fall color yellow.

FLOWERS. About ¼ in. (6 mm) in diameter, consisting of 5 white petals; perfect.

FRUIT. Drupe, ⅓ in. (8 mm) in diameter, spherical, red turning black, leathery, containing 2–4 nutlets; flesh thin, sweet, somewhat dry; September.

WOOD. Light brown, light, hard, not strong, close grained; commercially unimportant.

Figure 752. *Rhamnus caroliniana* foliage

HABITAT AND RANGE. Stream borders to limestone ridges from Virginia to western Florida, west to Texas, north to Kansas, east through the Ohio River Valley.

PROPAGATION. Seed, stratify 60–90 days at 33–41°F (1–5°C).

WILDLIFE VALUE. Fruit is good for songbirds and small rodents; foliage and stems are browsed by rabbit.

LANDSCAPE VALUE. Attractive small tree with dark green, shiny foliage and good display of fruit through late summer into autumn. Zones 5–9.

BEST RECOGNIZABLE FEATURES. Shiny, elliptic foliage; blotchy bark; naked, hairy buds.

Other buckthorns in the Central Hardwood Forests:

Rhamnus cathartica Linnaeus, European buckthorn. Small tree to 20 ft. (6 m) tall; bark shiny, silvery-gray to black; leaves simple, subopposite and opposite, elliptic, glossy dark green, with 3–5 distinct pairs of veins, crenate-serrate margin; buds brownish black, terminal lacking; twigs thorn tipped, lenticellate; flowers small, yellow-green; fruit a black, berry-like drupe, in clusters, poisonous to people. This species lacks ornamental characteristics and is a nuisance, but is an indestructible plant that

Figure 753. *Rhamnus cathartica* foliage

Figure 755. *Rhamnus cathartica* bark, medium-sized tree

Figure 754. *Rhamnus cathartica* fruit

grows on a wide range of soils. Native to Europe and western and northern Asia. Zones 2–7.

Rhododendron—rhododendron
ERICACEAE—heath family

Key to *Rhododendron*

1.   Leaves rounded at base; flowers purple or pink; restricted to highest elevations within range ... *Rhododendron catawbiense*
1.   Leaves tapered at base; flowers white; common along mountain streams and lower slopes of mountains ....
.... *Rhododendron maximum*

Rhododendron catawbiense Michaux   PLATE 95
Catawba rhododendron, mountain rosebay

HABIT. Large shrub or rarely small bushy tree, to 20 ft. (6 m) tall, with rounded crown.
BARK. Thin, red-brown, smooth when young, later peeling into thin scales.
TWIGS. Stout, glabrous, yellow-green turning brown in second season; pith homogeneous, pale to brownish, sometimes angled.
BUDS. Flower buds terminal, conical, pointed, yellowish green, less than 1 in. (2.5 cm) long; leaf buds smaller.

Rhododendron catawbiense

LEAVES. Evergreen, alternate, simple, 4–6 in. (10–15 cm) long, broad-elliptic, leathery, dark green and lustrous above, paler below; apex rounded to blunt; base rounded; margin entire; petiole stout.
FLOWERS. Bell shaped with 5 rounded lobes, 2¼ in. (6 cm) in diameter, waxy lilac purple or pink, in upright rounded clusters; late spring to early summer.
FRUIT. Capsule, 5-celled, ovoid, ½ in. (13 mm) long, long stalked; persisting through winter.
WOOD. Hard, close grained; used for turned objects, pipe bowls, fuel.

Figure 756. *Rhododendron catawbiense* foliage

HABITAT AND RANGE. High mountain slopes of the Allegheny Mountains, West Virginia, southwest to Georgia and Alabama in the southern Appalachian Mountains.

PROPAGATION. Fresh seed germinates if not covered by media, then sow on fine sphagnum and keep moist; cuttings require a hormone dip to root.

WILDLIFE VALUE. Foliage and twigs are browsed by whitetail deer; tree provides excellent year-round cover for birds and small game.

LANDSCAPE VALUE. Beautiful, large, evergreen shrub for moist, well-drained, acidic, cool (heavily mulched) soils; should also be kept out of strong winter sun. The "plain" species is rarely planted because there are so many varieties of the species and hybrids that are more reliable in winter hardiness and offer more popular colors. Dirr (1990) lists numerous varieties that have flower colors ranging from white, yellow, pink, lavender, purple, and red, to everything in between. Zones 4–8.

BEST RECOGNIZABLE FEATURES. Broad-elliptic leaves with rounded base; pinkish purple, bell-shaped flowers; typically in dense thickets at high elevations in the central and southern Appalachian Mountains.

Rhododendron maximum Linnaeus   PLATE 96
rosebay rhododendron, rosebay, great-laurel

HABIT. Dense shrub to bushy tree, 6–30 ft. (2–9 m) tall, often in thickets, with a short, crooked, and often prostrate bole supporting a round crown of stout contorted branches.

BARK. Light red-brown, smooth when young, becoming broken superficially into small, thin, appressed scales.

TWIGS. Stout, glabrous, dark green turning red-brown in second season and ultimately becoming gray tinged with red; pith continuous, brown or pale, sometimes angled.

BUDS. Flower buds terminal, to 1½ in. (4 cm) long, dark green, conical;

leaf buds smaller, with many imbricate scales; solitary.

LEAVES. Evergreen, alternate, simple, 4–10 in. (10–25 cm) long, oblong, leathery, dark green and shiny above, paler below; margin revolute; base tapered; apex pointed.

FLOWERS. White, pink, or rarely purple; in terminal clusters 4–6 in. (10–15 cm) in diameter with 16–24 flowers, individual flowers 1½ in. (4 cm) in diameter.

Rhododendron maximum

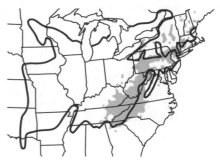

FRUIT. Capsule, ½ in. (13 mm) long, woody, 5-celled, ovoid; maturing in autumn, persisting through winter.

Figure 757. *Rhododendron maximum* foliage

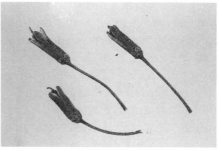

Figure 758. *Rhododendron maximum* fruit

Figure 759. *Rhododendron maximum* bark, small stem

Figure 760. *Rhododendron maximum* bark, large stem

WOOD. Light, clear brown, heavy, hard, strong, rather brittle, close grained; commercially unimportant.

HABITAT AND RANGE. Along streambanks and rocky slopes from Nova Scotia to Georgia and Alabama (mountain and upper Piedmont), west to Ohio, north to southern Ontario.

PROPAGATION. Cuttings.

WILDLIFE VALUE. Buds are eaten by grouse; leaves are eaten by deer; tree provides excellent cover.

LANDSCAPE VALUE. More colorful species and varieties of *Rhododendron* are usually available (e.g., *R. catawbiense*). Like *R. catawbiense*, suitable for moist, well-drained, acidic, cool (heavily mulched) soils and should be kept out of strong winter sun. Zones 3–7.

BEST RECOGNIZABLE FEATURES. Evergreen, elliptic, leathery leaves; terminal clusters of white flowers in midsummer; persistent clusters of woody seed capsules.

Rhus—sumac
ANACARDIACEAE— cashew family

Rhus typhina Linnaeus
staghorn sumac, velvet sumac

PLATE 97

HABIT. Thicket-forming small tree to large shrub, 15–30 ft. (5–9 m) tall, with a short bole, ascending branches, and a flat-topped crown.

BARK. Light brown, thin, and smooth when young becoming dark brown with lenticels and scales at maturity.

TWIGS. Stout, brown, densely covered with velvety hairs, clublike, somewhat triangular, brittle, exuding a white sticky sap when broken; leaf scars U shaped, nearly surrounding the buds, with many bundle scars; pith continuous, large, orange-brown.

Rhus typhina

BUDS. Terminal absent; laterals ⅛ in. (3 mm) long, hairy, alternate.

LEAVES. Alternate, pinnately compound, 12–24 in. (31–61 cm) long, green above, pale below, with 13–23 lanceolate leaflets 2–4 in. (5–10 cm) long; margin serrate; rachis stout, hairy; fall color orange-scarlet.

Figure 761. *Rhus typhina* foliage

Figure 762. *Rhus typhina* flowers

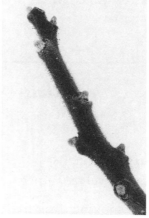

Figure 763. *Rhus typhina* fruit

Figure 764. *Rhus typhina* twig and buds

Figure 765. *Rhus typhina* bark, medium-sized stem

FLOWERS. Greenish, ⅛ in. (3 mm) in diameter, in upright, tight clusters to 8 in. (20 cm) long; dioecious.

FRUIT. Drupe, ⅛ in. (3 mm) in diameter, hairy, bright red, borne in erect, pyramidal clusters; persisting through winter; very tart.

WOOD. Orange to golden-brown, light, soft; commercially unimportant.

HABITAT AND RANGE. Abandoned fields, roadsides, clearings from Quebec and Ontario south to Iowa, Kentucky, and Tennessee.

PROPAGATION. Seed, scarify by soaking in sulfuric acid or hot water, or by mechanically filing the seed coat.

WILDLIFE VALUE. Fruit is eaten by some songbirds, grouse, quail, and small mammals.

LANDSCAPE VALUE. Would probably be more highly regarded if it was not so abundant on old fields and waste soils, and did not root sucker so profusely; tolerates all but water-saturated soils, has interesting texture and outstanding fall color. Zones 3–8.

BEST RECOGNIZABLE FEATURES. Stout, densely hairy stems that exude milky sap when broken; large, orange-brown pith; erect, red, persistent cluster of hairy drupes.

Other tree-size sumacs in the Central Hardwood Forests (features not mentioned are similar to *R. typhina*):

Rhus copallina Linnaeus, winged or shining sumac. Leaves with small, leaf-like wings along the rachis, leaf scars broadly crescent shaped; twigs slender to moderate, lenticellate, and with short, downy hairs; fruit pubescent. Native from Maine to Ontario, south to Texas and Florida. Zones 4–9.

Rhus copallina

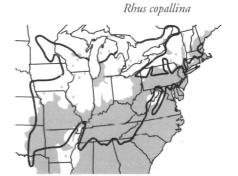

Figure 766. *Rhus copallina* foliage

Figure 767. *Rhus copallina* flowers

Figure 768. *Rhus copallina* bark, small stem

Figure 769. *Rhus copallina* bark, large stem

Rhus glabra Linnaeus, smooth sumac. Twigs glabrous, stout, often covered by a glaucous bloom, somewhat 3-sided; fruit not as hairy as *R. typhina*. Native from Maine to British Columbia, south to Florida and Arizona. Zones 2–9.

Rhus glabra

Figure 770. *Rhus glabra* foliage

Figure 771. *Rhus glabra* fruit

Figure 772. *Rhus glabra* twig and buds

Robinia—locust
FABACEAE—bean or pea family

Key to *Robinia*

1. Leaf rachis and fruit covered with sticky glands; flowers pinkish
    . . . . *Robinia viscosa*
1. Leaf rachis and fruit glabrous; flowers white . . . .
    . . . . *Robinia pseudoacacia*

Robinia pseudoacacia Linnaeus
black locust, yellow locust, locust

PLATE 98

HABIT. Medium sized tree, 40–70 ft. (12–21 m) tall, usually with low branching and several large, ascending branches that form an irregular, open crown, becoming more ragged with age.

BARK. Reddish brown to dark brown, deeply furrowed with interlacing ridges having a shreddy surface; inner bark orange and visible on old specimens.

TWIGS. Moderate to stout, dark brown, brittle, zigzag, smooth, angled, usually with stipular spines ½–1 in. (13–

Robinia pseudoacacia

25 mm) long in pairs at each node; pith continuous, white, often angled.
BUDS. Terminal absent; laterals ¹⁄₁₆ in. (2 mm) long, rusty brown to
brown, with 3–4 superposed, downy buds; covered by base of petiole
and later recessed in leaf scar and often hidden.

LEAVES. Alternate, pinnately compound, 8–14 in. (20–36 cm) long, elliptic, dull green above, pale below, with 7–11 leaflets 1–2 in. (2.5–5 cm)
long; margin with tiny bristle tip, entire; fall color yellow.

FLOWERS. White, fragrant, ¾ in. (19 mm) long; in drooping clusters 4–8
in. (10–20 cm) long; very showy; May.

FRUIT. Flat pod, 2–4 in. (5–10 cm) long, brownish black, narrow; seed
kidney shaped; September, persisting through winter.

WOOD. Dark yellow to brown, heavy, hard, strong; used for fence posts,
tool handles, fuel, erosion control plantings.

HABITAT AND RANGE. Abandoned fields, dry slopes, roadsides from south-

Figure 773. *Robinia pseudoacacia* foliage

Figure 774. *Robinia pseudo-acacia* flowers

Figure 775. *Robinia pseudoacacia* fruit and seed

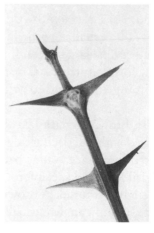

Figure 776. *Robinia pseudo-acacia* twig

Figure 777. *Robinia pseudo-acacia* bark, small tree

Figure 778. *Robinia pseudo-acacia* bark, medium-sized tree

Figure 779. *Robinia pseudoacacia* bark, large tree

ern New England, south to northern Alabama, north to southern Illinois; also Ozark Mountains in Missouri, Arkansas, and Oklahoma.

PROPAGATION. Seed, scarify by soaking in sulfuric acid 1 hour and rinsing thoroughly with water, or by mechanically filing the seed coat to allow water inside; no stratification needed.

WILDLIFE VALUE. Dens are used by songbirds and squirrel.

LANDSCAPE VALUE. Often weedy and short lived (due to insects and disease) in eastern United States, although some varieties appear to offer promise; an exceptional species for reclaiming all but flooded sites. Zones 3–8.

BEST RECOGNIZABLE FEATURES. Stipular spines in pairs at nodes; deeply furrowed bark with fibrous ridges; blue-green pinnately compound leaf; flat legume; fragrant white clusters of flowers.

Robinia viscosa Ventenat
clammy locust

HABIT. Thicket-forming shrub to small tree, to 30 ft. (9 m) tall.

Robinia viscosa

BARK. Smooth becoming furrowed, dark brown.

TWIGS. Dark reddish brown, with small stipular spines in pairs at some nodes; with sticky glands; leaf scars large, triangular or 3-lobed, raised; pith homogeneous, white.

BUDS. Terminal absent; laterals hidden, with 3–4 superposed, embedded under leaf scar, downy, naked.

LEAVES. Alternate, pinnately compound, 5–10 in. (13–25 cm) long, with 13–23 ovate leaflets; apex of leaflets bristle tipped; leaf petiole and rachis covered with sticky glands.

FLOWERS. Each raceme with 6–16 pink or flesh-colored flowers each with yellow blotch; flower stalk covered with sticky glands.

FRUIT. Winged pod, narrow, oblong, 2–3 in. (5–8 cm) long; seed bean-like, and mottled brown, covered with sticky glands.

HABITAT AND RANGE. Open forests, clearings, and waste places above 3000 ft. (900 m) elevation in North and South Carolina mountains.

PROPAGATION. Seed, scarify by soaking 24 hours in hot water or sulfuric acid.

WILDLIFE VALUE. Tree provides cover.

LANDSCAPE VALUE. Excellent choice to minimize soil erosion. Zone 3.

BEST RECOGNIZABLE FEATURES. Shorter leaves than *Robinia pseudoacacia*, but with more leaflets; fewer spines on twig than *R. pseudoacacia*; glandular, sticky hairs on fruit, twigs, and leaf rachises; rosy or flesh-colored flowers.

Salix—willow
SALICACEAE—willow family

Key to *Salix*

1.   Leaf margin finely serrate; petiole generally glandular at or near junction with blade 3
1.   Leaf margin irregular, lacking evenly spaced, fine serrations; petiole lacking glands . . . . *Salix discolor*
2(1).   Leaves strongly glaucous below 3
2.   Leaves green or only pale below . . . . *Salix nigra*
3(2).   Leaves and twigs somewhat pubescent; petioles typically ≤ 0.3 in. (6 mm) long . . . . *Salix caroliniana*
3.   Leaves and twigs glabrous; petioles typically > 0.3 in. (6 mm) long and up to 0.8 in. (19 mm) long . . . . . *Salix amygdaloides*

Salix amygdaloides Andersson
peach-leaf willow

HABIT. Shrub or small tree, 10–40 ft. (3–12 m) tall, with 1–3 often leaning trunks, 4–16 in. (10–41 cm) in diameter, and a narrow, rounded crown.

BARK. Thin, ½–¾ in. (13–19 mm) thick, reddish brown or darker in fissures of main stem; branches gray-brown.

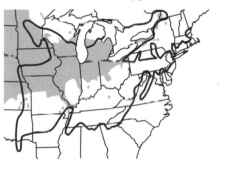

Salix amygdaloides

TWIGS. Slender, yellowish to orange-brown, glabrous, with pale lenticels, drooping at the tip, not brittle.

BUDS. Ovoid, pointed, ¼ in. (6 mm) long, yellowish but darker near apex, glabrous, lustrous.

LEAVES. Alternate, simple, 2–5 in. (5–13 cm) long, ½–¾ in. (13–19 mm) wide, lanceolate to lance-ovate, yellow-green to dark green above, glaucous below; petiole ½–¾ in. (13–19 mm) long; margin finely serrate; apex very long pointed; stipules absent, or occasionally small and deciduous early.

FLOWERS. Aments; borne on short, leafy peduncles.

FRUIT. Capsule, smooth, less than ¼ in. (6 mm) long, 2-valved, light reddish yellow.

WOOD. Brown heartwood, white sapwood, soft, weak.

HABITAT AND RANGE. Wet woods and swamps, alluvial soils, from Quebec west to Washington, south to Pennsylvania, Kentucky, and Texas.

PROPAGATION. Fresh seed germinates without pretreatment; cuttings root readily.

WILDLIFE VALUE. Wood is eaten and used by beaver; tree provides good cover for waterfowl.

LANDSCAPE VALUE. Excellent potential for wetland rehabilitation. Zone 4.

BEST RECOGNIZABLE FEATURES. Leaves glaucous below, with very long pointed apex; stipules absent.

Salix caroliniana Michaux
Carolina willow, Ward's willow, long-pedicelled willow

HABIT. Shrub or tree, to 30 ft. (9 m) tall, with a spreading, open, irregular crown.

BARK. Gray, deeply furrowed.

TWIGS. Slender, brittle, yellowish, becoming reddish or purplish with age, pubescent.

BUDS. Sharp pointed; scales overlapping, yellowish to dark brown.

LEAVES. Alternate, simple, 3–6 in. (8–15 cm) long, ½–1 in. (13–25 mm) wide, lanceolate, dark green above, densely glaucous below, often pubescent; petiole less than ½ in. (13 mm) long; teeth rounded and yellow

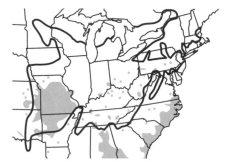

Salix caroliniana

Figure 780. *Salix caroliniana* foliage

Figure 781. *Salix caroliniana* bark, small tree

glandular; stipules ¼–½ in. (6–13 mm) long and winglike; base rounded; apex long pointed.

FLOWERS. Aments, up to 4 in. (10 cm) long, on leafy peduncles; scales yellowish.

FRUIT. Capsule, glabrous, ¼ in. (6 mm) long.

WOOD. Brown heartwood, white sapwood, soft, weak.

HABITAT AND RANGE. Along water courses and shores, from Florida to Texas, north to Maryland, West Virginia, southern Indiana, southern Illinois, Missouri, and Kansas.

PROPAGATION. Fresh seed germinates without pretreatment; cuttings root readily.

WILDLIFE VALUE. Wood is eaten and used by beaver; tree provides good cover for waterfowl.

LANDSCAPE VALUE. Excellent choice for wetland rehabilitation. Zones 5–10.

BEST RECOGNIZABLE FEATURES. Leaf glaucous below; toothed margin with yellow glands; stipules winglike, eventually deciduous.

Salix discolor Muhlenberg
pussy willow

PLATE 99

HABIT. Multistemmed shrub or small tree, 15–20 ft. (5–6 m) tall, with stout, ascending branches and an open, round crown.

BARK. Light brown to gray tinged with red, divided by shallow fissures into thin, platelike, oblong scales.

TWIGS. Stout, reddish to dark brown, smooth or thinly hairy when young; pith continuous.

Salix discolor

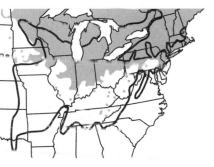

BUDS. Large, ⅜ in. (10 mm) long, dark reddish purple, lustrous, flattened, appressed, acute at apex, with single caplike scale.

LEAVES. Alternate, simple, 1½–4½ in. (4–11 cm) long, oblong to oblanceolate; bright green, glabrous above; blue green, glaucous, sometimes hairy below; margin toothed sparingly, especially about the middle.

FLOWERS. Aments; staminate are soft and silky before flowers open; late winter or early spring.

FRUIT. Capsule, 2-valved, one-celled, containing many silky-hairy seeds.

Figure 782. *Salix discolor* foliage

Figure 783.
Salix discolor
flowers,
pistillate

Figure 784.
Salix discolor
fruit,
immature

Figure 785. *Salix discolor* bark,
medium-sized tree

WOOD. Brown streaked with red, light, soft, close grained; commercially unimportant.

HABITAT AND RANGE. Swamps, streambanks, moist lowlands from Newfoundland west to central British Columbia, south to Idaho, east to Delaware, and in mountains south to eastern Tennessee.

PROPAGATION. Fresh seed germinates if uncovered and kept in moist media; cuttings root easily.

WILDLIFE VALUE. Buds are eaten by grouse; stems and foliage are browsed by beaver, rabbit, and deer.

LANDSCAPE VALUE. Excellent choice for wetland rehabilitation. Zone 2.

BEST RECOGNIZABLE FEATURES. Single caplike bud scale; multistemmed habit; soft, silky male flowers in early spring.

Salix nigra Marshall
black willow, swamp willow, willow

HABIT. Small tree, 30–40 ft. (9–12 m) tall, with a short bole and a spreading, open irregular crown.

Salix nigra

BARK. Dark brown to black, deeply furrowed with shaggy scales on old specimens.

TWIGS. Slender, pale orange to brownish red, darkening with age, brittle, smooth, becoming somewhat pendulous with age.

BUDS. Terminal absent; laterals ⅛ in. (3 mm) long, reddish brown, alternate, with one caplike scale, appressed to the stem.

LEAVES. Alternate, simple, 2–6 in. (5–15 cm) long, narrowly lanceolate, dark green and smooth above, pale below; margin finely serrate, red glandular; apex long pointed, often falcate; base wedge shaped; stipules large, persistent.

FLOWERS. Aments.

FRUIT. Capsule, 2-valved, ¼ in. (6 mm) long, reddish brown, borne in clusters 3–6 in. (8–15 cm) long.

WOOD. Light reddish brown, light, soft, weak; used for pulpwood, charcoal, veneer, flooring, boxes, crates.

HABITAT AND RANGE. Wet sites from New Brunswick to eastern Minnesota, south to southern Texas, east to northern Florida.

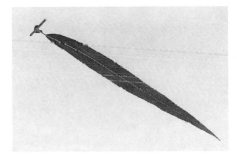

Figure 786. *Salix nigra* foliage

Figure 787. *Salix nigra* bark, small tree

Figure 788.
Salix nigra
bark,
medium-
sized tree

Figure 789.
Salix nigra
bark, large
tree

PROPAGATION. Seed germinates when mature; cuttings root with no pre-treatment.

WILDLIFE VALUE. Wood is eaten and used by beaver; tree provides good cover for waterfowl.

LANDSCAPE VALUE. Wood is brittle; trees tend to be messy and many tend to clog drains with extensive root systems. This is a fine genus of numerous species to plant around bodies of water or streams, but the use of these species should be greatly tempered around the home landscape. Zone 3.

BEST RECOGNIZABLE FEATURES. Single caplike bud scale; single-stemmed individuals; dark, shaggy bark; persistent stipules.

Other willows commonly planted in the regional landscape:
Salix babylonica Linnaeus, weeping willow. To 40 ft. (12 m) tall; leaves

Figure 790. *Salix babylonica* foliage

long, dark green, lance shaped, attached to pendulous branches that may touch the ground. Native to China. Zones 6–8.

Other tree-size willows in the Central Hardwood Forests (dozens of other more shrubby species also occur regularly through this region):

Salix bebbiana

Salix alba Linnaeus, white willow. Large tree to 80 ft. (24 m) tall; bark gray-brown, rough, ridged; leaves 2–4½ in. (5–11 cm) long, lanceolate or elliptic, finely serrate, shiny dark green above, whitish and silky below; twigs yellow to brown, flexible, often somewhat pendulous; fruit a capsule with a sharp-pointed apex. An important European timber species. Native to Europe and from North Africa to central Asia. Zones 2–8.

Salix exigua

Salix bebbiana Sargent, Bebb willow. Bushy tree to 20 ft. (6 m) tall; stout, ascending branches forming a broad round head; bark grayish, rough, scaly; leaves oblong to lanceolate, acute at apex, bluish green below and usually pubescent, to 3 in. (8 cm) long, margin entire and wavy; twigs slender and lenticellate. Zone 2.

Salix exigua Nuttall, sandbar willow. Large, thicket-forming shrub to small tree, to 20 ft. (6 m) tall; thin spreading branches forming a round-topped head; leaves narrow lanceolate, acuminate, 1½–4 in. (4–10 cm) long, minutely glandular-serrate above the middle, bluish green and glabrous above, white silky-hairy below; twigs slender, glabrous, red-brown. Zone 5.

Salix lucida

Salix lucida Muhlenberg, shining willow. Small tree to 20 ft. (6 m) tall, with erect branches forming a broad, round-topped symmetrical head; bark brown; leaves ovate-lanceolate, long-pointed apex, finely serrate, 3–5 in. (8–13 cm) long, leathery, smooth and lustrous above, paler below; petiole glandular at apex; stipules glandular on margin and often persisting during summer; twigs stout, glabrous, dark orange, shiny. Zone 2.

Salix petiolaris J. E. Smith, meadow willow. Shrub to small tree, to 10 ft. (3 m) tall; bark gray; leaves 2–4 or more in. (5–10 or more cm) long, narrow lanceolate, dark green and shiny above, glaucous beneath, margin finely serrate with gland-tipped teeth; twigs slender, usually glabrous. Zone 2.

Salix sericea Marshall, silky willow. Shrub with clustered stems, or small tree to 15 ft. (5 m) tall; bark brown; leaves 2–4 in. (5–10 cm) long, dark green and glabrous above, white-silky below; margins of largest leaves serrate to minutely serrate; twigs moderately slender, rather stiff, ascending; fruit, mature capsules silky and with blunt apex. Zone 3.

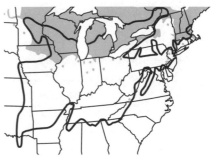

Salix petiolaris

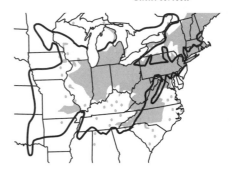

Salix sericea

Sambucus—elder
CAPRIFOLIACEAE—honeysuckle family

Key to *Sambucus*

1. Buds purple and globose; flowers in early spring; fruit red and matures in early summer; pith orange-brown . . . . *Sambucus racemosa*

1. Buds less conspicuous and pointed; flowers in summer; fruit blackish purple and matures in mid to late summer; pith white . . . . *Sambucus canadensis*

Sambucus canadensis Linnaeus
American elder, elderberry, common elder

PLATE 100

HABIT. Large shrub or small tree, to 15 ft. (3 m) tall, with an irregular crown of stout, spreading branches.

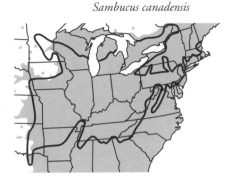

Sambucus canadensis

BARK. Light gray or brown with raised, warty lenticels.

TWIGS. Light green, stout, angled, prominently lenticellate, glabrous; leaf scars large, broadly crescent shaped or lobed; pith homogeneous, white.

BUDS. Terminal generally absent; laterals ⅛ in. (3 mm) long, conical, brown, with 4–5 pairs of scales.

LEAVES. Opposite, pinnately compound, 5–9 in. (13–23 cm) long, with 3–7 shiny, elliptic, bright green leaflets 1½–4 in. (4–10 cm) long; margin serrate; lowest pair of leaflets often 2- or 3-lobed.

FLOWERS. White, ¼ in. (6 mm) in diameter, fragrant, in upright flat cluster 4–8 in. (10–20 cm) wide; opening in summer.

FRUIT. Drupe, ¼ in. (6 mm) in diameter, black or purplish black, juicy, slightly sweet; maturing in late summer or early autumn.

HABITAT AND RANGE. Wet or moist soils in open areas throughout the eastern United States.

PROPAGATION. Seed, stratify in moist medium 60 days at 68°F (20°C), then 90–150 days at 41°F (5°C); softwood and hardwood cuttings generally root easily.

WILDLIFE VALUE. Fruit is eaten by more than 45 species of birds (e.g., grouse, pheasant, quail), whitetail deer, squirrel, and other rodents.

Figure 791. *Sambucus canadensis* foliage

Figure 792. *Sambucus canadensis* fruit

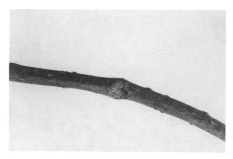

Figure 793. *Sambucus canadensis* twig

Figure 794. *Sambucus canadensis* bark, small stem

Figure 795. *Sambucus canadensis* bark, larger stem

LANDSCAPE VALUE. Good choice for wet soils and when there is interest in making jelly from fruit or attracting birds. Zones 3–9.

BEST RECOGNIZABLE FEATURES. Opposite, pinnately compound leaves; stout twig with white pith; large clusters of small, blackish berries; open, moist to wet sites.

Other elderberries in the Central Hardwood Forests:

Sambucus racemosa Michaux, red berried elder, scarlet elder. Typically an erect shrub to 12 ft. (4 m) tall. Distinguished from *S. canadensis* in having smaller leaves with fewer leaflets; buds globular and reddish purple in winter; pyramidal clusters of yellowish white flowers that open in early spring; smaller, pyramidal clusters of red berries in early summer; and brown pith. Common in moist, shaded forests. Zones 4–6.

Figure 796. *Sambucus racemosa* foliage

Figure 798.
Sambucus racemosa fruit

Figure 797. *Sambucus racemosa* flowers

Sapindus—soapberry
SAPINDACEAE—soapberry family

Sapindus drummondii Hooker & Arnott
western soapberry, wild chinatree, cherioni

HABIT. Large shrub or medium-sized tree, to 40 ft. (12 m) tall, with erect branches and a broad-oval crown of upright branches.
BARK. Gray to tan, long, narrow ridges that are scaly on surface, deep fissures, bitter and astringent.
TWIGS. Initially angled, becoming round, pale yellow-green, finely pubescent, lenticellate; leaf scars large, somewhat triangular, with 3 bundle scars; pith homogenous, white to pale brown.
BUDS. Terminal absent; laterals globular, with 2 overlapping scales often superposed.
LEAVES. Alternate, even pinnately compound, 5–8 in. (13–20 cm) long,

with 11–19 dull yellow-green leaflets
1½–3½ in. (4–9 cm) long, pubescent
beneath, lance shaped; base falcate;
apex acuminate; margin entire; rachis
slender, grooved, hairy; fall color yel-
low-gold.

Sapindus drummondii

FLOWERS. Diameter ⅛ in. (3 mm); usually with 5 rounded yellowish white
petals; in upright terminal panicles 6–
10 in. (15–25 cm) long.

FRUIT. Drupe (often berrylike), sub-
globose, about ½ in. (13 mm) in diameter; flesh translucent, yellow-
orange, turning black, developing lather when crushed in water, poisonous; seed round, black; persisting into winter.

WOOD. Light brown tinged with yellow, heavy, strong, close grained;
used for baskets, frames.

HABITAT AND RANGE. Moist clay soil or dry limestone uplands, from
southern Missouri, Kansas, New Mexico, and Arizona to Louisiana,
Texas, and northern Mexico.

PROPAGATION. Seed, scarify, then stratify 90 days at 41°F (5°C); a low
percentage of untreated seeds will likely germinate.

WILDLIFE VALUE. Tree provides cover for birds.

LANDSCAPE VALUE. Graceful shade tree with beautiful fall color. Should
be used more where it is reliably hardy; good for urban conditions, except
for fruit litter. Zones 5–9.

BEST RECOGNIZABLE FEATURES. Rough, deeply furrowed bark; pinnately
compound leaves with lance-shaped leaflets; large clusters of globose
yellow-orange "berries."

Sassafras—sassafras
LAURACEAE—laurel family

Sassafras albidum (Nuttall) Nees
sassafras

PLATES 101, 102

HABIT. Medium-sized tree, 40–70 ft. (12–21 m) tall, with a cylindrical
bole, an ovoid or columnar crown, and short stout, twisted branches.

BARK. Dark reddish brown to cinnamon-red, with deep irregular fissures, flat gray ridges, and thick-appressed scales; inner bark reddish orange, aromatic.

TWIGS. Moderately stout, curved upward at tips, bright green to yellowish green to red, with spicy odor and taste, hairy becoming smooth, shiny or with glaucous bloom; pith white, continuous, mucilaginous.

BUDS. Terminal ¼ in. (6 mm) long; laterals ⅛ in. (3 mm) long; green with red-tinged tip, globose or ovoid; scales keeled.

Sassafras albidum

LEAVES. Alternate, simple, 4–6 in. (10–15 cm) long, ovate to elliptic, bright green to blue-green above, glaucous and glabrous below, unlobed or 2- to 3-lobed frequently on the same tree; spicy odor when crushed; fall color orange, red, scarlet, yellow.

Figure 799. *Sassafras albidum* foliage

Figure 800. *Sassafras albidum* foliage

Figure 801. *Sassafras albidum* foliage

Figure 802. *Sassafras albidum* fruit

Figure 803. *Sassafras albidum* twig and buds

Figure 804. *Sassafras albidum* bark, medium-sized tree

Figure 805. *Sassafras albidum* bark, large tree

FLOWERS. Yellow, in terminal racemes; early spring.

FRUIT. Drupe, ½ in. (13 mm) in diameter, blue, club shaped, hairy; pedicel red; September.

WOOD. Dull orange-brown; soft, weak, brittle, durable; used for fence posts, cooperage, carvings, furniture; dried root bark used to make a spicy tea.

HABITAT AND RANGE. Abandoned farms, bottomlands, dry ridges from southeastern Maine to central Michigan and southeastern Iowa, south to eastern Texas, east to central Florida.

PROPAGATION. Seed, stratify 90–120 days at 33–41°F (1–5°C).

WILDLIFE VALUE. Fruit is eaten by songbirds.

LANDSCAPE VALUE. Tolerates wide range of site conditions; has unique form and beautiful fall color; no serious pest problems. Zones 4–9.

BEST RECOGNIZABLE FEATURES. Aromatic plant parts; variably shaped

foliage; contorted (generally) growth habit; upturned tips; bright green
new twig growth.

Sorbus—mountain-ash
ROSACEAE—rose family

Sorbus americana Marshall
American mountain-ash

PLATE 103

Sorbus americana

HABIT. Generally a small tree, to 30 ft.
(9 m) tall, with a narrow round-topped
crown.
BARK. Thin, light gray, irregularly broken into small, appressed, scaly plates,
aromatic when cut.
TWIGS. Stout, initially hairy but
becoming glabrous, brown tinged with
red, dotted with prominent lenticels;
leaf scars raised, narrowly crescent
shaped, with 3–7 (usually 5) bundle
scars in single curved line; pith homogeneous, red-brown, large.
BUDS. Terminal about ¾ in. (19 mm) long, conical, acute, dark red,
resinous; laterals about ¼ in. (6 mm) long, appressed.
LEAVES. Alternate, odd pinnately compound, 6–8 in. (15–20 cm) long,
with 13–17 lanceolate and sharp-pointed leaflets 2–4 in. (5–10 cm) long,
glabrous and dark yellow-green on upper surface, pale below; margin
serrate nearly to base; petiole dark green or red, 2–3 in. (5–8 cm) long;
petiole and rachis grooved; fall color bright clear yellow.
FLOWERS. Creamy white, ⅛ in. (3 mm) in diameter, arranged in flat clusters 3–4 in. (8–10 cm) in diameter; appearing after the leaves mature.
FRUIT. Pome, ¼ in. (6 mm) in diameter, subglobose, bright orange-red;
seed round at apex, acute at base, about ⅛ in. (3 mm) long.
WOOD. Pale brown, light, soft, weak, close grained.
HABITAT AND RANGE. Near swamps and on rocky soils and mountain
slopes from the southern Appalachian Mountains northwest to Manitoba and northeast to southern Labrador and Newfoundland.
PROPAGATION. Seed, stratify in moist medium 60–120 days at 38°F
(4°C).

Figure 806. *Sorbus americana* foliage

Figure 807. *Sorbus americana* fruit

Figure 808. *Sorbus americana* bark, small tree

Figure 809. *Sorbus americana* bark, medium-sized tree

Figure 810. *Sorbus aucuparia* foliage and fruit

WILDLIFE VALUE. Fruit is an important source of food for many small birds; twigs and leaves are browsed by moose.

LANDSCAPE VALUE. Good small tree for fall fruit color, on moist soil in colder regions of the Central Hardwood Forests. Zone 2.

BEST RECOGNIZABLE FEATURES. Alternate, pinnately compound leaves; large, white, flat clusters of flowers; clusters of orange-red fruit (a pome); stout twig with large, resinous, pointed terminal bud.

Other mountain-ashes in the Central Hardwood Forests:
Sorbus decora (Sargent) Schneider, showy mountain-ash. Small tree with spreading branches forming a round-topped crown, to 30 ft. (9 m) tall; leaves 4–6 in. (10–15 cm) long, pinnately compound, consisting of 7–13 ovate-lanceolate leaflets, dark bluish green above, pale below; flowers ¼ in. (6 mm) in diameter, in flat clusters; fruit subglobose, bright red, ½ in. (13 mm) in diameter. Infrequent and iso-

Sorbus decora

lated in northern portion of the region, abundant in eastern Canada. Regarded by some as most beautiful species of genus because of large, brilliant fruit display. Zones 2–5.

Other mountain-ashes commonly planted in the regional landscape:
Sorbus aucuparia Linnaeus, European mountain-ash. Medium-sized tree, to 40 ft. (12 m) tall, with broad crown. Similar to American mountain-ash except buds are woolly and fruit is orange-red. Numerous varieties available. Native from Europe to western Asia and Siberia. Zones 3–6.

Staphylea—bladdernut
STAPHYLEACEAE—bladdernut family

Staphylea trifolia Linnaeus
American bladdernut, bladdernut

PLATE 104

HABIT. Shrub or small tree, to 15 ft. (5 m) tall.
BARK. Gray with white linear fissures.

TWIGS. Initially pale green, becoming brown-purple then gray, moderately stout, rounded, glabrous; pith large, continuous, white.

BUDS. Paired at twig apex, opposite along stem, 4-scaled, solitary, ovoid, glabrous.

LEAVES. Opposite, 6–9 in. (15–23 cm) long, trifoliate, dark green above, paler and pubescent below; leaflets 1½–3 in. (4–8 cm) long, ovate; margin finely serrate.

FLOWERS. Length ½ in. (13 mm); white, in pendent racemes 4 in. (10 cm) long; midspring.

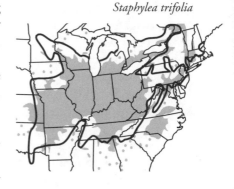

Staphylea trifolia

Figure 811. *Staphylea trifolia* foliage

Figure 812. *Staphylea trifolia* flowers and foliage

Figure 813. *Staphylea trifolia* fruit

Figure 814. *Staphylea trifolia* twig and buds

Figure 815.
*Staphylea
trifolia*
bark, small
stem

Figure 816.
*Staphylea
trifolia*
bark, large
stem

FRUIT. Capsule, 2 in. (5 cm) long, inflated, 3-lobed, light green during summer becoming brown at maturity; September.

WOOD. Commercially unimportant.

HABITAT AND RANGE. Rich, moist woods from southern Ontario to southern Quebec and New Hampshire, south to northwestern Florida, west to Oklahoma, north to southeastern Minnesota.

PROPAGATION. Seed, stratify 90 days at 68/86°F (20/30°C) night/day, then 90 days at 40°F (4°C); cuttings root easily.

WILDLIFE VALUE. Stems and foliage are browsed by rabbit, squirrel, other small rodents, and deer.

LANDSCAPE VALUE. Nothing outstanding, but would make a dense, low screen. Zones 3–8.

BEST RECOGNIZABLE FEATURES. Paired buds at tip of stem; opposite leaf arrangement; striped bark; bladderlike fruit; raceme of white flowers.

Stewartia stewartia
THEACEAE—tea family

Stewartia ovata (Cavenilles) Weatherby   PLATE 105
mountain stewartia, mountain-camellia

HABIT. Large shrub or small tree, 10–20 ft. (3–6 m) tall, with spreading branches and a bushy habit.

BARK. Slightly rough, dark gray-brown.

TWIGS. Slender, circular, glabrous, reddish brown to gray; pith spongy, round.

BUDS. Length ¼ in. (6 mm), usually with 2 outer, often hairy scales, solitary, superposed, spindle shaped.

LEAVES. Alternate, simple, 2½–5 in. (6–13 cm) long, ovate to ovate-oblong, thick, dark green above, pale and sparingly hairy below; margin finely toothed, hairy; petiole ½ in. (13 mm) long, hairy; fall color orange and red.

Stewartia ovata

FLOWERS. White with yellow anthers, 4 in. (10 cm) in diameter, very showy; July.

FRUIT. Capsule, ⅗–⅘ in. (15–20 cm) long, 5-angled, beaked, woody, hairy; calyx persistent.

Figure 817. *Stewartia ovata* foliage

Figure 818. *Stewartia ovata* flower

Figure 819. *Stewartia ovata* fruit

Figure 820. *Stewartia ovata* bark, medium-sized tree

WOOD. Commercially unimportant.

HABITAT AND RANGE. Moist, wooded slopes in the Appalachian Mountains from Kentucky to Virginia south to Florida and Alabama.

PROPAGATION. Seed, stratify 150–180 days at 68/86°F (20/30°C) night/day, then 60–90 days at 33–41°F (1–5°C); softwood cuttings collected in June or July and treated with a hormone dip.

WILDLIFE VALUE. Tree provides cover.

LANDSCAPE VALUE. Exceptional, but very uncommon, small tree because of showy midsummer flowers, vivid fall color, and beautiful form. Zones 5–9.

BEST RECOGNIZABLE FEATURES. Showy white midsummer flowers; small stature; fruit a 5-angled, woody capsule.

Styrax—snowbell
STYRACACEAE—snowbell family

Key to *Styrax*

1. Leaves more or less elliptic, more or less glabrous . . . .
    . . . . *Styrax americanus*
1. Leaves broader, typically obovate, pubescent below . . . .
    . . . . *Styrax grandifolius*

Styrax americanus Lamarck
American snowbell

PLATE 106

HABIT. Generally a rounded shrub or small tree, to 15 ft. (5 m) tall.

BARK. Thin, smooth.

TWIGS. Slender, glabrous, somewhat zigzag; leaf scars crescent shaped, with single bundle scar; pith homogeneous, green.

BUDS. Length to ⅛ in. (3 mm), naked, superposed, scurfy, blunt, brown, alternate.

LEAVES. Alternate, simple, 1–4 in.

Styrax americanus

Figure 821. *Styrax americanus* foliage

Figure 822. *Styrax americanus* bark, large tree

(2.5–10 cm) long, elliptic to obovate, 2-ranked, sparingly pubescent below; margin with few shallow teeth or none; base wedge shaped.

FLOWERS. White, bell shaped, ½ in. (13 mm) long, 5-lobed corolla; 10 stamens; 1–4 flowers per raceme; very showy; late May.

FRUIT. Drupe, ⅜ in. (10 mm) in diameter, obovoid, dry, gray-brown, hairy; September.

WOOD. Commercially unimportant.

HABITAT AND RANGE. Swampy woodlands from southeastern Virginia to central Florida, west to eastern Texas, north to southeastern Oklahoma, southeast Missouri, southern Illinois, southwestern Indiana, and western Kentucky.

PROPAGATION. Seed, stratify 150 days at 68/86°F (20/30°C) night/day, then 90 days at 41°F (5°C).

WILDLIFE VALUE. Tree provides cover.

LANDSCAPE VALUE. Beautiful tall shrub or small tree for cool, moist, acidic soils. Zones 5–9.

BEST RECOGNIZABLE FEATURES. White, bell-shaped flowers with 10 stamens; dry, hairy drupe; naked bud; single bundle scars.

Styrax grandifolius Aiton
bigleaf snowbell

HABIT. A broad shrub to 20 ft. (6 m) tall or occasionally a tree to 40 ft. (12 m) tall with a narrow round-topped crown.

BARK. Thin, smooth, dark red-brown to black.

TWIGS. Slender, initially covered with dense hair but becoming mostly glabrous, chestnut-brown; leaf scars crescent shaped, with one central bundle scar; pith homogeneous, green, small, rounded.

Styrax grandifolius

BUDS. Terminal absent; laterals about ⅛ in. (3 mm) long, acute, naked, scurfy, often superposed at nodes in groups of 3.

LEAVES. Alternate, simple, 2–5 in. (5–13 cm) long, thin, obovate, pale green and glabrous above, pale tomentose along veins below; apex acute; base rounded or wedge shaped; margin nearly entire or remotely serrate; petiole ¼ in. (6 mm) long, stout, pubescent.

FLOWERS. To 1 in. (2.5 cm) in diameter; fragrant, white, deeply lobed but bell shaped, in a raceme 5–8 in. (13–20 cm) long with 5–20 flowers; very showy; opening in early spring after the leaves are at least half grown.

FRUIT. Drupe, ¼ in. (6 mm) diameter, obovoid, densely hairy, dry; seed obovoid, dark orange-brown.

HABITAT AND RANGE. Low wet woods and borders of swamps from Virginia south to Florida and west to Georgia, Louisiana, and Mississippi.

PROPAGATION. Seed, stratify in moist medium 150 days at 68°F (20°C), then 90 days at 41°F (5°C).

WILDLIFE VALUE. Poor.

LANDSCAPE VALUE. Beautiful small tree for woodland setting. Zones 7–9.

BEST RECOGNIZABLE FEATURES. Veins on underside of leaf woolly; white, bell-shaped, deeply lobed flowers; green pith; naked scurfy buds; obovoid dry drupe.

Figure 823. *Styrax grandifolius* foliage

Symplocos—sweetleaf
SYMPLOCACEAE—sweetleaf family

Symplocos tinctoria (Linnaeus) L'Héritier de Brutelle
sweetleaf, horse-sugar   PLATE 107

HABIT. Large shrub or small tree, to 30 ft. (9 m) tall, with an open, rounded crown.

Symplocos tinctoria

BARK. Thin, ash-gray tinged with red, having narrow fissures and warty openings.

TWIGS. Stout, reddish brown to ash-gray, somewhat pubescent, with a few elevated lenticels, often with glaucous bloom; leaf scars half-round with one large, horizontal bundle scar (sometimes divided); pith chambered.

BUDS. Terminal about ⅛ in. (3 mm) long, ovoid, acute, brown; scale margin hairy. Laterals of 2 types: leaf buds small, conical, embedded, often superposed; flower buds globose, larger.

LEAVES. Alternate, simple, 5–6 in. (13–15 cm) long, oblong, leathery, dark green and lustrous above, pale and pubescent below; apex acute; base tapered; margin somewhat crenate-serrate or entire; petiole short, stout, slightly winged; sweet-tasting; persisting long into winter farther south.

FLOWERS. Creamy white, ½ in. (13 mm) long, fragrant, stamens exerted; opening in very early spring.

FRUIT. Drupe, ½ in. (13 mm) long, ovoid, dark orange-brown, dry; seed ovoid, pointed, with thin papery chestnut-brown coat; ripening in summer or early autumn.

WOOD. Light red or brown, light, soft, close grained.

HABITAT AND RANGE. Moist, rich soil in forests and along swamp margins, from sea level to 3500 ft. (1050 m) in mountains, from Delaware, south through North and South Carolina to Florida, west to eastern Texas and southern Arkansas.

PROPAGATION. Seed, stratify in moist medium 90–120 days at 68°F (20°C), then 90 days at 41°F (5°C).

WILDLIFE VALUE. Leaves are eaten by whitetail deer, cattle, and horses.

Figure 824. *Symplocos tinctoria* foliage

Figure 825. *Symplocos tinctoria* bark, small tree

Figure 826. *Symplocos tinctoria* bark, medium-sized tree

LANDSCAPE VALUE. Very early blooming, rather coarse-textured small tree for naturalized landscapes or woodland settings. Zones 7–9.

BEST RECOGNIZABLE FEATURES. Sweet-tasting leaves that are pubescent below; small white flowers; chambered pith; warty bark.

Taxodium—baldcypress
TAXODIACEAE—redwood family

Taxodium distichum (Linnaeus) Richard PLATE 108
baldcypress, cypress, swamp-cypress

HABIT. Large tree, 100–150 ft. (31–46 m) tall, with a buttressed, tapered, often fluted bole and an open pyramidal or flat-topped crown; woody growths of "knees" common around the tree on very wet sites.

Taxodium distichum

BARK. Reddish brown to ash-gray, fibrous, shreddy thin.

TWIGS. Terminal twigs slender, bearing axillary buds, light green on new growth becoming reddish brown, persistent; lateral twigs green, deciduous with needles still attached.

BUDS. Length 1/16–1/8 in. (2–3 mm), grayish brown to green, rounded with 2–4 overlapping, pointed scales.

LEAVES. Needles deciduous, alternate, 1/2–3/4 in. (13–19 mm) long, yellow-green, 2-ranked; fall color brown.

FRUIT. Cone, 1 in. (2.5 cm) in diameter, green changing to purple, resinous, disintegrating at maturity; stalk 1/2 in. (13 mm) long; scales shield shaped; September to October.

WOOD. Reddish brown heartwood, yellowish brown sapwood, light, soft, very durable, close grained; used for general construction, shingles, fence posts, cooperage, railroad ties, bridges.

HABITAT AND RANGE. Swamps and bottomlands from New Jersey to southern Missouri, except the Appalachian Mountains, south to eastern Texas, east to Florida.

PROPAGATION. Seed, soak in ethyl alcohol for 5 minutes, then stratify 90 days at 33–41°F (1–5°C).

WILDLIFE VALUE. Tree provides cover.

LANDSCAPE VALUE. Beautiful large tree for moist to wet soils. Zones 4–9.

BEST RECOGNIZABLE FEATURES. Deciduous, 2-ranked needlelike foliage; fibrous bark; round cone of shield-shaped scales that breaks up at maturity.

COMMENT. Dawn redwood (*Metasequoia glyptostroboides* H. H. Hu &

Figure 827. *Taxodium distichum* foliage

Figure 828. *Taxodium distichum* cones

Figure 829. *Taxodium distichum* twig

Figure 830. *Taxodium distichum* form

Figure 831. *Taxodium distichum* bark, small tree

Figure 832. *Taxodium distichum* bark, medium-sized tree

Figure 833. *Taxodium distichum* bark, large tree

Figure 834. *Taxodium distichum* lower bole and "knees"

Figure 835. *Metasequoia glyptostroboides* foliage

Figure 836. *Metasequoia glyptostroboides* cone

Cheng) looks very similar to our native baldcypress; however, the cone is long stalked and smaller, and the foliage on the supporting twigs is arranged oppositely. Thought to be extinct, dawn redwood was discovered growing in China in 1941 and was introduced into the United States in the late 1940s. Not unusual for this species to grow 3 ft. (1 m) per year; a beautiful tree if given room to grow. Zones 4–8. See Figures 835 and 836.

Thuja—aborvitae
CUPRESSACEAE—cypress family

Thuja occidentalis Linnaeus
northern white-cedar, aborvitae

HABIT. Medium-sized tree, 40–70 ft. (12–21 m) tall, with compact, irregular crown composed of short branches curved up towards the end; supported by a short, buttressed, fluted, noticeably tapered trunk.

Thuja occidentalis

BARK. Light red to grayish brown, thin, fibrous, shreddy, fissured into narrow connecting ridges.

TWIGS. Yellowish green and flattened, becoming reddish brown and round, "jointed"; buds minute, hidden.

LEAVES. Opposite, 1/16–1/4 in. (2–6 mm) long, scalelike, in pairs (4-ranked), side pair keeled, flat pair with gland-dot, flattened and fanlike, light yellow-green above, pale blue green below; tangylike odor when crushed.

FRUIT. Cone, 1/3–1/2 in. (8–13 mm) long, oblong, woody, erect, composed of 8–10 thin oval scales that are tipped with a small spine and spread upon maturity (4 scales fertile), reddish brown to yellowish brown.

WOOD. Pale yellow-brown, light, soft, brittle, durable, very coarse grained, fragrant; used in northern United States for fence posts, cooperage, woodenware, rails, railroad ties, shingles, small boats.

HABITAT AND RANGE. Swamps and rocky banks, from Quebec to Saskatchewan, south chiefly on limestone outcrop to Minnesota, Ohio, and the mountains of North Carolina to Tennessee.

PROPAGATION. Cuttings, taken in winter and treated with rooting compound; seed germinates when mature; other seed, stratify 30–60 days at 34°F (1°C).

WILDLIFE VALUE. Twigs and foliage are excellent deer browse; tree provides good cover.

LANDSCAPE VALUE. Excellent for a screen or foundation planting, especially some of the more compact, darker foliage varieties; tolerates wide range of conditions once established. Zones 2–8.

Figure 837. *Thuja occidentalis* foliage

Figure 838. *Thuja occidentalis* cone

Figure 839. *Thuja occidentalis* bark, small tree

Figure 840. *Thuja occidentalis* bark, medium-sized tree

Figure 841. *Thuja occidentalis* bark, large tree

Figure 842. *Thuja occidentalis* lower bole, large tree

Figure 843. *Platycladus orientalis* foliage

BEST RECOGNIZABLE FEATURES. Flattened evergreen foliage; small, erect, woody cones; fibrous bark.

Other aborvitaes commonly planted in the regional landscape: *Platycladus orientalis* (Linnaeus) Franco, Oriental arborvitae. Native to Korea, Manchuria, and northern China. Horticultural varieties exhibiting golden foliage and more compact form are widely planted, especially in the South. Similar to *Thuja occidentalis* except that branchlets of foliage are arranged in a very distinct, vertical plane; cones are larger and have thicker scales that are more strongly hooked; and seeds are wingless. Zones 5–9.

Tilia—basswood, linden
TILIACEAE—basswood family

Key to *Tilia*

1. Leaves glabrous or sparingly pubescent below . . . .
    . . . . *Tilia americana*
1. Leaves covered below with whitish or brownish hairs . . . .
    . . . . *Tilia heterophylla*

Tilia americana Linnaeus
American basswood, American linden, bee-tree

PLATE 109

HABIT. Large tree, commonly 70–90 ft. (21–27 m) tall, with a broad, round-topped head and a long, clear, cylindrical bole that is often surrounded by basal sprouts.

Tilia americana

BARK. Light gray and smooth, becoming dark gray and with distinct longitudinal fissures and narrow, flat topped, scaly ridges, often with some smooth patches.

TWIGS. Slender to moderate, glabrous, glaucous, somewhat zigzag, green to deep red the first year, becoming light brown to dark gray; pith pale, continuous, often angled.

BUDS. Terminal absent; laterals ¼ in. (6 mm) long, divergent, lopsided, green to dark red, broadly ovoid, with 2–4 visible scales (less than mulberry, more than persimmon); mucilaginous when chewed.

LEAVES. Alternate, simple, 4–8 in. (10–20 cm) long, heart shaped, coarsely toothed, shiny and dark green above, nearly hairless and paler below; apex acute; base asymmetrical; petiole 1–2 in. (2.5–5 cm) long; fall color pale yellow to brown.

FLOWERS. In early summer, borne on drooping stalks, pale yellow, fragrant (excellent source of nectar for honeybees, makes a superior honey).

FRUIT. Nutlike drupe, ½–1½ in. (1.3–4 cm) long, globose, densely tomentose, borne singly or in clusters on a common stalk attached midway to a leaflike bract; some persistent.

WOOD. Light brown with a tinge of red, soft, straight grained; used for woodenware, toys, paper pulp, furniture, boxes.

HABITAT AND RANGE. In rich, moist soils across the northern half of the eastern United States.

PROPAGATION. Seed (difficult), remove outer covering, scarify by soaking 15 minutes in sulfuric acid to overcome impermeable seed coat, then stratify in moist medium 90–120 days at 34–41°F (1–5°C).

WILDLIFE VALUE. Fruit is fair for quail and rodents; browse is fair for deer.

LANDSCAPE VALUE. Beautiful large shade tree for average (not extreme) sites. Zones 2–8.

BEST RECOGNIZABLE FEATURES. Large, heart-shaped leaves with asymmetrical base; reddish twigs and usually 2-scaled buds; bark with long, narrow ridges; clusters of fruit (woody, nutlike drupe) on leafy bract.

Figure 844. *Tilia americana* foliage

Figure 845. *Tilia americana* fruit

Figure 846. *Tilia americana* twig and buds

Figure 847. *Tilia americana* bark, small tree

Figure 848. *Tilia americana* bark, medium-sized tree

Figure 849. *Tilia americana* bark, large tree

Tilia heterophylla Ventenat
white basswood, linden, bee tree

HABIT. Large tree, to 80 ft. (24 m) tall, with a long, clear, sometimes buttressed bole.

BARK. Thick, deeply furrowed between grayish brown, flattened ridges that are scaly at surface.

TWIGS. Moderately stout, somewhat zigzag, red-brown to yellow-brown, glabrous, dotted with small pale lenticels; leaf scars half-round to crescent shaped, with several scattered bundle scars; stipule scars prominent; pith homogeneous, white.

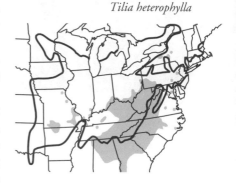

Tilia heterophylla

Figure 850. *Tilia heterophylla* foliage

Figure 851. *Tilia heterophylla* bark, small and medium-sized stems

Figure 852. *Tilia heterophylla* bark, large stem

BUDS. Terminal absent; laterals ¼ in. (6 mm) long, pointed, dark reddish, mucilaginous, 2–3 outer scales that are glabrous except for hairs along margin.

LEAVES. Alternate, simple, 3–5½ in. (8–14 cm) long, ovate, dark green and smooth above, covered with dense white or pale brown hairs below; apex long tapered; base obliquely heart shaped or flattened; margin finely glandular, dentately toothed.

FLOWERS. Pale yellow, in clusters of 10–20.

FRUIT. Nutlike, about ⅓ in. (8 mm) long, leathery, ellipsoidal, densely hairy.

WOOD. Light, soft; used for cabinets, specialty items, furniture, plywood, interior trim.

HABITAT AND RANGE. Lower slopes of mountains on moist, but well-drained soils, from West Virginia to northwestern Florida, Alabama, and southern Indiana, scattered into Missouri and Arkansas.

PROPAGATION. Seed (difficult), remove outer covering, scarify by soaking 10–15 minutes in sulfuric acid, then stratify in moist medium 90 days at 35°F (2°C).

WILDLIFE VALUE. Twigs are browsed by whitetail deer; nectar collected by bees makes a prized honey.

LANDSCAPE VALUE. Good for large areas like parks or very big lawns; otherwise, size and lack of outstanding ornamental characteristics limit use. Zones 5–9.

BEST RECOGNIZABLE FEATURES. Flattened, asymmetrical leaf base; densely hairy leaf underside; light gray bark with long, narrow fissures.

Other basswoods commonly planted in the regional landscape:
Tilia cordata Miller, littleleaf linden. To 70 ft. (21 m) tall; with smaller foliage. Some very attractive varieties. Commonly planted. Native to Europe. Zones 3–7.

Figure 853. *Tilia cordata* foliage

Figure 854. *Tilia* ×*euchlora* foliage

Figure 855. *Tilia tomentosa* foliage

Tilia ×euchlora K. Koch, Crimean linden. To 60 ft. (18 m) tall. Native to Europe. The cultivar 'Redmond' makes a good urban tree, as do most basswoods. Zones 3–7.
Tilia tomentosa Moench, silver linden. To 70 ft. (21 m) tall; underside of foliage white tomentose. Makes a very good urban tree. Native to Europe. Zones 4–7.

Toxicodendron—poison-sumac
ANACARDIACEAE—cashew family

Toxicodendron vernix (Linnaeus) Kuntze
poison-sumac, poison-dogwood, poison-elder

PLATE 110

CAUTION: All plant parts contain a volatile oil that may cause severe dermatitis upon contact.

Toxicodendron vernix

HABIT. Shrub to small tree, 25 ft. (8 m) tall, with low branching and a narrow crown.
BARK. Light brown to dark gray, mottled, thin, smooth or slightly fissured, with horizontally elongated lenticels.
TWIGS. Stout, orange-brown to gray, glabrous, glaucous, lenticellate; leaf scars large, broadly triangular; upper margin not surrounding bud (as for *Rhus* spp.); sap watery, becoming dark after exuding from cut stem (sap milky white for *Rhus* spp.); pith homogenous, brownish.

Figure 856. *Toxicodendron vernix* foliage

Figure 857. *Toxico-dendron vernix* fruit

Figure 858. *Toxico-dendron vernix* twig and buds

Figure 859. *Toxico-dendron vernix* bark, medium-sized stem

BUDS. Terminal about ¼ in. (6 mm) long (terminal absent for *Rhus* spp.), conical, pointed at apex, purplish, consisting of a few, downy scales.

LEAVES. Alternate, pinnately compound, 7–14 in. (18–36 cm) long, with 7–13 leaflets, dark green and shiny above, pale below, elliptic to ovate, acuminate, short stalked; margin entire; rachis red; petiolule red; fall color scarlet to orange.

FLOWERS. Often dioecious; small, greenish yellow; drooping, slender panicles in axillary clusters 8 in. (20 cm) long.

FRUIT. Drupe, ¼ in. (6 mm) in diameter, globose, yellowish white, shiny, glabrous; seed pale yellow; persisting into spring.

WOOD. Light yellow streaked with brown, light, soft, coarse grained.

HABITAT. Swamps and margins of bogs, from southern Maine west to southeastern Minnesota, south to Illinois and central Florida.

WILDLIFE VALUE. Fruit is eaten by many bird species.

Figure 860. *Toxicodendron radicans* foliage

Figure 861. *Toxicodendron radicans* fruit

LANDSCAPE VALUE. Interesting but very poisonous (to touch) small tree that resembles a young white ash, with alternate foliage. Outstanding fall color.

BEST RECOGNIZABLE FEATURES. Mottled bark; alternate, pinnately compound, shiny leaves with red rachis; axillary, white clusters of fruit; margin of bogs.

Toxicodendron radicans (Linnaeus) Kuntze, poison-ivy. CAUTION: All plant parts contain a volatile oil that may cause severe dermatitis on contact. Furthermore, burning wood with this liana attached results in smoke containing this oil, which, when inhaled, can cause much misery. Alternate, trifoliate leaves; brownish twigs with aerial rootlets where attached to trees; naked, elongated, angular, tan buds; yellow-white clusters of berries in autumn; either a liana (vine) supported by taller vegetation or a short, upright shrub.

Tsuga—hemlock
PINACEAE—pine family

Key to *Tsuga*

1.   Needles basically 2-ranked; cones < 1 in. (2.5 cm) in diameter
. . . . *Tsuga canadensis*
1.   Needles more radially aligned on twig; cones ≥ 1 in. (2.5 cm) in diameter . . . . *Tsuga caroliniana*

Tsuga canadensis (Linnaeus) Carrière
eastern hemlock, Canada hemlock, hemlock spruce

HABIT. Medium-sized to large tree, 60–90 ft. (18–27 m) tall, with a conical crown and drooping terminal leader; dead limbs persisting on bole.

Tsuga canadensis

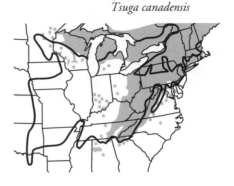

BARK. Reddish brown, flaky or scaly when young, becoming widely ridged and deeply furrowed with age; freshly cut surfaces show purplish streaks.

TWIGS. Slender; terminal leader often droops to one side; lateral branches turn up at the ends.

LEAVES. Needles ¼–¾ in. (6–19 mm) long, borne in flat sprays (2-ranked), blunt, shiny green above, pale green with 2 white bands below; petiole minute.

FRUIT. Cone, ½–¾ in. (13–19 mm) long, pendent, light brown; scales thin with a smooth, rounded margin.

WOOD. Light brown, light, splintery, knotty, coarse grained; used for pulp, crates, rough construction.

HABITAT AND RANGE. Cool, moist sites from Nova Scotia to southern Ontario, south to northern Alabama and Georgia.

PROPAGATION. Seed, stratify 60–120 days at 33–41°F (1–5°C).

WILDLIFE VALUE. Seed is fair for songbirds and mice; tree provides good cover for deer and smaller animals.

LANDSCAPE VALUE. Very graceful and beautiful large evergreen for cool, moist, well-drained sites. Zones 3–7.

BEST RECOGNIZABLE FEATURES. Leaves appear 2-ranked and have 2 white stomatal bands beneath; slender and drooping terminal leader that results

Figure 862. *Tsuga canadensis* foliage

Figure 863. *Tsuga canadensis* cones

Figure 864. *Tsuga canadensis* bark, small tree

Figure 865. *Tsuga canadensis* medium-sized tree

Figure 866. *Tsuga canadensis* bark, large tree

in a curved tip; small cones with smooth scale margin; cut ridges of bark with purple streaks.

Tsuga caroliniana Engelmann
Carolina hemlock

HABIT. Medium-sized tree, to 50–70 ft. (15–21 m) tall, with crown consisting of short, stout, often pendulous branches that form a compact pyramid.
BARK. Deep furrows separated by thick, rough, broad, flat ridges.
TWIGS. Slender, light orange-brown, pubescent.
BUDS. Length ⅛ in. (3 mm), obtuse, dark chestnut-brown, pubescent.
LEAVES. Needles about ½ in. (13 mm) long; dark green, lustrous, grooved

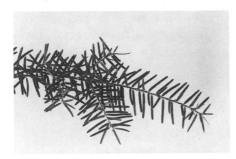

Figure 867. *Tsuga caroliniana* foliage

Figure 868. *Tsuga caroliniana* foliage and cones

Figure 869. *Tsuga caroliniana* cones

Figure 870. *Tsuga caroliniana* bark, medium-sized tree

above; covered by white bands of stomata below; margin entire; arranged radially around twig; falling during their fifth year.

FRUIT. Cone, to 1½ in. (4 cm) long, light brown, oblong, on short stout stalks; scales narrow-oval.

WOOD. Pale brown ringed with red, light, soft, not strong, brittle, coarse grained.

HABITAT AND RANGE. Rocky streambanks at moderate elevations in the southern Appalachian Mountains from southwestern Virginia to northern Georgia.

PROPAGATION. Seed, stratify in moist medium 60–120 days at 40°F (4°C).

WILDLIFE VALUE. Seed is fair for songbirds and mice; tree provides good cover for deer and smaller animals.

LANDSCAPE VALUE. Beautiful specimen tree for moist, well-drained, rich soils in sheltered locations. Zones 4–7.

BEST RECOGNIZABLE FEATURES. Cones twice the size of *Tsuga canadensis;* needles not as flattened on twig as for *T. canadensis;* coarser texture overall than *T. canadensis;* very restricted natural range.

Ulmus—elm
ULMACEAE—elm family

Key to *Ulmus*

1.   Branchlets often with corky wings 2
1.   Branchlets lacking corky wings 5
2(1).   Trees flower in spring 3
2.   Trees flower in late summer or autumn 4
3(2).   Leaves ≤ 3 in. (8 cm) long; samara about 0.3 in. (6 mm) in diameter .... *Ulmus alata*
3.   Leaves often to 4 in. (10 cm) long; samara to 0.8 in. (19 mm) in diameter .... *Ulmus thomasii*
4(2).   Leaves ≤ 2 in. (5 cm) long; entire samara pubescent .... *Ulmus crassifolia*
4.   Leaves ≥ 2 in. (5 cm) long; only margin of samara pubescent . ... *Ulmus serotina*
5(1).   Leaves glabrous or finely pubescent; buds and stem brown; samara elongate and deeply notched at apex; bark has alternating layers of brown and white in cross section .... *Ulmus americana*
5.   Leaves scabrous; buds dark purple, stems gray; samara round and basically not notched at apex; bark lacking white layers in cross section .... *Ulmus rubra*

Ulmus alata Michaux
winged elm, cork elm, wahoo

HABIT. Medium-sized tree, 40–50 ft. (12–15 m) tall, with a short bole and a spreading, oblong crown.
BARK. Brown-gray, shallowly fissured with flat, long, narrow scaly ridges of alternating brown and tan layers.
TWIGS. Gray-brown to red-brown, smooth, with orange lenticels, slender, often with 3 corky wings; leaf scars with 3 bundle scars.

BUDS. Length ⅛ in. (3 mm), narrow, brown, acute, imbricate; glabrous; flower buds globose.

LEAVES. Alternate, simple, 1–3 in. (2.5–8 cm) long, ovate-oblong to oblong-lanceolate, dark green and smooth above; pale and hairy in axils below; petiole ¼–½ in. (6–13 mm) long; base asymmetrical; margin unequal, doubly serrate; fall color yellow.

FLOWERS. Greenish, ⅛ in. (3 mm) long; appearing before the leaves unfold.

Ulmus alata

FRUIT. Samara, ¼ in. (6 mm) in diameter, reddish, winged, hairy; spring.

WOOD. Light brown, hard, heavy, moderately strong, difficult to split, close grained; used for crates, boxes, tool handles; not a significant timber species.

HABITAT AND RANGE. Upland sites from southeastern Virginia through

Figure 871. *Ulmus alata* foliage

Figure 872. *Ulmus alata* twig

Figure 873. *Ulmus alata* bark, small tree

Figure 874. *Ulmus alata* bark, medium-sized tree

Figure 875. *Ulmus alata* bark, medium-sized tree

the coastal plain and Piedmont to eastern Texas, north to Missouri, east to central Kentucky.

PROPAGATION. Seed, some germinates upon maturity; other seed, stratify in moist medium 60–90 days at 41°F (5°C).

WILDLIFE VALUE. Browse is good for deer.

LANDSCAPE VALUE. Attractive medium-sized shade tree. Zones 6–9.

BEST RECOGNIZABLE FEATURES. Winged branches; leaf surface smooth above, hairy below.

Ulmus americana Linnaeus
American elm, white elm, soft elm

HABIT. Large tree, once commonly 80–100 ft. (24–31 m) tall, with a long, clear bole, a spreading, vaselike crown, and drooping branches; larger trees with buttressed base, especially in bottomland habitats.

BARK. Gray to gray-brown, layered in cross section alternating cream and reddish brown; on upland sites, fissured with narrow, flat ridges; on bottomland sites, scaly with a scalloped appearance.

Ulmus americana

TWIGS. Dark red-brown, smooth or lightly hairy, lenticellate; leaf scars elevated, with 3 bundle scars.

BUDS. Terminal absent (as for all *Ulmus* spp.); laterals ⅛ in. (3 mm) long,

Figure 876. *Ulmus americana* foliage

Figure 877. *Ulmus americana* flowers

Figure 878. *Ulmus americana* fruit

Figure 879. *Ulmus americana* twig and buds

Figure 880. *Ulmus americana* form, summer

Figure 881. *Ulmus americana* upper bole, summer

Figure 882. *Ulmus americana* bark, small tree

Figure 883. *Ulmus americana* bark, medium-sized tree

Figure 884. *Ulmus americana* beetle galleries associated with Dutch elm disease

reddish brown, smooth or lightly hairy, acute or only slightly rounded.
LEAVES. Alternate, simple, 3–6 in. (8–15 cm) long, ovate-oblong; dark green, shiny, smooth or rough above (hairy on new growth); hairy or smooth below; petiole ¼–½ in. (6–13 mm) long; base asymmetrical; margin doubly serrate; fall color bright yellow.
FLOWERS. Perfect, on slender stalks; appearing in early spring before the leaves.
FRUIT. Samara, ½ in. (13 mm) long, green to brown, hairy only along edge, with a terminal notch; spring.
WOOD. Light brown, heavy, hard, strong, tough, difficult to split, coarse grained; used for containers (dairy and poultry supplies), slack cooperage, curved portions of furniture.
HABITAT AND RANGE. Moist upland and bottomland sites from Newfoundland to Florida, west to Texas, north to Saskatchewan.

PROPAGATION. Seed, some germinates upon maturity; other seed, stratify in moist medium 60–90 days at 41°F (5°C).

WILDLIFE VALUE. Following death by Dutch elm disease and elm yellows, this species is excellent for woodpeckers.

LANDSCAPE VALUE. Although some varieties are supposedly resistant to Dutch elm disease, elm yellows can still can kill any specimen. Zones 2–9.

BEST RECOGNIZABLE FEATURES. Leaf surface smooth above; vase-shaped form, drooping branches; white and reddish brown layers in cross section of bark; dark colored buds and stem.

COMMENT. Still very common in wet forests throughout the eastern United States though Dutch elm disease and elm yellows have caused tremendous losses of this species in cities and forests across North America. Trees are able to flower and fruit at an early age, assuring the survival of this species in the forest despite diseases.

Ulmus crassifolia Nuttall
cedar elm, basket elm

HABIT. Large tree, 80–100 ft. (24–31 m) tall, with a buttressed base, a fluted bole, and a crown of long pendulous branches forming a cone-shaped head.

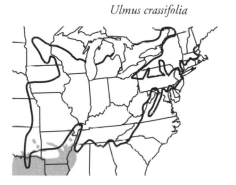

Ulmus crassifolia

BARK. Silvery-gray to brown-gray, often tinged with purple, broken into thin, flat brittle scales.

TWIGS. Slender, light reddish brown, pubescent, lenticellate; having 2 corky, lustrous brown wings; leaf scars elevated, semicircular, with 3 bundle scars; pith homogeneous.

BUDS. Terminal absent; laterals ⅛ in. (3 mm) long, broadly ovoid, acute, chestnut-brown; scales imbricate.

LEAVES. Alternate, simple, 1–2 in. (2.5–5 cm) long, elliptic to ovate, thick, leathery; dark green, lustrous, and roughened above; pubescent below; base wedge shaped, asymmetrical; apex acute or rounded; margin doubly serrate; petiole short, stout, densely hairy; fall color bright yellow.

FLOWERS. Perfect; opening in late summer to early autumn.

FRUIT. Samara, to ½ in. (13 mm) long, oblong, green, deeply notched at apex; margin covered with white hair; ripening in autumn.

WOOD. Light brown tinged with red, heavy, hard, strong, brittle; used for lumber.

HABITAT AND RANGE. Typically on bottomland soils in southern Arkansas, western Mississippi, and northern Louisiana into eastern Texas.

PROPAGATION. Seed, stratify in moist medium 90 days at 41°F (5°C).

WILDLIFE VALUE. Fruit is eaten by grouse, turkey, squirrel, and other rodents.

LANDSCAPE VALUE. Attractive tree with small glossy dark green leaves; withstands infertile, dry, heavy soils. Zones 7–9.

BEST RECOGNIZABLE FEATURES. Bark not fissured; corky, pubescent twigs; small leaves, roughened on surface; deeply notched samara that matures in autumn; hairy bud scales.

Ulmus rubra Muhlenberg
slippery elm, red elm, soft elm

PLATE 111

HABIT. Medium-sized tree, 60–70 ft. (18–21 m) tall, with a short, usually branched bole, ascending branches, and a wide, flat-topped crown.

Ulmus rubra

BARK. Dark brown to gray, with light and dark reddish brown layers and shallow fissures with flat ridges; inner bark slippery when chewed.

TWIGS. Slender to stout, ash-gray, lenticellate, hairy, rough; twig bark difficult to break cleanly; inner surface slippery when chewed; leaf scars with 3 bundle scars.

BUDS. Length ¼ in. (6 mm), dark purplish to reddish brown, hairy; leaf buds acute; flower buds rounded with orange tips.

LEAVES. Alternate, simple, 4–7 in. (10–18 cm) long, obovate to oblong, dark green and very sandpapery (scabrous) above, lighter green and hairy below; petiole ¼–½ in. (6–13 mm) long, stout; base asymmetrical; margin doubly serrate; fall color dull yellow.

FLOWERS. Perfect; appearing before the leaves in early spring.

FRUIT. Samara, ¾ in. (19 mm) in diameter, winged, circular, green; seed hairy; wing smooth; spring.

WOOD. Dark brown or red, hard, strong, durable, easy to split, very close grained; used for furniture, crates, boxes, rough flooring, farm implements, gates.

HABITAT AND RANGE. Upland or bottomland sites from Maine to Minnesota, south to eastern Texas, east to South Carolina.

PROPAGATION. Seed, some germinates upon maturity; other seed, stratify in moist medium 60–90 days at 41°F (5°C).

Figure 885. *Ulmus rubra* foliage

Figure 886.
Ulmus rubra flowers

Figure 887.
Ulmus rubra fruit

Figure 888.
Ulmus rubra bark, small tree

Figure 889.
Ulmus rubra bark, medium-sized tree

Figure 890.
Ulmus rubra bark, large tree

WILDLIFE VALUE. Tree provides cover.

LANDSCAPE VALUE. Not as graceful and stately as American elm; susceptible to Dutch elm disease and elm yellows. Zones 3–9.

BEST RECOGNIZABLE FEATURES. Sandpapery leaf; rough hairy light gray twigs and hairy dark red buds; slippery inner bark (mucilaginous); bark cross section with brown layers only (light brown and dark brown).

Ulmus serotina Sargent
September elm, red elm

HABIT. Medium-sized tree, to 60 ft. (18 m) tall, with a broad crown of pendulous branches.

Ulmus serotina

BARK. Light grayish brown or reddish brown, with scaly, flat ridges and shallow fissures.

TWIGS. Slender, pendulous, glabrous, shiny, brown, lenticels white, often winged; leaf scars elevated, semicircular, with 3 bundle scars.

BUDS. Terminal absent; laterals ½ in. (13 mm) long, ovoid, acute, dark chestnut-brown, glabrous.

LEAVES. Alternate, simple, 3–4 in. (8–10 cm) long, oblong, thin; yellow-green, glabrous, and shiny above; pale below; pubescent along midrib and large veins; apex acute; base very asymmetrical; margin doubly crenate-serrate; petiole short, stout; fall color clear orange-yellow.

FLOWERS. Perfect; opening in September, generally 3–4 weeks after *Ulmus crassifolia*.

FRUIT. Samara, about ½ in. (13 mm) long, light green, oblong-elliptic, covered with silvery-white hair, deeply divided at apex.

WOOD. Light red-brown, hard, very strong, tough, close grained; used locally for fuel.

HABITAT AND RANGE. Rare and local on limestone hills and riverbanks over a very scattered range in Kentucky, Tennessee, northwestern Georgia, northern Alabama, northern Mississippi, Arkansas, and eastern Oklahoma.

PROPAGATION. Seed, stratify in moist medium 90 days at 41°F (5°C).

WILDLIFE VALUE. Seed is eaten by turkey, grouse, pheasant, and rodents; twigs and buds are browsed by whitetail deer (not first choice).

LANDSCAPE VALUE. Limited. Zone 5.

BEST RECOGNIZABLE FEATURES. Leaves yellow-green and glabrous above, pale below; corky twigs; deeply notched samara covered with silvery-white hairs; glabrous bud scales.

Ulmus thomasii Sargent
rock elm, cork elm

HABIT. Medium-sized tree, 50–70 ft. (15–21 m) tall, with a clear bole, a short, narrow crown, and drooping branches.

Ulmus thomasii

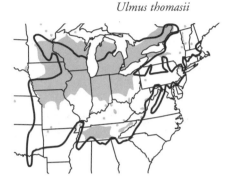

BARK. Gray-brown, fissured with wide, scaly ridges, layered in cross section with tan and reddish brown.

TWIGS. Slender, gray to gray-brown, usually with 2–4 irregular corky wings, smooth or slightly hairy; leaf scars with 3 bundle scars.

BUDS. Length ¼ in. (6 mm), reddish brown, smooth or lightly hairy, very sharp pointed.

LEAVES. Alternate, simple, 2–4 in. (5–10 cm) long, ovate-oblong, 2-ranked, dark green and smooth above, light green and hairy below; base asymmetrical; margin doubly serrate; tip elongate; fall color bright yellow.

FLOWERS. Perfect; appearing before the leaves in early spring.

FRUIT. Samara, ¼–¾ in. (6–19 mm) long, winged, flat, green, notched at tip, hairy over entire surface; April to May.

WOOD. Light clear brown, often tinged with red, heavy, hard, strong,

Figure 891. *Ulmus thomasii* foliage

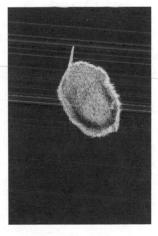

Figure 892. *Ulmus thomasii* fruit

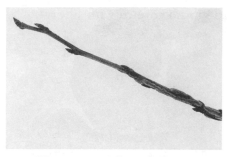

Figure 893. *Ulmus thomasii* twig

Figure 894. *Ulmus thomasii* bark, small stem

Figure 895. *Ulmus thomasii* bark, medium-sized tree

tough, close grained; used for containers, crates, furniture (especially curved portions), veneer.

HABITAT AND RANGE. Upland sites, ridges, and limestone outcrops, scattered from central New York to Minnesota, south to Missouri, east to western Virginia.

PROPAGATION. Seed, some germinates upon maturity; other seed, stratify in moist medium 60–90 days at 41°F (5°C).

WILDLIFE VALUE. Tree provides cover.

LANDSCAPE VALUE. Susceptible to Dutch elm disease. Zones 2–7.

BEST RECOGNIZABLE FEATURES. Very sharp pointed buds; irregular corky wings on branches; dry, rocky sites.

Other elms commonly planted in the regional landscape:
Ulmus carpinifolia Ruppius ex Suckow, smooth leaf elm. Has typical

Figure 896. *Ulmus parvifolia* foliage

Figure 897. *Ulmus parvifolia* bark

"elm" leaf, though form of tree varies. Native to Europe and Asia. Some varieties are planted in the region. Zones 5–7.

Ulmus glabra J. Hudson, Scotch elm. Has typical "elm" leaf, though form of tree varies. Native to Europe and Asia. Some varieties are planted in the region. Zones 4–6.

Ulmus parvifolia Jacquin, Chinese elm. A beautiful, sturdy tree that flowers in autumn; it is much longer lived than *U. pumila*, and with age, the bark exhibits a unique mottling of various colors. Numerous varieties are becoming available. It is native to northern and central China, Korea, and Japan. Zones 4–9.

Ulmus pumila Linnaeus, Siberian elm. Often incorrectly called Chinese elm, though it is quite distinct from the true Chinese elm. With age, Siberian elm develops a deeply furrowed, silvery-gray bark; flower buds dark purplish, conspicuous throughout winter before opening in early

Figure 898. *Ulmus pumila* foliage

Figure 899. *Ulmus pumila* bark

spring. Unfortunately, this species is indiscriminately planted; it has brittle wood, minimal pest and disease resistance, and can become quite a weed problem. Native to eastern Siberia and northern China. Zones 4–9.

Vaccinium—blueberry
ERICACEAE—heath family

Vaccinium arboreum Marshall
tree sparkleberry, farkleberry, tree-huckleberry

PLATE 112

Vaccinium arboreum

HABIT. Small bushy tree, to 20 ft. (6 m) tall, with crooked branches forming a dense, irregularly round-topped crown; less often a large shrub.
BARK. Dark brown to purple-brown with thin, long, shreddy, interlacing ridges.
TWIGS. Numerous, very slender, light red and pale pubescent, becoming nearly glabrous and reddish brown to dark red, somewhat angled; pith white, continuous.
BUDS. Terminal absent; laterals ¹⁄₁₆ in. (2 mm) long, rounded, solitary, imbricate, reddish brown.
LEAVES. Tardily deciduous to evergreen, alternate, simple, ½–2 in. (1.3–5 cm) long, oblong to circular, dark green and lustrous above, paler below; margin nearly entire; fall color red.
FLOWERS. In drooping racemes, 2–3 in. (5–8 cm) long; white, bell shaped; in midspring.
FRUIT. Berry, ¼ in. (6 mm) in diameter, globose, black, lustrous, 10-seeded, slightly astringent yet pleasant tasting; ripening in early autumn, persisting into winter.
WOOD. Light brown tinged with red, heavy, hard, very close grained; used for pipes, tool handles, novelties; commercially unimportant.
HABITAT AND RANGE. Typically in the understory, streams in moist sandy soil or in dry rocky uplands from Virginia south to central Florida, west to Texas, and north to southeastern Kansas.
PROPAGATION. Softwood cuttings root easily.

Figure 900. *Vaccinium arboreum* foliage

Figure 901. *Vaccinium arboreum* bark, small stem

Figure 902. *Vaccinium arboreum* bark, larger stem

WILDLIFE VALUE. Fruit is excellent for grouse, turkey, squirrel, small rodents, and raccoon; browse is good for rabbit and deer.

LANDSCAPE VALUE. Good choice to attract wildlife, on dry to wet sites; attractive bark and glossy foliage turning red in autumn give it year-long beauty. Zones 7–9.

BEST RECOGNIZABLE FEATURES. Shiny black berries in early autumn; shiny, dark green leaves; bush habit; exfoliating bark.

Viburnum—viburnum
CAPRIFOLIACEAE—honeysuckle family

Key to *Viburnum*

1.   Petioles winged .... *Viburnum lentago*
1.   Petioles without wings 2
2(1).   Petioles nearly glabrous; inflorescence short stalked; buds rufous pubescent .... *Viburnum prunifolium*
2.   Petioles of early leaves rusty tomentose; inflorescence sessile; buds rusty tomentose .... *Viburnum rufidulum*

Viburnum lentago Linnaeus   PLATES 113, 114
nannyberry, blackhaw, sheepberry, wild raisin, nannyplum

HABIT. Small tree or large shrub, to 20 ft. (6 m) tall, with a short crown; often with multiple, straight stems and drooping crown.
BARK. Gray or gray-brown, smooth, becoming scaly and loose with age; ill scented when cut.
TWIGS. Slender, green, hairy on new growth.
BUDS. Length 1 in. (2.5 cm), valvate, reddish brown to gray, densely hairy, pointed.

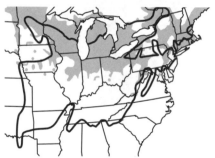

Viburnum lentago

LEAVES. Opposite, 3–4 in. (8–10 cm) long, ovate, dark green and shiny above, yellowish green and hairy below with small black dots; tip acute; margin finely toothed; petiole wide with wavy margin and often hairy.
FLOWERS. White, ¼ in. (6 mm) in diameter, with 5 fused petals, in branched clusters at twig tips; clusters 3–5 in. (8–13 cm) across; fragrant; May to June.
FRUIT. Drupe, ½ in. (13 mm) diameter, rounded, slightly flattened, shiny, black or bluish black; persisting into winter.
WOOD. Light brown, brittle; commercially unimportant.
HABITAT AND RANGE. In old fields or woodland edges with full sunlight from southern Canada, Lake states, and the northern Appalachian Mountains to Virginia.

Figure 903. *Viburnum lentago* foliage

Figure 904.
*Viburnum
lentago*
bark,
medium-
sized stem

PROPAGATION. Seed (difficult), stratify 150–270 days at 68/86°F (20/30°C) night/day, then 30–60 days at 33–41°F (1–5°C).

WILDLIFE VALUE. Fruit is excellent high-energy food for birds and mammals.

LANDSCAPE VALUE. Excellent small tree to attract wildlife; tolerates great range of site conditions. Zones 2–8.

BEST RECOGNIZABLE FEATURES. Opposite, toothed leaves with pointed tip and black dots below; long-pointed, valvate bud.

Viburnum prunifolium Linnaeus
blackhaw

PLATE 115

Viburnum prunifolium

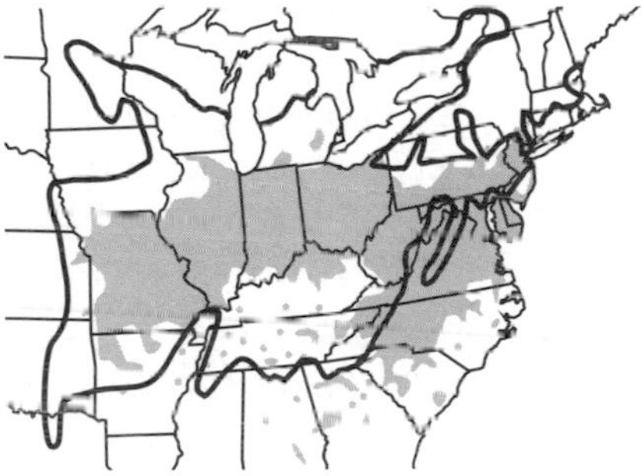

HABIT. Small tree or large shrub, 10–20 ft. (3–6 m) tall, with stiff, spreading branches.

BARK. Dark brown to black, with very blocky, "alligator hide" appearance.

TWIGS. Slender, gray-brown with orange lenticels, smooth, short, stiff, often exhibits right angle, opposite branching; pith continuous, pale.

BUDS. Length ½ in. (13 mm), reddish gray to lead-gray, smooth or scurfy covered by a purplish pubescence, valvate, sharp pointed; flower buds terminal, flask shaped.

LEAVES. Opposite, simple, 2–3 in. (5–8 cm) long, broad-elliptic to ovate, shiny and dark green above, pale below, smooth or lightly hairy; margin serrate; fall color bright red.

Figure 905. *Viburnum prunifolium* foliage

Figure 906. *Viburnum prunifolium* bark, large stem

FLOWERS. White, ¼ in. (6 mm) in diameter, in upright flat-topped clusters 4 in. (10 cm) wide.

FRUIT. Drupe, ¼–½ in. (6–13 mm) in diameter, ovoid, bright blue-black with a whitish bloom, borne on red stalks in cymes; seed oblong; September to October.

WOOD. Reddish brown, heavy, hard, brittle; commercially unimportant.

HABITAT AND RANGE. Moist or dry sites in open, rocky woods, fencerows, and thickets from Connecticut to Michigan, south to Texas, east to Florida.

PROPAGATION. Seed (difficult), stratify 150–270 days at 68/86°F (20/30°C) night/day, then 30–60 days at 33–41°F (1–5°C).

WILDLIFE VALUE. Fruit is excellent for songbirds, grouse, turkey, quail, rodents, rabbit, raccoon, and deer.

LANDSCAPE VALUE. Tolerates dry soils very well, sun or shade; an attractive, small tree with year-round ornamental features. Zones 3–9.

BEST RECOGNIZABLE FEATURES. Light purplish colored buds; stiff, straight branches; "alligator hide" bark.

Viburnum rufidulum Rafinesque
rusty blackhaw, bluehaw, rusty nannyberry

HABIT. Shrub or small tree, 10–20 ft. (3–6 m) tall, with a short bole and an open, round crown.

BARK. Similar to blackhaw.

TWIGS. Slender, gray-brown with small red lenticels, covered with rusty red hairs; pith continuous.

BUDS. Length ¼–½ in. (6–13 mm), rusty red, woolly, valvate, opposite.

LEAVES. Opposite, simple, 2–4 in. (5–10 cm) long, ovate to obovate, dark green and shiny above, rusty hairy below, thick; margin serrate; petiole winged and with rusty pubescence; fall color bright red.

FLOWERS. Similar to blackhaw.

FRUIT. Drupe, ¼ in. (6 mm) in diameter, bright blue with a waxy bloom, borne on red stalks in drooping clusters; seed oblong.

WOOD. Dark orange-brown, hard, strong, brittle, close grained; commercially unimportant.

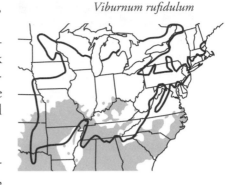

Viburnum rufidulum

Figure 907. *Viburnum rufidulum* foliage

Figure 908. *Viburnum rufidulum* bark, small stem

Figure 909. *Viburnum rufidulum* bark, large stem

HABITAT AND RANGE. Moist or dry sites in open, rocky woods, fencerows, or thickets from Virginia to Missouri, south to Texas, east to Florida.
PROPAGATION. Seed (difficult), stratify 150–270 days at 68/86°F (20/30°C) night/day, then 30–60 days at 33–41°F (1–5°C).
WILDLIFE VALUE. Fruit is excellent for songbirds, grouse, turkey, quail, rodents, rabbit, raccoon, and deer.
LANDSCAPE VALUE. Tolerates dry soils very well, sun or shade; an attractive, small tree with year-round ornamental features. Zones 5–9.
BEST RECOGNIZABLE FEATURES. Rusty, red, woolly buds; "alligator hide" bark.

Other viburnums in the Central Hardwood Forests:

Viburnum dentatum Linnaeus, arrowwood. Typically a much-branched shrub or rarely a small tree to 10 ft. (3 m) tall found in moist to dry soils in rather open areas; bark gray; leaves opposite, 1–3½ in. (2.5–9 cm) long, ovate or rounded, acute at apex, hairy on underside; twigs slender, usually hairy; flowers white, ¼ in. (6 mm) in diameter, in clusters 2–3½ in. (5–9 cm) wide, in late spring to early summer; fruit < ½ in. (< 13 mm) in diameter, rounded or elliptic, blue or blue-black, juicy, containing a large flattened stone. Zones 2–8.

Viburnum nudum Linnaeus, possumhaw viburnum. Large shrub or rarely a small tree to 20 ft. (6 m) tall, in moist soil; mature bark smooth; twigs glabrous, shiny, red-brown; buds covered with rusty scales, flower buds narrow and long pointed; leaves opposite, 4–6 in. (10–15 cm) long, thick, shiny, dark green, broad-elliptic, with entire or slightly crenulate margin, rusty pubescent midrib (lower side) and petiole; flowers white or creamy, ¼ in. (6 mm) in diameter, in long-stalked flat clusters 2–4 in. (5–10 cm) wide, from early May to mid-June; fruit globose, ¼ in. (6 mm) in diameter, pink finally ripening to bright blue. Zones 5–9.

Viburnum trilobum Marshall, American cranberrybush. Large shrub or small tree with arching stems forming a dense, round-topped crown, to 15 ft. (5 m) tall; bark gray; leaves opposite,

Viburnum nudum

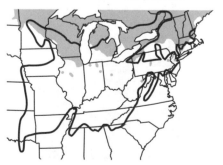

Viburnum trilobum

Figure 910. *Viburnum dentatum* foliage

Figure 911.
*Viburnum
nudum*
foliage

Figure 912. *Viburnum trilobum* foliage

broadly wedge shaped, 2–4 in. (5–10 cm) long, sharply 3-lobed, sharp
pointed at tip, margin coarsely dentate; petioles with pair of slender
thick-tipped stipules at base and several small club-shaped glands near
apex; twigs glabrous; buds plump, green, glabrous; flowers white, in flat-
topped clusters, outer flowers sterile and much larger than inner, fertile
flowers; fruit round or ellipsoid, orange to red, juicy, berrylike. Strongly
resembles the European cranberrybush (*V. opulus*), which is widely
planted in eastern United States. Zones 2–7.

Zanthoxylum—prickly-ash
RUTACEAE—rue family

Zanthoxylum americanum Miller   PLATE 116
common prickly-ash, toothache-tree, northern prickly ash

HABIT. Thicket-forming shrub to small tree, to 20 ft. (6 m) tall, with a rounded crown.

Zanthoxylum americanum

BARK. Smooth, gray to brown.

TWIGS. Brown to gray, slender, zigzag, with fragrance like lemon when crushed; pubescent when young, becoming glabrous; spines paired, stout, about ⅓ in. (8 mm) long; leaf scars rounded or triangular, slightly raised, with 3 circular or C-shaped bundle scars; pith homogenous, white.

BUDS. Terminal present; small, woolly, reddish brown, globose, superposed.

LEAVES. Alternate, pinnately compound, 5–10 in. (13–25 cm) long, with 5–11 leaflets 1–2 in. (2.5–5 cm) long, dark green, ovate to elliptic; apex blunt, nearly sessile; margin somewhat crenate, with tiny transparent dots; bitter aromatic when crushed; rachis with 1–2 spines.

FLOWERS. Dioecious; yellowish green, axillary clusters.

FRUIT. Capsule, elliptic, brown, splits along one side, stalked; seed one, shiny, black.

WOOD. Yellow, hard; commercially unimportant.

HABITAT AND RANGE. Moist soils along streamsides; dry, rocky uplands; fencerows; and forest edges; from southern Quebec to eastern North Dakota, south to South Carolina, Georgia, and Oklahoma.

PROPAGATION. Seed, stratify 120 days at 41°F (5°C); also, transplant root suckers.

WILDLIFE VALUE. Fruit is eaten by some birds; tree provides good cover.

LANDSCAPE VALUE. Limited unless a nasty barrier is wanted or poor soil conditions prevent little else from growing. Zones 3–7.

BEST RECOGNIZABLE FEATURES. Rusty, woolly buds; prickle along rachis; pinnately compound leaf; thicket-forming.

Figure 913. *Zanthoxylum americanum* foliage

Figure 914. *Zanthoxylum americanum* flowers

Figure 915. *Zantho-xylum ameri-canum* twig

Figure 916. *Zantho-xylum ameri-canum* bark, medium-sized stem

Glossary

Accessory buds. Buds beside or above the true bud at a node.

Achene. A dry, indehiscent, one-seeded fruit (e.g., individual fruits that make up ball-like structure of *Platanus*).

Acorn. A thick-walled nut with a woody cuplike base (e.g., *Quercus*).

Acuminate. Sharp pointed.

Acute. Having an apex whose sides are straight and taper to a point.

Aggregate fruit. A fruit developing from several carpels of a single flower (e.g., *Magnolia*, *Platanus*).

Alternate. Pertaining to leaf or bud arrangement in which there is one bud or one leaf at a node.

Ament. A spike bearing unisexual flowers without petals.

Angiosperm. A plant whose seeds are borne within a matured ovary.

Angled. With evident ridges, not smoothly rounded.

Anther. Pollen-bearing portion of stamen.

Apetalous. Without petals.

Apex. The tip or terminal end.

Apical. Pertaining to the apex or tip.

Apophysis. That part of the cone scale that is visible when the cone is closed.

Appressed. Pressed against the stem.

Aril. A fleshy appendage nearly or completely surrounding the seed.

Armed. Having a sharp defense (e.g., thorns, spines, prickles, barbs).

Aromatic. Fragrantly scented; often spicy.

Arcuate. Leaf veins that arch upward toward the apex of the leaf.

Asymmetrical. Not symmetrical.

Attenuate. Long tapering.

Auriculate. Having earlike lobes at base.

Awl shaped. Tapering to a slender stiff point.

Axil. The upper angle between a petiole of a leaf and the stem from which it grows.

Bark. The external group of tissues, from the cambium outward, of a woody stem; varying greatly in appearance and texture.

Berry. A fleshy, indehiscent, pulpy, multiseeded fruit resulting from a single pistil (e.g., *Asimina triloba*).

Bipinnate. Twice pinnate.

Blade. The expanded part of leaf; the lamina.

Bloom. A waxy coating found on stems, leaves, flowers, and fruits, usually of a white to gray cast and easily removed.

Bole. Stem of a tree.

Bract. A reduced or modified leaf, from the axil of which arises a flower or inflorescence.

Bristle. A stiff hair.

Bud. A structure of embryonic tissues that will become a leaf, a flower, or both, or a new shoot.

Bundle scar. Seen in the leaf scar, the broken ends of the woody vascular strands that connected the leaf and stem.

Bur. A prickly seed covering.

Buttress. In reference to a tree bole, a projection or flaring near the lower portion of the main bole.

Calyx. Sepals, collectively; outermost flower whorl.

Capitate. Shaped like a head or lollipop.

Capsule. A dry, dehiscent fruit produced from a compound pistil (e.g., *Catalpa*).

Carpel. A floral leaf bearing ovules along the margin.

Catkin. An inflorescence, really a spike, generally bearing only pistillate flowers or only staminate flowers, which eventually fall from the plant entire.

Chambered pith. Divided into empty horizontal chambers by cross partitions.

Chevron. Black, triangular patches on bark below point of branch insertion.

Ciliate. Fringed hairs.

Coarse-grained wood. In reference to texture, wood that has relatively large vessels or pores.

Collateral buds. Accessory buds to either side of the true lateral bud at a node.

Common name. Regionalized names that may or may not be recognized elsewhere. The primary common name listed here is that given by Little (1979).

Complete flower. A flower that has corolla, calyx, stamens, and one or more pistils.

Compound leaf. A leaf of two or more leaflets.

Cone. A fruit having several woody, leathery, or fleshy scales, each bearing one or more seeds, and attached to a central axis.

Conical. Cone shaped.

Coniferous. Cone bearing.

Continuous pith. Solid and without interruption.

Cooperage. Vessels formed of staves and hoops (e.g., casks, barrels, tubs).

Corolla. Petals, collectively; usually the conspicuous colored flower whorl.

Corymb. A short, broad, flat-topped inflorescence.

Couplet. Two successive lines.

Crenate. Margin with rounded teeth.

Crenulate. Margin with minute rounded teeth.

Crown. The upper mass or head of a tree.

Cruciform. Shaped like a cross.

Cyme. Broad, flat-topped flower cluster, with central flowers opening first.

Deciduous. Falling off.

Decurrent. Extending down the stem.

Dehiscent. Splitting open.

Deliquescent. The primary axis or stem much branched.

Deltate. Triangular shaped.

Dentate. Toothed, teeth pointing outward.

Diaphragmed pith. Having horizontally elongated cells with thickened walls spaced throughout the pith.

Dichotomous. Forking regularly by pairs.

Dimorphic. Two forms.

Dioecious. Having unisexual flowers, with flowers of each sex confined to a separate plant.

Dissected. Divided in narrow, slender segments.

Divergent. Spreading very wide apart.

Doubly serrate. Bearing serrations that bear minute teeth on their margins; each tooth bearing smaller teeth.

Downy. Pubescent with fine, soft hairs.

Drupe. A fleshy, indehiscent fruit having a seed enclosed in a stony endocarp.

Elliptical. Shaped like an ellipse.

Emarginate. Apex with shallow, broad notch.

Endocarp. The inner layer of the pericarp.

Entire. Having a margin without teeth, notches, or lobes.

Epicormic shoot. Foliage attached directly to main stem of tree.

Evergreen. Having green foliage throughout the year (but not necessarily a conifer).

Excrescence. An abnormal outgrowth.

Excurrent. Stem or trunk continuing to the top of the tree.

Exfoliating. Peeling away.

Exserted. Extending beyond.

Exotic. Foreign, not naturalized.

Falcate. Sickle shaped.

Family. A group of genera; family names end with the suffix -aceae; families are grouped into orders.

Fascicle. A close cluster.

Fibrous. Having long narrow shreds or flakes.

Filament. Stalk of stamen bearing the anther at its tip.

Fine-grained wood. In reference to texture, wood that has relatively small vessels or pores.

Fissured bark. Torn lengthwise, with vertical furrows.

Flaking. Shreddy, with shorter fragments.

Fleshy (fruit). Pulpy or juicy at maturity.

Flower. An axis bearing one or more pistils, or one or more stamens, or both.

Fluted. Having rounded lengthwise ridges, resembling flexed muscles.

Follicle. A dry, dehiscent fruit opening only along one suture and the product of a single carpel.

Fruit. A matured ovary; a seed-containing unit characteristic of angiosperms.

Furrowed (bark). Having longitudinal channels or grooves.

Genus. A group of species, structurally or phylogenetically related.

Glabrous. Not hairy.

Gland. Generally, any small knob or wart that is a normal part of the plant; technically, a surface or protuberance that secretes a substance.

Glaucous. Covered with a waxy bloom or whitish material that rubs off easily.

Globose. Having a round or spherical shape.

Gymnosperm. A plant bearing naked seeds without an ovary.

Habit. The general aspect or mode of growth of a plant.

Habitat. The place a plant naturally grows.

Heartwood. Mature and dead wood.

Hoary. With a close white pubescence.

Imbedded buds. Completely or partially sunken in the bark.

Imbricate. Overlapping.

Imperfect flower. A flower that lacks a calyx, corolla, stamens, and/or pistils.

Indehiscent. Not opening regularly.

Indeterminate. Pertaining to a specific floral arrangement (inflorescence) in which flowers open progressively from the base upward.

Inflorescence. A characteristic floral arrangement or flower cluster.

Interlacing. Said of bark when ridges and furrows have overall appearance of connected diamonds.

Introduced. Brought intentionally from another region for purposes of cultivation.

Involucre. A cluster of bracts enclosing a flower or inflorescence.

Keeled. Ridged, like the bottom of a boat.

Lanceolate. Lance shaped (i.e., much longer than wide and pointed at tip).

Lateral bud. A bud borne in the axil of a previous season's leaf.

Lead. Choice within a dichotomous key.

Leaf. The whole organ of photosynthesis, characterized by an axillary bud most of the year.

Leaflet. A foliar element of a compound leaf.

Leaf scar. The mark remaining after the leaf falls off a twig.

Legume. A dry, dehiscent fruit opening along both sutures and the product of a single carpel.

Lenticel. A small corky spot on young bark made of loosely packed cells.

Lobe. A division of a leaf, calyx, or petals cut to about the middle.

Lustrous. Shiny.

Margin. The edge of a leaf.

Mesocarp. Middle layer of fruit wall.

Monoecious. Having unisexual flowers, with flowers of both sexes on the same plant.

Mucilaginous. Slimy.

Multiple fruit. A fruit formed from several flowers into a single structure having a common axis.

Naked bud. A bud without scales.

Native. Original to an area.

Naturalized. Thoroughly established, but originally from a foreign area.

Node. A joint on a stem, represented by point of origin of a leaf or bud.

Nut. A dry, indehiscent, one-celled, one-seeded fruit having a hard and bony mesocarp.

Nutlet. A small nut.

Oblanceolate. Lance shaped except widest near apex.

Oblique. Asymmetrical base of leaf.

Obovate. Reverse of ovate (i.e., the terminal half broader than the basal).

Obovoid. Reverse of ovate (i.e., the terminal half broader than the basal).

Obtuse. Blunt.

Opposite. Pertaining to leaf or bud arrangement in which there are two buds or two leaves at a node across from each other.

Orbicular. Rounded.

Ovary. Enlarged basal portion of the pistil, which becomes the fruit.

Ovate. Egg shaped, like an oval.

Ovoid. Egg shaped.

Ovule. The egg-containing unit of an ovary, which after fertilization becomes the seed.

Palmate. Radiating fanlike from a common point, as in palmately compound leaflets (e.g., *Aesculus*).

Panicle. A pyramidal, many-branched inflorescence.

Pedicel. An individual flower stalk in an inflorescence.

Peduncle. Stalk of a single flower or of an entire inflorescence.

Pendent. Hanging.

Pendulous. Hanging.

Perfect flower. Having both functional stamens and pistils.

Pericarp. The ovary wall.

Persistent. Remaining attached (e.g., fruit, twigs, leaves).

Petal. One unit of the inner floral envelope or corolla, usually colored and more or less showy.

Petiole. Leaf-stalk.

Petiolule. Leaflet-stalk.

Pinnate. Compounded with the leaflets or segments along each side of a common axis or rachis; featherlike.

Pistil. Central organ of the flower, typically consisting of ovary, style, and stigma.

Pistillate flower. A flower with no functional stamens.

Pith. The central part of a twig, usually lighter or darker than the wood.

Platy. Bark that has relatively large, wide flat or curved ridges.

Pod. A dry, dehiscent fruit.

Pome. A type of fleshy fruit resulting from a compound ovary (e.g., *Malus*).

Prickle. An excrescence of bark that is small, weak, and spinelike.

Pseudo-terminal bud. Seemingly the terminal bud of a twig, but actually the upper-most lateral bud with its subtending leaf scar on one side and the scar of the terminal bud often visible on opposite side.

Pubescent. Covered with short soft hairs.

Raceme. An indeterminate inflorescence comprised of a central rachis bearing pedicelled flowers.

Rachis. Axis bearing leaflets.

Recurved. Curved downward or backward.

Resinous. Secreting a viscid exudate.

Reticulate. A network of interlacing lines.

Revolute. Rolled towards the bottom side.

Ridges (bark). Raised areas of bark.

Ring-porous wood. Wood of an angiosperm, which has an abrupt change in pore size between wood produced early in growing season versus wood produced later in that growing season.

Root sucker. A shoot that arises from the root system of an individual plant.

Rufous. Reddish brown.

Samara. A dry, indehiscent fruit bearing a wing (e.g., *Acer*).

Sapwood. The young living wood.

Scabrous. Rough or gritty to the touch.

Scale (bud). A small vestigial leaf; thin, membranelike covering.

Scalloped (leaf margin). Rounded indentations.

Scarify. Removing part or all the impermeable covering of certain seeds by concentrated sulfuric acid or a mechanical means (e.g., file, sandpaper).

Scientific plant name. Consists of a genus name and specific epithet.

Scurfy. A scaly or branlike deposit.

Seed. A fertilized ripened ovule that contains an embryo.

Sepal. Outermost flower structures which usually enclose the other flower parts in the bud.

Serrate. Saw-toothed, the teeth pointing forward.

Sessile. Without a stalk.

Sheath. Thin tissue present at needle bases and binding the (conifer needle) needle bundles.

Shreddy bark. Divided into fragile, thin, narrow sheets.

Simple leaf. A leaf with only one leaflet.

Singly serrate. Bearing a single set of teeth.

Sinus. The space or indentation between two lobes.

Slack cooperage. A wooden container that will not hold liquids.

Softwood cutting. Emerging shoot that is cut for propagation purposes.

Spatulate. Shaped like a spatula (i.e., very broad near apex and narrow towards base).

Species. A natural group of plants composed of similar individuals that can produce similar offspring.

Specific epithet. The second term of a plant's scientific name, referring to the species.

Spike. An inflorescence comprised of a central axis having sessile flowers.

Spine. An excrescence of stems; strong and sharp-pointed; a modified stipule.

Spongy (pith). Porous.

Spur. A short, stubby branchlet.

Stalked (bud). A bud whose outer scales are attached above the base of the bud axis.

Stamen. Flower structure made up of an anther and a stalk or filament.

Staminate flower. A flower with only functional stamens.

Stellate. Starlike.

Stem. The primary axis of a plant having foliage and flowers.

Sterigmata. Peglike projections onto which *Picea* needles are attached.

Stigma. Receptive portion of the pistil to which pollen adheres.

Stipule. A basal appendage of a petiole, usually one at each side, often ear-like.

Stipule scar. A pair of marks left after the stipules fall off, to either side of the leaf scar.

Stolon. A horizontal stem that can root and produce a new plant.

Stratify. Storing seed in mixture of moist peat, sand, or other water-retentive media under cold temperatures, usually 34–40°F (1–4°C), and/or warm temperatures, usually 68–86°F (20–30°C), for specific periods of time.

Striate. With fine longitudinal lines, channels or ridges.

Strobilus. A conelike structure.

Style. The slender column of tissue that arises from the top of the ovary and through which the pollen tube grows.

Submerged bud. A bud hidden by the petiole or embedded in the leaf scar.

Superposed. Having one or more buds immediately above the lateral bud.

Sutures. Lines along which a dehiscent fruit can open.

Syncarp. A fruit from united carpels.

Terete. Cylindrical, or circular in cross section.

Terminal bud. A bud at tip of stem.

Thorn. A modified twig that has tiny leaf scars and buds.

Tight cooperage. A wooden container that will hold liquids.

Tomentose. Densely woolly, the hairs soft and matted.

Trifoliate. Compound leaf having three leaflets.

Truncate. Flattened, perpendicular to midrib.

Twig. The shoot of a woody plant representing the growth of the current season.

Two ranked. Alternate leaves all in one plane.

Umbel. An inflorescence from which pedicels originate from same point.

Umbo. A conical projection arising from the surface.

Undulate. Wavy-margined.

Unisexual flowers. Of one sex only.

Valvate. Meeting by the edges without overlapping.

Vestigial. A degenerate or imperfectly developed organ or structure having little or no utility.

Villous. Long, silky, straight hairs.

Whorled. Three or more (leaves or buds) at a node.

Wood. A dead, hard xylem tissue.

Bibliography

Bailey, L. H. 1949. *Manual of cultivated plants*. Macmillan Company, New York, 1116 p.

Barnes, B. V., and W. H. Wagner, Jr. 1981. *Michigan trees*. University of Michigan Press, Ann Arbor, Michigan, 383 p.

Bir, R. E. 1992. *Growing and propagating showy native woody plants*. University of North Carolina Press, Chapel Hill, North Carolina, 192 p.

Blakeslee, A. F., and C. D. Jarvis. 1911. *New England trees in winter*. Storrs Agricultural Experiment Station, Storrs, Connecticut, 576 p.

Braun, E. L. 1950. *Deciduous forests of eastern North America*. Blakiston, Philadelphia, Pennsylvania, 596 p.

Brown, C. L., and L. K. Kirkman. 1990. *Trees of Georgia and adjacent states*. Timber Press, Portland, Oregon, 292 p.

Brown, H. P. 1921. *Trees of New York State. Native and naturalized*. New York State College of Forestry Technical Publication No. 15, Syracuse University, Syracuse, New York, 401 p.

Bryson, R. A., and F. K. Hare. 1974. The climates of North America. Pages 1–47, *in* R. A. Bryson and F. K. Hare, editors. *Climates of North America*. Vol. 11, *World survey of climatology*. Elsevier Scientific Publishing Company, New York.

Core, E. J., and N. P. Ammons. 1958. *Woody plants in winter*. Boxwood Press, Pacific Grove, California, 218 p.

Core, H. A., W. A. Cote, Jr., and A. C. Day. 1976. *Wood structure and identification*. Syracuse University, Syracuse, New York.

Court, A. 1974. The climate of the conterminous United States. Pages 193–343, *in* R. A. Bryson and F. K. Hare, editors. *Climates of North America*. Vol. 11, *World survey of climatology*. Elsevier Scientific Publishing Company, New York.

Curtis, J. T. 1959. *The vegetation of Wisconsin*. University of Wisconsin Press, Madison, Wisconsin.

Delcourt, P. A., and H. R. Delcourt. 1979. Late Pleistocene and Holocene distributional history of the deciduous forest in the southeastern United States. Pages 79–107, *in* H. Lieth and E. Landolt, editors. *Contributions to the knowledge of the flora and vegetation in the Carolinas*, Vol. 1. Stiftung Rub'l, Zurich.

Dirr, M. A. 1990. *Manual of woody landscape plants* (4th ed.). Stipes Publishing Company, Champaign, Illinois, 1007 p.

Dirr, M. A., and C. W. Heuser, Jr. 1987. *The reference manual of woody plant propagation. From seed to tissue culture.* Varsity Press, Athens, Georgia, 239 p.

Duncan, W. H., and M. B. Duncan. 1988. *Trees of the southeastern United States.* University of Georgia Press, Athens, Georgia, 322 p.

Elias, T. S. 1980. *Trees of North America.* Van Nostrand Reinhold Company, New York, 948 p.

Fenneman, N. M. 1938. *Physiology of eastern United States.* McGraw-Hill Book Company, New York.

Flint, H. L. (no date). *Landscape plants for the central Midwest.* Department of Horticulture, Purdue University, West Lafayette, Indiana.

Gleason, H. A., and A. Cronquist. 1991. *Manual of vascular plants of northeastern United States and adjacent Canada* (2nd ed.). New York Botanical Garden, Bronx, 910 p.

Greller, A. M. 1988. Deciduous forest. Pages 288–316, *in* M. G. Barbour and W. D. Billings, editors. *North American terrestrial vegetation.* Cambridge University Press, Cambridge, England.

Halfarce, R. G., and A. R. Shawcroft. 1989. *Landscape plants of the Southeast* (5th ed.). Sparks Press, Raleigh, North Carolina, 426 p.

Harlow, W. M. 1946. *Fruit key and twig key.* Dover Publications, New York, 56 p.

Harlow, W. M., E. S. Harrar, J. W. Hardin, and F. M. White. 1991. *Textbook of dendrology* (7th ed.). McGraw-Hill Book Company, New York, 501 p.

Harrar, E. S., and J. G. Harrar. 1962. *Guide to southern trees* (2nd ed.). Dover Publications, New York, 709 p.

Hartmann, H. T., and D. E. Kester. 1990. *Plant propagation, principles and practices* (5th ed.). Prentice-Hall, Englewood Cliffs, New Jersey, 647 p.

Hightshoe, G. L. 1978. *Native trees for urban and rural America.* Iowa State University Research Foundation, Ames, Iowa.

Hosie, R. C. 1973. *Native trees of Canada* (7th ed.). Canadian Forestry Service, Environment Canada, 380 p.

Hunt, C. B. 1974. *Natural regions of the United States and Canada.* W. H. Freeman and Company, San Francisco, California.

Leopold, A. 1966. *A Sand County almanac.* Ballantine Press, New York, 295 p.

Li, Hui-lin. 1972. *Trees of Pennsylvania.* University of Pennsylvania Press, Philadelphia, Pennsylvania, 276 p.

Lindsey, A. A., and L. K. Escobar. 1976. *Eastern deciduous forest.* Vol. 2, *Beech-maple region.* Inventory of natural areas and sites recommended as potential natural landmarks. U.S. Department of the Interior, National Park Service, publication 1481, Natural history theme studies, no. 3.

Little, E. L. 1971. *Atlas of United States trees.* Vol. 1, *Conifers and important hardwoods.* Misc. Pub. No. 1146, USDA Forest Service, Government Printing Office, Washington, D.C.

Little, E. L. 1976. *Atlas of United States trees.* Vol. 4, *Minor eastern hardwoods.* Misc. Publ. No. 1342, USDA Forest Service, Government Printing Office, Washington, D.C.

Little, E. L. 1979. *Checklist of United States trees.* Agriculture Handbook 541. USDA, Washington, D.C., 375 p.

Little, E. L. 1980. *The Audubon Society field guide to North American trees, eastern region.* A. A. Knopf, New York, 714 p.

Martin, A. C., H. S. Zim, and A. L. Nelson. 1951. *American wildlife and plants. A guide to wildlife food habits.* Dover Publications, New York, 500 p.

Miller, H. A., and S. H. Lamb. 1985. *Oaks of North America.* Naturegraph Publishers, Happy Camp, California, 327 p.

Mohlenbrock, R. H. (no date). *Forest trees of Illinois.* State of Illinois Department of Conservation, Division of Forestry, 178 p.

Muenscher, W. C. 1950. *Keys to woody plants* (6th ed.). Comstock Publishing Associates, Ithaca, New York, 108 p.

Petrides, G. A. 1988. *A field guide to eastern trees. Eastern United States and Canada.* Houghton Mifflin Company, Boston, Massachusetts, 272 p.

Preston, R. J. 1976. *North American trees* (3rd ed.). MIT Press, Cambridge, Massachusetts, 399 p.

Preston, R. J., and V. G. Wright. 1976. *Identification of southeastern trees in winter.* North Carolina Agriculture Extension Service, Raleigh, North Carolina, 113 p.

Rehder, A. 1940. *Manual of cultivated trees and shrubs* (2nd ed.). Macmillan Company, New York, 996 p.

Sargent, C. S. 1965. *Manual of the trees of North America,* Vols. 1 and 2. Dover Publications, New York.

Schopmeyer, C. S., editor. 1974. *Seeds of woody plants in the United States.* Agriculture Handbook 450. Government Printing Office, Washington, D.C., 883 p.

Soper, J. H., and M. L. Heimburger. 1985. *Shrubs of Ontario.* Royal Ontario Museum, Toronto, Canada, 495 p.

Stupka, A. 1964. *Trees, shrubs, and woody vines of Great Smoky Mountains National Park*, University of Tennessee Press, Knoxville, Tennessee, 186 p.

Swanson, R. E. 1994. *A field guide to the trees and shrubs of the southern Appalachians.* Johns Hopkins University Press, Baltimore, Maryland, 399 p.

Trelease, W. 1931. *Winter botany* (3rd ed.). Dover Publications, New York, 396 p.

Wharton, M. E., and R. W. Barbour. 1973. *Trees and shrubs of Kentucky.* University of Kentucky Press, Lexington, Kentucky, 582 p.

Young, J. A., and C. G. Young. 1986. *Collecting, processing, and germinating seeds of wildland plants.* Timber Press, Portland, Oregon, 236 p.

Young, J. A., and C. G. Young. 1992. *Seeds of woody plants in North America.* Dioscorides Press, Portland, Oregon, 407 p.

Index to Scientific and Common Names